WAR POWER, POLICE POWER

D1610922

WAR POWER, POLICE POWER

Mark Neocleous

EDINBURGH
University Press

Edinburgh University Press Ltd
The Tun – Holyrood Road
12 (2f) Jackson's Entry
Edinburgh EH8 8PJ
www.euppublishing.com

Typeset in Palatino Light by
3btype.com, and
printed and bound in Great Britain by
CPI Group (UK) Ltd, Croydon CR0 4YY

A CIP record for this book is available from the
British Library

ISBN 978 0 7486 9236 1 (hardback)
ISBN 978 0 7486 9237 8 (paperback)
ISBN 978 0 7486 9238 5 (webready PDF)
ISBN 978 0 7486 9239 2 (epub)

CONTENTS

ACKNOWLEDGEMENTS

On 13 May 1985, police in Philadelphia acted against the MOVE organisation, a group of mostly black activists espousing a mixed philosophy of communal living, vegetarianism, animal rights and black liberation. During the police action a stand-off ensued at the property that was the MOVE's home and headquarters. Water was first poured into the house to 'flush out' the residents and shots were then fired, with the police using semi-automatic weapons. After 90 minutes of shooting, the police action shifted: they bombed the property. In this exercise of state power, six adults and five children were burned alive. The bombing also had the effect of burning down some 60 houses in the block; eyewitnesses described the whole area as looking like a war zone. An official commission established by the Mayor to investigate what happened issued a Report the following year. Although it found that the bombing was 'unconscionable', no criminal charges were brought against the state or police: unconscionable it may have been, but it could not officially be considered a crime. Yet if it was not a crime, what kind of act was it?

The image on the cover of this book is based on the police bombing in Philadelphia and was created by elin o'Hara slavick. I am grateful to elin for permission to use the image.

I am also grateful to: Tyler Wall for his persistence in sending me snippets of information on matters pertaining to air power, his willingness to share his extensive knowledge of drones, and his general support for the project that this book has become; George Rigakos and other colleagues in the anti-security collective for pursuing the arguments regarding pacification – 'the book' on pacification has yet to be written, but that project seeps into this book here and there; my colleagues on the *Radical Philosophy* Editorial Collective for allowing me to test the argument out at various points; Susan Marks, Maia Pal and Hayley Gibson for comments on the argument concerning international law; Yari Lanci, Caroline Holmqvist, Colleen Bell and Jan Bachmann for opportunities to pursue the argument about air power, and Michael D. Smith for in turn pushing that line of enquiry; James Brassett and Nick Vaughan-Williams for the initial chance to open the question of trauma and resilience.

Several people were unstinting in offering time, space and hospitality well beyond what is regarded as the norm in academic circles. Matthew Hughes offered countless sources and resources from inside the world of military history as well as more general support as a good friend and colleague; Rob Crawford allowed me to test three different aspects of the argument in the book across two days at the University of Washington; during a trip to the University of Winnipeg Steven Kohm, Heidi Rimke and George Rigakos helped me exercise what some might call my 'resilience' but what I prefer to think of as revolutionary will; Oktay Dursun, Deniz Özçetin, Burak Özçetin and Dinçer Demirkent enabled me to communicate in and through three days in Ankara; Valerie Kerruish at the ASFPG in Hamburg twice offered time and space to pursue parts of the argument, and occasionally saw through the magic. For seeing through the whole thing I am, as ever, heavily in debt to DB, KK, PC and, in the final few months of writing, LL.

INTRODUCTION

For the War Machine rolls on, never stopping, never resting, never sleeping, on and on, always rising, always consuming, always devouring. On and on, the War Machine rolls on, across the fields and through the forests, on and on, over looted house and over stripped corpse, on and on, and from severed hand into bloody hands, forever-bloody hands, money passes, money changes, money grows.

David Peace, *Occupied City* (2009)

In 2005 yet another book was published on that perennial theme loved by military theorists, strategic thinkers and IR scholars: 'the art of war'. Called *The Utility of Force: The Art of War in the Modern World*, the book was written by a British General with 40 years' experience in the British army and as NATO Supreme Commander, and was published as a cheap paperback to reach a wide audience. It begins with a stark statement: 'war no longer exists'. Conflict, confrontation and combat continue, but 'the entire concept of war ... has changed'.[1] It sounds like a provocation, a neat rhetorical device with which to open a book on war, until one realises that the author is far from alone in making such a claim. A report on the lessons of the Kosovo campaign published by the Centre for Strategic and International Studies in Washington claims that 'it may be that one of the lessons of modern war is that war can no longer be called war'.[2] Likewise, when asked in an interview in 2010 whether the war in Iraq was effectively over, one US General who had worked as Senior Serving Officer in Iraq for four years replied: 'War is a very different concept. This is a – I call it more of an operation, not a war.'[3]

More of an 'operation' than a 'war'? 'Operation' here performs the same role as a whole host of other terms which have quickly come to the fore, and then sometimes just as quickly disappeared, to discuss military conflict and politically organised violence: 'persistent conflict', 'quasi-war', 'pseudo war', 'measures short of war', 'counterinsurgency', 'civic action', 'grey area operations', 'reprisals', 'state of belligerency', 'state of hostilities', 'asymmetrical war', 'effects-based operations' and 'military operations other than war'. War, it seems, can take many forms, but rarely now does it get given the simple label 'war'. On this basis it is not surprising that commentators have noted that almost anything can be called 'war' except the actions that used to be called 'war'.[4] So even if it has not quite 'ceased to exist',[5] war appears to have at least 'lost its well-defined contours'.[6] War, it seems, is 'in crisis'.[7]

This crisis has had an impact on the ways in which critical thinkers talk about war, for a new consensus seems to have emerged concerning a supposed continuity between the conditions of war and peace. Alain Badiou, for example, suggests that the category 'war' has become so obscured that it 'has rendered war and peace indistinguishable'. 'In the end', notes Badiou, contemporary wars 'are not really distinguishable from the continuity of "peace"'. Antonio Negri and Eric Alliez likewise comment that 'peace appears to be merely the continuation of war by other means', adding that because peace, 'otherwise known as global war ... is a permanent state of exception', war now 'presents itself as peace-keeping' and has thereby reversed their classical relationship.[8] Their reference to a concept made popular following Giorgio Agamben's *State of Exception* is far from unusual in this new consensus since, according to Agamben, in the state of exception the distinction between war and peace becomes impossible.[9] Likewise, according to Slavoj Žižek, in 'the new wars ... it will not even be clear whether it is a war or not. Somehow life will go on and we will learn that we are at war, as we are now'.[10] 'We no longer have wars in the old sense of a regulated conflict between sovereign states' but, rather, either 'struggles between groups of *Homo sacer* ... which violate the rules of universal human rights, do not count as wars proper, and call for "humanitarian pacifist" inter-vention by Western powers' or 'direct attacks on the USA or other representatives of the new global order, in which case, again, we do not have wars proper, merely "unlawful combatants" criminally resisting the forces of universal order'. Hence 'the old Orwellian motto "War is Peace" finally becomes reality'.[11]

For a sense of how wide this consensus now is one need only cite a few more examples from a diverse range of publications: Ulrich Beck claims that 'the differences between war and peace, the military and police, war and crime … are from within and without, completely annulled'; Daniel Ross argues that an analysis of democratic violence shows that 'peacetime and wartime … are increasingly convergent'; Rey Chow suggests that war is now the very definition of normality itself; Gopal Balakrishnan claims that the invasion and policing of 'rogue states' means that 'a long-term epistemic shift seems to be occurring which is blurring older distinctions between war and peace'; and François Debrix argues that the reason the war machine permeates everyday culture is because the distinction between peace and war has broken down.[12] At the same time, leading peace thinkers claim that the concept of peace is also in crisis.[13]

I have no interest in challenging this account about the convergence of war and peace in itself; as will be seen, despite its apparent boldness it is in fact a fairly uncontroversial position to hold. But these claims do rely on a problematic historical assumption, in that they rely on the idea of a 'classical' age in which war and peace were indeed distinguishable. That is, they assume that the destabilisation of 'war' and 'peace' is somehow *new*; hence the references to wars in 'the past', in the 'old sense' and in the 'classical' age. The nebulous nature of some of these phrases is remarkable, given the implied radicalism of the insight being expressed. Worse, in accepting the very claim made by the major Western powers that everything has indeed changed from the time when the distinction between war and peace was supposedly categorical and straightforward, this account also reinforces the general fetish of '9/11' as *the* political event of our time.

It may be that there really was a 'classical age' when the concept and condition of war was clear, but I doubt it. Felix Grob's book *The Relativity of War and Peace*, published in 1949, offers countless examples of states engaged in mass militarised killing of enemies but either denying or sometimes just not knowing whether or not they were at war, and more than a few international lawyers in the mid-twentieth century also pointed out the artificial nature of the distinction between war and peace. Quincy Wright, writing as a lawyer in one of the major liberal democracies, pointed out in 1932 that 'a state of war may exist without active hostilities, and active hostilities may exist without a state of war', while Carl Schmitt, writing as a lawyer in one of the major fascist regimes, claimed a few years later that 'the concept of war today has … become a problem', in that 'it is now impossible to distinguish between not only the just and unjust war, but also between "war" and "not-war"'. That is, he adds, if 'war can even be said to exist'. Georg Schwarzenberger attacked the presumption of the 'abnormal' or 'alternative' character of war in 1943, arguing that states were continually in a *status mixtus* between peace and war, and in 1954 Philip Jessup proposed that international law recognise a status 'intermediate' between peace and war.[14]

The history books and the law books are replete with comments along these lines. Thus when in 1968 leading international lawyer Elihu Lauterpacht reflected on the conflicts in Korea, Vietnam and Yemen, he could claim that in a technical-legal sense the protracted fighting in those conflicts was not war.

> True, in two of these situations many of the 'laws of war' were applied, and in particular the Geneva Conventions of 1949. That fact, however, does not change the conflicts in to 'war' in the strict sense, since those Conventions contain certain provisions that they shall apply in case of hostilities as well as in case of war. In other technical respects these conflicts did not enjoy the legal status of 'war'. In particular, there was no 'declaration of war'; in the case of the one conflict which was terminated, the Korean conflict, there was no 'treaty of peace'; and in none of the three cases was there any attempt on the part of the belligerents to require states not immediately involved to adopt positions of 'neutrality'.[15]

Taking a longer historical view, we find the same point being made time and again. Three examples: following naval battles between the US and the French in 1798 the official French position was that there had been no war, the US Attorney General agreed, and the Supreme Court later called it a 'limited' or 'imperfect' war; during the 1827 naval battle of Navarino, the British, French and Russian fleets attacked the Turco-Egyptian fleet, destroying some 60 ships and killing 4,000 men, but the British Foreign Secretary said they were not at war; following the declaration of support for Turkey from France and England in Turkey's war with Russia in 1853, Secretary Lord Clarendon said that 'we are not at war, because war is not declared – we are not strictly at peace with Russia … I consider that we are in the intermediate state'.[16]

It is therefore fair to say that the consensus among critical theorists about a *recent* elision of war and peace is rooted in a deep historical misconception. Indeed, as I have shown at length elsewhere, the whole logic of 'security' underpinning bourgeois modernity is that despite being conjoined with 'peace' (in the mantra of 'peace and security') it constantly reiterates the idea that peace is a form of war.[17] So one basic point to be made and pursued in the chapters which follow is that from a critical perspective the distinction between war and peace has *always* been questionable. The fact that the distinction remains so dominant, however, suggests that it is still doing rather a lot of political work. One of the purposes of this book is to challenge that work, and thereby offer a critique of liberal ideology and its language of 'peace'. The more specific and political aim of this book, however, is also to use this challenge as the basis for a critique of war power.

To take up questions of war requires first and foremost recognition of the powerful sway of received ideas and dominant narratives through which we are supposed to think about it. These ideas and narratives – what C. Wright Mills once called the 'military definition of reality' – get repeated easily and endlessly, and ultimately constrain new and more radical ways of thinking about war.[18] More importantly, critical theorists on the Left have too easily bought into the idea of war as articulated in international relations (IR) and strategic studies and have thus been driven by an agenda not of the Left's own making, replicating a very narrow idea of war as formal military engagement between states and aping IR and strategic studies in becoming little more than a series of footnotes to Clausewitz. The problem might be seen in what is missing from the narrow conception of war. First, such a conception has traditionally designated colonial warfare as 'unconventional' or a 'small wars' affair, thereby managing to dismiss what has in fact been 'by far the most common form of warfare in the modern world'.[19] To give an example of the way this dismissal works, one need only note that between 1815 and 1914 'there was not one month in which British forces were not engaged somewhere across the world',[20] and yet the period in question is still widely described in British history books as the 'hundred years peace'. This is because the 'engagements' were merely 'small wars'. 'Small wars', in other words, is the category used by liberal theory and mainstream war studies to describe the violence through which millions have been slaughtered and resources of whole continents appropriated; so 'small' is such warfare, in fact, that even the writing on 'total war' more or less completely omits it. The reason that such an extensive organised violence in the process of systematic colonisation can be sidelined in this way is deeply connected to the second absence in the narrow conception of war: the structural and systematic violence through which capitalist order has been constituted and accumulation secured.

All of which is to say that radical thinking about the war power must address the question of capital; conversely, it is also a way of saying that radical thinking about capital must address the question of war.[21] This book therefore aims to take discussion of the war power away from the mundane familiarity of what counts as 'war studies', its sub-fields such as military history and strategic studies, its adjacent fields such as IR and geopolitics, and its broader ideological underpinnings in liberal theory. This book instead starts at a difference place: by thinking of war as inseparable from the history of capitalist domination. This book therefore seeks to understand the war power in terms of what is, after all, the most fundamental and violent conflict in human history: the class war.

In a speech at Elberfeld in 1845, Frederick Engels commented on 'present-day society, which … produces a social war of all against all'.[22] This was a major theme of *The Condition of the Working Class in England*, published the same year, which describes 'the social war, the war of each against all … openly declared'. Everywhere is barbarous indifference, hard egotism and nameless misery: 'every man's house is a state of siege, everywhere reciprocal plundering under the protection of the law', meaning that 'everywhere [is] social warfare'. Such comments appear as a gloss on the perpetual war of the state of nature as described by Hobbes, but Engels points to the class dimension of this war. 'Let us proceed to a more detailed investigation of the position in which the social war has placed the non-possessing class', an investigation which takes in the miserable condition of the working class, the deaths from overwork and malnutrition, and the use of the law against any attempt on the part of the working class to resist such conditions. 'Is this social war, or is it not?' asks Engels, adding that 'it is in the interest of the bourgeoisie to conduct this war hypocritically, under the guise of peace'.[23] Marx likewise refers to 'civil war in its most terrible aspect, the war of labour against capital'[24] and in *Capital* writes of the struggles over the working day as a 'protracted and more or less concealed civil war between the capitalist class and the working class'.[25] As joint-authors of the *Manifesto of the Communist Party*, Marx and Engels also write of the 'more or less veiled civil war' that takes place in bourgeois society with the development of the proletariat.[26]

Mainstream studies of war tend to assume that when Marx and Engels use the term 'war' in these ways they do so in a rhetorical sense.[27] But much as Marx and Engels do delight in more than the occasional rhetorical flourish,[28] their claims about the social war are meant to be taken seriously. Hence when in *Capital* Marx comments that 'force is the midwife of every old society which is pregnant with a new one', and that force 'is itself an economic power'[29] the term Marx uses is *Gewalt*, better understood as 'violence', and he is describing the systematic colonisation of the social world by capital and the violence which creates, re-creates and permanently disciplines the proletariat. The violence is a form of war, a global and permanent process that Marx analyses through the lens of 'primitive accumulation', as we shall see in Chapter 2.

Yet are we not constantly told that capital, trade and private property are signs of a healthy commercial order, and that a healthy commercial order is in an inherently co-constitutive relationship with peace? Is this not one of the central claims of liberalism and its law?

According to mainstream IR and political theory, liberalism sets out its stall as a politics of peace. The so-called 'liberal peace' thesis assumes that if all societies were liberal (that is, less barbaric, less communist, less totalitarian, less terroristic, less fascist) then the world would be at peace and the mythical liberal entity known as 'security' would prevail. On this view, war is something that emerges from *outside* of liberal society. This book will instead suggest that liberalism has from its inception been a political philosophy of war, has been fully conscious of this and, as a consequence, has sought to bury this fact under various banners: 'peace and security'; 'law and order'; 'police'. To accept the idea that there was a 'classical age' where the distinction between war and peace did make sense is thus to accept one of liberalism's major myths, one which circulates widely in academic discourse as part of 'the liberal peace' hypothesis: that peace is the focal dynamic of civil society, that capitalism and peace go hand in hand, that law and the state exist in order to realise this 'liberal peace' within civil society, and that international law exists to ensure peace between states. This series of conjoined myths has served to gloss over what Michael Dillon and Julian Reid call the 'liberal way of war'.[30] To gloss over, that is, the violence *of* the liberal peace and liberalism's own mechanism for producing order and policing subjects. Like its siblings 'security', 'law and order' and 'police', 'peace' is from a critical perspective politically suspicious.

'If we look beneath peace, order, wealth, and authority ... will we hear and discover a sort of primitive and permanent war?' In asking this question Michel Foucault launched a project exploring the ways in which we might consider war as the matrix for techniques of domination. Noting Clausewitz's well-known formulation that war is the continuation of politics by other means, Foucault insists that we invert the formulation: politics is the continuation of war by other means. On this view, the task of political power lies in the perpetual inscription of relations of force through a form of unspoken warfare called 'civil peace'. It is not so much 'politics' that is the continuation of war by other means, then, but that 'peace' is, alterations in which are merely episodes, factions and displacements in war. We 'have to interpret the war that is going on beneath peace', because 'peace itself is a coded war'.[31]

Before developing these points we might note that Foucault's comments are not quite as much of an inversion of Clausewitz as Foucault thinks. Clausewitz's thinking around the formulation that war is the continuation of politics in another form concerns the question of whether war is an art or science. For Clausewitz, war is not a science such as maths or astronomy, in which the subject is pure knowledge, and in that sense the term 'art of war' is more appropriate. Yet 'strictly speaking', he says, 'war is neither an art nor a science', but 'is part of man's social existence'. This has a number of implications. First, 'rather than comparing it [war] to art we could more accurately compare it to commerce, which is also a conflict of human interests and activities'. Second, war 'is *still* closer to politics, which in turn may be considered as a kind of commerce on a larger scale', and which means that 'the main lines along which military events progress, and to which they are restricted, are political lines that continue throughout the war into the subsequent peace'; 'how could it be otherwise?', Clausewitz adds, as if he thought he was stating the obvious.[32] Third, if war is indeed a continuation of politics by other means then the 'politics' Clausewitz has in mind is one which takes war to be as one of the highest forms of experience, with an existential vitality, as his 1812 'Political Declaration' and his private letters make clear.[33] These issues aside (and to underscore the point just made about footnotes to Clausewitz, this is the last time he will be mentioned in this book) if it is indeed the case that the political lines of war continue into the subsequent peace, and peace itself is a coded war, then 'keeping the peace' has to be understood anew, and it has to be understood anew through the concept which has historically been central to it as an idea: police.

In 2006 the US Army and Marine Corps updated their *Counter-insurgency Field Manual* for the first time in 25 years. Building on documents such as a joint Department of Justice and the Department of Defense memorandum of understanding built around a 'growing convergence between the technology required for military operations and the technology required for law enforcement', the Manual holds that 'warfighting and policing are dynamically linked' and that the 'roles of the police and military forces ... blur'.[34] Such blurring is now central to military planning.[35] Thus when state personnel use phrases such as 'more of an operation, not a war' they almost always suggest that the operation in question looks and feels like something called 'police'. 'Police' has thus become a central feature of the discursive trope through which the war power is now simultaneously invoked and elided.

This contemporary connection between the war power and the police power reinforces, though is in turn also reinforced by, the increasing use of rather loose concepts within academia and journalism, such as 'world policeman', 'world sheriff', 'global gendarme', 'globocop', 'police-keeping', 'soldiers as cops', 'the blue in the green' and 'blue geopolitics'. Such terminology is found far and wide across the political spectrum.[36] It is also found far and wide across the disciplines: international relations, international law, criminology, socio-legal studies, and social and political theory all have a story to tell about 'criminology meeting international relations', the coming together of the 'military model' and the 'criminological model', of 'war-fighting' turning into 'crime-fighting', and 'warfare' converging with 'crimefare'.[37] The problem with much of the work in this field, however, is that it has an incredibly impoverished concept of police power. All that seems to happen in this work is that IR scholars give a nod in the direction of criminology, and criminologists send a little wink in the direction of IR, and both doff their caps to political theories of war, but all that emerges is a series of rather dull claims about the 'militarisation of policing' and the 'policization of the military' or the coming together of 'high-intensity policing' with 'low-intensity warfare'. For a critical theory of war power, police power and capital accumulation, these banalities get us precisely nowhere.

This can perhaps best be seen in the work of the critical thinkers already cited who suggest that war and peace are coming together, for the almost universal assumption they make is that one can see war and peace coming together in the way war now looks like police. According to Badiou, governments now oppose terrorism within the symbolic register of 'policing'; according to Agamben, 'a particularly destructive *jus belli* ... cloak[s] itself in a seemingly modest "police operation"'; according to Paul Virilio, 'the military class is turning into an internal super-police'. The most influential work, however, has been that of Hardt and Negri. In *Empire* Hardt and Negri suggest that 'war is reduced to the status of police action', with the US acting as the 'international police power'. 'Today the enemy, just like war itself, comes to be banalized', and by 'banalized' they mean 'reduced to the status of routine police repression'. Lest we be unclear about their meaning, they repeat the point four years later in *Multitude*, where they tell us again that war is 'reduced to police action'.[38] Yet what is this 'reduction' exactly? We are told neither why the process needs to be understood as 'reduction' nor what 'reduction' means, in any real sense. What appears in these debates, then, is a rather basic, narrow and ultimately very liberal concept of police. It is the concept of police found in 'police studies'.

Police studies is centrally concerned with something called '*the police*', an institution it claims was invented in the early nineteenth century to deal with crime and enforce the law. But as I have argued at length elsewhere, this was a meaning imposed on the term 'police' by an increasingly hegemonic liberalism in the late-eighteenth century. There is, however, a much older and broader conception of police, the central concern of which was 'good order' in the broadest possible sense, including crime and law enforcement but extending through the regulation of trade and commerce, the discipline of labour, the process of education and training, welfare and health, the minutia of social life and, of course, anything understood as breaching the 'peace'. In some of my earlier work I sought to recover this older and broader concept of police from the backwater of 'police studies' and to place it at the heart of a critical theory of state power. The point was to suggest that 'police' has to be understood less in terms of the institution called *the* police and more in terms of the broad range of powers through which social order is fabricated and subjects constituted – the police power – exercised by a range of agencies of policing situated throughout the state and the institutions for administering civil society.[39] This is the search for the 'well-ordered police state',[40] one which takes in the maintenance of the body politic as a whole[41] and offers an overarching principle for creating a social body out of individual subject-citizens best captured in the Latin phrase used by Foucault when grappling with the idea of police: *omnes et singulatim* (everyone together and each individually).[42] More than anything, however, this is a concept of police 'as a bundle of measures that *make work possible and necessary* to all those who could not live without it'.[43]

The police power thus involves a set of apparatuses and technologies constituting political order in general and the law of labour in particular. This gives us an expanded concept of police that enables us to make sense of the fabrication of bourgeois order and is the very reason why that concept so central to police, namely security, is the fundamental concept of bourgeois society.[44]

In *The Fabrication of Social Order* I held back from thinking through one of the obvious issues: what does such a concept of police power mean for our understanding of the international? More specifically: what does such a concept mean for our understanding of what goes by the name of 'international police'? Asking such questions forces us to situate the police power in relation to the war power. Now, the question of the connection between the war power and the police power is one that arises in Foucault's work. Foucault is undoubtedly the thinker who had done most to put a broad concept of 'police' back in the centre of political thinking. The series of engagements with the police idea, through *History of Madness, The Birth of the Clinic* and other texts, gets developed most fully in the two lecture series Foucault gave between 1977 and 1979, now published as *Security, Territory, Population* and *The Birth of Biopolitics*.[45] At the same time, and as I have already pointed out, Foucault sought to think social relations through the model of war. This has become clear from the publication of various lecture series through the 1970s prior to *Security, Territory, Population* and *The Birth of Biopolitics*. For example, the great confinement which in *History of Madness* had been a *police* matter gets treated in the 1973–4 lectures on psychiatric power as a *battlefield*.[46] In further lectures Foucault develops this focus to consider politics as the continuation of war by other means. This approach to thinking politics through war and thinking war politically is reinforced in Foucault's more substantive works such as *The History of Sexuality*, but most notably in *Discipline and Punish* where he takes as his model a perpetual battle rather than contract and which uses war (and not punishment, despite the book's familiar motifs) for understanding power.

One can therefore read Foucault as sometimes thinking about power through the lens of police and sometimes through the lens of war. Yet there is something fundamentally strange about Foucault's work in this regard, in that these really do seem to be two different lenses. In other words, he never really does very much to connect his concepts of police and war, such as offering an exploration of how these two apparatuses might be considered together, within each other, alongside each other or implicated in one another. In *'Society Must Be Defended'*, for example, he talks at some length about war yet gives just a couple of passing and somewhat superfluous references to police. In the lectures two years later, published as *Security, Territory, Population*, he talks about both police and war and yet for the most part discusses them separately. He speaks of 'two great assemblages': 'a military-diplomatic apparatus, on the one hand, and the apparatus of police … on the other'. And although he suggests that there is a relation between police and 'European equilibrium' maintained by the military-diplomatic assemblage and that these two apparatuses had to 'maintain a relation of forces, and then the growth of these forces' in a way which links them under the sign of 'security', he for the most part keeps them apart, even going so far at one point to characterise the Italian state as a state of military-diplomacy but not police.[47]

There is I think a potential in Foucault's work which is never quite realised, namely to consider the war power and the police power in conjunction.[48] That it remains unrealised is witnessed by two features of the scholarship in this field. On the one hand, there is now a substantial and important body of work stemming from an engagement with Foucault which has sought to mobilise the original concept of police for new insights in political and historical sociology.[49] However, aside from maybe three short attempts,[50] it has not been widely used to grapple with the *international* dimension of police powers or what it means to speak of war and police coming together. On the other hand, there is now a growing body of work within IR and geopolitics which has sought to bring Foucault's work to bear on questions of war and international order. Yet virtually none of this work utilises Foucault's account of the police power.[51] More often than not, 'police' just never appears. Worse, when it does appear it is as *the* police – in the narrow, liberal and decidedly non-Foucauldian conception of mainstream police studies. Despite employing Foucault, this work has more or less completely forgone any attempt to use the broader and far more productive concept of police, and thus all of the critical potential in exploring the war–police nexus is lost.

In other words, the 'war-is-becoming-police' approach found across the disciplines and in the various attempts to think critically about war does little genuinely to bring 'war' and 'police' together and sheds little light on either; more or less replicating the liberal conception of police, it comes closer to mystifying rather than explaining. Critical theory needs an argument that works on and with the nexus of war power and police power. This is an argument that assumes that war and police are *always already* together, that treats the war power and the police power as predicative on one another. This is therefore not a book about an institution called 'the military' and how it connects to an institution called 'the police'. From a critical perspective, such a distinction is irrelevant, pandering as it does to a general liberal tendency replicated throughout the social and political sciences, namely the simplifying of the complexity of state power into distinct dichotomies: law versus administration, constitutional versus exceptional, normal versus emergency, courts versus tribunals, legislative versus executive, state versus civil society and, of course, military versus police. Rather, we need to think of war and police as *processes* working in conjunction as state power.

By thinking through the war power in conjunction with the police power, and the police power as dealing with a condition of *disorder*, the war power can more easily be read in terms of the fabrication of order. This is an analysis of the way war imbricates itself into the fabric of social relations as a form of ordering the world, diffracting into a series of micro-operations and regulatory practices to ensure those nebulous targets of bourgeois desire: security, order and accumulation.

Mitchell Dean has argued that in the terms of the original police science we can see some important differences between police and war: police confronts a situation of disorder rather than an enemy; when police does concern an enemy, it is as a source of disorder rather than as an enemy per se. In this light, the main concern of police is the constitution of order rather than defeating the enemy.[52] True as this is, it obscures a double unifying connection between the police power and war power in this regard, a connection which will run through this book. On the one hand, we need to grasp the exercise of the police power in constant *war* against the 'enemies of order'. Police treatises, texts, speech and action never cease telling us of the constant police wars being fought against the disorderly, unruly, criminal, indecent, disobedient, disloyal and lawless.[53] On the other hand, we also need to grasp the *ordering* capabilities of the war power. 'War is the motor behind institution and order', as Foucault puts it.[54] Just as the police power is not reducible to *the* police but depends on a whole range of technologies to form the social order, so the war power is not reducible to the military but depends on a whole range of technologies to do the same.[55] If, as it has been said, warfare can best be defined with one word – *formation*[56] – then we might say that what is always under formation is order: social order, international order, the order of accumulation.[57] This is therefore a book about technologies of war power and police power in the formation of capitalist order; it is therefore also a book about the violence of accumulation and its legitimisation in liberal ideology. The fabrication of bourgeois order *is* war.

This is, however, *not* a book about the 'war on terror'. Although I do discuss the 'war on terror' at various points and use some of its features as a springboard for my wider argument – we live, after all, in a time in which liberals seem to be falling over each other in the rush to explain why the war machine must keep rolling on and on – it is now fairly obvious that the 'war on terror' has little to do with defeating 'terror', whatever that might mean, and rather a lot to do with shaping civil society and the social order: with making and remaking citizens and/as subjects, with re-forming populations into new modes of security and technologies of governing and, more than anything, with establishing new grounds for accumulation. The war on terror is thus treated as the contemporary instantiation of the combination of war power and police power.

It will be clear from this Introduction that this book seeks to distance the reader from the familiarity of the disciplines in which war and police are 'obviously' studied. Obviousness more often than not reveals itself as a function of power,[58] a means of policing the act of writing, and nowhere is this clearer than in what passes as 'war studies', 'police studies', IR and criminology. This book therefore seeks to break with the obvious, or at least what is presented as obvious in the disciplinary formations of the modern University. The value of a thought really needs to be measured by its distance from the obvious and the familiar.[59] Or as Flaubert once said, 'the worth of a book can be judged by the strength of the punches it gives and the length of time it takes you to recover from them'.[60]

Chapter 1

WAR AS PEACE, PEACE AS PACIFICATION

Don't forget the real business of the War is buying and selling. The murdering and the violence are self-policing, and can be entrusted to non-professionals. The mass nature of wartime death is useful in many ways. It serves as spectacle, as diversion from the real movements of the War. It provides raw material to be recorded into History, so that children may be taught History as sequences of violence, battle after battle, and be more prepared for the adult world. Best of all, mass death's a stimulus to just ordinary folks, little fellows, to try 'n' grab a piece of that Pie while they're still here to gobble it up. The true war is a celebration of markets.

Thomas Pynchon, *Gravity's Rainbow* (1973)

The story of Henry Dunant is well known, but bears retelling. Dunant is famous for having founded the Red Cross in 1864, an international society to provide immediate care for those wounded in war, and for which he received the Nobel Peace Prize in 1901. The story goes that Dunant's idea came to him in the aftermath of the battle of Solferino, where Napoleon was assisting the Italians in trying to drive the Austrians out of Italy. Having witnessed the scene of bloodshed, Dunant published *Un Souvenir de Solferino* (1862), in which he described in detail the misery of the battle and proposed a new society to alleviate the suffering of soldiers and to care for the wounded. In February 1863 the Geneva Society for Public Welfare took his suggestion on board and began to promote the idea, and Dunant spent time travelling across Europe to garner support. In August 1864 twelve nations signed an international Treaty at Geneva guaranteeing the treatment of medical personnel as neutrals, the free movement of medical supplies, and an international emblem of a red cross on a white background under which such medical workers would operate. And, so the story goes, a hero of international humanitarian law is said to have been born.[1]

One lesser known part of the story is that the reason Dunant encountered the wounded and dying on the battlefield at Solferino was that he had been travelling to meet with Napoleon to negotiate over water rights for part of Algeria. The reason the water rights were needed was that the Financial and Industrial Company of Mons-Gémila Mills in Algeria, of which Dunant had recently become President, needed the water to fully exploit the land there. Dunant was carrying on a family tradition: he was a colonialist; the project in Algeria was just one of many such colonial projects in which he had a personal investment. Frédéric Mégret has noted that in the history of international law there is no one quite as 'sacred' as Henry Dunant. And yet this most sacred figure in international law turns out to have a very direct relationship to colonialism.[2]

There is an aspect of international law that international lawyers prefer to ignore, one which IR also conveniently omits from most of its analyses, that security studies largely sidelines and which liberalism likes to deny is constitutive of liberalism as a doctrine: colonialism.[3] The reason for this is clear: it is an aspect that points directly to the violence of international law and the fact that the real historical content of international law is a war over resources.

Mainstream claims about the role and function of international law are founded on but also sustain the idea that law in general is the basis of 'peace and security': without law, there is only violence. Hence in terms of geopolitics, international law is seen as a high point of universal ethics, war as the high point of pure violence; law protects, war kills. 'Law is, essentially, an order for the promotion of peace', says Hans Kelsen. 'The law makes the use of force a monopoly of the community. And precisely by doing so, law ensures peace'. What this means, in effect, is that 'law is … an ordering for the promotion of peace in that it forbids the use of force in relations among the members of the community'.[4] In this view, war and law are antithetical, law is the counter to war, and so law and peace come together. This has been reinforced more recently in the stress on the United Nations as a mechanism of 'peace and security'.

Peace and security: both are supposedly 'good things', uncontrovertibly beneficial, and must remain unchallenged. Both come draped in law. This is the juridical illusion perpetuated by liberalism, by ideas about the international rule of law in 'cosmopolitan democracy', 'global democratic governance' and 'humanitarianism'. It is also reinforced in the claim made by radicals and progressives that some wars are 'illegal', most notably since 2001 as part of a political mobilisation against the 'war on terror'. This illusion is also one of the things against which this book intends to argue. In this chapter and the next I work through some aspects of this illusion in order to shape an argument about the integral relationship between war and law.

'OUR WAR ... IS PERMANENT'

'The prevailing view in the study of international law is that it emerged in Europe in the period after the Peace of Westphalia (1648)', notes one textbook. On this view, after 1648 there emerged a new collective security order in which disputes would be settled by legal adjudication.[5] But starting an analysis of international law with 1648 plays on the idea that international law is somehow a product of Western states meeting together to agree some common principles of sovereignty and territorial right. In so doing, it reinforces 'the myth of 1648'.[6] 'International scholars have made much of 1648', notes David Kennedy. 'Using that date to mark the beginning of their discipline, they have generally treated earlier work as immature and incomplete – significant only as a precursor for what followed'.[7] For example, the textbook just cited, *Akehurst's Modern Introduction to International Law*, mentions colonialism and recognises the substantive inequalities behind the formal equality of international law, but does so only in the context of colonialism from 1648 and specifically within the 'great powers' struggle of the eighteenth and nineteenth centuries.[8] But the issue at stake needs to be traced back beyond Westphalia, to the law of nations from 1492 to 1648, and thus to the *wars* of early colonialism. In this context the work of Francisco de Vitoria and Hugo Grotius is crucial.

Vitoria's work is regarded as one of the first statements of a universalist and humanitarian conception of international law. He is often regarded as the first to have 'proclaimed a "natural" community of all mankind and the universal validity of human rights', to have presented a 'courageous defence of the rights of the Indians' against the Spanish, and to have laid down an early case for 'humanitarian intervention'.[9] This reading of Vitoria is rooted in his conception of 'the whole world which is in a sense a commonwealth' and the idea of a law of nations which would have 'the sanction of the whole world'.[10] Put simply: Vitoria was a liberal. Indeed, notes James Brown Scott, Vitoria 'could not help being a liberal. He was an internationalist by inheritance. And because he was both, his international law is a liberal law of nations'.[11] One reason for this interpretation is that Vitoria's 'humanist' tendencies meant his work was established against the more explicitly violent policies of Spanish colonialism: 'No business shocks me or embarrasses me more than the corrupt profits and affairs of the Indies … I do not understand the justice of the war'.[12] A second reason is his claim that the Indians had rights of *dominium*. Sinners and non-believers as they might be, they are nonetheless 'not impeded from being true masters, publicly and privately' and so 'could not be robbed of their property'.[13] One of the reasons Vitoria thought the Indians had rights of dominium, and a third reason for the interpretation of Vitoria as providing one of the first statements of a liberal humanitarian international law, is because he considered the Indians as human beings: the Indians are not monkeys but 'are men, and our neighbours', so 'it would be harsh to deny to them … the rights we concede to Saracens and Jews'.[14]

In suggesting that non-Christians are somehow equal to Christians, Vitoria challenges the idea of a universal Christian order administered by the Pope within which the Indians could be characterised as heathens and their rights and duties determined accordingly. He thereby disallows religion as the basis for war against the Indians or rule over them. Yet although the Indians are like the Spanish, their social, economic and political practices, including nudity, the consumption of raw food and cannibalism, mean they diverge from universal norms in such a way as to also make them unlike the Spanish.[15] The Indian appears to have some of the social and cultural characteristics of civilised life, yet as an 'Indian'[16] is markedly uncivilised; the Indian shares the characteristics of a universal humanity, yet is also set clearly apart. Thus the 'Indian problem' became the basis of a discussion about the relations between different groups of humans within a 'republic of all the world'. In effect, as Anghie points out, the problem for Vitoria was not one of managing order between formally equal sovereign states, but a question of constituting order among culturally different entities.[17] It is this tension between the claims of natural law against behaviour that is somehow 'unnatural' and the necessity of understanding *others* within the framework of a universal humanity which runs though Vitoria's two 1539 lectures on the Indians and on the laws of war.[18] And it is this tension which begins to reveal the conjunction of violence and law running through the liberal imperialism which emerges and in which the idea of 'peace' becomes a key theme.

Inspired by the dynamics of Spanish territorial possession, Vitoria places colonial domination – and thus dispossession – at the heart of international law. At the heart of this domination and dispossession are the laws of war and peace but also the question of 'free trade'. According to Vitoria, the natural rights and duties of the law of nations are society and fellowship, trade and commerce, communication, participation regarding things in common, and the freedom to travel. Because trade is essential to human communication and to the exchange and develop-ment of human knowledge, the right to maintain lines of communication through trade and exchange is a right of natural law. Hence 'the Spaniards have the right to travel and dwell in those countries, so long as they do no harm to the barbarians', and 'they may lawfully trade among the barbarians, so long as they do no harm to their homeland'. A refusal by the Indians to trade with the Spaniards constitutes a refusal to maintain 'natural' lines of communication, and is barbarism. Moreover, 'if there are any things among the barbarians which are held in common both by their own people and by strangers, it is not lawful for the barbarians to prohibit the Spaniards from sharing and enjoying them'. The reason for this is based in part on the principle of trade and in part on the idea that in natural law a thing which does not belong to anyone becomes the property of the first taker. What this means is that should the barbarians try to deny the Spaniards what is theirs by the law of nations and natural law then 'they commit an offence against them'.[19]

If Vitoria's argument is a major contribution to some kind of emergent international law of nations, then it is equally an important contribution to an emergent discourse of political economy centred on commerce and accumulation. Not only were the trade routes themselves of huge historical and geopolitical significance, but they also led to the intro-duction of huge quantities of gold and silver into the European markets, such that major European marketplaces such as Seville, Antwerp, Lyon and Venice became centres of routine speculation for profit and accumulation. At the same time, Spanish *cambistas* (money exchanges) were beginning to issue credit and letters of exchange enabling merchants to travel without having to carry large quantities of money with them, all of which Vitoria also thought permissible.[20] It is in this context of commerce, trade, profit and accumulation that Vitoria helps shape natural law arguments for conquest, since for Vitoria the right to engage in commerce and trade is a natural right. As Robert Williams points out, within the totalising discourse of a universally obligatory natural law of nations, the profit motive occupies an extremely privileged status, in the sense that *not* engaging in trade is treated as contrary to the mutual self-interests shared by all humankind.[21] And this motivation must be allowed to triumph over common property rights. Put simply: customary land use by the Indians has to be treated as an *illegitimate* form of property. Any indigenous 'law of the commons' must therefore be abolished and replaced by the law of private property, and dispossession legitimised on the grounds of natural law.

It is this dispossession and replacement of common property with private property that becomes central to the colonising project and to bourgeois political economy thereafter, and is the point at which the question of liberal war becomes crucial. According to Vitoria, the Spaniards have the right to defend themselves against the offences committed by the Indians by availing themselves of the other main right of the law of nations: to go to war. 'If the barbarians ... persist in their wickedness and strive to destroy the Spaniards, they may then treat them no longer as innocent enemies, but as treacherous foes against whom all rights of war can be exercised'.[22] In making this argument Vitoria's lecture broke new theoretical ground for Western colonising thought, providing a natural law source of Spain's right – and, by implication, any other state's right – to engage in war against native peoples and to rule in the New World as a means of securing the right to commerce. If the law of nations emerged to deal with war, then the war in question was one of accumulation.

For the argument to be developed in this book it is significant to note that this liberal war of accumulation was recognised from the outset as permanent. 'Our war against the pagans is ... permanent', claims Vitoria, on the grounds that the pagans/Indians 'can never sufficiently pay for the injuries and losses inflicted'.[23] Moreover, and because of this, '*a prince may do everything in a just war which is necessary to secure peace and security*', including plundering the goods of the innocent, killing the innocent, enslaving the women and children, and even to the point of annihilation:

> War is waged to produce peace, but sometimes security cannot be obtained without the wholesale destruction of the enemy. This is particularly the case in wars against the infidel, from whom peace can never be hoped for on any terms; therefore the only remedy is to eliminate all of them who are capable of bearing arms, given that they are already guilty.[24]

Vitoria's law of nations, then, in essence a formulation of the legality of the principle of accumulation as the conquest of the world, gives us two options: permanent war in search of free trade, or absolute destruction of the enemies of such trade.

That Vitoria has been so highly regarded within international law reveals the extent to which the violence of early colonial war was central to the constitution of international law. It would be difficult to overstate the influence of Vitoria's arguments as his work filtered into the political and legal discourse of Europe. His lectures were published in Latin versions in Lyons in 1557, in Salamanca in 1565 and in Golstadt in 1580, and the'New Laws of the Indies'promulgated by Charles V in 1542 were heavily dependent on Vitoria's arguments. His various'proofs'of the laws of nations and their implications for colonial domination filtered through the work of his pupils and into the writings of a range of English thinkers and colonists, many of which, such as George Peckham's *True Reporte, Of the late discoveries, and possession, taken in the right of the Crowne of England, of the Newfound Lands* (1583), helped rearticulate Vitoria's claims into a set of terms more amenable to Protestant state- and empire-building. They can also be found in Alberico Gentili's work on the law of nations in the last two decades of the sixteenth century and, as we shall see, his arguments are appropriated by Grotius.[25] Onuma Yasuaki sums it up by saying that Vitoria's theory 'exhibits a prototype of normative justification of international law which remained basically the same for the next four centuries'.[26]

In this light, James Brown Scott's description of Vitoria as a *liberal* is both interesting and historically important. A leading law scholar, Scott was solicitor to the US Department of State (1906–9), acted as Trustee and Secretary to the Carnegie Endowment for International Peace

(1910–40), served as advisor to the US delegation to the second Hague Peace Conference of 1907, was President of the American Institute of International law (1915–40), wrote several major works on international law and the various Hague Peace conferences, edited and thereby made newly available a series of translations of the 'classics' of international law (including Vitoria's), helped establish the Permanent Court of International Justice in 1921, and served under President Woodrow Wilson. In pursuing the idea that Vitoria is a liberal, Scott sought to draw a link between the liberalism of the sixteenth century law of nations and the liberalism of early twentieth-century US foreign policy. The 'discovery' of America, in his view, gave birth to a modern law of nations which was originally Catholic but had now become entirely laicized in liberal form. For that reason, he sought to situate Vitoria within this liberal tradition.

Now, Scott's argument has been widely challenged. Arthur Nussbaum, for example, is just one of many who have responded by pointing out the supposedly 'illiberal' things Vitoria has to say or tries to justify.[27] Yet the argument of Nussbaum and others is founded on the rather naïve assumption that liberalism could never engage in something so 'illiberal' as systematic violence against weaker and even unarmed opponents for merely commercial reasons. Nussbaum's argument is founded, in other words, on a modern political myth: that liberalism is inherently peaceful. But leaving aside some of the issues in Scott's reading of Vitoria, it seems to me that Scott gets it more or less spot on: Vitoria is a liberal. But what both Scott and Scott's challengers fail to see is that *this is the very reason* Vitoria defends the practice of war against the Indians. To understand why, Vitoria really needs to be understood in terms of the wider tradition of liberal imperialism and the simultaneous creation of durably pacified social spaces that were then becoming established in Europe.

PACIFICATION: WAR AND LAW, POLICE AND ORDER

Much has been made of what J. G. A. Pocock has called 'the Machiavellian moment' in the history of political thought, in which a new language was forged addressing the problems associated with constituting a republic of liberty through a dialectic of virtue and fortune.[28] Mikael Hornqvist has shown that this republican ideal of freedom was deeply implicated in the imperial project, in which acquisition becomes the touchstone of liberty. For in the century leading up to Machiavelli, as well as in the years to follow, writer after writer had stressed the importance of empire to liberty: Bruni on the right to lordship over the world; Dati on the centrality of empire to security and economic order; Palmieri on the links between civic unity and increase of empire; Savonarola on the importance of the empire to ancient Rome; the list is long and well-documented by Hornqvist. Thus when Machiavelli lays down the basic tenets of Roman and Florentine republicanism – namely that a city has two ends, one to acquire, the other to be free – he draws on and summarises a position that had become well-established over the previous century. This tradition assumes that liberty 'entails a commitment to empire understood as a defense and a militant extension of true liberty in a hostile world'. In concrete terms, this 'translates into a pursuit of territorial security which justifies the intervention in the political life of neighbouring states and the subjugation and annexation of foreign lands'. Far from being contrary values, notes Hornqvist, liberty and imperial acquisition are understood as together constituting the dual end of the healthy republic.[29] The liberal and 'humanitarian' concept of a world of universal being presupposes an expansive polity which, in generating a politics of acquisition, produces new enemies and thus requires the exercise of violence. For there can be no empire of liberty without arms. The art of politics is the art of war, as Machiavelli puts it in the only one of his major works to be published in his lifetime (in 1521). Or as he puts it in his better-known work: the successful Prince 'takes as his profession nothing else than war and its laws and discipline'.[30] This art of war is in Machiavelli's mind central to imperial politics, but also links back to the discipline of liberty needed for internal order.

Empires of 'liberty' are always already empires of violence. 'Violence is not an epiphenomenon of the Machiavellian Moment', notes Mick Dillon. Nor is it merely instrumental to the realisation of liberty. In the Machiavellian Moment, rather, liberty 'cannot even be thought outside of the killing required for it to be. Its very grid of intelligibility is that provided by strategically inspired violence, and specifically by the need to say how much killing is enough to realise and sustain political freedom'. Seen in this light, the Machiavellian moment is liberty written as a logos of war.[31]

This logos of war gets written into the emerging law of nations, and it does so because it is violence carried out in the name of peace, security and accumulation. 'The aim of war is peace and security', says Vitoria, over and again. War is waged specifically for the defence of property, for the recovery of property and in revenge for an injury, and it is waged more generally 'to establish peace and security'.[32] This is used to justify offensive as well as defensive war.

> The purpose of war is the peace and security of the common-wealth ... But there can be no security for the commonwealth unless its enemies are prevented from injustice by fear of war. It would be altogether unfair if war could only be waged by a commonwealth to repel unjust invaders from its borders, and never to carry the conflict into the enemies' camp.

Indeed, pre-empting the idea of a 'humanitarian war' that would emerge centuries later, Vitoria insists that war might be carried out 'for the good of the whole world'.[33]

The significance of Vitoria's idea that war is made for peace and security lies in the fact that it was being articulated at the very start of a crisis in the European international legal order that was both reflected in and constituted by the practice of 'peace' as a key principle in the emerging law of nations (and which therefore generated a new set of practices for 'peace treaties').[34] The colonial wars which gave rise to this law of nations were increasingly taking on the ideological form of peace. Concomitantly, this was a key moment in the development and structural transformation of the state. The prolonged cumulative effect of new weapons technology, new disciplinary provisions, fortifications, increase in the size of armies and navies, and the changes in tactics and strategy which these developments aided and abetted, including a fiscal centralisation necessary to sustain these developments, meant that not only was the development of state power being accelerated as the monarchs and republics of Europe centralised and nationalised, most notably in the major colonising powers of England, Spain, the Netherlands and France, but that it was being accelerated as a war power.[35] And as a war power it received philosophical legitimation in a variety of forms: from the new and decidedly Machiavellian 'military arithmetic' found in the work of writers such as Girolamo Cataneo in Italy and Thomas Digges in England, to the most sustained commentaries on the nature of sovereignty, such as Bodin's *Six Books of a Commonweale* (1576) and Botero's *Ragion di Stato*

(1589), both of which suggest that military discipline and training in arms are necessary for war with other nations and for disciplining one's own subjects.[36]

Yet this *war power* was also compelled to declare itself a *power for peace*, in a way that distinguished it from the feudal order it was increasingly usurping.

Feudalism, as its name suggests, was founded on the feud. The feud constituted a form of enmity, understood as the negation of friendship and thus the opposite of peace; the feud was 'un-friendship' (*Unfreundschaft*).[37] Now, one of the older terms for feud and enmity was the Germanic *Werra* and its Latin, Romance and English forms *gwerra*, *guerre* and *war*. Hence there was no legal distinction between feud and war: violence was the distinguishing mark – the *obviously* distinguishing mark – of the feudal system, pervading and shaping the social and ideological order and providing the social definition of the feudal ruling class.[38] In such an order there could be no distinction between the feud/war as a conflict between sovereign entities and the feud/war within those same entities. An order rooted in the feud could have no distinction between the threat from outside the territory and the lawbreaker within: both were enemies. Within this schema, a discourse about violence as some kind of 'problem' was simply not possible. Brunner notes that this 'whole basic pattern of peace and feud persisted even as late as the sixteenth century'. The Church, kings and princes tried to restrict or suppress the feud, passing more and more prohibitions on feuding, most of which had little effect. Simply prohibiting the feud was not enough. What was needed 'was a structural transformation of the state itself'.[39]

Thus it was only once the feudal order had collapsed and the absolutist state began to pioneer the professional army that the question of violence came to be addressed as a political issue by the 'intelligentsia'; 'peace', in other words, could be placed on the ideological agenda. Humanists such as Erasmus suggested that an unjust peace be better than a just war, statesmen and sovereigns came to talk about a universal peace rather than perpetual war, some of them adopting *beati pacifici* ('blessed are the peacemakers') as their motto or styling themselves as *Rex Pacificus*, and pageants lauding peace increasingly took place with a pomp that would have been unthinkable just a century earlier. Catherine de Medici, for example, took on the mantle of peacemaker using symbols of peace such as the rainbow or the Juno (arranger of peace-bringing marriages), and Charles V fashioned himself as the new Augustus, the emperor of peace: the famous painting of him by Titian has him riding through a landscape conveying the peaceful calm after a raging battle, while a sculpture of him by Leone y Pampeo has him 'dominating over fury'.[40]

The issue here is not just a monarchical jockeying for the image of 'peacemaker', for the question of peace resonated culturally and intellectually. It has been noted, for example, that the mid-sixteenth century saw a proliferation of peace poetry,[41] and, as Ben Lowe has shown, as that century progressed 'peace' was becoming more complex and adaptable as an idea and more entrenched as a societal ethic. In personal form it was associated with charity, mercy and piety; in its religious mode it connoted tranquillity as part of a rigorous Christian ideal; in a more 'political' mode it meant the restoration of order and stability along with an end to lawlessness. Most importantly, in becoming conjoined with a set of ideas associated with the rise of new forms of commerce and accumulation which liberalism would later use to claim an intimate and fundamental connection between peace and capital ('commercial order' as *doux commerce*), it connoted certain practical benefits to the nation. It was a discourse of peace outside and distinct from 'just war' doctrine and centred on the idea of the nation-state.[42] Even manuals of military method were now required to incorporate a peace ethic,[43] as the world of commerce and the market laid claim to be a condition of 'peace and security' and offered the foundations of a political structure to protect that condition.

'War appears to be as old as mankind, but peace is a modern invention', the nineteenth-century liberal jurist Sir Henry Maine once commented.[44] An invention, that is, that came about amid the increasing monopolisation of violence by the developing state and one which could be shaped and utilised by the state to help justify the violence under its control. The discourse of peace thus came to *permeate* the discourse of war in the very century in which war was being treated as an ineradicable feature of politics, as a necessity for the security of the state, and in which the 'permanent-war machine' was being perfected. A book such as Thomas Becon's *New Pollecye of War* (1542, published under his pseudonym Theodore Basille) could be retitled for its second edition later that year *The True Defense of Peace* and then reissued under its old title again after Becon's death without anyone finding anything odd in the changes.[45] The changes are indicative of the extent to which 'peace', as an increasingly seductive ideal to the martial mentality of the European ruling elites, had to be subsumed under the logic of war. Hence, on the one hand, even a staunch 'pacifist' such as Erasmus ends up accepting the right to wage war, not least for the 'tranquillity' and 'stability' of the Christian republic and to 'punish delinquents'; that is, for dealing with internal dissent and rebellion.[46] On the other hand, even a staunch defender of the 'art of war' such as Machiavelli also writes of the 'arts of peace', to be exercised externally against one's enemies in the hope of breaking them down (due to the fact that 'the cause of union is fear and war') and internally as a mechanism for internal order (his example is to have the people believe in religion), and it is clear from his discussion that the arts of peace are continuous with the arts of war.[47] As much as it is often said that war made the state and the state made war, so too might we say that 'peace' made the state and the state made peace. The war machine is a peace machine; the peace machine is a war machine.

'Peace' derives from the Middle English and Old French *pais*, and is adapted from the Latin *pacem*, itself derived from *pax*. *Pax* was central to the articulation and development of the imperial theme in this period (as understood in terms of the *Pax Romana*, and as it would later be understood in terms of the *Pax Britannica* and *Pax Americana*). But in the Roman tradition, *pax* has as much affinity with the word 'dominance' as it does 'peace'. For the Romans *pax* did not presuppose some kind of equality. A Treaty declaring 'peace' generally meant the unconditional surrender of the defeated state, notes Gerardo Zampaglione, which is why expressions such as 'to impose the peace' and 'to dictate the peace' were common and remain so. The use of such words indicated nothing less than the victory of the Roman army and the unconditional surrender of the enemy.[48] What is connoted by the word *pax*, and thus 'peace', is not an absence of conflict or making of a pact but, rather, the imposition of hegemony and domination achieved through conquest and maintained by arms.[49] 'The peace imposed by Rome became the principal ideological justification for the empire', notes Zampaglione, adding that 'almost all the Roman writers agreed that spreading peace among mankind meant subjecting other peoples to Roman dominion'. Subjecting them, that is, to Roman 'security'.[50] In going hand in hand with *imperium*, *Pax* was and is a victor's peace achieved by war and conquest.

All of which is a way of saying that peace needs to be understood as legitimate violence: a coded war.[51] But what might this mean for our understanding of that institution that we are told is charged with 'keeping the peace', namely police? The question requires a long answer, one which weaves its way in and out of the chapters of this book.

Let us note here that the category 'police' came to the fore in European thought at this very moment. Its connotations were the legislative and administrative regulation of the internal life of a community to promote general welfare and the condition of good order. The instructions and activities considered necessary for the maintenance of good order were known as 'police ordinances', 'Policey Ordnung' or 'Polizeiordnungen' and referred to the management and direction of the population by the state. Police becomes the foundation of the fabrication of social order. The image of the well-ordered state developed because the breakdown of the feudal order, as an order in which exploitation and domination were united, turned into an increasingly capitalist order in which the unity of political domination and economic exploitation gets broken. Politico-legal coercion gets concentrated in a centralised (and militarised) national unit while economic coercion gets displaced onto the new regime of accumulation. This generates the fundamental police problem: how to generate a peaceful and secure order of lawful obedience amid the apparent disorder and insecurity of bourgeois society.

The problem of police is also very much the problem of the city. At this moment historically the growth of towns generated concern over forms of behaviour made possible by urbanisation: gambling, drinking, adultery, blasphemy and, of course, the 'wandering' poor. More generally, fears were expressed about a 'dissolute condition of masterlesse men' created from the collapse of feudal order, 'without subjection to Lawes' and with no 'coercive Power to tye their hands'.[52] The massive de-population following the Black Death of 1349 led to a doubling of wages and an increase in the mobility of labour, along with the transformation of a large number of labour services into cash rents. With the increased mobility of labour, displaced labourers could slip away from their manors and demand more wages as 'free' labour. Worse, such creatures were thought to be behind the rise of popular disturbances throughout Europe during the sixteenth century. This conjunction of 'disorderliness' and 'criminality' was connected to the idea of 'rebellion' against the very structures of life and modes of being that were being imposed by the state and the new regime of accumulation, and even against the political order itself.

Together, the 'criminal-disorderly-rebel' constituted the *lawless* creature. According to the *Oxford English Dictionary* (*OED*) this is the period that 'lawless' becomes widely used, pertaining to 'disorderly' and 'disobedient' as well as the absence of law. As the security problem of the age, the lawless creature was the police problem. But the lawless creature was also thought to be *at war with the social order*. Thus 'outlawry' came to be practised as a police power, in the sense that one could be 'outlawed' as punishment, but outlawry also came to form the foundation of police wars thereafter. The declaration of 'outlawry' is 'a declaration of war by the commonwealth against an offending member', as Frederick Pollock and Frederic William Maitland put it. And this police war was designed as a means of 'compelling submission to authority'.[53] This also stems from the fact that war was considered to be a form of punishment and that for the most part the punishment was concerned with crimes against property (a point which we shall develop in the chapter to follow).[54]

All of which is to say that it is impossible to understand the development of the concepts of war and peace in this crucial period of state formation and capital accumulation without connecting them to the concept of police. As writers as diverse as Marx, Weber, Foucault and Elias have variously shown, the birth of the age of nations as military organisations defending the sovereign and the population also saw the birth of political tactics for the policing of subjects within states. This is why the history of the army is the 'epitome of the whole history of civil societies' (Marx) and why the fundamental reference point of the 'military dream of society' (Foucault) is not warfare against distant enemies similarly organised but, rather, the police of the internal territory.[55] The war power and the police power need to be grasped alongside, as part of and in conjunction with one another.

Now, this process was worked out in different ways in different states, but the general tendency is clear: the process as a whole facilitated a functional integration of the powers of the modern state operating under the sign of peace and security. The process concerns not just the violent crushing of opposition (though it certainly involves that), nor just a question of which 'force' does the crushing (military, paramilitary, police?), but is also very much about the shaping of the behaviour of individuals, groups and classes, and thereby ordering the social relations of power around a particular regime of accumulation, a process constituting the'peace and security'of social order; the peace agreement, in the form of the *law of the peacekeeper*, was never clearer than when applied internally. This is the meaning of police that eventually becomes central to its whole history and logic: the fabrication of *durably pacified social spaces*, to use Elias's phrase, organised around the ideas of 'peace', 'order' and 'security' and within which new forms of commerce and accumulation could flourish.[56] If peace is a coded war, it is coded as pacification.

One does not hear too much about 'pacification' these days. One reason for this is its replacement with'peacekeeping':'one small but clear signpost of change in the twentieth century has been the growing use of the word"peacekeeping"in place of"pacification"'.[57] A second reason is that it is a term that many like to dismiss as a euphemism or dishonest misnomer for armed attack, occupation, torture and repression.[58] George Orwell makes the point in an essay on political writing:

> In our time, political speech and writing are largely the defense of the indefensible … Political language has to consist largely of euphemism, question-begging and sheer cloudy vagueness. Defenceless villages are bombarded from the air, the inhabitants driven out into the countryside, the cattle machine-gunned, the huts set on fire with incendiary bullets: this is called *pacification*.[59]

Such dismissal is often a result of the blatantly obvious acts of violence carried out under the label of 'peacekeeping' and, more recently, 'counterinsurgency'in the twentieth and now twenty-first centuries.

Yet there is a longer story to tell. The *OED* cites the Edicts of Pacification of 1563 and 1570, and the Edict of Nantes in 1598 as the first examples of the word'pacification'. The dates of the first usage – and by the end of that century there had been so many Edicts of Pacification that King Henry IV of France issued an Edict on the Edicts[60] – are important. Philip II came to believe that the violence being meted out in the conquest of the colonies was causing a certain discontent among his own people. He therefore proclaimed in July 1573 that all further extensions of empire be termed'pacifications'rather than'conquests'.

Discoveries are not to be called conquests. Since we wish them to be carried out peacefully and charitably, we do not want the use of the term 'conquest' to offer any excuse for the employment of force or the causing of injury to the Indians ... Without displaying any greed for the possessions of the Indians, they [the 'discoverers', 'conquerors'] are to establish friendship and cooperation with the lords and nobles who seem most likely to be of assistance in the pacification of the land.[61]

The history of 'discovery' as an ideological gloss on conquest and dispossession is too well known to bear repeating here, but Philip's use of the term 'pacification' is historically significant. As Tzvetan Todorov notes, the conquests themselves are not to be stopped, but the idea of 'conquest' is to be replaced with 'pacification'.[62] The violence remains unchanged, but in taking from the Roman tradition of imperial glory through military domination, in which *pax* implied 'pacification', it was understood in terms of the verb 'pacificate', now obsolete but which in the sixteenth and seventeenth centuries meant 'to make peace'. In citing the Edicts of Pacification of the late sixteenth century, the *OED* describes the powers used by a prince or state 'to put an end to strife or discontent ... the action or fact of pacifying or appeasing; the condition of being pacified; appeasement, conciliation'. It then suggests this is 'a process or operation (usually a military operation) designed to secure the peaceful cooperation of a population or an area where one's enemies are thought to be active'. It thus proposes that to pacify is 'to reduce to peaceful submission'. The *OED* also notes the emergence of 'peace-keeper' and 'peacemaker' in the very late sixteenth century.

This *making* and *keeping* of the peace set in train a range of practices that would continue to be refined through the following four centuries of pacification projects; in effect, the four centuries of the making of the bourgeois world. Philip II held that the pacifying conquerors:

are to gather information about the various tribes, languages and divisions of the Indians in the province ... They are to seek friendship with them through trade and barter, showing them great love and tenderness and giving them objects to which they will take a liking ... In order that the Indians may hear the faith with greater awe and reverence, the preachers should convey the Cross in their hands and should be wearing at least albs or stoles

… The preachers should ask for their children under the pretext of teaching them and keep them as hostages; they should also persuade them to build churches where they can teach so that they may be safer. By these and other means are the Indians to be pacified and indoctrinated, but in no way are they to be harmed, for all we seek is their welfare and their conversion.[63]

Is this pacification an act of *war*? Clearly: yes. Yet it also concerns the gathering of information about the population, the teaching of trades, education, welfare provision, ideological indoctrination and, most importantly, the construction of a market. These activities concern the practices constitutive of the social order of modernity. Put another way: we need to understand pacification as *productive*,[64] in the sense that it implies the construction of a new social order as well as the crushing of opposition to that construction. This is why the discourse of pacification is replete with phrases such as 'reconstruction', 'rural construction', 'revolutionary reconstruction', 'civic action', 'civil operations' and so on. These are terms expressing the 'productive side' of power, as Foucault might have said and President Johnson more or less did say about the pacification of Vietnam: the 'other war', as he called pacification, is 'a war to build as well as to destroy'.[65] At the heart of pacification, then, are the kinds of practices we associate with the police power: the fabrication of social order, the dispersal of the mythical entity called 'security' through civil society and the attempt to stabilise the order around the logic of peace and security. If 'pacification' is a euphemism for anything, it is 'police'.

This becomes clear in the theory and practice of Captain Bernardo de Vargas Machuca in his command of Spanish colonial projects in the late sixteenth century. It is notable that his major work, *Milicia Indiana* (1599), which is to all intents and purposes the world's first manual of counter-revolutionary warfare, appears amid the so-called 'military revolution of the sixteenth century' and midway between the appearance of Vitoria's and Grotius's work on the laws of war, since Machuca's arguments identify pacification as a feature of war that has been omitted from the standard accounts of the military revolution, which focus on the centralisation of violence and the bureaucratisation and discipline of standing armies. Machuca's concern was not that of militarily organised national units facing another, but of an empire confronting recalcitrant and rebellious indigenous populations. To fight these populations Machuca advocated adopting their fighting methods, learned by him 'after twenty-eight years … employed in pacifications in the Indies'. The manual thus describes a world of skirmishing and ambushing, of fighting on the move, of a 24-hour 'hunt' against enemy 'hunters'.[66] This is the war of militias as part of an expanding global empire. It is a war for the pacification of those peoples which empire would necessarily have to destroy or control. On the one hand, Machuca thought such war needed to be brutal and bloody, with what we now know to be fairly standard atrocities associated with colonialism, including the burning alive of rebels, summary executions and the occasional drowning of babies, all justified by Machuca in the familiar terms of colonial conquest: because the war is just, because the Indian rebellion requires punishment, and because the Indians are 'with no reason, depraved and without honor' and are 'even more brutish than irrational animals'. On the other hand, Machuca insists that 'fair treatment' must be granted the Indian: the 'distributing and assigning the Indians to their encomiendas' must be done with the approval of the native lords of the land, the Indians should be granted herds, gifts and care, commanders must carry out censuses. Most of all, they must be governed in 'peace'.[67]

If pacification is a euphemism for police, then what of law?

'Law is not pacification', says Foucault. Well, no, not least because pacification is also very much about culture and ideology ('hearts and minds'), productivity and development ('modernisation'), welfare and sexuality (from population censuses to sex manuals), and much more. But for Foucault, law is not pacification because 'beneath the law, war continues to rage in all the mechanisms of power'.[68] With this comment, Foucault's unwillingness to deal properly with the question of law comes to the fore: looking 'beneath' the law is one of Foucault's ways of implying that law is not important to questions of power-war. Yet to try to understand war without recourse to the question of law is a serious mistake, as Foucault ultimately came to acknowledge.[69] It is far more the case that *through* the law, and through law's fractured relationship to police, war continues to rage. Such a claim *does* require grappling with law, as it means grappling with the violence and war that take place through law and police but which law and police manage to mask, and often manage to mask in the name of 'peace'. Contra Foucault, law *is* pacification. Moreover, and even more contra Foucault, this was the crowning achievement of liberalism and its international law, which is articulated most clearly in the idea that there are *rights of war* as well as peace, as we have begun to argue in relation to Vitoria, which we will now pursue in the work of Grotius, and which we will pursue further in Chapter 2.

'THERE IS NOTHING REPUGNANT TO WAR'

The Rights of War and Peace [*De Iure Belli ac Pacis*] (1625) by Hugo Grotius is widely taken to have created an important set of claims about a system of international law applicable and acceptable to all states. His book, quickly translated into Dutch, English, French, German, Spanish, Swedish, Chinese and Japanese, and published in just under fifty Latin editions, is often said to be the first to articulate the idea of an international society held together by some universally applicable rules, and to be the foundation of the law of nations as it develops in the seventeenth century. Called the 'jurist of humanity' by Vico, Grotius is still referred to in textbooks as the 'father' of a liberal law of nations – James Brown Scott's influence is once again important here – and it has been said that Grotius's thinking underpins more recent developments such as The Hague Peace Conference of 1899 (during which a wreath was placed on his tomb), The Hague Peace Conference of 1907, the League of Nations Covenant, the Kellogg–Briand Pact, the Geneva conference of 1949 and the United Nations Charter.[70] He also receives high praise from liberals such as John Locke and Adam Smith: the latter notes that 'Grotius seems to have been the first who attempted to give the world any thing like a regular system of natural jurisprudence, and his treatise on the laws of war and peace ... is perhaps at this day the most compleat work on this subject'; we shall turn to Locke's appropriation of Grotius's work in the chapter which follows.[71] Grotius was thus a good liberal; he was also author of a series of works offering a juridical foundation for wars of accumulation.

Grotius was a classically trained scholar who worked as official historiographer to the assembly governing the Province of Holland, subsequently becoming Attorney General and then Pensionary of Rotterdam with a seat in the States. The Dutch were then leaders in both capital accumulation and military technique, and well trained in using violence to break the resistance of indigenous peoples.[72] Grotius's family included cousins who had been Directors of the United East India

Company and admirals in its service, and his father was responsible for nominating one of the seats on the company's Board. Grotius's early writings are also smattered with praise for Dutch sailors carrying the war with Spain into Spanish territories. 'In these circumstances', notes Richard Tuck, 'it was not surprising that he was led to write a major apology for the whole Dutch commercial expansion into the Indies'.[73]

This apology began following the capture in 1603 of a Portuguese ship carrying commodities to the value of over 3 million guilders from Japan, China, Mexico and Peru. The size of the capture, carried out by a ship in the service of the United East India Company, was unprecedented and brought home to contemporaries that the United Provinces, having formerly been engaged in a war of rebellion and self-defence against Spanish power in the Netherlands, was now engaged in a war of aggression. In 1605 this aggression increased as the Dutch took a fort at Amboyna from the Portuguese and began to make various parts of Asia reliant on Dutch capital. In other words, 'the Dutch were not waging a defensive war in the Indies to protect either their homeland or existing trade patterns: they were waging an offensive war, in order to open up trade routes and make a lot of money'.[74] In this context Grotius wrote a treatise which has become known as *De Iure Praedae Commentarius* [*Commentary on the Law of Prize and Booty*]. The text is often known through the title of a separate pamphlet based on Chapter 12, *Mare Liberum* [*The Freedom of the Seas*], which was prepared by Grotius for the Company in 1608 in order to placate those shareholders whose religious feelings meant they were troubled by the use of force to obtain such 'prize'.[75] But Grotius's own title for the work as a whole was in fact the same as Vitoria's famous lecture: *De Indis*.[76]

To argue that the East India Company's action was a just act, Grotius defended the idea of the freedom of the seas and the right to engage in just war: he asserted the *mare liberum* against the *mare clausum*. But the issue concerned not just the sea. The European powers entering the commercial and political world of the East Indies found there a network of organised states. This allowed Grotius to emphasise the legal status of the East Indian communities within the law of nations when he came to defend the rights of the Dutch against the Portuguese claims to the East Indies.[77] The dispute is thus legal, not theological. Against the idea that the Pope is 'lord of the East Indian lands' with authority to give away the land as 'an unrestricted act of donation', Grotius argues that the Pope

'ought to be content with his spiritual jurisdiction'. Moreover, any
decision made by the Pope, such as the one made by Alexander VI in
1492 drawing a line of demarcation between the Spanish and
Portuguese, is an attempt to arbitrate a local dispute and so 'will not
affect the other peoples of the world' (C, pp. 309–11). All of this allows
Grotius to avoid treating the East Indies as if in some kind of legal
vacuum and the easy option of resolving the problem summarily via
reference to Papal power. It is this dimension of his work that historians
most frequently stress when they treat him as one of the key founders
of international law.

Grotius's solution to the particular problem in the East Indies, but
also the general problem of the law of nations and war, lies in 'the very
fount of nature' (C, pp. 17–18). The state is morally identical to the
individual in nature, and so the powers possessed by the state are the
same powers possessed by the individual in the state of nature. These
are the powers of sovereignty. What follows from this is that states and
individuals may use violence in the same ways and for the same ends,
most notably in their self-defence and for purposes of security. In other
words, the first fundamental law of nature is 'that *It shall be permissible
to defend* [one's own] life and to shun that which threatens to prove
injurious'. But Grotius also believes this grants private trading companies
as much right to wage war as more 'obvious' sovereign entities. Early
modern trading companies were essentially instruments of policy, for in
granting 'economic' rights to the corporation the state granted it a degree
of sovereign authority too. Such corporations were constituted by the
state in order to act in the manner of the state, and were thus granted
criminal and civil jurisdiction within the territories which they came to
police. Thus just as the English East India Company was given the task
of performing all those acts of government in those regions under its
jurisdiction, so the charter of the Dutch East India Company granted it
the prerogative rights, privileges and powers of the Dutch state.[78] This
included the right and power to make war, and Grotius's text was
written with the intention of justifying this right and power.[79] Hence just
as 'we find that Nature … withholds from no human being the right to
carry on private wars', so 'no one will maintain that the East India
Company is excluded from the exercise of that privilege, since whatever
is right for single individuals is likewise right for a number of individuals
acting as a group' (C, p. 302).

The problem, however, is that such an argument alone could hardly justify the violence exercised in the Indies, which had clearly not been carried out for purposes of 'defence'. The second law of nature, however, is 'that *It shall be permissible to acquire for oneself, and to retain, those things which are useful for life'*. This law, Grotius suggests, is 'an admission that each individual may, without violating the precepts of nature, prefer to see acquired for himself rather than for another, that which is important for the conduct of life' (*C*, p. 23). Grotius is suggesting that it is a right of self-preservation possessed by individuals which allows them to acquire as many goods as possible so long as this does not deny others their own legitimate ownership (*C*, p. 27). On this basis Grotius could begin to defend Dutch action in the Indies, based on the right to trade. Citing Vitoria a number of times in support, Grotius suggests that 'the right to engage in commerce pertains equally to all peoples' (*C*, p. 304). The same freedom that Vitoria sanctioned for Spanish Catholics vis-à-vis the non-Christian Indians, Grotius advanced for Dutch Protestants vis-à-vis Portuguese and Spanish Catholics, and the same argument would be used by English Protestants against the Dutch: 'under the law of nations, the following principle was established: that all men should be privileged to trade freely with one another' (*C*, p. 354).[80] Thus the right to commerce is part of natural law, so 'the Portuguese, even if they were the owners of the regions sought by the Dutch, would nevertheless be inflicting an injury if they prevented the Dutch from entering the regions and engaging in commerce' (*C*, p. 30; also p. 401).

To stop such trade the Portuguese would have to show that they owned the seas across which the Dutch were sailing, but for Grotius one can claim as property only those things which one can occupy, consume or transform. 'Those things which are incapable of being occupied, or which never have been occupied, cannot be the private property of any owner, since all property has its origin as such in occupancy'. This is reinforced by the idea that there are some things which are so constituted by nature that they might be used by a range of persons (and 'persons' here includes corporations) (*C*, p. 320). The example Grotius gives of such 'things' include air (an issue to which we turn in Chapters 5 and 6), running water and the sea. 'The sea is an element common to all, since it is so vast that no one could possibly take possession of it, and since it is fitted for use by all' (*C*, p. 322). Thus the fisherman may claim property over the fish he has caught, but not the sea from which he has caught it, although he may 'fence in a fishing-pool for himself in some small portion of the sea' (C, p. 325). 'In short', says Grotius, 'the sea is included among those things which are not articles of commerce, that is to say, the things that cannot become part of anyone's private domain' (C, p. 328).[81]

The term 'domain' here is important.

> It must be understood that, during the earliest epoch of man's history, ownership [*dominium*] and common possession [*communion*] were concepts whose significance differed from that now ascribed to them. For in the present age, the term 'ownership' connotes possession of something peculiarly one's own, that is to say, something belonging to a given party in such a way that it cannot be similarly possessed by any other party; whereas the expression 'common property' is applied to that which has been assigned to several parties, to be possessed by them in partnership (so to speak) and in mutual accord, to the exclusion of other parties. Owing to the poverty of human speech, however, it has become necessary to employ identical terms for concepts which are not identical. Consequently, because of a certain degree of similitude and by analogy, the above-mentioned expressions descriptive of our modern customs are applied to another right, which existed in early times. Thus with reference to that early age, the term 'common' is nothing more nor less than the simple antonym of private [*proprium*]; and the word 'ownership' denotes the power to make use rightfully of common [i.e. public] property. (C, p. 315)

Grotius is playing on the idea that dominium is taken now to mean private property, in the sense of ownership, but that the term originally meant the power to use what was not privately possessed.[82] Thus *'neither the sea itself nor the right of navigation thereon can become the exclusive possession of a particular party'*; rather, access must be available to all *'by the command of the law of nations'* (C, p. 300).

Tuck suggests that the extreme originality of Grotius's view here is not often recognised. Most modern histories of the law of the sea propose that the freedom of the seas in its Grotian form was an ancient doctrine. In fact, Tuck suggests that the universal view prior to Grotius was that states could claim jurisdiction over waters connected to their territory and that such jurisdiction allowed rulers to regulate traffic on the water to the extent of a de facto ban.[83] Grotius's argument was pitched at the general theoretical level concerning rights of jurisdiction –'we have shown it to be impossible that any private right over the sea itself should pertain to any nation or private individual'– but also had significant practical implications, since it meant that'the Portuguese have not established a private right over that part of the sea which one traverses in sailing to the East Indies' (C, p. 331). But what applies to Dutch–Portuguese relations applies equally to Dutch–Indian relations, and the implications of this are important because it means that although Grotius claims for the East Indians a legal status within the law of nations on the grounds of sovereignty, he also claims for the Europeans access to East Indian territory on the grounds of a fundamental right to trade. Grotius's argument about war needs to be read as an argument concerning property as much as it concerns sovereignty.[84]

Grotius claims to have shown that'a just cause of war exists when the freedom of trade is being defended against those who would obstruct it'. Hence 'the Dutch had a just cause for war against the Portuguese'(C, p. 363). And since the rights of nature are rights claimed by individuals and groups of individuals as well as states, so 'private individuals are not prohibited from undertaking a war'. As such, it was 'permissible for the Dutch East India Company to attack in war the individual Portuguese' (C, pp. 377, 380). Now, on the one hand Grotius uses this argument to suggest that'there is nothing to prevent a war from being private for one side, public for the other' (C, p. 377). On the other hand, he very quickly notes that'although … this conflict could have been waged as a private war, and a just one too, it is nevertheless accurate to say that in actual fact it is a public war and that the prize in question was acquired in accordance with public law' (C, p. 392). Thus 'whatever acts could have been committed by private individuals under the law of nations … those individuals shall now be held to have committed with retroactive public authorization and in the circum-stances equivalent to a decree of war' (C, p. 424). As Pashukanis notes, in Grotius's argument sovereign states are counterposed to one another in exactly the same way as individual property owners with equal rights, allowing him to treat relations between states as relations between *the owners of private property*.[85] This is what provides the argument for the justice of the war, but the specific point that 'the war which is being waged by the Dutch East India Company is just' (C, p. 388; also pp. 421, 436) has wider implications, in that Grotius is suggesting that there exists a fundamental right to exercise violence in order to ensure that trade routes remain open and that commerce remains 'free'.

This provides the foundation for the argument in *De Iure Belli ac Pacis* where, notwithstanding a slight shift in his account of free trade and some complicated theological twists and turns between the two texts, much of the substantive argument develops the main points in *De Indis*.[86] *De Iure Belli ac Pacis*, however, does transform the claims about the laws of nature into claims about war, for the fundamental right of self-preservation gets turned into a claim about war being 'agreeable' to nature.

> Among the first Impressions of Nature there is nothing repugnant to War; nay, all Things rather favour it: for both the End of War (being the preservation of Life or Limbs, and either the securing or getting Things useful to Life) is very agreeable to those first Motions of Nature; and to make use of Force, in case of Necessity, is in no wise disagreeable thereunto. (*RWP*, I. II. I, p. 183)[87]

Reason, then, 'does not prohibit all Manner of Violence, but only that which is repugnant to Society', and that which is repugnant is that which 'invades another's Right' (*RWP*, I. II. I, p. 184). Far from outlawing violence, liberalism seeks to regulate it and see that it is exercised for just reasons, offering an argument not against war, but *for* war conducted in the right manner and for the right reasons. This argument in Book 1 comes back into play in telling detail in the discussion of land ownership and punishment in Book 2.

In *De Indis* Grotius had been concerned with the law of the sea, which had been the issue most pressing on the policies of the East India Company. In *De Iure Belli ac Pacis* he focuses increasingly on the question of land, coming to the view that if the sea could not be owned by those who travelled across it, then perhaps neither could the land. This is manifestly *not* an argument for common property ownership, which for Grotius is 'no longer approved of'. God 'gave to mankind in general a Dominion over Things', but this is not really property as such: even if one were to call it 'common property', such use of things and land only 'supply the Place of Property', he says. This is the 'primitive Simplicity' of the state of nature, confirmed by 'the Account we have of some People of *America*' (*RWP*, II. II. II, p. 421). For Grotius, 'Men did not long continue in this pure and innocent State of Life'. Labour and industry led to the assigning of portions of lands to different families, and it is this division and ownership that 'was the Original of Property'. Although God gave to mankind in general dominion over things, he also allowed that 'every Man converted what he would to his own use'.

> Property … resulted from a certain Compact and Agreement, either expressly, as by a Division; or else tacitly, as by Seizure. For as soon as living in common was no longer approved of, all Men were supposed, and ought to be supposed to have consented, that each should appropriate to himself, by Right of first Possession, what could not have been divided. (*RWP*, II. II. II, pp. 421, 423, 426–7)

It is this exclusive right that deserves to be called property. Moreover, it is this right that allows for appropriation.

> If there be any waste or barren Land within our Dominions, that also is to be given to Strangers, at their Request, or may be lawfully possessed by them, because whatever remains uncultivated, is not to be esteemed a Property, only so far as concerns Jurisdiction, which always continues the Right of the antient People. (*RWP*, II. II. XVII, p. 448)

This is clearly a reference not to land in the 'cultivated' realm of Europe, but to those areas called 'waste', a point to which we turn in the following chapter. Indeed, the logic of his argument is that this is a right that can not be claimed by the Indians, working as they are with a system 'in Place of property'. Grotius is thus no longer discussing the relationship between commercial states but between commercial states, corporations and 'non-commercial' peoples living with a different form of subsistence. This connects with Grotius's argument regarding the right to travel, to trade and to use that which is not being made *proper* use of – hence the importance of *usus* [use] as the step between *possessio* [the act of taking possession] and *dominium* [ownership]. 'So likewise a free Passage ought to be granted to Persons where just Occasion shall require, over any Lands and Rivers, or such Parts of the Sea as belong to any Nation'. This argument applies to those who might be travelling in order 'to traffick with some distant People', and applies also to 'Goods and Merchandize, for no Body has a Right to hinder one Nation from trading with another distant Nation'. Grotius also claims it applies to those who 'being expelled their own country, [might] want to settle in some uninhabited Land' (*RWP*, II. II. XIII, pp. 438–9, and II. II. XIII, p. 446).

Tuck shows the extent to which this shift was a direct reflection of a shift in the nature of Dutch colonialism. From around 1619 onwards the East India Company began to forcibly annex territory without the agreement of native rulers, and Dutch policy more generally underwent a similar shift in the light of competition from England and France.[88] But the issue is not just Dutch colonialism; after all, Grotius received plenty of offers of employment from various states across Europe, accepted some of them (working for France before eventually ending up in the Swedish diplomatic service), and the book is dedicated to the King of France. It is colonial war in general, and thus appropriation and accumulation, that is the issue. This is why commentators have pointed out that despite Grotius's work being a work on the laws of war and peace, war is the all-inclusive and over-riding phenomenon.[89] But the important point is that since the theory of war is a theory of property, the over-riding phenomenon in fact turns out to be nothing less than the war of accumulation. If Grotius is the founder of liberal international law, as many suggest, then we may have to admit with Ellen Meiksins Wood that liberal international law has since its inception had 'as much to do with advocating as limiting war, and as much to do with profit as with justice'.[90]

Grotius was hardly new in this, for he builds on and cites not only Vitoria but also Roman law and Canon law. As James Whitman points out, Roman texts largely assumed that war was a mode of acquiring property rights, Canon texts often eliminated everything other than material considerations in the causes of war, and plenty of medieval jurists argued that wars were a form of litigation over property between sovereigns.[91] (It is for this reason punishment figures so heavily in the early thinking about the laws of war, as we shall see in Chapter 2, and why 'booty' retains such a central place in the legal texts on just war, including Grotius's.) Yet Grotius was writing during a crucial period of commercial development, imperial rivalry and capitalist dispossession of peoples. Grotius obscures the origin of property in violence with that classic technique of natural law liberalism, namely the proposition that private property is both natural and develops through the gradual progress of man (*C*, p. 317). Under the auspices of an increasingly non-theological notion of natural law, the law of nations was understood by Grotius as legitimising the needs of the new expansionist nation states, corporations and forms of private property which had arisen on the ruins of the mediaeval world.[92] If Grotius really is an 'ideologue of empire',[93] it is because the law of nature and nations had forged a just war theory harmonised with, and even transformed into an expression of, the new social order being organised around accumulation.[94]

De Iure Belli ac Pacis has a status as one of the definitive liberal statements of just war, international law and liberal peace. Yet the law of peace is for Grotius almost incidental to the law of war. His only concern, ultimately, is that the 'licentiousness' into which war has degenerated comes to an end and that from hereon war be 'not rashly and unjustly begun, nor dishonourably carried on' (*RWP*, Preliminary Discourse, XXVIII–XXIX, pp. 105–6). Yet even then, this attempt to end licentiousness and conduct war honourably and justly opens the door to a new set of measures 'necessary to the obtaining our just Rights' (RWP, III. I. II. p. 1186), which turns out to include the forms of violence in the name of 'military necessity' presented in the third volume of *De Jure Belli ac Pacis*: killing unarmed soldiers, killing innocent inhabitants of enemy territory, decimating civil populations, seizing their goods, pillaging and laying waste, burning and destruction, mistreatment of prisoners and the random sacking of sacred places. Even slavery gets legitimised in the law of nations laid out by Grotius.[95] Grotius thus equips liberalism with the fundamental right to make war in the name of peace, security and accumulation. Reading his work in the light of what we have already said about Vitoria, it is becoming clear that the history of liberal thought needs to be read in terms of the history of capitalist violence.

'There is a kind of violence within liberalism', notes Tuck, 'in which liberty and warfare (both civil and international conflict) were bound together'.[96] What makes this binding sometimes hard to discern is that liberalism likes to separate the idea of violence from the idea of liberal politics. Liberalism wants to be able to threaten violence while denying or masking the violence it inflicts in the name of liberal order. This is why law comes to play such a central role in liberalism. Its ideology of the rule of law works by rendering certain kinds of violence illegitimate and illegal and other kinds of violence legitimate and legal. The legal construction and moral justification of violence channels it into certain forms of activity engaged in by certain kinds of people and for certain kinds of reasons.[97] This conjoined threat and mask of violence forms the foundation of 'just war' theory and the 'administration of justice'. The foundation, that is, of the war power and the police power.

As we have seen so far in this chapter and as we shall continue to explore through the chapters which follow, the split between law and violence is pure ideology; law and violence flow into one another. Violence constitutes law by providing the occasion and method for founding legal orders, giving it a reason for being (as the regulator of force and coercion), and providing a means through which law acts. This is the 'lawmaking character' of violence, as Benjamin calls it.[98] Violence is thus not some kind of legal aberration, but is central to law; not exceptional, but quotidian. Violence is one means through which law acts in the world and law is one means by which violence gets carried out.[99] In geopolitical terms, this is a way of saying that international law was from the outset a *strategic asset* in the conduct of war, the legal form through which capitalist states and corporations fought for domination over the world and to order the world for accumulation.[100] We therefore need to consider law as facilitating rather than restricting war.[101] War is 'woven into the law', as Gros puts it, but law is equally woven into war. In the very act of the violence of war, law is reaffirmed rather than undermined. The contemporary interest in war as a juridical operation, what has been called 'lawfare', 'warlaw' or 'juridical warfare', tends to treat this warp and weft of law and war as somehow a recent development,[102] but they have been woven together since the birth of early modern political thought, the birth of the laws of nations and, concomitantly, the transition of feudalism to capitalism. International law assumes the appearance of a device invented to end the violence of war when in fact *war is international law in action.*[103] To mask this fact, international law arrives dressed in the garb of peace and security, law and order (and, as we shall see in Chapter 4, 'civilisation').

The history of liberalism and its order is the history of a violence structured in certain ways, one which binds international war and civil conflict together, which therefore binds the war power to the police power, and in which the violence of accumulation is central. Which is a way of saying that war is integral to capital as a material formation and the very concept of liberty that lies at the heart of liberalism. The development of the early law of nations into what becomes 'international law' was nothing less than the translation onto the international domain of some basic tenets of liberal theory at the very moment of liberal theory's emergence.[104] To pursue this argument requires rethinking the liberal theory of property as a philosophy of the war of accumulation, a rethinking which, in turn, asks further questions of the relationship between colonialism and international law and demands that we consider one of the most fundamental wars of liberal modernity: the war on waste.

Chapter 2

WAR ON WASTE; OR, INTERNATIONAL LAW
AS PRIMITIVE ACCUMULATION

═══════

Waste is a religious thing.

There is a curious connection between weapons and waste ...
Because waste is the secret history, the underhistory ...
Don DeLillo, Underworld (1998)

In the chapter on the genesis of industrial capital in Volume 1 of *Capital*, Marx writes:

> The discovery of gold and silver in America, the extirpation, enslavement and entombment in mines of the indigenous population of that continent, the beginnings of the conquest and plunder of India, and the conversion of Africa into a preserve for the commercial hunting of black skins, are all things which characterize the dawn of the era of capitalist production. These idyllic proceedings are the chief moments of primitive accumulation. Hard on their heels follows the commercial war of the European nations, which has the globe as its battlefield ... These methods depend in part on brute force, for instance the colonial system. But they all employ the power of the state, the concentrated and organized force of society, to hasten, as in a hothouse, the process of transformation of the feudal mode of production into the capitalist mode, and to shorten the transition. Violence is the midwife of every old society which is pregnant with a new one. It is itself an economic power.[1]

Marx here highlights the fact that capitalism is not a spontaneous order and that, in contrast to the myth of an idyllic origin of private property, in actual history'conquest, enslavement, robbery, murder, in short, force, play the greatest part' (*C1*, p. 874). What is at stake here, then, is the constitution of bourgeois order through the violence of what Marx calls 'primitive accumulation'. This is a term through which Marx seeks to grasp the 'police methods' used to forcefully separate people from a means of subsistence other than the wage. But it is a process which also appears to incorporate the very thing that animates international law, namely war, and the very thing that animates critical international legal theory, namely colonisation.

In 1996 Anthony Carty suggested that one of the major deficiencies in mainstream international legal theory is that 'no systematic undertaking is usually offered of the influence of colonialism in the development of the basic conceptual framework of the subject'.[2] Carty was highlighting the fact that in mainstream studies of international law, colonialism was for a very long time – indeed, since the inception of international law – either ignored or figured only as a problem, a phenomenon about which international law must have some rules or would have to develop some even better rules. As David Kennedy put it in the same year, when colonialism *had* been tackled as an issue in international law it was treated as either a rare and aberrational feature or as part of a mythical 'pre-legal' world of war and ideology.[3] Neither claim was entirely true, in that there had already been a number of works seeking to identify the centrality of colonialism to international law.[4] But the remarkably small amount of work on colonialism and international law prior to the mid-1990s has been dwarfed by the enormous body of literature which has since emerged. Writing in the same year as Carty and Kennedy, for example, Anthony Anghie pressed home the centrality of the colonial to international law and, since then, a huge and generally impressive body of work has reasserted and extended the argument.[5] It is no exaggeration to say that if there is one abiding achievement of 'new approaches to international law', 'Third World approaches to international law' and 'critical international legal theory' in the last twenty years, it has been to place colonial warfare at the heart of international law: the violence of colonialism is now seen, at least among the *critical* wing of the international legal community, as 'continuing, systematic, and ingrained in international law'.[6]

Yet one of the features of this body of work is that 'accumulation' often goes unmentioned and, more specifically, the concept of primitive accumulation is nowhere. Take a few examples. First, the set of critical essays edited by Fleur Johns, Richard Joyce and Sundhya Pahuja, called *Events: The Force of International Law*.[7] One has to get through close on 200 pages before one gets any mention of accumulation of any sort, and then it really is only a mention, made almost in passing. Note too that despite the various historical 'events' in the book, from the debate at Valladolid in 1550, the Peace of Westphalia, the levée en masse in France in 1793, the Paris Commune of 1871, the moment of decolonisation, and so on, accumulation gets mentioned only in the two essays on the recent/current place of the World Trade Organization. Accumulation in general gets in, then, but not as history, and it seems to barely count as part of international law. And thus 'primitive accumulation', as a critical concept, is nowhere. Similarly, Anne Orford's edited text on *International Law and its Others* also contains some very good essays, but mentions accumulation *even less* than *Events*; which is to say: *not at all* – not one reference to accumulation, let alone primitive accumulation. The themes of 'responsibility', desire, violence', 'conflict', the 'liberal individual' and the 'sovereign state' are all there, and there is much talk of 'others' – savages, barbarians, mobs, races, subalterns – but not accumulation. We get plenty of references to Schmitt, and even his description of land appropriation as a constitutive process of international law, but very few to Marx and his description of land appropriation as central to capitalist accumulation. The desire to situate the collection at the 'disruptive edges' of the discipline are expressed and the logic of critique is asserted as the key method, but it is Kant rather than Marx who gets cited as the authority in this regard.[8] Likewise, Anthony Anghie's excellent book on imperialism and international law discusses savages and races but not primitive accumulation, as is the case with Anghie's earlier essays,[9] and even China Miéville's extended analysis of international law from a Marxist perspective avoids using 'primitive accumulation' apart from in one fleeting reference. 'Fleeting' is also the way one might describe the one appearance of 'primitive accumulation' in *Law and Globalization from Below*, in which colonial exploitation figures widely.[10]

Finally, we might note that the set of essays edited by Susan Marks as *International Law on the Left*, a book dealing explicitly with Marxism and international law (the book's subtitle is '*Marxist Legacies*'; some of the chapters are developed from a symposium on Marxism and international law held at The Hague in 2003 and then published by the *Leiden Journal*

of International Law under the heading of 'Marxism and international
law'), has next to nothing to say about primitive accumulation.[11]
Anthony Carty's contribution to the book cites David Harvey on the
need for a general re-evaluation of the role of primitive accumulation in
the long historical geography of capital, but not much is made of it there
and next to nothing is said about it in the rest of the book.[12] Thus even
a major collection bringing specifically Marxist analyses to bear on the
question of international law appears uninterested in the idea of
'primitive accumulation'.

   This last example points us to a broader issue in critical international
legal thought as it has sought to highlight the centrality of colonial
violence to international law: Marx appears, but in a strangely mute
form. This muteness is most obvious concerning one of the central
categories through which he spoke about 'the colonial' as capital and
capital as colonisation, namely 'primitive accumulation'. Let me give two
examples of attempts by key figures within critical international legal
studies to discuss what Marx might offer international legal theory. First,
Martii Koskenniemi's article 'What Should International Lawyers Learn
from Karl Marx?', reprinted as a chapter in the collection of essays edited
by Marks. The discussion there is centred on a demand for 'international
justice' that Koskenniemi thinks can be developed out of Marx's work,
with no mention of primitive accumulation. This is despite the fact that
Marx has absolutely nothing to say about 'international justice', yet
devotes a fair amount of *Capital* to primitive accumulation. But by
connecting the 'international justice' he thinks underpins international
law to Marx's argument concerning a universal class which can redeem
itself only through the total redemption of humanity, Koskenniemi
performs a remarkable feat in which international law is said to offer an
'emancipatory promise' of the very kind Marx thought needed to be
brought about by a revolutionary class. This perverse treatment of Marx
is compounded in a recent article on empire and international law in
which the latter's role in creating 'a structure of human relationships that
we have been accustomed to label "capitalism"' is outlined, yet which
ignores Marx entirely despite the fact that Marx's life work concerns the
very same structure of human relationships called 'capital', despite the
fact that he analyses these relationships through the lens of colonisation,
and despite the fact that he uses the category 'primitive accumulation'
to do so.[13]

The second example is the recent work of B. S. Chimni. In his earlier book *International Law and World Order* Chimni mentions Marx on primitive accumulation, yet does so only in passing and solely with reference to a historical period he calls 'old colonialism' between 1600 and 1760. There is thus no attempt to integrate the category into the wider attempt to 'clarify and articulate a Marxist theory of international law' in the book. Indeed, his description of a period of primitive accumulation during 'old' colonialism more or less limits the category to understanding 'the emergence of the capitalist order';[14] but as we shall see, there is far more to the category than this. Chimni has since published 'An Outline of a Marxist Course on International Law' and a 'Prolegomena to a Class Approach to International Law'.[15] Yet in the 'Outline Course' no discussion of primitive accumulation occurs; indeed, accumulation itself barely gets mentioned.[16] By the time of the 'Prolegomena to a Class Approach to International Law' the possibility of using Marx for the purposes of critical international legal theory diminishes even further. Chimni suggests that 'a central feature of capitalism is … its inherent tendency to spatial expansion', but 'this fact was not integrally factored into Marx's understanding of capitalism'. This is a bizarre claim, since Marx time and again points to capital's tendency to spatial expansion. But Chimni makes his point in order to claim that because of this gap in Marx's work, 'the interaction between capitalism and the colonies remains an area of silence for Marxist theory'.[17] This is an even more bizarre claim since it requires us to ignore several hundred pages in Marx's work (and several thousand pages of Marxist work) on precisely that issue.

Set alongside each other, the claims made by Koskenniemi and Chimni suggest something deeply troubling about how international law – including and especially its *critical* wing – wants us to think about Marx.[18] So there is a general issue which underpins this chapter: the inability of critical international legal theory to use Marx properly, fully, coherently, in a way which might strengthen and deepen some of the political claims made by critical international legal theory. Which is to say: to use Marx in a way that might allow us to develop a genuinely Marxist critique of international law. This is what I shall attempt in this chapter. I extend the critique of law begun in the previous chapter by developing the links between international law and the colonial made by critical international legal theory, but I do so by otherwise eschewing the main lines of enquiry taken by legal scholarship. Instead, I bring to bear on the issue Marx's thinking about *colonisation* as a *process* rather than 'the colonies' as a place. Colonisation as a process is a way of speaking about primitive accumulation by grasping it as systematically engrained in capital as a social relation. In so doing, the chapter also seeks to develop the reading of accumulation as war, and thus of liberalism as a philosophy of war.

The chapter therefore explores the deep and nuanced connections between law and political economy on which the process of systematic colonisation depends and without which liberal order could not be produced. I engage in this exploration through what I shall call the war on waste that animates liberal theory and practice. In the process, I aim to reveal the secret of Marx's *Capital*, the secret of capital and the secret of systematic colonisation. All of which takes us, albeit in a very roundabout way, to the secret of international law.

THE SECRET OF SYSTEMATIC COLONISATION

It is not often noticed that Volume 1 of *Capital* ends with the revelation of a secret. The final chapter is called 'The Modern Theory of Colonization' and, after several pages discussing colonisation, the final paragraph of the chapter, and therefore the final paragraph of the book as a whole, ends as follows:

> However, we are not concerned here with the condition of the colonies. The only thing that interests us is the secret discovered in the New World by the political economy of the Old World, and loudly proclaimed by it: that the capitalist mode of production and accumulation, and therefore capitalist private property as well, have for their fundamental condition the annihilation of that private property which rests on the labour of the individual himself; in other words, the expropriation of the worker. (*C1*, p. 940)

Note that Marx is interested less in 'the colonies' as such and more in the process of colonisation and thus the secret which the colonies reveal.

To understand the importance of Marx's rhetorical device in this final paragraph we might first want to note that *Capital* is in many ways nothing less than a book of secrets. Several minor secrets are revealed

through the pages of the book: the 'secret history' of the Roman
Republic, the 'secret purpose' of the Chinese *assignats*, the 'secret
foundations of Holland's wealth in capital', the secret dungeons on
Celebes, 'the secret of the flourishing state of industry in Spain and Sicily
under the rule of the Arabs', the secret of Henry VII's lack of success, the
'secret of [bourgeois] "sympathy" for widows, poor families and so on',
'the secret of the capitalists' complaints about the laziness of the working
people' (*C1*, pp. 176, 224, 388, 631, 649–50, 880, 916, 920). There is clearly
something that animates Marx about letting us in on a secret. This might
explain why Marx's famous discussion of the fetishism of the commodity
in Chapter 1 is in fact a revelation of the fetishism *'and its secret'* (*C1*,
p. 163, my emphasis).

Yet the secret of the fetish is but one part of the really big secret
revealed in the whole book. This is the 'secret which vulgar economics
has so far obstinately refused to divulge' and thus 'the secret source of
the harmonious wisdom of … free-trade optimists'. Or, in other words,
it is 'the secret of profit-making [that] must at last be laid bare' (in order,
these are *C1*, pp. 745, 706, 280). What is it? What is the secret?

Marx tells us: 'The secret of the expression of value', he says – that is,
the 'secret hidden under the apparent movements in the relative values
of commodities' – lies in how capital manages labour. And that, at its
core, reveals 'the secret of making a profit', namely 'the appropriation
of unpaid labour' (in order, *C1*, pp. 152, 168, 743). In other words, 'the
secret of the self-valorization of capital resolves itself into the fact that
it has at its disposal a definite quantity of the unpaid labour of other
people' (*C1*, p. 672). Hence 'the innermost secret of English capital … is
to force down English wages' and 'the secret of why it happens that the
more they [workers] work, the more alien wealth they produce'. This is
'the true secret of producing efficient workpeople' (*C1*, pp. 748, 793, 613).
Then again, he also says that 'the formation of surplus-value by surplus
labour is no secret' (*C1*, p. 352). Well, no, it is certainly no secret now that
Marx has spent a thousand pages exposing it. But then at least he has
done so in the hope that human beings can decipher the hieroglyphic of
value and 'get behind the secret of their own social product' (*C1*, p. 167).

So the revelation of the secret of the colonies in the final paragraph
of the final chapter of the book turns out to be a key political manoeuvre
on Marx's part: significant for our understanding capital *as a whole*, so to
speak, as well as capital in the colonies themselves: its 'innermost secret,

the hidden basis of the entire social edifice'.[19] This is what Marx calls 'the great secret of systematic colonization'. The term 'systematic colonization' is taken by Marx from Edward Gibbon Wakefield's influential studies of colonial accumulation. Wakefield was the key figure in a movement of the 1830s which sought to revive the 'lost art of colonization' (rooted in the need to use and improve 'waste land' and 'waste countries'), but Marx is keen for us to grasp this art as the fundamental secret of primitive accumulation. Why? First, because the secret revealed, that 'the supply of labour *must* be constant and regular', is 'the truth about capitalist relations in the mother country' as well as the colonies (*C1*, p. 932); 'systematic colonization' thus captures a *process* inherent to capital, not a place. And, second, because for Wakefield the art of colonisation and the art of accumulation are bound together as part of the art of war.[20]

The chapter called 'The Modern Theory of Colonization' is the eighth chapter of Part Eight of the book. Part Eight as a whole is called 'So-Called Primitive Accumulation' and it begins with a chapter called 'The Secret of Primitive Accumulation'. Primitive accumulation is the process that constitutes capitalist social relations as the separation of the bulk of the population from the means of production.[21] This process is of obvious crucial historical importance, since without separating workers from the means of production capital could not have come into being; without such separation there could be no capitalist accumulation. Workers must therefore be 'free' in a double sense: free to sell their labour power, but also 'free' from owning the means of production.

Marx begins his analysis of 'so-called primitive accumulation' by claiming that it plays the same role in political economy as primitive sin does in theology.

> Adam bit the apple, and thereupon sin fell on the human race. Its origin is supposed to be explained when it is told as an anecdote about the past. Long, long ago there were two sorts of people: one, the diligent, intelligent and above all frugal elite; the other, lazy rascals, spending their substance, and more, in riotous living … Thus it came to pass that the former sort accumulated wealth, and the latter sort finally had nothing to sell but their own skins. And from this primitive sin dates the poverty of the great majority who, despite all their labour, have up to now nothing to sell but themselves. (*C1*, p. 873)

Marx's ironic turn of phrase is designed to open up the important move he makes, one in which he shifts from mocking the concept as used by Smith to using it as a serious concept in its own right,[22] in a way that enables him to avoid the story told in the tender annals of political economy, where primitive accumulation is simply assumed and in which 'the idyllic reigns from time immemorial', and instead to argue that in actual history violence is integral to the process. The history of capital is 'written in the annals of mankind in letters of blood and fire' (C1, pp. 874–5).

What this means, in effect, is that *Capital* needs to be read 'as a treatise on the structural violence that capitalism inflicts'.[23] Marx addresses this violence at length in the chapter on 'the genesis of industrial capital', the sixth chapter of Part Eight on primitive accumulation where, as we have seen, he connects the extirpation and enslavement of human beings during the conquest of the colonies to the wider commercial wars of the European nations. The point he wants to make is that the colonies, the national debt, the modern tax system and the whole system of protection rely on the coercive power of the state to bring about the transformation of the feudal mode of production into the capitalist mode. Capital comes into the world 'dripping from head to toe, from every pore, with blood and dirt' (C1, p. 926). As Rosa Luxemburg points out, capitalism is always and everywhere engaged in a war of annihilation against every non-capitalist form that it encounters.[24] The structural violence in question, then, is a war with the whole globe as its battlefield. In this context, the mere expropriation of the land and resources was often not enough to create the proletariat, since many preferred vagabondage and 'crime' to the misery of wage-labour, and so there developed a series of police powers through which 'the fathers of the present working class were chastised for their enforced transformation into vagabonds and paupers' (C1, p. 896). The powers in question include Acts outlawing vagabondage, begging, wandering and myriad other 'offenses', but also includes Acts of enclosure in which laws were passed separating people from subsistence on the land and its resources. The 'freeing' of the peasantry into wage-labour is the *forcing* of the peasantry into wage-slavery; liberation is subjugation. Capital demands 'Let there be workers!'[25] and sets about forging them.

We need to be clear about what is at stake here, especially given that the early law of nations was centrally concerned with the question of war. For what Marx is suggesting is that the mechanism through which people were made to work within the conditions posited by capital *is a form of war*. That is: class war. And it is class war conducted through *police power*:

> Henry VIII, 1530: Beggars who are old and incapable of working receive a beggar's licence. On the other hand, whipping and imprisonment for sturdy vagabonds. They are to be tied to the cart-tail and whipped until the blood streams from their bodies, that they are to swear on oath to go back to their birthplace or to where they have lived the last three years and to 'put themselves to work' ... By 27 Henry VIII the previous statute is repeated, but strengthened with new clauses. For the second for vagabondage the whipping is to be repeated and half the ear sliced off; but for the third relapse the offender is to be executed as a hardened criminal and enemy of the common weal.
>
> Edward VI: A statute of the first year of his reign, 1547, ordains that if anyone refuses to work, he shall be condemned as a slave to the person who has denounced him as an idler. The master shall feed his slave on bread and water, weak broth and such refuse meat as he thinks fit. He has the right to force him to do any work, no matter how disgusting, with whip and chains. If the slave is absent a fortnight, he is condemned to slavery for life and is to be branded on forehead or back with the letter S; if he runs away thrice, he is to be executed as a felon. The master can sell him, bequeath him, let him out on hire as a slave, just as any other personal chattel or cattle. If the slaves attempt anything against the masters, they are also to be executed. Justices of the peace, on information, are to hunt the rascals down ...
>
> Elizabeth, 1572: Unlicensed beggars above 14 years of age are to be severely flogged and branded on the left ear unless some one will take them into service for two years; in case of a repetition of the offence, if they are over 18, they are to be executed, unless some one will take them into service for two years; but for the third offence they are to be executed without mercy as felons. Similar statutes: 18 Elizabeth, c. 13, and another of 1597.

Remaining with the English case, Marx goes on:

> James I: Any one wandering about and begging is declared a

rogue and a vagabond. Justices of the peace in Petty Sessions are authorised to have them publicly whipped and to imprison them for six months for the first offence, and two years for the second. Whilst in prison they are to be whipped as much and as often as the justices of the peace think fit … Incorrigible and dangerous rogues are to be branded with an R on the left shoulder and set to hard labour, and if they are caught begging again, to be executed without mercy. These statutes, legally binding until the beginning of the eighteenth century.

And in case his reader thinks this is peculiar to England, Marx adds that 'there were similar laws in other European states'.

By the middle of the seventeenth century a kingdom of vagabonds (*royaume des truands*) had been established in Paris. Even at the beginning of the reign of Louis XVI, the Ordinance of 13 July 1777 provided that every man in good health from 16 to 60 years of age, if without means of subsistence and not practising a trade, should be sent to the galleys. The statute of Charles V for the Netherlands (October 1537), the first Edict of the States and Towns of Holland (10 March 1614), the *Plakaat* of the United Provinces (26 June 1649) are further examples of the same kind.

And on it goes through a series of 'terroristic laws' (Marx's term again) perfected across four centuries of capitalist development and through which 'agricultural people [were] first forcibly expropriated from the soil, driven from their homes, turned into vagabonds, and then whipped, branded, tortured by laws grotesquely terrible, into the discipline necessary for the wage system' (C1, pp. 896–8). The creatures who would haunt the bourgeois mind at this point historically, the vagabonds, paupers, criminals, street peddlers, as well as their social cousins who will later emerge, the undeserving poor, the squeegee merchants, the feral youth, the delinquent, will be the ones on which *war will be declared* time and again – war on crime, war on scroungers, war on poverty, war on squeegee merchants, war on delinquency – but also the ones subject most directly to the police power, as such (vague) social identities were assumed to constitute disorderliness and criminality in the bourgeois mind.

Parallel to this creation of 'free proletarians' is the 'theft of the common lands', conducted through the concomitant process of 'the Parliamentary form of robbery'. Through 'decrees by which the landowners grant themselves the people's land as private property', known as Acts of enclosure, the land is, in essence, stolen from the people through the law. Marx cites text after text from the economic literature of the time acknowledging that, as one pamphlet put it, 'the circumstances of the lower ranks of men are altered in almost every respect for the worse', in that 'they are reduced to the state of day-labourers and hirelings … [and] their subsistence in that state has become more difficult' (*C1*, pp. 885, 887–8).

Now, the enclosures movement was historically one of the areas in which classical political economy most obviously overlapped with classical legal theory. Which is a way of saying: the question of enclosures was a fundamental issue in the law of property. The sixteenth through to the eighteenth centuries might also be described as the period in which property law was being perfected. Notwithstanding the development of the joint-stock company in the nineteenth century and changes brought about with new technologies in the twentieth, the essence of property law was developed during the period of the rise of capital in which enclosures were crucial. The same period also saw the development of international law, in the form of the 'law of nations' and in terms of the legal justification for the exercise of force linked to a right. This combined (if uneven) historical development was of huge political importance, and in order to develop my argument concerning law and war I want to suggest that the key categories through which enclosures came to be justified legally were key categories of bourgeois ideology and political economy, and that *these same categories were central to international law*. 'Enclosure' thus connotes war as well as the law of private property; or, better still, *the law of private property as war*. It is here that the work of John Locke and the idea of waste become important.

Why Locke? And why waste?

Although widely understood to be one of the first key thinkers of bourgeois political thought, Locke is rarely considered in debates about international law and order. Despite his praise for Grotius and his appropriation of many of Grotius's key ideas, Locke is often missing from widely used texts on political theory and international relations. On the rare occasions he is discussed, it is usually in terms of just war theory,[26] or to suggest that he laid the foundations for a liberal concept of peace.[27] This omission is perhaps even more surprising given the emergence of a 'colonial reading' of Locke[28] and a related literature on liberalism and empire.[29] The reason for the oversight or omission would seem to be because of a widespread assumption that Locke's main concern is not war but property and the construction of a peaceful political order in which property ownership may flourish: 'Securing our navigation and trade [is] more the interest of this kingdom than wars, or conquests', he notes.[30] Hence Ellen Meiksins Wood suggests that Locke's 'theory of colonization is not a theory of war or international law but a theory of private property, which applies both at home and abroad'.[31] Yet there is a sense in which this misconstrues the extent to which Locke's theory of private property is *simultaneously* a theory of war. Or to put that another way, that he wrote with both the 'domestic' and the 'international', the 'inside' and the 'outside', in mind. It thus misconstrues the extent to which Locke, continuing the line of thought established by Vitoria and Grotius, contributed to the liberal justification for war based on its assumptions about capitalist modernity. At the core of these assumptions is the category 'waste'.

Waste has been suggested by Zygmunt Bauman to be a key characteristic of modernity: just as weeds are the waste of gardening, so 'mean streets the waste of town-planning, dissidence the waste of ideological unity, heresy the waste of orthodoxy, strangerhood the waste of nations-state building'.[32] My interest here is in the idea of the 'waste' of the commons, because, *pace* Bauman, in bourgeois thought the most significant 'waste' of modernity is the uncultivated land and idle labour that the commons represents. In being understood as 'waste', such things have been thought to require elimination, and the elimination of waste comes from its *improvement*. Drawing these points together, I want to suggest that the outcome of this bourgeois obsession with improving uncultivated (waste) land and idle (waste) labour has been nothing less than a *war on waste*. This war, I also suggest, was central to the wars of accumulation, to liberal just war theory, and thus to international law.

It is well known that the idea of the state of nature is crucial to Locke's theory. Many writers have suggested that such a state was for Locke either a 'logical abstraction' or 'an ahistorical condition'.[33] In fact, there is a third possibility: 'In the beginning all the world was *America*'. For Locke, Indians 'in the Woods of America … are perfectly in a State of Nature', since 'if *Josephus Acosta*'s word may be taken ... in many parts of *America* there was no Government at all'; the '*Kings* of the *Indians* in *America*' command their armies but 'exercise very little Dominion, and have but a very moderate Sovereignty'. The reason the Indians lack the institutions of political society is because their simple way of living confines their desires within narrow bounds and so generates few controversies and so no need for laws to decide them. Their system of property ownership, in other words, is such that they have 'no temptation to enlarge their Possessions of Land, or contest for wider extent of Ground'.[34]

Such a reference to enlarging possessions or land hints back to Locke's argument that God has given the world to men in common and that everyone is free to exercise their labour 'to make use of it [the World] to the best advantage of Life, and convenience'. This is in accordance with the natural law of preservation and can be carried out without the consent of others. For Locke, the 'civilized' part of mankind recognises that 'God gave the World to men in Common; but ... it cannot be supposed he meant it should always remain common and uncultivated'. God directed man 'to subdue the earth, i.e. improve it for the benefit of Life', and thus 'gave it to the use of the Industrious and rational ... not to the Fancy or Covetousness of the Quarrelsom and Contentious. He that had as good left for his Improvement'. This reinforces the idea that '*As much Land* as a Man Tills, Plants, Improves, Cultivates, and can use the Product of, so much is his *Property*' (*TT*, II, sects. 26, 30, 32, 34).

This reference to subduing and improving the land is important. Locke time and again refers to 'improvement' both in and of itself, as in 'improvement, tillage or husbandry', or through some other term which for Locke is synonymous to improvement: 'cultivation', 'pasturage', 'tillage', 'planting', 'husbandry'. These are the things the Indians fail to do. The Indians, he says, 'whom Nature having furnished as liberally as any other people, with the materials of Plenty, *i.e.* a fruitful Soil, apt to produce in abundance, what might serve for food, rayment, and delight; yet for want of improving it by labour, have not one hundredth part of the Conveniences we enjoy. Worse, in failing to labour on their land the Indians fail to create anything of any value. The transformation of 'waste' into value 'is all the Effect of Labour', a bushel of wheat on Indian land being worth barely one-thousandth of a bushel of wheat in England (*TT*, II, sects. 41, 43).

It might be said, then, that the ethos of 'improvement' is nothing less than the cornerstone of Locke's political philosophy *as* a philosophy of empire.[35] But one of the defining features of this language of empire is its description of the sheer waste that comes with land and nature going 'unimproved'. 'Land that is left wholly to Nature, that hath no improvement of Pasturage, Tillage, or Planting, is called, as indeed it is, *wast*' (*TT*, II, sect. 42).

> Whatsoever he tilled and reaped, laid up and made use of, before it spoiled, that was his peculiar Right; whatsoever he enclosed, and could feed, and make use of, the Cattle and Product was also his. But if either the Grass of his Inclosure rotted on the Ground, or the Fruit of his planting perished without gathering, and laying up, this part of the Earth, notwithstanding his Inclosure, was still to be looked on as Waste, and might be the possession of any other. (*TT*, II, sect. 38)

This is an argument that Locke applies directly to the condition of the Indians: 'there are still *great Tracts of Ground* to be found, which (the Inhabitants thereof not having joined with the rest of Mankind, in the consent of the Use of their common Money) *lie waste*' (*TT*, II, sect. 45). In other words, by virtue of the fact that they do not use money, the Indians allow land to 'waste'.

That this portrait is based on rather flimsy 'evidence' from a selection of travelogues, bears little relation to the real activities in which the Indians engaged,[36] and is at odds with Locke's own experience of colonial property, from which he made a profit despite some land remaining uncultivated,[37] reveals just how much Locke needed this argument as part of his political economy. But as we shall see, it is also important to his arguments concerning the wars of conquest.

Initially at least, it is the avoidance of waste that explains and justifies commerce: it is a 'foolish thing, as well as dishonest', for a person to hoard more than they might use. So if the person 'bartered away Plumbs that would have rotted in a Week, for Nuts that would last good for his eating a whole year, he did no injury; he wasted not the common Stock'; the important thing is that 'nothing perished uselessly'. For Locke, exceeding the bounds of just property lies not 'in the largeness of his Possession, but the perishing of any thing uselessly in it' (*TT*, II, sect. 46).

Hence money acts as part of the foundation of social life by being a mechanism for the exchange of things that might otherwise perish and be wasted.

> Supposing an Island, separate from all possible Commerce with the rest of the World, wherein there were but a hundred Families, but there were Sheep, Horses, and Cows, with other useful Animals, wholesome Fruits, and Land enough for Corn for a hundred thousand times as many, but nothing in the Island, either because of its Commonness, or Perishableness, fit to supply the place of *Money*.

The abstract example is used to suggest that in such a condition there could be no basis for enlarging one's possessions, yet the abstractness of the discussion is illustrated with reference to America.

> I ask, What would a Man value Ten Thousand, or an Hundred Thousand Acres of excellent *Land*, ready cultivated, and well stocked too with Cattle, in the middle of the in-land Parts of America, where he had no hopes of Commerce with the other Parts of the World, to draw *Money* to him by the Sale of the Product? It would not be worth the inclosing, and we should see him give up again to the wild Common of Nature. (*TT*, II, sect. 48)

Similarly, he stresses the importance of agriculture as a productive form of labour compared to hunting by constant reference to 'the vacant places of *America*' (*TT*, II, sect. 36). The general claim about the benefits of appropriation is also connected to the example of America.

> For I aske whether in the wild woods and uncultivated wast of America left to Nature, without any improvement, tillage or husbandry, a thousand acres will yield the needy and wretched inhabitants as many conveniences of life as ten acres of equally fertile land doe in Devonshire where they are well cultivated? (*TT*, II, sect. 37)

It is clear, then, that Locke's argument is focused on the waste that uncolonised and unimproved land might represent, a focus that reflects his deep concern over waste in general. As he put it in *Some Thoughts on Education*: 'I think people should be accustomed from their cradles to … spoil or waste nothing at all'.[38] Commenting to Locke's first biographer on Locke's character, Lady Masham noted that 'waste of anything he could not bear to see'.[39] Locke, as Bhikhu Parekh comments, 'was deeply haunted by the idea of waste'.[40]

Yet Locke was far from alone here. Neil Wood points out that Locke's arguments concerning property cannot be fully grasped unless read in the context of the wider seventeenth-century discourse of improvement.[41] The 'gentleman's desire', noted the House of Lords in 1607, was 'improvement',[42] and the century which followed proved the Lords right. Francis Bacon had set the scene in *The Advancement of Learning* (1605), with the idea of learning being 'improved and converted by the industry of man',[43] which kick-starts a whole 'improvement industry': Walter Blith's *The English Improver, Or a New Survey of Husbandry* (1649), which then became *The English Improver Improved* (1652); an anonymous tract called *Waste Land's Improvement* (1653); Andrew Yarranton's *The Improvement Improved* (1663); Samuel Fortrey's *England's Interest and Improvement* (also 1663); William Carter's *England's Interest Asserted, in the Improvement of its Native Commodities* (1669); John Smith's *England's Improvement Revived* (1670); Carew Reynell's *The True English Interest, or An Account of the Chief National Improvements* (1674); Roger Coke's *England's Improvements* (1675); another work by Yarranton called *England's Improvement by Sea and Land* (1677); A. Newbold's *London's Improvement and the Builder's Security Asserted* (1680); John Houghton's *A Collection of Letters for the Improvement of Husbandry and Trade* (1681). This list could go on, and could be expanded to include weekly journals such as *A Collection for the Improvement of Husbandry and Trade*. According to Paul Slack, the British Library catalogue reveals that the number of holdings including 'improve', 'improvement' and related terms in their titles rises from nine published before 1641, to 55 published between 1641 and 1660, 72 published between 1661 and 1680, 109 published between 1681 and 1700, 139 published between 1701 and 1720, and 185 published between 1721 and 1740.[44] 'Improvement of wastes and forests' was the slogan of the age, notes Joan Thirsk.[45]

The *Oxford English Dictionary* (OED) notes that 'improvement' refers in its original meaning to 'the turning of a thing to profit or good account; making the most of a thing for one's own profit', and specifies that in its earliest sense it was applied to the cultivation of land. Where terms such as 'subdue' or 'multiply' had Biblical sources,[46] 'improve', 'improver' and 'improvement' connoted technical agricultural innovations to increase productivity by the enclosure and cultivation of waste land. From thereon the idea of 'improvement' would play a central role in liberal thinking and the ideological development of the bourgeois class. Mark Girouard takes up the theme:

> Methods of commerce could be improved, by the provision of better quays, docks and warehouses. Manufacture could be improved, by new techniques such as the application of steam power, and that subdivision of labour which amazed visitors to Birmingham in the mid-century. Transport could be improved, by the formation of canals, the building of bridges, and the making of turnpike trusts. Agriculture could be improved, by enclosure and better methods of farming. Towns could be improved, by the paving, lighting, straightening and widening of streets, the formation of new streets, the destruction of medieval town walls, the provision of water. Country houses could be improved, by being rebuilt or remodelled in a purer taste, or given a new setting of idyllic parkland. The arts could be improved, by enlightened patronage and the founding of academies. The condition of the poor could be improved, by the provision of schools, hospitals, and better prisons.[47]

As well as expanding to include such a range of reforms, the term resonated with the legal expectation that land be privately held and practically used,[48] and was later extended to what Sarah Tarlow calls 'the moral sense of self-cultivation', cutting across and oscillating between economic profit and moral benefit, encouraging the idea of discipline, resonating through the 'self-help' literature, and making a fundamental connection between the material and psychological processes of change.[49] By the eighteenth century, in other words, 'improvement' had become a key category of capitalist modernity, permeating political thought, political economy and property law.[50]

Now, the idea of the 'improvement of waste' was increasingly used to challenge customary rights and to underpin the whole enclosures movement.[51] Enclosures were argued for on the grounds that unenclosed land was waste land. The *OED*'s second definition of 'improvement' is 'the turning of land to better account, the reclamation of waste or unoccupied land by inclosing', and by the time Blackstone came to write his *Commentaries on the Laws of England* (1765–9), a text which helped shape the legal foundations of the colonies, he could comment that the term used in law to signify enclosure, 'approving', is an ancient expression 'signifying the same as "improving"' and the lord of the manor 'may enclose so much of the waste as he pleases', waste being defined as 'uncultivated forest or desert'.[52] The belief was that if left unimproved the wasted commons would generate a masterless, idle and disorderly mass, with the consequence that enormous profits were being lost. England has 'many hundreds of acres of waste and barren lands', notes Samuel Hartlib, on which 'many thousands of idle hands' go without working.[53] For Timothy Nourse, in *Campania Fóelix, or, a Discourse of the Benefits and Improvements of Husbandry* (1700), the argument to 'uncommon wast grounds' was based on the fact that the 'common people' are 'rough and savage … and refractory to Government, insolent and tumultuous', while for Adam Moore, in *Bread for the Poor… Promised by Enclosure of the Wastes and Common Grounds of England* (1653), the commons led the poor to 'Begging, Filching, Robbing, Roguing, Murthering, and whatsoever other Villaines their unexercised brains and hands undertake'.[54] 'Common fields are the seat of disorder, the seed plot of contention, the nursery of beggary', noted one anonymous writer.[55] Enclosure, another anonymous writer notes, would therefore be 'an effectual tendency to the anticipation and suppression of many robberies, thefts, burglaries, rapes, and murders, which do much annoy this Commonwealth, and do receive their nourishment and encourage-ment from those vast, wild, wide forests'. This tract, called *Waste Land's Improvement* (1653), distinguishes the order of enclosures from the 'wild howling wildernesses' and 'deformed chaos' of the disorderly wastes, and warns that unless Parliament divides the wastes and provides work for the poor they 'may in time make England's wastes a receptacle and harbour for troops of assassinating rogues like the Tories in Ireland, and the Moss-troopers in Scotland'.[56] The commons, on this view, equals disorder. But the main reason the commons equals disorder is because of the idleness said to result, which was distinctly at odds with the concept of 'improvement'. To leave people idle was to leave them to 'waste' in the same way that the land might be 'wasted'. Appropriating the word from characterisations of land, Gervase Markham proposes in *The English Husbandman* (1613) to use as unskilled employees 'some Boyes and Girles, or other waste persons', using 'waste' to mean 'offscourings, dregs, worthless people', dated by the *OED* as emerging in the very late sixteenth century.[57] For John Bellars, the poor are like the scraps of pastry that cooks clip off the edges of pies and tarts: they 'appear wast and useless'.[58] For the ruling class, wasted land, wasted labour and wasted time went hand in hand, and what the reformers, jurists, merchants and publicists saw in the idleness of the poor was waste. Enclosure would therefore provide employment for idle people and masters for the 'masterless men' without obedience or discipline.[59]

What was at stake in these debates was the subsistence economy of the propertyless commoners, for whom 'waste' meant access to a variety of things and opportunity to acquire the raw materials to make others. Incorporated under the 'waste' of the commons were practices such as gleaning after harvest; grazing animals; catching wild animals; gathering wood and dung for fuel; picking rushes and reed to make into baskets, mats and thatch; procuring sand for use in scouring and for absorbing grease; acquiring herbs for cooking and medical use; picking nuts, fruit and berries; taking loose wool caught on bushes to use in blankets and clothes. The open-field system also allowed villagers to use strips of land in a field that had not been fenced in. Moreover, beyond providing a fundamental means of subsistence, the commons was also a form of reciprocity and mutuality between commoners; Tawney calls it 'practical communism'.[60] In other words, the struggle against 'waste' was a key moment in capitalism's war of annihilation against every non-capitalist form that it encounters. This was a war over the separation of the bulk of the population from the means of subsistence outside the wage and thus between rival models of labour and subsistence: a war between a rights-based model founded on the custom of providing the direct producers with some measure of immediate access to the means of production, and a model of absolute property giving the direct producers access to subsistence only through the mediation of the wage form; a war between usage for human need and the reification of usages into property to be exchanged; a war between the communism implicit in the commons and the primitive accumulation of capitalist modernity.[61]

What was at stake in the war on waste, then – and thus in Marx's account of primitive accumulation – is nothing less than an attack on the basic defences protecting the growing army of labourers from their proletarianisation. Such warfare – 'the expression is not too modern or too strong', notes Tawney[62] – was thus central to the invention of capital as *class war*, and thus occupies a pivotal position in the creation of the proletariat and the fabrication of bourgeois order.

The idea of the need to eliminate waste could carry such force not only because it could transform the socio-economic structure and propulsion to work under the power of 'clock-time' – that is 'bourgeois time'[63] – but also because of the way in which it operated and continues to operate within a moral economy of order: what counts as the *proper* use of nature and thus nature as *property*, what counts as the *proper* use of one's own person (labour) and time and thus *propriety*, and thus what counts as a *proper order*.[64] And in connoting what is *out of order*, waste is by definition also a question of *police power*.

Thus we find that in Britain during the eighteenth century a number of Improvement Acts were passed. Beatrice and Sydney Webb calculate that between 1689 and 1835 almost 300 new statutory bodies were formed under the rubric of 'Improvement Commissions' with widespread powers of urban governance. With approximately 100 of these in London and most of the others in urban centres, they offer evidence of 'improvement' as the ideological foundation of urbanisation. But it is significant that the Improvement Acts were also known as 'police acts' and the Improvement Commissions were sometimes known as 'police commissions'. Often described as the first forms of local government – 'the term "police" at that time almost synonymous with the later term, "local government"', notes T. A. Critchely – these forms of administration were essentially 'bodies of police' tasked with paving, cleansing, lighting, sewering, watching and generally 'improving' their towns, all organised under the general rubric of good order. So common was the idea that the Improvement Acts were police acts that they were often understood as the 'Improvement Act police'.[65] The war on waste and for improvement was thus always already a police measure: the war power folds once more into the police power as we find ourselves back on the terrain of the durably pacified social spaces in the previous chapter.

This is also why the *fence* was of such importance in the texts of Locke and other writers of the time.[66] 'Private property rests altogether on partitioning', notes Marx, and the fence was historically a key enactment of such partition. As the mark of enclosure the fence is simultaneously a visible symbol of a landscape 'improved' by its conversion into private property, a violent remarking of space and a fundamental ceremony of possession.[67] The fence constitutes an order or property and thus, by definition, a policed zone constituted by law. But English law in the eighteenth century also regarded the breaking of a boundary such as a fence or hedge to be a form of trespass and held that when an actual fence was broken force must have been required. The act of breaking a fence was understood to have been undertaken *vi et armis* (with force and arms),[68] and so was an act of war. The fenced-in space, as enclosure, constitutes a police zone subject to the rights of war.

On the one hand, then, I am arguing that one has to read the question of 'domestic waste' in terms of the early class war which created and disciplined the proletariat, a war on the ante- and anti-capitalist condition of the workers. This filtered into bourgeois thought wholesale, as a legal regime of private property consolidated the assumptions about property built into liberal philosophy, legal theory and the ideology of liberty. On the other hand, I want now to suggest that this set of ideas was also fundamental to international law.

As we have seen in Chapter 1, the attempt to create a modern legal regime governing the relations between emerging nation-states occurred in the context of the 'settlement' of the New World and the encounter with indigenous peoples as well as other states as enemies. Indeed, the encounter with other states was often via the encounter with other peoples in those territories. However, this encounter concerned not just questions of sovereignty and legal title by conquest, as per mainstream international law, or imperialism and racial supremacy over 'the other', as per critical international law (which is of course not to say that these questions and processes were not operative), but was in fact central to the process of primitive accumulation. Hence the same ideas about 'improving' the waste lands of the Old World were applied to the waste lands of the New World: the hunters and gatherers on the waste lands of England had their counterparts on the waste lands of else-where.[69] 'We have *Indians* at home, *Indians* in *Cornwall*, *Indians* in *Wales*, *Indians* in *Ireland*', claimed leading Puritan colonist Roger Williams in 1652.[70] Unsurprisingly then, the analogy between the need to expropriate idle and unproductive workers and idle and unproductive Indians became standard in political discourse.

The underlying logic was that the colonised failed to properly 'occupy' a fenced space as 'territory', and so had a tendency to range rather than inhabit. They 'range a great deal of ground', says Hobbes, rather than cultivating 'a little Plot with art and labour'.[71] William Bradford, Governor of the Plymouth plantation, writes of the land being 'devoyd of all civill inhabitants', consisting only of 'salvage and brutish men, which range up and down'.[72] In his hugely influential contemporary account of the settling of Virginia, Samuel Purchas describes the American natives as 'more wild and unmanly than that unmanned country, which they range rather than inhabite', and connects 'ranging rather than inhabiting' with Devil-worshipping, brutishness and bloody wickedness.[73] His fellow colonialist Robert Cushman thought that Indian 'land is spacious and void, and there are few, and do but run over the grass, as also do the foxes and wild beasts'. Such an unsettled life was thought to reveal the bestial nature of the natives, but also to mark the difficulty of pacifying them, notes Stephen Greenblatt.[74] Yet pacification became possible through the war on waste.

English lawyer, farmer and founder of the colony at New England, John Winthrop, for example, proposes that the Lord gave the earth to man to be 'tilled and improved', but that 'savage people ramble over much land without title or property', meaning that 'they inclose no ground, neither have they cattell to maintayne it, but remove their dwellings as they have occasion, or as they can prevail against their neighbours'. But since 'that which is common to all is proper to none', surely 'Christians have liberty to go and dwell among them in their waste lands and woods?'[75] The same point is made time and again: 'The Savages murmured at our planting in the Countrie', notes George Percy, but were answered: 'Why should you bee offended … as long as they hurt you not, nor take anything away by force, they take but a little waste ground'.[76] God 'abhorreth all willful waste' and so compels us 'to enter into a void and desolate country, overgrown with woods, thickets, and otherlike … having lien waste, untouched and untilled' (Richard Eburn); the Indians are 'a hindrance to Industry' and their waste lands 'Nurseries of Idleness and Insolence' (John Bellers); that there can be no argument against a 'peaceable colony, in a Wast country, where the people do live but like Deere in heards' (William Symonds); that because Indian land is 'spacious and void' and the Indians 'do but run over the grass', the land is 'idle and waste', 'all spoils, rots, and is marred for want of manuring, gathering, ordering, &c' (Robert Cushman); that 'the wast and vast uninhabited growndes' of Virginia need improving, because although the Indians reside there they do not 'knowe howe to turne to any benefitt' and so the land 'lyes ... vayne and idle before them' (William Strachey); or that the 'waste firme of America' needs planting (Richard Hakluyt).[77] As these comments suggest, the colonising impulse simply assumed the 'Indian', like the peasant, to be incapable of occupying and improving land as private property, and hence left everything to waste. 'In both cases', notes Christopher Hill, 'some unfortunates had to lose out in the interests of rational improvement'.[78] This logic saturated colonial thought at the time[79] and the discourse of systematic colonisation thereafter.[80]

In the colonial context, then, the discourse of sovereignty and the discourse of improvement merge.[81] This is why the very same idea is found in the key texts of international law, as Locke himself recognised. In his recommendation of reading matter to anyone who wishes to be 'instructed on the natural rights of men, and the original and foundations of society, and the duties resulting from these', Locke offers us Grotius as one of the prime sources.[82] That he does so is telling. In a text published in 1622 and read far less than *De Iure Belli ac Pacis*, Grotius made the following observation: 'If God has granted us something', he says, 'we are not commanded to cast it into the sea, as some philosophers imprudently did; nor to let it lie useless by us, nor yet to lavish it away'.[83] Appropriation, in Grotius's view, is justified where there is 'waste or barren Land'. Far from being a throwaway comment in a text that is now largely unread, this view runs through his major work on the laws of war and peace three years later. As we saw in the previous chapter, that book is founded on the idea that Locke will eventually take from Grotius, namely that although God 'gave to mankind in general a Dominion over Things', God also allowed that 'every Man converted what he would to his own use' and so *common* property ownership is 'no longer approved of'. 'As soon as living in common was no longer approved of, all Men were supposed, and ought to be supposed to have consented, that each should appropriate to himself, by Right of first Possession, what could not have been divided'. This generates an exclusive right, and this exclusive right in turn allows for the appropriation of anything that might be 'waste'. Things which are 'uncultivated' or 'untilled' become open to appropriation in order that they might not be wasted (*RWP*, II. II. IV, p. 432).

> If there be any waste or barren Land within our Dominions, that also is to be given to Strangers, at their Request, or may be lawfully possessed by them, because whatever remains uncultivated, is not to be esteemed a Property ... *They commit no Crime who cultivate and manure the untilled Part of a Country. (RWP,* II. II. XVII, p. 448)

Jurisdiction over land may be alienated by a People should that land be 'uninhabited and waste' (*RWP*, II. VI. VII, p. 572). In Volume III of the book Grotius returns to the theme, insisting that there shall be no recompense for those losing possessions which they had 'either wasted or alienated' (*RWP*, III. X. VI, p. 1419). And Grotius's criticism of appropriation concerns those who appropriate and accumulate lands which 'were *not* waste and desolate' (*RWP*, II. II. XVII, p. 449, emphasis added). Thus in addition to the observation made in the previous chapter concerning Grotius's claim that there exists a fundamental right to wage war to appropriate certain types of territory not being 'properly' used by indigenous peoples, the point here is that being 'properly' used means not being wasted.[84] It is this which underpins the argument for war, albeit declared, regulated and exercised in a way which renders it 'just'.[85]

This same idea finds its way into other texts on the law of nations. Vattel, for example, whose *Law of Nations* (1758) followed Grotius in aiming to show that 'war, founded on justice, is a lawful mode of acquisition',[86] describes the cultivation of the soil as 'an obligation imposed by nature on mankind'.

> The whole earth is destined to feed its inhabitants; but this it would be incapable of doing if it were uncultivated. Every nation is then obliged by the law of nature to cultivate the land that has fallen to its share ... Those nations ... who inhabit fertile countries, but disdain to cultivate their lands, and choose rather to live by plunder, are wanting to themselves ... There are others, who, to avoid labour, live by hunting, and their flocks. This might, doubtless, be allowed in the first stages of the world, when the earth, without cultivation, produced more than was sufficient to feed its small number of inhabitants. (*LN*, Bk I, Chap. VII)

Unsurprisingly, Vattel's argument is from the Americas: 'Though the conquest of the civilized empires of Peru and Mexico was a notorious usurpation, the ... people of those extensive tracts rather ranged through than inhabited them'. This ranging, involving a level of idleness which Vattel despises (*LN*, Bk I, Chap. VI; Bk I, Chap. VIII; Bk I, Chap. XII; Bk I, Chap. XX; Bk III, Chap. I), means that 'the establishment of many colonies on the continent of North America might, on their confining themselves within just bounds, be extremely lawful' (*LN*, Bk I, Chap. VIII).

> All mankind have an equal right to things that have not yet fallen into the possession of any one; and those things belong to the person who first takes possession of them. When, therefore, a nation finds a country uninhabited, and without an owner, it may lawfully take possession of it. (*LN*, Bk I, Chap. XVIII)

At this point Vattel adds a comment regarding waste, and there follows what Vattel calls the 'celebrated question':

> It is asked whether a nation may lawfully take possession of some part of a vast country, in which there are none but erratic nations whose scanty population is incapable of occupying the whole? We have already observed, in establishing the obligation to cultivate the earth, that those nations cannot exclusively appropriate to themselves more land than they have occasion for, or more than they are able to settle and cultivate. Their unsettled habitation in those immense regions cannot be accounted a true and legal possession; and the people of Europe, too closely pent up at home, finding land of which the savages stood in no particular need, and of which they made no actual and constant use, were lawfully entitled to take possession of it, and settle it with colonies. (*LN*, Bk I, Chap. XVIII)

Since the earth 'belongs to mankind in general, and was designed to furnish them with subsistence', colonisation is allowed: 'we do not, therefore, deviate from the views of nature, in confining the Indians within narrower limits' (*LN*, Bk I, Chap. XVIII). Peoples and nations which choose not to cultivate their lands, despite those lands being fertile, are not only 'wanting to themselves' but are also 'injurious to all their neighbours' and, as such, 'deserve to be extirpated as savage and pernicious beasts' (*LN*, Bk I, Chap. VII).

What we find in yet another of the key texts of international law, then, is an overlap, reiteration and further juridical underpinning of arguments found in colonial thinking and major works of bourgeois political philosophy. Despite his distance from Grotius – it has been claimed that whereas Grotius wrote the international law of absolutism, Vattel wrote the international law of political liberty[87] – Vattel also structures part of his argument concerning international law around questions of subsistence and in categories taken from bourgeois political economy and the logic of enclosures. Both writers operate and reinforce a conceptual opposition of improvement versus waste that ranks alongside the opposition of civilisation versus barbarism in the history of political thought. The conceptual opposition in question was a crucial ideological foundation for the war of accumulation against the poor and the systematic colonisation of the world by capital.

What this means, in effect, is that the ways in which the international order and its legal regime were violently constituted through the sixteenth and seventeenth centuries can be understood as part and parcel of the process Marx calls 'primitive accumulation'. To the extent that international law *embodies* the violence of colonialism, it also embodies the violence of primitive accumulation. This is why the central theme that so animated the early law of nations, the question of *just war*, is shot through with the categories of the war on the commons and the language of enclosures. In the bourgeois mind, *the global war of accumulation was the archetypal just war*. To put that another way: in the bourgeois mind, the class war was historically a just war. International law was a key weapon used in this war.

THE SECRET POLICE WAR: CRIMINALS, SLAVES, WORKERS

The chapter on the state of nature at the beginning of the *Second Treatise* is regarded as one of the classic chapters in the history of political thought, outlining as it does the liberal case for natural rights. Yet the key question dealt with by Locke in the chapter – which is, in effect, the first substantive chapter of the *Second Treatise* – concerns the right of punishment. To justify such a right the simplest claim would have been to say that it is derived from the limited rights of citizens over others once political society has been created and derived from the doctrine of tacit consent which Locke articulates elsewhere in the *Second Treatise*.[88]

But making this claim would have meant Locke abandoning the doctrine that he wishes to hold: that there is a natural right to punish. For Locke, this implies that every man has in the state of nature the right to punish a murderer with death. This power to punish is '*to secure* Men from the attempts of a Criminal' and is necessary because the criminal has 'renounced Reason' and so figures as a savage beast, equivalent to 'the *Lyon* or *Tyger*'. In this context, Locke makes an important additional claim: he says that beasts such as the *Lyon*, the *Tyger* and the criminal can be understood as having 'declared War against all Mankind' (*TT*, II, sect. 10). The criminal is at war with society; with the criminal, as with the lion or tiger, security is impossible.

Now, despite Locke twice conceding that this doctrine concerning punishment is a 'strange' one (*TT*, II, sects. 9 and 13), it is in fact lifted from some of the key liberal texts in international law. In other words, the liberal doctrine concerning the right to *punish* figures as part of a set of claims about the rights of *war*. In the *Commentary* Grotius describes a natural right to punishment as well as dominion.

> Is not the power to punish essentially a power that pertains to the state? Not at all! On the contrary, just as every right of the magistrate comes to him from the state, so has the same right come to the state from private individuals … Therefore, since no one is able to transfer a thing that he never possessed, it is evident that the right of chastisement was held by private persons before it was held by the state. The following argument, too, has great force in this connexion: the state inflicts punishment for wrongs against itself, not only upon its own subjects but also upon foreigners; yet it derives no power over the latter from civil law; and therefore, the law of nature, or law of nations, is the source from which the state receives the power in question. (*C*, pp. 136–7)

This argument means that the private application of force is not entirely ruled out, as we saw in the previous chapter, but it also feeds into the account of punishment in Book II of the *De Iure Belli ac Pacis* where, alongside defence and the recovery of property, punishment is a fundamental part of the international right of war. Since natural law is the foundation of the law of nations, so the natural law of punishment applies within the law of nations.

We must also know, that Kings, and those who are invested with
a Power equal to that of Kings, have a Right to exact Punishments,
not only for Injuries committed against themselves, or their
Subjects, but likewise, for those which do not peculiarly concern
them, but which are, in any Persons whatsoever, grievous
Violations of the Law of Nature or Nations. For the Liberty of
consulting the Benefit of human Society, by Punishments, which
at first, as we have said, was in every particular Person, does now,
since Civil Societies, and Courts of Justice, have been instituted,
reside in those who are possessed of the supreme Power.

He goes on:

We follow the Opinion of *Innocentius*, and others, who hold that
War is lawful against those who offend against Nature; which is
contrary to the opinion of *Victoria*, *Vasquez*, *Azorius*, *Molina*, and
others, who seem to require, towards making a War just, that he
who undertakes it be injured in himself, or in his State, or that he
has some Jurisdiction over the Person against whom the War is
made. For they assert that the Power of Punishing is properly an
Effect of Civil Jurisdiction; whereas our opinion is, that it proceeds
from the Law of Nature. (*RWP*, II. XX. XL, pp. 1021–2, 1024–5)

Grotius's examples of the kind of actions which break the law of nature
and which thus lend themselves to punishment even by those not
injured by the actions themselves include being inhuman to one's
parents, cannibalism, piracy, killing settlers, engaging in tyrannical rule
and generally being 'like Beasts': 'war may be justly undertaken' against
such people (II. XX. XL, pp. 1022–4).

So, one source for Locke's strange doctrine is Grotius's work on the
laws of war. But when in his *Thoughts Concerning Education* Locke
recommends Grotius to anyone who wishes to be instructed on duties,
rights and the foundations of society, he says that the one book better
than Grotius's *De Iure Belli ac Pacis* is Pufendorf's *On Natural Law and
the Law of Nations*. And in that text we find a similar 'strange' doctrine of
punishment related once again to war. After outlining the need to 'try
every means before arms' and the need to exercise patience with those
injuring us, Pufendorf declares that the one who does the injury 'has

broken off all relations of humanity'. 'By avowing that he is my enemy – and this is the case when he attacks me with injuries and shows no signs of repentance – he gives me, so far as he is able to, an unlimited freedom of action against him'. The 'affair must be decided by blows', and 'it will be proper to withstand him even to his death'.[89]

All of this tells us something important about Locke's 'international theory'. Locke's claim in Chapter II that 'Governments all through the World, are in a State of Nature' is often taken as a suggestion that his conception of war is the conventional one found in IR, that war is what takes place between militarily organised nation-states, which is what makes him an 'international theorist'. Yet this is not the real substance of his argument. Rather, he is more animated by the continued existence of criminality following the creation of political society. So the arguments concerning punishment and war are deeply connected, and in a complicated way; moreover, and to complicate the matter further, they are bound up with the argument concerning slavery.

Locke says that:

> *By the Fundamental Law of Nature* ... one may destroy a Man who makes War upon him, or has discovered an Enmity to his being, for the same Reason, that he may kill a *Wolf* or a *Lyon*; because such men are not under the ties of the Common Law of Reason, have no other Rule, but that of Force and Violence, and so may be treated as Beasts of Prey, those dangerous and noxious creatures, that will be sure to destroy him, whenever he falls into their Power. (*TT*, II, sect. 16)

This is not just about the murderer, and nothing to do with the relations between Governments of the world, but refers to anyone who might have a 'sedate setled Design, upon another Man's Life': not just the thief who may use force to take our money but even 'any one that joyns with him in his Defence'. Moreover, Locke's claim that '*Force without Right, upon a man's Person, makes a State of War*', appears initially to concern the state of nature: 'force, or a declared design of force upon the Person of another, where there is no common Superior on Earth to appeal to for relief, *is the State of War*'. And yet within a few lines Locke adds that force without right makes a state of war '*both where there is, and is not, a common Judge*' (*TT*, II, sect. 19, last emphasis added). And this

'Right to destroy that which threatens me with Destruction' extends to the most heinous threat of all: that of the man 'who attempts to get another Man into his Absolute Power'. For as well as counting as criminal in itself, and thus a form of war, such an act would, of course, also 'make me a Slave' and so 'put [me] into a State of War' (*TT*, II, sects. 16–18).[90]

These moves between punishment and warfare conjure up an image of a social body saturated by war. This situation is intensified with the introduction of money, which generates the opportunity of increasing one's possessions and thus increasing the range of crimes and the general levels of enmity.[91] Political power in this sense is a *permanent war* against the criminal and in defence of private property. Thus in addition to the point made in the previous chapter, that the lawless creature was so thought to be *at war with the social order*, we might also say that for liberalism punishment always 'preserves something of the battle'.[92]

Moreover, making war runs into the more general hostility implicit in the idea of 'enmity' – 'The *State of War* is a State of Enmity' (*TT*, II, sect. 16) – and, as such, constitutes a permanent threat, for even the more 'sedate and setled' forms of enmity constitute a form of warfare. This permanence is taken further by the contrast of the innocent with the noxious rather than the guilty. And the 'noxious' is illustrated again with the example of wild beasts of prey outside of any possible political order. Wolves, lions and other dangerous creatures offer a threat not because they are likely to break the law – in the way that they might be 'guilty' compared to 'innocent' – but because they constitute a pure physical threat to property and life.

Locke's comments on the colonial situation in America and war against the Indians are similarly mapped out in terms of the doctrine of punishment-as-war.

> *Touching War, we see that* Abraham *Commanded an Army of* 318 *Souldiers of his own Family* … Is it not possible for a Man to have 318 Men in his Family, without being Heir to *Adam*? A Planter in the *West Indies* has more, and might, if he pleased (who doubts) Muster them up and lead them out against the *Indians*, to seek Reparation upon any injury received from them. (*TT*, I, sect. 130)

This comment is from the *First Treatise* and thus, in essence, part of the argument against Filmer. Yet its core assumption is centred on the political economy of land and labour that was by then becoming entrenched in bourgeois political thought and which Locke more than anyone was doing so much to develop. On this view, since European planters possess the right to execute the law of nature, Indian resistance to the exercise of such right is a *crime* and an act of *war*. Against such a 'crime' and an act of 'war', the colonial powers have a right to seek 'reparations'. At the same time, a further implication of Locke's argument concerning waste and improvement is that any resistance to the taking of waste land turns the natives into the aggressors, which reinforces the belief that the European project is a 'just war'.[93] The violence of war and the violence of punishment are thus rolled together on the grounds of the political economy of land and labour.

This raises the question of slavery. Commentary on Locke's theory of slavery in the *Two Treatises* is remarkably narrow, focusing as it does on trying to reconcile the opening lines of the text, where Locke condemns slavery, with those sections where he clearly condones it. But this approach to Locke on slavery ignores its debt to the history of writings on the laws of war. Aristotle held that 'the art of acquiring slaves, I mean of justly acquiring them … [is] a species of hunting or war', Justinian's *Institutes* of Roman law held slavery to be an institution under the law of nations, and from such sources it was widely accepted that capture in war was the major justification of slavery.[94] Locke says that conquerors in an unjust war '*never* come to *have a right over the Conquered*', but that captives taken in a just war can rightfully be enslaved: '*Slaves* … being Captives taken in a just War' forfeit their lives, liberties and estates. If we take the standard definition of 'war' to imply inter-state military conflict then this would seem to mean that Locke is implying that captives taken in an inter-state European war would rightly become slaves. But if Locke's condemnation of slavery in the first sentence of the *Two Treatises* is to be taken seriously, this is clearly not what he is intending. Rather, he is intending to justify slavery, which can only mean that black slaves are justifiably enslaved because they were taken as captives in a just war. Not only does this mean that the forays of corporations such as the Royal Africa Company count as just wars,[95] but it also implies that the more general global war of accumulation being conducted by states and corporations is also just.

This is why the condition of slavery is, for Locke, an exercise of the war power. The slave has no property, is outside the compact, and is therefore under a form of despotism. But since 'it arises not from Compact', what Locke calls 'despotical power' is 'the state of war continued'. Furthermore, although Locke suggests that the slave is outside of civil society, the bulk of his argument presupposes the place of the slave within civil society through being 'united under the Domestick Rule of a Family' (*TT*, II, sects. 24, 85, 86, 172, 175, 176). Thus the state of war that is slavery rumbles on through any civil society which allows slavery. At the same time, Locke would also have been more than familiar with arguments that slave resistance is not only illegal but also, as an 'unjust' rebellion, a form of war. Hobbes, for example, had argued that 'Rebellion, is but warre renewed', and Algernon Sydney had already pointed to the fact that 'rebellion' 'is taken from the Latin *rebellare*, which signifies no more than to renew a war'.[96] Locke suggests that 'those who set up force again in opposition to the Laws, do *Rebellare*, that is, bring back again the state of War, and are properly Rebels'. 'Rebellion being an opposition, not to Persons, but Authority ... those, whoever they be, who by force break through, and by force justifie their violation of them, are truly and properly *Rebels*' (*TT*, II, sect. 226). As Secretary to the Lords Proprietors of Carolina (1669 to 1675), Secretary and Treasurer to the Council for Trade and Foreign Plantations (1673 to 1676), and Commissioner for the Board of Trade and Plantations (1696 to 1700), Locke read and summarised the various communications, requests and orders that circulated between the key offices of state and the colonising authorities in America, Barbados, Jamaica and elsewhere,[97] and would therefore have known that rebellion and related activities (conspiracies, spontaneous revolts, planned revolts, revolts fought from rebel hideouts and often lasting several years) were a more or less permanent feature of slave societies and constituted a condition of permanent war. He would have understood the various punishments meted out by the colonial rulers (including burning alive, beheading, dismembering and hanging) as a means of fighting the rebellion, the extent to which territories were essentially governed through the militia – some two thousand 'militia tenants' were installed on Barbados plantations after 1696, with no manual labour duties to perform but with the sole function of policing slavery – and the ways in which the colonial militia exercised a crucial police power over the slaves.[98] In seventeenth-century America, it has been said, 'every colonist was a policeman' and the colony itself 'more like an army camp than a civilian community'.⁹⁹ Colonial discourse also presupposed that Indian society was one of 'constant warfare'.¹⁰⁰

The fact that despite his commitment to private property Locke remains wedded to the idea of slavery, that slavery is the state of war continued, and that slave rebellions are a form of intensified warfare, reinforces the idea that any social order which allows slavery is by definition an order of perpetual war, and any rebellion by those in the condition of slavery or its associated subservient conditions reinforces this war status.

This issue becomes even more complex when one realises that although Locke distinguishes between slave and servant, he sometimes also uses the second term to refer to the slave proper. He describes 'Slaves bought with Money', but also speaks of a Planter's 'Power in his Family over Servants, born in his House, and bought with his Money' (*TT*, I, sects. 13 and 131). Locke would have been familiar with Grotius's arguments that although slavery is against nature, humans can become slaves 'in Consequence of some Crime', as well as his claim that 'there were many People formerly, who, sensible of their own Weakness and Incapacity for getting a Livelihood, voluntarily submitted themselves Slaves to others' (*RWP*, III. VII. I, p. 1360 and II. V. XXVII, p. 557). But this oscillation between slavery and servitude is also a reflection of the extent to which degrees of 'quasi-slavery' existed in England and elsewhere, partly a remnant of villeinage, partly an outcome of the law failing to distinguish theoretically between a slave and a serf, and partly due to the various Vagrancy Acts which facilitated the idea of slavery as a form of punishment, as we saw earlier, indicative of the ways in which the categories of slave, servant, vagabond and worker were permeable. Even when such laws were repealed, pockets of indentured labour remained: English law made the violation of many 'free' labour contracts punishable with imprisonment, and workers would only be released once they were willing to return to their employers and complete the service in question, often for a year and sometimes more since additional days' service could be imposed because of the absence. This was transplanted into the colonial law of America, such that in both England and colonial America 'contractual labor' existed in varying degrees of 'unfreedom'.¹⁰¹ And it should be noted that Locke was not averse to recommending forced labour as a solution to the problem of England's ill-disciplined and

recalcitrant workers – as Commissioner on the Board of Trade Locke
wrote a memorandum on the poor law along these lines in 1697.[102]

What all of this means, of course, is that rebellion by the propertyless
at home – and Locke would have known full well that the pre-eminent
form of rebellion in England took the form of protest and riot against
enclosures[103] – registers in the same way as rebellion by slaves in the
colonies: as war. In effect, the necessity of the state in Locke's argument
is comprehensible only through the logic of war, exercised in permanent
fashion against rebellious slaves, antagonistic Indians, wayward workers
and, of course, the criminal more broadly defined.[104] Liberal government,
constituted supposedly for 'peace and security', turns out to be nothing
less than a permanent exercise of the war power against these unsocial
and lawless elements. Seen through the lens of sovereignty, these
elements are the enemies of security; through the lens of property, they
are the enemies of improvement; through the lens of police, they are
disorderly. The outcome can only be war and war again: war against the
waste of the commons; war against forms of existence outside the
political economy of private property; war on the worker-slave; war on
the enemies of bourgeois order. Liberal sovereignty is constituted for
just such a war. And yet, at the same time, liberalism will constantly hold
back from calling it 'war'. It is thus in many ways the secret war of
bourgeois history. Which is precisely why it is so often conducted
through the police power (the logic being: if we call it 'police' then it can't
be 'war'). The *police* action against these disorderly, unruly and lawless
elements becomes central to the very *secrecy* of the war.

In the chapters to follow I turn to some of the ways in which this
police war gets conceptualised: as 'liberal peace', as 'civilisation', as
'international police'. Given that those chapters have some things to say
about the current 'war on terror', I want to finish this chapter by
returning more directly to the question of international law and the
current conjuncture.

THE SECRET OF INTERNATIONAL LAW

One of the most common refrains among commentators writing about
the 'war on terror' is that the war illustrates the enduring impact of
imperialism in the international system. Terms such 'empire', 'empire lite',
'imperial peace', 'new imperialism', 'the Empire's new clothes', imperial

sovereignty', 'military empire' and the 'new colonial' now dominate analyses of international order and 'an imperial global state' in the making. As a consequence, the refrain is often that the war breaks international law, is therefore illegal, and that those pursuing it are, in effect, war criminals.[105] I want to suggest, instead, that to make sense properly of this 'colonial present'[106] we need to grasp it as part of the logic of primitive accumulation and, moreover, that doing so reveals precisely the point about international law being made in the previous chapter and this: that it facilities rather than threatens the war of accumulation.

We need first to distance ourselves from the tendency in commentaries on Marx's work to treat primitive accumulation as either a period of transition from feudalism to capitalism or as pertaining to the early history of the colonies. Both views are encouraged by the convention of translating '*ursprüngliche*' as 'primitive' rather than 'original' or 'previous'. '*Ursprüngliche*' was Marx's translation of Smith's 'previous', which those translating Marx's work into English rendered as 'primitive'. The fact that the discussion of primitive accumulation requires a discussion of enclosures as well as colonisation encourages this view, since the tendency has been to view both enclosures and colonisation as historical acts. The general tendency runs: *before* capitalism there is colonisation and enclosures – in other words, there is 'primitive' accumulation – which form the preconditions of capitalism by creating and developing markets, but that once the job is done we can stop talking about enclosures or colonisation (and thus we can stop talking about primitive accumulation).[107] In fact, contra this tendency, we need to understand primitive accumulation as the foundation of capital not just historically but *permanently*.

Marx notes:

The capital-relation presupposes a complete separation between the workers and the ownership of the conditions for the realization of their labour. As soon as capitalist production stands on its own feet, it not only maintains this separation, but reproduces it on a constantly extending scale. The process, therefore, which creates the capital-relation can be nothing other than the process which divorces the worker from the ownership of the conditions of his own labour; it is a process which operates two transformations,

whereby the social means of subsistence and production are
turned into capital, and the immediate producers are turned into
wage-labourers. So-called primitive accumulation, therefore, is
nothing else than the historical process of divorcing the producer
from the means of production. It appears as 'primitive' because it
forms the pre-history of capital, and of the mode of production
corresponding to capital. (*C1*, pp. 874–5)

Marx's use of 'pre-history' here is misleading, since it does indeed
suggest that the process is somehow 'over'. But the gist of the passage
suggests that Marx is interested in capital in terms of the historical
presuppositions of capital's becoming: capital *presupposes* the divorce of
workers from the conditions of the realisation of their labour and as soon
as capital is able to stand on its own two feet it not only maintains this
divorce but *reproduces it on a constantly extending scale*. Hence Marx's
comment elsewhere that 'accumulation merely presents as a continuous
process what in primitive accumulation appears as a distinct historical
process'.[108] The presuppositions of capital 'primitively appeared as
conditions of its becoming' but 'now appear as results of its own realization, reality, as *posited by it – not as conditions of its arising, but as results
of its presence*'.[109] Or as he puts it in Volume 3 of *Capital*, it is the 'divorce
between the conditions of labour on the one hand and the producers
on the other that forms the concept of capital, as this arises with
primitive accumulation', adding that this 'subsequently appear[s] as a
constant process in the accumulation and concentration of capital'.[110]

   In other words, 'primitive accumulation' refers not to a period in the
emergence of capitalist relations or a transitory phenomenon characteristic of the 'prehistory' of capital prior to its 'developed' or 'civilised'
stage but, rather, to capitalism's need permanently to form markets and
re-create labour supplies. Because primitive accumulation is a
permanent process in the colonisation of the world by capital, the term
refers to the historical process that constitutes capitalist relations as a
whole.[111] As Balibar puts it, the analysis of primitive accumulation is 'the
genealogy of the elements which constitute the structure of the capitalist mode
of production'.[112] As the presupposition of capital, primitive accumulation
'is not just the historical starting point of capital but, qua coercive
proletarianization, central to its essence',[113] and it has been rightly
pointed out that the chapters on 'so-called primitive accumulation' with

which *Capital* ends form a decisive overview of the entire set of problems concentrated in the relation called 'capital' itself.[114] If so, then we need to understand primitive accumulation not as a historical process exhausted at the consolidation of capitalism but, rather, a *permanent feature of accumulation* and an *integral component of class war*.[115] The separation of labourers from the conditions of labour independent of capital *is* (not just *was*) the social constitution of capitalist social relations. And this helps us make sense of the permanence of systematic colonisation, at the heart of which is the accumulation of capital and not merely one powerful 'imperial' state.

On this view, to criticise the 'war on terror' for violating international law is to miss the point completely, for what is most obvious about the war is not the violation of this or that aspect of international law but, rather, the brutality with which resources have been appropriated and peoples proletarianised. This situates the war on terror within the wider frame of contemporary accumulation strategies. For example, in Iraq, generations of farmers operated in an essentially unregulated, informal seed supply system, whereby farm-saved seed and the free innovation with and exchange of planting materials among farming communities was standard agricultural practice. Yet the Coalition Provisional Authority established after the invasion of Iraq changed the law (with Order 81), making it illegal for Iraqi farmers to reuse seeds harvested from new varieties registered under the law. As the GRAIN organisation noted in an opinion piece on the *war* against Iraqi farmers, 'the purpose of the law is to facilitate the establishment of a new seed market in Iraq, where transnational corporations can sell their seeds, genetically modified or not, which farmers would have to purchase afresh every single cropping season'. In other words, the historical prohibition of private ownership of biological resources was to be replaced by a new patent law allowing a system of monopoly rights over seeds, with the rights in question almost certain to be held by multinational corporations.[116] This was reinforced by the new constitution established for the country in October 2005, which requires that the state in Iraq manages the Iraqi economy in accordance with modern – that is, 'liberal' – economic principles and to ensure the development of the private sector; a commitment to capitalist accumulation is now a constitutional requirement for Iraq.

The generation of a new seed market in Iraq must be situated in the context of TRIPS (Trade-Related Aspects of Intellectual Property Rights).

Operating under the auspices of the World Trade Organization (but pushed through by major corporations within the multinational information industries and their lobbying group the Intellectual Property Committee), TRIPS enacts an ideology of commodified intellectual property rights, such that ideas and genetic material might be treated as such and managed by monopolies through patent and copyright law. Resources once used by peoples on a collective basis thereby become appropriated as property for accumulation, from the Indian *neem* plant now patented for oral hygiene use to the West African *karité* butter now appropriated by the cosmetics industry. For such a process to work the legal status of the resources has to be changed from being the common property of indigenous communities to being the patented property of corporations: the 'intellectual commons' becomes private property, human need gets over-ridden by accumulation and profit, and the war on terror continues the war on waste.

Yet TRIPS also needs to be set alongside other international arrangements such as the North American Free Trade Agreement (NAFTA), which allows the dumping of heavily subsidised food products by US-based corporations onto the markets of other countries within the Agreement. In Mexico alone this has led to the ripping from producers of an estimated $1 billion a year in earnings and to the forcible dispossession of some two million farmers of their means of subsistence (and who, as migrants, thereby become a 'security problem'). The World Bank and the IMF impose 'structural reforms' on whole nations, usually involving massive cuts in public spending, the privatisation of anything that looks remotely like 'the commons' or communal control of the means of subsistence, the separation of workers from the resources for anything like an alternative mode of being beyond capital, job losses and the closure of public facilities such as schools and hospitals, the elimination of state subsidies on basic commodities relied on by the poor, enforcing mobility on the labour force (albeit within the requisite security measures), the devaluation of local currencies (thereby pushing up the prices for imported goods), the opening up of economies to foreign ownership, the modernising (that is, liberalising) of financial systems, the dismantling of the labour laws that might have provided workers with even the most basic of rights and generally divorcing workers from the terrain on which their organisational power might be built, and removing environmental laws protecting resources and farming. This is the lens through which what is taking place across the globe as a 'war on terror' – but in the name of 'peace and security' – needs to be seen. Much as these developments can often appear and feel new, given that the warfare in question is heavily mediated by international institutions such as the IMF and World Bank, they have long and deep roots in formulations established by Vitoria, developed by Grotius and refined by Locke.

This process has unsurprisingly been called the 'new enclosures' or the 'second enclosure movement', but as Retort point out, the only term which properly describes this complex rearticulation of imperial war, military neoliberalism and international law is 'primitive accumulation'.[117] Now, as David Harvey observes, it seems peculiar to call an ongoing process 'primitive' accumulation (hence Harvey's opting for 'accumulation by dispossession'), but the point stands either way: that 'all of the features of primitive accumulation that Marx mentions have remained powerfully present within capitalism's historical geography'.[118] 'Primitive accumulation' is in this sense a far more powerful term than the other phrases used by critics, radicals and activists, such as plunder, piracy or privatisation,[119] not only because it treats accumulation as war but also because such terms usually involve clinging desperately to the idea of international law as some kind of defence against the violence in question. 'We cannot forget the universal promise of international law' is the common refrain, connecting precisely to the view that in the 'war on terror', as in any war, we must engage in 'speaking law to power'.[120] But reading this contemporary combination of war and law as primitive accumulation reiterates the point made in Chapter 1: that the violence in question is built into the very fabric of international law. The violent dispossession and proletarianisation of peoples in the war on terror needs to be understood as part and parcel of the systematic colonisation of our world.

The beauty of 'systematic colonization' as an idea is that it grasps capital as a social relation and the conjunction of war and law as class power. Marx was interested in the secret of systematic colonisation as the secret of accumulation. Might this also be the secret of international law? Evgeny Pashukanis once pointed out that international law has always sought to hide its class character, and one might say the same about capital.[121] Perhaps capital and international law share the very same secret: the very secret of the class war?

Chapter 3

'O EFFEMINACY! EFFEMINACY!': MARTIAL POWER, MASCULINE POWER, LIBERAL PEACE

The army has its uses
In times of civil crisis
'Allo boys! Seen any action?
Hey boys, seen any action?

Bond together with your mate
Against the common enemy
Gang of Four, 'He'd Send in the Army' (1980)

'Real men' are back. That is, 'real men' are back according to a certain kind of commentary on the 'war on terror'. In the *Wall Street Journal* the following story ran just one month after the attacks on the World Trade Center in 2001:

A certain style of manliness is once again being honored and celebrated in our country since Sept. 11. You might say it suddenly emerged from the rubble of the past quarter century, and emerged when a certain kind of man came forth to get our great country out of the fix it was in.

I am speaking of masculine men, men who push things and pull things and haul things and build things, men who charge up the stairs in a hundred pounds of gear and tell everyone else where to go to be safe. Men who are welders, who do construction, men who are cops and firemen. They are all of them, one way or another, the men who put the fire out, the men who are digging the rubble out, and the men who will build whatever takes its place.

And their style is back in style. We are experiencing a new

respect for their old-fashioned masculinity, a new respect for physical courage, for strength and for the willingness to use both for the good of others.

For the writer, such men have 'a very old-fashioned sense of what it is to be a man, and ... that sense is coming back into style because of who saved us on Sept. 11'. This was 'very good for our country'. Why? Because 'manliness wins wars'.[1]

The writer was far from alone. Three weeks after the attack the *New York Times* was talking about a new 'muscular role for government' (30 September 2001), and the media was desperate to declare the return of the kind of man who might carry out such a muscular role: 'The Return of Manly Men' (*New York Times*, 28 October 2001), 'Hooray for Men' (*Washington Times*, 1 January 2002), 'Real Men Back in Style' (*San Francisco Chronicle*, 4 August 2002), 'Real Men: They're Back' (*The American Enterprise*, September 2003), with special features on 'The Return of Manly Leaders and the Americans Who Love Them', 'Why We Need Macho Men', 'Me Man, Me Hunt' and 'The Manliness of Men'.[2] Key political figures were recast in masculine terms: Donald Rumsfeld, for example, was 'The Stud' and 'America's New Pin-Up', according to the *National Review* (31 December 2001), and George W. Bush and his advisors were cast as superheroes in *Vanity Fair* (February 2002). At the same time, those doing 'man's work' such as fighting fire, fighting crime, fighting terror – take note: always *fighting* – were cast as the new heroes of our time.[3]

In this cultural remasculinisation US President Bush, who after the attacks had commented on America having 'gone soft', 'impotent' and 'flaccid',[4] took the time to praise the British Prime Minister for his 'balls',[5] commentators such as David Halberstam commented on the new 'muscularity' of American society,[6] and political scientists such as Harvey Mansfield articulated the idea that the world needs to rediscover and restore the confidence and command of manly men.[7] The decade ended with a new British Prime Minister, David Cameron, espousing a 'muscular liberalism' which, although ostensibly about multi-culturalism, was in reality about being 'muscular' enough to fight a war on extremism.[8] Concomitantly, this fanfare for a new masculinity was accompanied by announcements of the defeat of feminism: although few went as far as the Reverend Jerry Falwell in actually blaming feminists (along with gays and abortionists) for the attack, military historian Martin van Creveld declared that feminism would be one of the principal losers in the war on terror,[9] while journalists argued that 'the feminist movement, already at low ebb, has slid further into irrelevancy'.[10]

Why did such a reassertion of manliness come about in a period of intensified war and accumulation? A number of feminist critiques have noted that the concern over a supposed feminisation and collapsing masculinity that had resonated in American politics since the 'loss' of Vietnam came into sharper focus with the 'loss' of the World Trade Center on 11 September 2001.[11] But one of the key achievements of feminist work in general has been to show just how much the war power and the police power both thrive on and sustain a logic of masculine protection.[12] Taking this body of work as my touchstone, I use it to develop part of the argument in the previous chapters concerning capitalism, liberalism and war. I do so by taking up and challenging one of the claims made in the 'liberal peace' thesis.

The 'liberal peace' thesis is now a standard trope in the political discourse of international theory. In this discourse, liberalism and peace are presented as entwined philosophies and conjoined histories. One of the key arguments in the thesis is that commerce and free markets are the foundation of peace. In essence, then, the liberal peace thesis is also a claim for capitalism's essentially pacific grounds, sometimes known as the *doux commerce* thesis. 'The more completely capitalist the structure and attitude of a nation, the more pacifist ... we observe it to be', notes Joseph Schumpeter, and we should note too the class implications of this argument, for it is usually taken to imply that the bourgeois class's interest in accumulation makes it somehow more oriented to peace: 'the industrial and commercial bourgeoisie is fundamentally pacifist', Schumpeter insists.[13]

The idea that 'peace would encourage trade; trade would encourage peace', as Michael Howard puts it, and thus the idea that the world would be much more peaceful if it were much more capitalist, is now almost a received wisdom, and it has its roots in a reading of eighteenth-century liberalism as centred on a conception of 'economic man' keen to get on with the business of making money within civil society and thus desperate to avoid war.

Here, for the first time, is sounded the note which was to

dominate so much liberal thinking about war and peace during the following two centuries. Wars arose because of international misunderstandings, and because of the dominance of a warrior-class. The answer to both lay in free trade – trade which would increase the wealth and power of the peace-loving productive sections of the population at the expense of the war-oriented aristocracy, and which would bring men of different nations into constant contact with one another.[14]

This view is repeated, albeit with various nuances, in work after work in IR. 'The classical liberals were right', we are told, in their belief that 'trade … increased the prosperity and political power of the peaceful'.[15] The view has also filtered into textbooks, which tend to repeat uncritically the idea that liberal internationalism has its roots in the eighteenth-century liberal appetite for free trade and peace rather than the more militarily offensive policies of mercantilism.

One standard technique in this argument is to cite Kant's suggestion in 'Perpetual Peace' that 'the *spirit of commerce* … cannot exist side by side with war'.[16] But beyond citing Kant, the usual claim is that the roots of the conjunction of liberalism and peace lie in the 'free trade friendliness' of the liberal political economy of the Scottish Enlightenment, which combined a new and compelling theory of commerce and trade with the language of universal peace.[17] The key figures and ideas referred to in this regard are Adam Smith's account of 'commercial man' and Adam Ferguson's account of 'civil society'. One finds time and again the idea that 'Adam Smith provided the foundations for the arguments for free trade pacifism';[18] that 'the political doctrine of international peace is a parallel to the economic doctrine of Adam Smith';[19] that 'the wealth of nations conditions the liberal peace';[20] that 'the decisive step' towards peace was made possible by 'the adoption of barter or exchange';[21] that 'from Adam Smith to its contemporary proponents, liberal thinkers … believe that trade and economic intercourse are a source of peaceful relations among nations';[22] and that 'peace and free markets' have their roots in the work of Smith.[23] Or one finds claims that the theory and practice of peace is rooted in the Enlightenment's conception of 'civil society' as a 'peace project',[24] with reference usually made to Ferguson's *Essay on the History of Civil Society*.[25] Such arguments have become core to the liberal peace thesis and, as a consequence, virtually a whole discipline or set of related disciplines around IR have bought into the idea that one of the key historical and intellectual roots of the liberal peace thesis is the account of commercial civil society in the Scottish Enlightenment.

I aim to challenge this received wisdom by arguing that it overlooks the importance which eighteenth-century liberalism attached to martial values. This attachment concerns the ability to wage war to secure the nation in the most effective way. As such, central to the development of ideas about liberty, commerce and civil society is the question of military organisation and the relative advantages of militias or standing armies. Exploring the contours of this very specific dispute about military organisation, however, reveals a much more general concern for martial virtues running through the work of the same thinkers. In particular, these thinkers articulate a strong sense that martial virtue is somehow *threatened* by new forms of accumulation. In the process of expressing this concern, eighteenth- century liberalism revealed a militaristic strand that is so deep and strong that it cannot be dismissed or ignored as a side issue. And yet this is precisely what most of the IR literature on 'liberal peace' does. Sometimes the received wisdom is simply repeated without mentioning war at all, sometimes the issue of martial values is noted but quickly dismissed –'these observations' about martial virtues 'are not critical'[26] – and sometimes the issue is noted but ignored.[27] This tendency either to dismiss or ignore the issue is reinforced by careful selection of the sources for edited texts on classical political thought and IR, which then helps shape the next generation of students to think in exactly the same way about eighteenth-century liberalism.[28]

This chapter therefore has a number of aims. First, I seek to show that a fuller engagement with the eighteenth-century Scottish Enlightenment debunks one of the foundational myths of the liberal peace thesis. Some critics have criticised IR in general and the 'liberal peace' theorists in particular for failing to engage seriously in the history of ideas, despite their frequent reference back to the 'classics', and have claimed that this failure is especially the case with the Scottish Enlightenment.[29] My argument here reinforces that criticism: the classical liberals were complex thinkers and subtle writers, and the liberal peace theorists have systematically ignored the complexities and subtleties. Second, I aim to develop further the connection made in the previous chapters between liberalism, accumulation and war by showing that this particular historical moment in liberal thinking, supposedly a highpoint in the development of the liberal peace doctrine, in fact reveals that the liberalism of the time was animated by a desire to maintain military virtues *as virtues*.[30]

In developing these points I also seek to make a third claim. A major current in the political discourse of the time held that the military virtues in question were under serious threat from one of the outcomes of an increasingly commercial and liberal order: the rise of effeminacy. J. G. A. Pocock once claimed that the term 'effeminacy' has perhaps been a little neglected in debates about the eighteenth century, and in particular the rise of commerce and private property.[31] Since Pocock made his claim, a number of writers have pointed to the role of effeminacy in a whole range of debates: from French fanciness, through to the social role of the 'dandy', the 'molly', the 'fop' and the 'sodomite', all somehow emblematic of the crisis of masculinity. The huge body of work in this field has shown the extent to which questions of effeminacy and masculinity underpinned ideas about citizenship and national strength in the eighteenth century. I aim to show that the problem of effeminacy was also at the heart of liberal thinking about the relationship between accumulation and the war power: underpinning the liberal conception of war was a concern that a peaceful commercial order might become just a little too emasculated, and that in undermining the 'manly' virtues of discipline, courage and strength, effeminacy threatened the value of military prowess and national strength. Thus a fourth point will be that the contemporary claim that 'men are back' and that we are now witnessing a new masculine spirit in the 'war on terror' might therefore reveal more than those who articulate it realise, for it might illustrate nothing less than the conflation of masculine and martial power underpinning the global war of liberal modernity.

'WAR … IS THE EXERCISE OF A LIBERAL SPIRIT'

In a number of ways, the opening chapter of Adam Ferguson's *Essay on the History of Civil Society* constitutes a milestone in the history of political thought. By focusing on 'civil society' as the object and product of 'civilization', Ferguson presents the emergence of a social order of the division of labour, commerce, the arts, and a well-regulated system of government. Taken together these constitute a condition of liberty and peace: 'We may, with good reason, congratulate our species on their having escaped from a state of barbarous disorder and violence, into a state of domestic peace and regular policy'.[32] It is this connection between the liberty of commercial society and peace that has filtered into the claim that the intellectual roots of the 'liberal peace' thesis can be found in part in eighteenth-century arguments about civil society. Yet this tells only part of the story.

A decade before the publication of the *Essay on the History of Civil Society* Ferguson published a much shorter and much less well-known pamphlet: *Reflections Previous to the Establishment of a Militia* (1756). The year of publication of the *Reflections* is important. In 1754 a new debating society of intellectuals had been formed, called the Select Society, including among its members key figures of the Scottish Enlightenment such as Ferguson, Smith and David Hume. From its very formation the main subject to which the Society repeatedly returned was the question of national defence and military organisation. For many Scots this question was especially important given the ease with which the Young Pretender's army had advanced in Scotland during the 1745 rebellion and the subsequent suppression of the militia by Parliament. By 1756 the focus of the question had been narrowed down: at the heart of the debate were the differing natures and relative advantages of militias compared to standing armies. Such debates overlapped with the reintroduction of the English Militia Bill in the House of Commons that year and a wider public agitation for such an introduction, heightened by the fact that a threatened invasion by the French in March led to the government sending for German troops to support them against the French.[33] But the issue of the relative advantages of militias compared to standing armies raised a more general issue: the compatibility of a military spirit in general within a commercial nation committed to liberty. Amid this discussion there appeared Ferguson's *Reflections*.

In the pamphlet Ferguson argues that although commercial society has become more peaceable and better-mannered, with 'Quarrels decided by the Edge of the Sword' decided now by 'Suits at Law', this has been at the loss of 'that martial spirit which prevailed in the early Ages of our Country'.[34] In the past, government was founded on military subordination and a militia. But 'the Perfection now attained in every Art, and the Attention required to furnish what is demanded in every Branch of Business, have led away from the military Profession great Numbers of our People'. We have 'gone too far', he says, in pursuit of trade;

Scotland has become a 'Nation of Manufacturers'. 'We labour to acquire Wealth ... but neglect the Means of defending it'. Ferguson is thus concerned that the commercial life has softened the people and damaged the martial spirit: 'The Hearts of our People are not Steel, they are softened by a Disuse of Arms, by Security, and pacific Employments'. This softness and pacific mode of being 'tempts an invasion': 'a few Banditti from the Mountains, trained by their Situation to a warlike Disposition, might over-run the Country'. The task, he says, is to find a way 'to mix the military Spirit with our civil and commercial Policy'. Ferguson thus argues for a militia, formed from the body of the people (albeit with the attendant caution over involving the lower orders). In contrast to the softening of the people, Ferguson sees the possibility of 'every man ... deriving military Spirit more from the Use of Arms'.[35]

It is this theme of the militia as both a better defence of the country and a mechanism for mixing the military spirit with commercial policy that runs through Ferguson's *Essay*. In fact, it is a theme that animated him through his whole life: 'no subject has been more in my thoughts than the danger of making the Use of Arms a Separate Profession', he wrote towards the end of the century.[36] We need to bear in mind that between the publication of the *Reflections* and the *Essay* there were continued and extensive militia agitations, most notably through 1760 and 1762. In 1762 a new club was formed in Edinburgh, called The Poker Club, of which Ferguson was a member along with Smith, Hume and Henry Home (Lord Kames). The main aim of The Poker Club was to agitate for a Scottish Militia, which it continued to do for over twenty years. In other words, it would be no exaggeration to say that in the ten years running up to the publication of Ferguson's *Essay* the question of military organisation in general and a militia in particular was at the heart of public debate, and that Ferguson and his friends and associates were at the heart of it. Indeed, one might argue that it is here that one finds one of the core themes of Scottish Enlightenment discourse.

One of the main themes of the *Essay* is the difference between the organisation of violence in primitive and civilised society. War in primitive society is the business of everyone and a perpetual feature of the social order, but the development of commerce and the arts has led to 'the departments of civil government and of war being severed' (*E*, p. 151). This separation between civil and military government is a necessary feature of the development of civil society 'where, from a regard to the welfare of our fellow-creatures, we endeavour to pacify their animosities' (*E*, p. 25). The process of pacification, however, comes at a cost, for it has separated the citizen from the warrior.

For Ferguson, the roots of conflict are found in human nature: just as animals play out some of the conflicts that dominate their lives, 'man too is disposed to opposition, and to employ the forces of his nature against an equal antagonist'. Hence 'sports are frequently an image of war'. Such sentiments 'are dispositions most favourable to mankind' in that they 'animate the warrior in defence of his country'. And the defence of the country is fundamental to the development of liberal order, with civil society formed through war: 'without the rivalship of nations, and the practice of war, civil society itself could scarcely have found an object, or a form' (*E*, p. 24). This shift of aggression from the 'natural' to the politically organised is important, since 'the sense of a common danger, and the assaults of an enemy, have been frequently useful to nations, by uniting their members more firmly together' (*E*, p. 22). 'We applaud, as proceeding from a national or party spirit, what we could not endure as the effect of a private dislike'. Indeed, the creation of organised fighting is one of the most profound developments of civil society: 'amidst the competitions of rival states … we have found, for the patriot and the warrior, in the practice of violence and stratagem, the most illustrious career of human virtue'. Ferguson then spells out precisely the point I have been making about liberalism: that 'war itself, which in one view appears so fatal, in another is the exercise of a liberal spirit' (*E*, p. 25).

Thus Ferguson's comment regarding the move from barbarous disorder and violence to domestic peace and regular policy is in part designed to highlight a potentially huge problem:

> We may, with good reason, congratulate our species on their having escaped from a state of barbarous disorder and violence, into a state of domestic peace and regular policy; when they have sheathed the dagger, and disarmed the animosities of civil contention; when the weapons with which they contend are the reasonings of the wise, and the tongue of the eloquent. But we cannot, mean-time, help to regret, that they should ever proceed, in search of perfection, to place every branch of administration behind the counter, and come to employ, instead of the statesman and warrior, the mere clerk and accountant. (*E*, p. 225)

This fear that the warrior in man has been lost with the growth of the accountant is in many ways the ultimate concern animating Ferguson's *Essay*, and is closely connected to the rise of commercial order: 'the enjoyment of peace … and the prospect of being able to exchange one commodity for another, turns, by degrees, the hunter and the warrior into a tradesman and a merchant' (*E*, p. 180). The danger in the fact that 'we have mingled politeness with the use of the sword' and subsumed the 'civilities of peace into the practice of war' (*E*, pp. 198–200) is that we forget how to use the sword and fight the war.

As well as concerning social structure and the division of labour, the issue is thus also one of human character and the virtue of being – or, in commercial order, the possibility of *remaining* – a warrior. There is a danger, for Ferguson, in making 'a kind of separation between the civil and the military character'.

> The subdivision of arts and professions, in certain examples, tends to improve the practice of them, and to promote their ends. By having separated the arts of the clothier and the tanner, we are the better supplied with shoes and with cloth. But to separate the arts which form the citizen and the statesman, the arts of policy and war, is an attempt to dismember the human character … By this separation, we in effect deprive a free people of what is necessary to their safety. (*E*, pp. 229–30)

The division of labour that is so crucial to commercial order and a liberal civil society is thus, in another fundamental way, also a *threat* to that order. As he puts it elsewhere in the *Essay*:

> In the progress of arts and of policy, the members of every state are divided into classes; and in the commencement of this distribution, there is no distinction more serious than that of the warrior and the pacific inhabitant; no more is required to place men in the relation of master and slave. Even when the rigours of an established slavery abate, as they have done in modern Europe, in consequence of a protection, and a property, allowed to the mechanic and labourer, this distinction serves still to separate the noble from the base, and to point out that class of men who are destined to reign and to domineer in their country. (*E*, p. 150)

Hence Ferguson's articulation of a conception of civil society as liberal, commercial and peaceful is also very much a demand that we *remix* – to use the term from the *Reflections* – the military spirit with the commercial policy. It is for this reason that Duncan Forbes suggests that in a rather unexpected way all the leading themes of the *Essay* meet in the forum of the militia question, and others have argued that the *Essay* is in many ways an extension of the themes outlined by Ferguson in the militia pamphlet.[37]

All of which is to say that 'civil society', the concept for which Ferguson is best known and which today is so central to liberal peace theory, is shot through with the concept of war, to the extent that, as Ferguson puts it, without war civil society could scarcely have found its form. The purely pacific citizen is thus in some senses a poor citizen, a 'dismembered character'. Or, to put it another way, the good citizen – the liberal, commercially driven citizen – needs to remain a warrior. The search, for Ferguson, was to combine the civility of commercial civil order with a more traditional form of aggression, which is also why nobility is still so important to Ferguson, despite the material importance of the increasingly hegemonic bourgeois class.[38]

In this context we might briefly note that the feeling among Ferguson's friends was that he personally 'relished military valour'[39] and that this relish remained present through his whole life. One anecdote told by Walter Scott and repeated by Ferguson's biographers describes the young Ferguson, during his time as Chaplain of the First Highland Regiment of Foot, with sword in hand, leading the column of men at the battle of Fontenoy.[40] As the Chaplain he addressed the soldiers prior to their battles with Jacobite forces, emphasising in his Sermon their masculine duty to defend the country and protect 'Security and Liberty as a treasure'. So taken was he by his own argument in the Sermon that he published it in English translation the following year.[41] Some fifty years later Ferguson commented to a friend that the Napoleonic wars were a reminder that 'it is more fortunate to have our Lot amidst great Events than in times of undisturbed tranquillity'.[42] And, reflecting back on his life, Ferguson suggested as his own epitaph: 'He lived a great statesman and Warriour',[43] repeating a couplet which he was fond of using in the *Essay* (E, pp. 124, 151, 188, 189) and to which he returned in various experimental though unpublished essays: 'the Warriour too is a Statesman' he says in one such essay, while in another, called 'Of

Statesmen and Wariours', he pursues the idea that the skills, attributes, aims and knowledge of warriors and statesmen must be unified.[44] As we shall now see, Ferguson's desire to press the liberal case for the virtues of the warrior was far from isolated.

In the *Lectures on Jurisprudence* delivered in the early 1760s (at the same time as the creation of The Poker Club), Adam Smith takes as his starting point 'the first and chief design of all civill governments', which in the *Wealth of Nations* becomes 'the first duty of the sovereign': that of 'protecting the society from the violence and invasion of other independent societies ... by means of a military force'.[45] In the *Lectures* he comments on the necessity that 'an armed force should be maintained' but that 'various species of armed forces' and 'the different sorts of militias and train'd bands' are suited to different types of government. This treatment is only properly developed in the *Wealth of Nations* where Smith comments that preparing military force in times of peace and employing it in time of war 'is very different in the different states of society, in the different periods of improvement' (*LJ*, pp. 6–7; *WN*, p. 689). As with other writers such as Ferguson, Smith argues that in the more primitive states of society every man was naturally a warrior, but that a shift in the techniques of both production and arms has brought about a division of labour: on the one hand, it is now impossible for those engaged in commerce and trade to give up their employment to fight without serious loss; on the other hand, the art of war has shifted such that it is now a skilled task. As society progresses, the art of war necessarily becomes more and more complicated, to the point that it has become 'necessary that it should become the sole or principal occupation of a particular class of citizens, and the division of labour is as necessary for the improvement of this, as of every other art' (*WN*, p. 697). The theme, then, is the same as the one that concerned Ferguson, yet the argument turns out to be subtly different.

Despite his long membership of The Poker Club, Smith was drawn to the conclusion that the commercial order made a standing army inevitable. He identifies 'two methods by which the state can make any tolerable provision for the public defence'.

> It may either, first, by means of a very rigorous police, and in spite of the whole bent of the interest, genius and inclinations of the people, enforce the practice of military exercises, and oblige either

all the citizens of the military age, or a certain number of them, to
join in some measure the trade of a soldier to whatever other trade
or profession they may happen to carry on.

Or, secondly, by maintaining and employing a certain number
of citizens in the constant practice of military exercises, it may
render the trade of a soldier a particular trade, separate and distinct
from all others. (*WN*, p. 698)

Because arms, military exercises and martial skills are now so specialised,
regular troops are required. Thus for Smith a standing army is the only
means by which civilisation can be defended: 'a militia … in whatever
manner it may be disciplined or exercised, must always be much inferior
to a well disciplined and well exercised standing army' (*WN*, pp. 699–
700).[46] Smith makes the point that this is especially the case given the
barbarous nature of some nations: 'When a civilized nation depends for
its defence upon a militia, it is at all times exposed to be conquered by
any barbarous nation'. The historical examples show that 'a well-
regulated standing army is superior to every militia'. Hence 'it is only by
means of a standing army … that the civilization of any country can be
perpetuated, or even preserved for any time'. And just as it is only by
means of a standing army that a civilised nation can be defended, 'so it
is only by means of it, that a barbarous country can be suddenly and
tolerably civilized' (*WN*, pp. 705–6).

These comments have been the subject of much debate, not least
because according to some interpretations it is one of the issues about
which Smith and Ferguson had a fundamental disagreement. In a letter
to Smith following the publication of the *Wealth of Nations*, Ferguson
wrote that 'You have provoked, it is true, the church, the universities, and
the merchants, against whom I am willing to take your part; but you have
likewise provoked the militia, and there I must be against you'.[47] There is
some evidence that Smith was misunderstood on this point. Or at least,
Smith certainly claims that he had been misunderstood. This seems to
be the case in Smith's response to an attack on him along these lines by
Alexander Carlyle, in his *Letter from a Gentleman to his Grace the Duke of
Buccleugh on National Defence*, published in 1778, in which he criticises
Smith over the question of a standing army rather than a militia. In a letter
to Andreas Holt two years later Smith seems confused by the attack:

When he Wrote his book, he had not read mine to the end. He fancies that because I insist that a Militia is in all cases inferior to a well regulated and well disciplined standing Army, that I disapprove of Militias altogether. With regard to that subject, he and I happen to be precisely of the same opinion.[48]

Smith is especially surprised given that he has been told that the man is 'one of my acquaintance', a comment which suggests he thinks anyone who knows him would know that he does not disapprove of militias (as indeed might be further evidenced by the fact that he had once argued that the ringleaders of 'mobs' opposing the militia should be hanged).[49]

Whether Ferguson and Smith may or may not have diverged in their views on the militia is tangential to the argument here, which is that regardless of the pros and cons of actual military structures the question of martial virtues and military values was at the heart of their thought. One can see this from Smith's *Theory of Moral Sentiments* where he comments on the martial spirit of those soldiers who 'cheerfully sacrifice' themselves 'to the prosperity of a greater system'.[50] In the same work he refers to war and civil faction as 'the two situations which afford the most splendid opportunities for the display of public spirit'. It is the martial spirit that animates a well-ordered public world: 'War is the great school for both acquiring and exercising ... magnanimity' (*TMS*, pp. 232, 239). This view gets developed through the *Lectures* and into the *Wealth of Nations*.

In the *Lectures*, Smith comments that one 'bad effect of commerce is that it sinks the courage of mankind, and tends to extinguish the martial spirit'. With the increasing division of labour, 'war comes to be a trade also'. 'The defence of the country is therefore committed to a certain sett of men who have nothing else to do' with the danger that 'among the bulk of the people military courage diminishes' (*LJ*, p. 540). Thus, as he puts it in the *Wealth of Nations*, the real problem is that the arts of war become so specialised that 'military exercises come to be as much neglected by the inhabitants ... and the great body of the people becomes altogether unwarlike' (*WN*, p. 697).

This concern over the decline of martial valour sheds light on the famous passage in the *Wealth of Nations* in which Smith comments on the disturbing effects of the division of labour. The passage runs as follows:

> The man whose whole life is spent in performing a few simple operations, of which the effects too are, perhaps, always the same … has no occasion to exert his understanding, or to exercise his invention … He naturally loses, therefore, the habit of such exertion, and generally becomes as stupid and as ignorant as it is possible for a human creature to become. The torpor of his mind renders him not only incapable of relishing or bearing a part in any rational conversation, but of conceiving of any generous, noble, or tender sentiment … Of the great and extensive interests of his country, he is altogether incapable of judging; and unless very particular pains have been taken to render him otherwise, he is equally incapable of defending his country in war. The uniformity of his stationary life naturally corrupts the courage of his mind.

The passage has gone down as an early insight into the damaging effects of capital and thus an indication of liberal concern for human well-being under industrial production. Yet the passage ends with the claim that the uniformity of the worker's life means the worker will 'regard with abhorrence the irregular, uncertain, and adventurous life of a soldier'. In other words:

> His [the worker's] dexterity at his own particular trade seems, in this manner, to be acquired at the expense of … intellectual, social, and martial virtues. But in every improved and civilized society this is the state into which the labouring poor, that is, the great body of the people, must necessarily fall, unless government takes some pains to prevent it. (*WN*, p. 782)

The final comment is suggestive: Smith invokes the intervention of the sovereign in order that the great body of the people do not lose their martial virtues.

This explains Smith's recommendation of military exercises as part of a country's education programme.

> In the progress of improvement the practice of military exercises, unless government takes proper pains to support it, goes gradually to decay, and together with it, the martial spirit of the great body

of the people, the example of modern Europe sufficiently demon-
strates. But the security of every society must always depend, more
or less, on the martial spirit of the great body of the people. (*WN*,
pp. 786–7)

On the one hand, this is again an argument about the virtues of standing
armies and militias: 'In the present times, indeed, that martial spirit
alone, and unsupported by a well-disciplined standing army, would not,
perhaps, be sufficient for the defence and security of any society. But
where every citizen had the spirit of a soldier, a smaller standing army
would surely be requisite'. On the other hand, however, Smith
acknowledges that notwithstanding the complications of the militia
question, the main point is the wider benefit that comes from nurturing
the martial spirit: 'Even though the martial spirit of the people were of
no use towards the defence of the society, yet to prevent that sort of
mental mutilation, deformity and wretchedness, which cowardice
necessarily involves … from spreading themselves through the great
body of the people', the martial spirit really must be attended to by
government; so damaging is the weakening of the martial spirit among
the people that Smith compares it to the spread of leprosy. Moreover,
nurturing the martial spirit among the people 'would necessarily
diminish very much the dangers to liberty' (*WN*, p. 787). Liberty, in effect,
depends on the martial spirit, but the key is to combine 'war and faction'
as 'the best schools for forming every man to this hardiness and firmness
of temper' with our 'sensibilities to the pleasures, to the amusements
and enjoyments' of liberty, commerce and the arts (*TMS*, pp. 245–6). It
is for this reason that Smith proposes that as well as teaching the
working class basic skills such as reading, writing and accounting,
schooling also provides for 'the acquisition of … military and gymnastic
exercises'. It was only 'by imposing upon the whole body of the people
the necessity of learning those exercises, that the Greek and Roman
republicks maintained the martial spirit' (*WN*, p. 786).

The extent to which this whole issue is central to Smith's work can
be seen in the new section added to his revised edition of the *Theory of
Moral Sentiments*. First published in 1759, the *Theory of Moral Sentiments*
went through several editions before having some 'principal alterations'
for an edition published just before Smith's death in 1790. Most significant of these is Part Six, which Smith describes in the 'Advertisement' of

the edition as 'altogether new', and where he reinforces the view that he had been developing through the *Lectures* and the *Wealth of Nations* concerning the importance of the martial spirit (*TMS*, p. 3).

Thus Smith's argument for a standing army came with the concern that the martial spirit would be lost, and he therefore sought to maintain such a spirit without turning to the militia as a solution. Yet the principle is the same: this is a *liberal martial spirit*. Peace may be necessary for the commercial arts, but 'the art of war', he says, 'is certainly the noblest of all arts' (*WN*, p. 697), and one can hear in his comment the echoes of Ferguson's vision of war as the 'exercise of a liberal spirit'. Together they reveal the importance attached by the thinkers of the eighteenth-century Scottish Enlightenment to military valour and martial virtues. 'None of the leader thinkers of the Scottish Enlightenment believed in perpetual peace, either as a practical possibility or as an ideal, not even Adam Smith', notes Forbes, adding that 'they were well aware of the creative as well as the destructive role of war in the development of civilization'.[51] One might say that the key problematic of the social and political theory of the Scottish Enlightenment is to ensure a property regime that is both liberal and bellicose: liberal power as war power, and vice versa.

PEACE: AN EFFEMINATE LUXURY

Late in the eighteenth century and some five years after writing his *Reflections on the Revolution in France*, Edmund Burke wrote a series of letters to members of Parliament, which together constitute the *Letters on a Regicide Peace*. Early in the first letter he comments on the practical vigour displayed by England against the French. 'Never did the masculine spirit of England display itself with more energy ... than at the time when frivolity and effeminacy had been at least tacitly acknowledged as their national character by the good people of this kingdom'.[52] The comment about a masculine spirit revealing itself at a time when effeminacy seems to have been acknowledged as the national character might be put down as one of Burke's rhetorical strokes and an indication of the gendered nature of his political ideas. In fact, there is more at stake.

Burke's comment is made in the light of a reference earlier in the same paragraph to the 'eloquent writer and ingenious speculator Dr Brown' who, in 'an elaborate philosophical discourse', proved 'that the distinguishing features of the people of England had been totally changed, and that a frivolous effeminacy was become the national character'. The 'Dr Brown' in question is John Brown and the 'philosophical discourse' to which Burke refers is Brown's *Estimate of the Manners and Principles of the Time* (1757). That Burke could refer to Brown's book in such a shorthand fashion is an indication of how well known it had become: 'nothing could be more popular than that work', says Burke, without feeling any need to give the title of a book which had run to seven editions and been extracted in journals such as *The Gentleman's Magazine* and *London Magazine*.

Brown's main theme in the *Estimate* was the effect on the 'spirit of liberty' of the relationship between the general character of the people and national decline. This was understood through the category of 'effeminacy'. The 'ruling character of the present Times is that of a vain, *luxurious* and *selfish* EFFEMINACY' and the 'luxurious and effeminate Manners in the Higher Ranks'. An effeminate nation is 'a Nation which resembles Women', he suggested, and a direct effect of the increase in commerce: the 'exorbitant Degree of Trade and Wealth ... naturally tends to produce luxurious and effeminate Manners'. The key issue for Brown was 'the natural Effects of these effeminate Manners, on Fleets and Armies', which he thought would make the nation 'Prey to the Insults and Invasions of our most powerful Enemies'. Yet it is also the fear of rebellion within that drives his concern: 'How far this dastard Spirit of Effeminacy hath crept upon us, and destroyed the national Spirit of Defence, may appear from the general Panic the *Nation* was thrown into, at the late *Rebellion*'.[53]

Brown was far from alone in articulating this concern. The *Oxford English Dictionary* records the rise of 'effeminate' and 'effeminacy' from the late sixteenth century. A standard criticism of those monarchs who portrayed themselves as 'peace-makers', noted in Chapter 1, was that they were effeminate and therefore reducing the nation as a whole to effeminacy. For example, when James succeeded Elizabeth to the throne he terminated the war against Spain, sought a more pacifist foreign policy, styled himself *Rex Pacificus* and liked to cite the motto *Beati pacifici*. As a result, 'James was also known for his effeminacy'; that is, 'to his critics and opponents, pacifism and effeminacy went together'.[54] Likewise, in 1690 a pamphlet called *The Secret History of the Reigns of K. Charles II and K. James II* attacked Charles for seeking to 'weaken and make soft the military temper of the people by debauchery and effeminacy, which generally go hand in hand together'. The court of William III was also a focus for gossip concerning its effeminate and homosexual atmosphere.[55] This was thought to be filtering through the whole social order: 'Men, they are grown full as effeminate as the Women', noted one radical pamphlet in 1703.[56] The problem was embodied in figures such as the 'dandy', the 'molly' and the 'fop'. The term 'molly' had first been used for female prostitutes, but soon came to refer to the sodomite, with roots in the Latin *mollis* meaning 'soft', which gives us the root of 'mollify', while 'fop' was originally an alternative to 'fool' but by the late seventeenth century began to connote a preoccupation with frivolities such as fashion and thus an effeminate mode of being, with the fop himself becoming emblematic of the crisis of masculinity.[57] Lurking in the shadows of this debate is the figure of the sodomite[58] and the emerging figure of what would eventually become known as the homosexual.[59] Such figures and practices were all taken as somehow emblematic of a crisis of masculine power but also connected to the core reason for the crisis: effeminacy.[60] The question of effeminacy thus came to occupy centre stage in the eighteenth-century Enlightenment.

In his *Characteristics of Men, Manners, Opinions, Times*, first published in 1711, the third Earl of Shaftesbury sought to reconcile 'manly liberty' with the 'goodly order of the universe' by arguing for a softness, serenity and harmoniousness among men. But he was concerned that a man should not have so much softness that it turns into 'effeminacy as unfits him to bear Poverty, Crosses or Adversity'. Shaftesbury had been tutored by John Locke, who had sought to discourage 'effeminacy of spirit' in his *Thoughts on Education*,[61] and Shaftesbury extended this by associating effeminacy with laziness, fondness, exaggerated pity, weakness, sloth, supineness and 'looseness of a thousand passions'.[62] Thus the refinement of manners needed to be developed alongside 'boldness', 'good muscling' and 'strong reason' lest it succumb to effeminacy. Reinforced by the new revised edition of Shaftesbury's text in 1732, effeminacy was by mid-century widely seen as central to the problem of national weakness and political impotence. As Kathleen Wilson comments, 'a variety of observers, from almanac writers and journalists to playwrights, philanthropists and village shopkeepers decried the nation's corrupted and "effeminate" spirit, which threatened the collapse of distinctions between public and private, men and women, and resulted in displays of national "impotency" abroad and ignominious imperial decline'.[63]

Effeminacy thereby became one of the pejorative terms of the discourse of civic humanism,[64] and did so by becoming a way of articulating concerns about martial power and military organisation. The ancient Greek term for 'manliness', *andreia*, was also the root of the term for 'courage', with the two terms coming together in the warrior. In the Roman tradition, *virtus* was constructed from the Latin *vir*, 'adult male human', connoting manliness and military valour; only later did it acquire the meaning of moral virtue. Part of the problem of sovereignty – kingly sovereignty in the early modern period but also the sovereignty of the autonomous male in the seventeenth and eighteenth centuries – centred on the gendered connection between the *vir* and *virtus*, with its meaning defined by the excluded sphere, populated by the non-warrior (boys, girls, eunuchs, hermaphrodites, slaves) and thus effeminate figure.[65] The fundamental problem faced by the civic humanism of eighteenth-century liberalism, namely that the conditions of human life had become so driven by commerce and commercial values that virtue might never be fully realised,[66] has to be seen in terms of the masculine and martial nature of virtue as it was understood.

In many ways, then, we are back on the terrain of the Machiavellian liberal moment discussed in Chapter 1, understood now in terms of the dynamic conjunction of military virtue and manly vigour as part of one's civic duty, or what R. Claire Snyder calls Machiavelli's 'fusion of *armed masculinity* onto republican citizenship'.[67] If 'Machiavelli's most characteristic, central, and frequently invoked concept is that of *virtù*', which he uses because it connotes manliness as well as energy, effectiveness and virtuosity, then '*effeminato* (effeminate) is one of his most frequent and scathing epithets', notes Hannah Pitkin.[68] What might be called an eighteenth-century neo-Machiavellian liberal political economy appropriated this dynamic wholesale.[69] Well, not quite wholesale. For mediating between the effeminate and the martial was the idea of 'luxury'.

Despite being 'a word of an uncertain signification',[70] and despite having some staunch defenders (Bernard Mandeville in *The Fable of the Bees*, for example), luxury had by the mid-century become 'the defining issue of the early modern period'.[71] In particular, it had become 'an omnicompetent explanation-cum-scapegoat for various social ills'.[72] Such ills were many, and Till Wahnbaeck has shown how seventeenth-century English, French and German dictionaries associated luxury with superfluity, excess, lust, lechery. Most of all, the dictionaries replicated 'the Greek notion of luxury as rendering man effeminate'.[73] John Brown, for example, tends to run effeminacy and luxury together, as we have seen. So too does Shaftesbury.[74] Others follow suit: 'effeminate wealth has shattered our age with venal luxury', John Millar put it in 1771,[75] an idea which he later used to reconstruct the history of English government, citing Smith in the process.[76] Here too is William Russell in his highly popular *History of Europe*:

> So great an influx of wealth, without any extraordinary expendi-
> ture, or call to bold enterprise, must soon have produced a total
> dissolution of manners; and the British nation, overwhelmed with
> luxury and effeminacy, might have sunk into an early decline. The
> martial spirit, which seemed to languish for want of exercise, was
> revived by the war.[77]

The major concern, however, is the one implied in Russell's final sentence: that the combined power of effeminacy and luxury was leading to a decline in military virtue and martial prowess. Rousseau put the point succinctly in the first *Discourse*: 'luxury spreads, true courage flags, military virtues disappear'. By the second *Discourse* the rise of sociability is associated with the rise of an 'effeminate way of life'.[78] This linkage was central to the liberal Enlightenment, and it is therefore unsurprising to find that it permeates the work of Ferguson and Smith.

Ferguson notes the dangers of 'the opiates of effeminacy, or a servile weakness, founded on luxury' and historical examples abound of cases where despotic tribes have easily taken over 'effeminate provinces' (*E*, pp. 103–4). Developing this idea later in the *Essay* he notes that Europe in particular is in danger from those mercenary and disciplined armies ready to 'traverse the earth', and what are most at risk are the 'effeminate kingdoms and empires' (*E*, p. 153). 'We are not ... to conclude, that luxury, with all its concomitant circumstances, which either serve to favour its increase, or which, in the arrangements of civil society, follow it as consequences, can have no effect to the disadvantage of national manners'.

If that respite from public dangers and troubles which gives a leisure for the practice of commercial arts, be continued, or increased, into a disuse of national efforts; if the individual, not called to unite with his country, be left to pursue his private advantage; we may find him become effeminate, mercenary, and sensual. (*E*, p. 250)

It is significant that the key concept for which Ferguson became known, 'civil society', was at this time closely connected to the debate about effeminacy, since one of the features of the new spaces of civil society, such as coffee houses, was that 'owing to the presence of so many women and the lack of traditional masculine recreations … these new public spaces were perceived to erase distinctions between the sexes and they threatened to make men "effeminate"'.[79]

The threat was thought especially to affect character and intellect. 'That weakness and effeminacy of which polished nations are sometimes accused, has its place probably in the mind alone', notes Ferguson. Much depends, for man and animal, on the physical environment and the kind of labour exercised. 'Delicate living, and good accommodation, are not found to enervate the body', a problem which affects 'the children of opulent families, bred in effeminacy'. In contrast, 'Wholesome food, and hard labour, the portion of many in every polished and commercial nation, secure to the public a number of men endued with bodily strength, and inured to hardship and toil'. Hence experiments have shown that all that is needed to allow the opulent to retain their strength is that children of the opulent spend a little more time subsisting in the forest and imitating the arts of the savage, thereby 'recovering' the knowledge and experience which 'it has cost civilized nations many ages to unlearn' (*E*, p. 228).

When the bulky constituents of wealth, and of rustic magnificence, can be exchanged for refinements; and when the produce of the soil may be turned into equipage, and mere decoration; when the combination of many is no longer required for personal safety; the master may become the sole consumer of his own estate: he may refer the use of every subject to himself; he may employ the materials of generosity to feed a personal vanity, or to indulge a sickly and effeminate fancy. (*E*, p. 252)

For Ferguson, monarchy is always in danger of being corrupted by luxury, resulting in 'a fatal dissolution of manners, under which men of every condition … have no remains of real ambition'. With 'neither the elevation of nobles, nor the fidelity of subjects' men 'have changed into effeminate vanity' (*E*, p. 251). Thus the integrity of manners in Sparta is contrasted to 'the weakness of nations sunk in effeminacy' (*E*, p. 161). Comparing 'tribes of warlike barbarians' with civilised society, Ferguson comments that what makes us regard them with contempt or even horror is 'our sense of humanity, our regard to the rights of nations, our admiration of civil wisdom and justice, even our effeminacy' (*E*, p. 155).

The fact that for Ferguson civil society is formed of war, then, is in part designed to reiterate that civil society must remain a 'manly' state of affairs. 'This "manly" state of things was deliberately poised against the model of tranquil, feminine domesticity', notes Fania Oz-Salzberger, adding that Ferguson 'had little time for the female version of human nature, and even less time for what later thinkers were to call the "feminine principle" in the rise of western civilization'.[80] A similar point might be made regarding Smith's commercial order.

In the *Theory of Moral Sentiments* Smith comments that the happiness of individual and society is dependent on the character of men as well as the contrivances of art and the institutions of civil government.

> The prudent, the equitable, the active, resolute, and sober character promises prosperity and satisfaction, both to himself and to every one connected with him. The rash, the insolent, the sloth-ful, effeminate, and voluptuous, on the contrary, forebodes ruin to the individual, and misfortune to all who have any thing to do with him. (*TMS*, p. 187)

There is therefore a huge amount at stake in the issue of effeminacy, threatening as it is to both individual and social well-being. Smith comments too that 'perhaps the delicate sensibility required in civilized nations sometimes destroys the masculine firmness of character' (*TMS*, p. 209). But this reference to the effeminate side of consumption is not just about the fact that wealth is, in the end, a 'mere trinket of frivolous utility' (*TMS*, p. 181). It also connects to his arguments about war: 'the external graces, the frivolous accomplishments of that impertinent and foolish thing called a man of fashion, are commonly more admired than the solid and masculine virtues of a warrior' (*TMS*, p. 63). This is not a straightforward comparison between a man so rooted in commerce that he becomes an effeminate man of fashion and the more masculine warrior. Rather, Smith's point is that commercial society as a whole has this emasculating effect: it produces 'weak men' (*TMS*, p. 117). Hence he contrasts the Spartan discipline of the savage, faced by constant danger, and thus resistant to the kinds of feelings of, say, love and grief that the civilised age allows expression. 'The weakness of love, which is so much indulged in ages of humanity and politeness, is regarded among savages as the most unpardonable effeminacy' (*TMS*, p. 205). Smith is here picking up on the complexities surrounding shows of emotion in an age in which we are supposed to have become more sympathetic, an age in which 'if we shed any tears, we carefully conceal them, and are afraid, lest the spectators, not entering into this excessive tenderness, should regard it as effeminacy and weakness' (*TMS*, p. 46). Thus in terms of Smith's theory of moral sentiments, one of the negative consequences of commercial society is that its main actors will end up lacking the kind of manly virtue which we even now, in a sentimental age, still admire: 'the man, who under the severest tortures allows no weakness to escape him, vents no groan, gives way to no passion which we do not entirely enter into, commands our highest admiration' (*TMS*, pp. 30–1). This point is explained by Smith with constant recourse to the army and military life, as in his comments on the sentiment which is deeply impressed 'upon every tolerably good soldier' or the idea that 'war and faction are certainly the best schools for forming every man' (*TMS*, pp. 138, 244).

Commentators have noted that the 'spectator' at the core of Smith's theory of moral sympathy and the autonomous subject that dominates Smith's theory of commercial order are both unquestionably male.[81] We might add that permanently threatening this autonomous male, his liberties, property, arts and government, is the effeminacy that lies in the luxurious wealth of commercial society. When in the *Lectures* Smith comments that one bad effect of commerce is that it sinks the courage of mankind and tends to extinguish the martial spirit, the issue is the combined development of luxury with effeminacy (*LJ*, pp. 189, 202). 'Having their minds constantly employed on the arts of luxury', he says, men 'grow effeminate' (*LJ*, p. 540). For Smith, the historical evidence of this is incontrovertible: it is weaker (that is, more effeminate) nations which get conquered easily (*LJ*, p. 158). Commenting on the rise of the

Italian republics, Smith notes that 'as soon as arts, etc. were improvd, there was an intire decradation and loss of courage in the whole state'. He adds that 'whenever therefore arts and commerce engage the citizens, either as artizans or as master trades men, the strength and force of the city must be very much diminished' (*LJ*, pp. 231–2). In the *Theory of Moral Sentiments* he uses this to explain why the Italians have historically relied too heavily on mercenaries. Thus, the problem of effeminacy is a problem for military organisation. The trick is to balance the experience of 'war and faction' as 'the best schools for forming every man to this hardiness and firmness of temper' and for 'curing him of the opposite weaknesses', with our 'sensibilities to the pleasures, to the amusements and enjoyments' of liberty, commerce and the arts (*TMS*, pp. 245–6). On this view current citizens are an 'effeminate and puny set of mortals', depending as they do on goods such as glass to allow heat and light and without which the country would be uninhabitable (*LJ*, p. 339). This reference to the 'present effeminate and puny set of mortals' makes its way into the drafts of the *Wealth of Nations*, albeit tweaked a little to 'effeminate and delicate race of mortals'.[82]

This same connection between and concern with effeminacy and luxury is made by writer after writer and, moreover, is always connected to the war power. Five further examples will suffice.

First, Lord Kames, close friend of Ferguson and Smith and a leading figure in the Scottish Enlightenment, notes that 'where arts, manufactures, and commerce, have arrived at perfection, a pacific spirit prevails universally'. But he sees this as a danger on the grounds that now 'not a spark of military ardor' remains 'nor will any man be a soldier'.[83] Kames argues that militias are the right military form for a people at liberty and a standing army 'is dangerous to liberty', but the real danger is that nations with a pacific spirit will tend to have recourse to mercenary troops – a sure sign of a nation that has become too weak and vulnerable. More generally, luxury and effeminacy go hand-in-hand, along with a set of related weaknesses such as softness, selfishness and sloth. On the one hand, 'by accumulating wealth, a manufacturing and commercial people become a tempting object for military conquest'; on the other hand, the same wealth tends to make them effeminate, and 'by effeminacy become an easy conquest'. In stark contrast to the 'original adventurers' whose 'piety, exalted courage, and indefatigable industry' made them 'more than men', the current 'indolence, sensuality, and effeminacy' of the commercial world has 'rendered their successors less than women', a view which Kames uses to read the whole history of decline and fall of empires and monarchs: from 'the luxury and effeminacy of a great monarchy' which left 'no appetite for war, either in the sovereign or in his subjects' through to empires being 'poisoned with sensual pleasure' and run by 'voluptuous and effeminate' princes and monarchs.[84]

> The voluptuousness and effeminacy of the late kings of Persia, has rendered that kingdom a prey to every bold invader … A nation corrupted with luxury and sensuality is a ready morsel for every invader. The potent Assyrian monarchy, having long subsisted in peace without a single enemy, sunk into sloth and effeminacy, and became an easy prey to the kings of Media and Babylon. These two nations, in like circumstances of sloth and effeminacy, were in their turn swallowed up.[85]

Through close on 1,000 pages of similar sketches of the history of man Kames offers accounts of how 'Asiatic luxury and effeminacy … got hold of the Greeks and Macedonians before the Roman invasion' and 'rendered them easy prey', or of how the Whidah in Guinea likewise 'produced luxury and effeminacy' and so became easy prey to enemies. Ultimately, for Kames, even the anarchy of perpetual war is better than 'effeminacy produced by long peace'.[86]

The second example is George Turnbull's work on 'liberal education'. Written with Locke's *Thoughts Concerning Education* in mind, Turnbull makes clear that the liberal way is also a 'truly manly way'. He writes of the 'liberal and manly temper' being forged through 'liberal, manly exercises', and spends a great deal of time on the importance of having a 'manly air', a 'manly carriage', a 'manly steadiness', a 'manly vigour' and 'manly conversation'. He returns time and again to the idea of 'manly intrepidity', not least when the man is handling arms. This stress on manliness is intended to save the good citizen from the 'effeminate life of pleasure' generated by 'luxury, pomp and magnificence', from 'corruption and effeminate pleasures', and from 'effeminate music' and other 'trifling, gaudy entertainments'; likewise, allowing children to complain 'weakens and effeminates [their] minds'.[87]

The third example is from William Thornton who, in a pamphlet on the choice between a militia and a standing army, makes a claim for a militia on the basis of the problem of effeminacy. 'It is said, The people of this Country are so effeminated by Luxury, as to be averse to Arms, consequently, not likely to enter a Militia'. For Thornton, the reverse is the case: a militia would help the people avoid becoming 'too effeminate for Arms'. This is despite the fact that, as it stands, the problem of effeminacy is a real one, as evidenced by the strength of the New England militia's ability to battle the Indians and the French compared to the inability of 'old England' to deal with 5,000 highlanders and a few Frenchmen. 'When they [the New England colonists] were invaded … by an Army of 20,000 French and Indians, the New England Militia, untainted with the corrupt and lying Politics of their effeminated Mother-Country, immediately took to their Arms and made the Enemy fly before them'.[88]

The fourth example is John Millar's comment, noted above, that 'effeminate wealth has shattered our age with venal luxury'. This is linked by him to the view that 'industry breeds effeminacy and this in turn makes a people lose their martial spirit and come to rely on mercenaries'. He gives as a historical example the ancient republics which owed their liberty to the narrowness of territory and small number of people, which together allowed them to abolish the power of petty princes 'before their effeminacy or industry had introduced the practice of maintaining mercenary troops'.[89] In his later work on the origins of English government Millar also comments on the way the Romans indulged their troops too much and so allowed them to become effeminate, how Severus built strong armies by avoiding recruiting from effeminate inhabitants of Italy, and of how the regular government of commercial order means citizens are 'seldom employed in fighting' and thus 'likely to lower their estimation of military talents'.[90]

Fifth, and finally, one might note how the theme runs through the political debates and intellectual context surrounding the creation of the American republic. Gordon Wood has traced how the virtues of the ancient republics were looked at for lessons in what made them great or destroyed them, and what was noted was the importance of 'the character and spirit of their people'. 'The virile martial qualities – the scorn of ease, the contempt of danger, the love of valor – were what made a nation great'. Within this set of beliefs, 'the obsessive term was luxury, both a cause and a symptom of social sickness'. The early republicans quickly bought into the idea that 'the love of refinement, the desire for distinction and elegance eventually weakened a people and left them soft and effeminate … unfit and undesiring to serve the state'.[91] Thus John Adams warns of the dangers of when 'Elegance, Luxury and Effeminacy begin to be established'.[92] A year after the revolution Adams comments that maybe a defeat of the army by the British might not be such a bad thing, as it 'would cure Americans of their vicious, and luxurious, and effeminate appetites, passions and habits', which together constituted 'a more dangerous army to American liberty than Mr. Howe's'.[93] Even into the 1780s the Americans were still deliberating over the issue. 'Throughout all the secular and religious jeremiads of the eighties the key term was "luxury"'.[94] 'Luxury, Luxury, the great source of dissolution and distress, has here taken up her dismal abode', noted the *Boston Independent Chronicle* in 1787, adding that what luxury was destroying above all was the 'native manliness … which is the spring and peculiar excellence of a free government'.[95] The Federalists pursued this against any radical democratic alternatives to the kind of republic being forged in America in the latter decades of the eighteenth century, where male economic failure was evidence of effeminacy.[96]

Lest these five examples, alongside the claims of Smith, Ferguson and the others cited, are not sufficient, one can point to similar claims elsewhere: in Edward Gibbon's *Decline and Fall of the Roman Empire*, where military defeat is usually put down to 'effeminate natives', 'effeminate tyrants', 'effeminate Indians', 'effeminate troops' and 'effeminate leaders';[97] in Tom Paine's characterisation of the court of Louis XV as 'remarkable only for weakness and effeminacy';[98] in Mary Wollstonecraft's comment that 'the present system of war has little connection with virtue … being rather the school of *finesse* and effeminacy, than of fortitude';[99] and in Kant's suggestions that although 'a prolonged peace favours the predominance of a mere commercial spirit' so it also 'tends to degrade the character of the nation' and bring 'a debasing self-interest, cowardice, and effeminacy'.[100]

There is, then, in the philosophy of liberal war and liberal philosophy of war, and thus in the wars of accumulation which underpin liberalism, an implacable logic of masculinity. The men – the *manly* men – who dominate the political landscape in general and the military landscape in particular, which is to say the manly men who control the war power, those warriors, generals, theorists, strategists and security intellectuals, must never have their manliness undermined, especially by the liberal commercial order they seek to defend and from within which the threat to their manliness might come.[101] Targeting effeminacy therefore performs an important function in reasserting the manliness in question. The charge of 'effeminacy' and the associated anxieties about changing identities enables the articulation of a worldview which is at the very least implicitly but, more often than not, fairly explicitly misogynistic and homophobic, projecting and protecting a notion of manliness as a social norm at the heart of the war power. As is well known, this gets confirmed in the striking antipathy towards women, effeminacy and homosexuality which characterises military organisations as well as the minds of military thinkers, strategic theorists and security intellectuals. The point here, however, is that this appears as a very liberal notion of manliness as a social norm, or, indeed, a notion of manliness as a liberal social norm.

The bourgeois and liberal citizen-subject-soldier is thereby expected to engage in strenuous martial activity to help overcome the insecurities and debilities generated by the commercial order on which the bourgeois depends. Thus one aspect of the war power is the struggle to define and occupy the 'masculine' position while emasculating ('effeminizing') and thus marginalising the other. This is what we might call, after Foucault, the *deployment* of the category of effeminacy as an *enactment* of a martial masculinity whose distinguishing characteristic is its liberal power.[102] A deployment, that is, for liberal wars of accumulation and for a capitalist order as an 'imagined fraternity' of masculine and martial men. Unsurprisingly, 'effeminacy' therefore also becomes associated with a range of liberal enemies and threats to order: the enemy of all nations, the pirate – 'in his dark nature there was a touch of the feminine, as in all the greatest pirates', notes J. M. Barrie of Captain Hook[103] – the communist, the anarchist and the rebellious colonial subject.[104] In terms of classical liberalism, then, it might be argued that the war power and its underlying martial values can be realised only through citizen-subjects who are themselves role models for liberal masculinity.

LIBERAL PEACE OR LIBERAL POLICE? TOWARD THE POLICE OF CIVILISATION

'O Effeminacy! Effeminacy! Who wou'd imagine this could be the *Vice* of such as appear no inconsiderable Men?'[105] Such was the concern of Shaftesbury early in the eighteenth century. I have been arguing in this chapter that this concern permeated liberal political discourse for the rest of the century and that the reason the thinkers I have considered thought effeminacy a vice is because they believed that, along with associated vices such as luxury, it undermined one of the virtues thought fundamental to a social order organised on the basis of private property: a martial spirit. The extent of this concern is indicative of the extent to which these eighteenth-century liberals believed in and perpetuated the tradition of thought which emphasised the creative role of war in the development of civilisation and the shaping of the character of human (though quintessentially male) beings. At the heart of the 'liberal peace', then, is nothing less than the question of how to maintain order as a realm of liberty and property such that the new liberal virtues of civil society did not threaten the more established virtues of a masculine martial power.

This argument somewhat undermines one of the fundamental historical claims made within the liberal peace thesis, namely that the conceptual underpinning of liberal peace lies in part in the eighteenth-century Scottish Enlightenment's conception of commercial man and civil society. The association between liberalism and peace was a product of the more doctrinaire 'free traders' of the nineteenth century peddling the myth of a link between peace and trade.[106] From there, the idea of a liberal vision of peace rooted in an image of economic order became a piece of received wisdom. Too many IR theorists have accepted this received wisdom uncritically and perpetuated it unthinkingly, systematically ignoring the importance which the eighteenth-century liberals attached to military valour and martial virtues.

I have elsewhere argued that liberalism's key concept is less liberty and more security, and nowhere is this clearer than in eighteenth-century liberal thought.[107] Yet 'security' in the work of liberalism is never a reference to a 'passive' form of 'defense', but rather connotes an *active militaristic* practice, as Michael Shapiro puts it.[108] To reiterate the point being made in previous chapters: liberalism has been committed to the violence of war as the exercise of the liberal spirit since its inception (whichever date one wishes to put on that inception), which is one of the reasons why as war powers liberal states have been so willing to deploy violence in the name of liberty and accumulation. Within and around this exercise, the 'liberal peace' thesis operates as a modern political myth, offering nothing less than an ideological gloss over classical liberalism's violence.

As well as an active militaristic practice, security for liberalism also connotes an active police power.[109] Hence as much as effeminacy and luxury resonated through the liberal debate about the war power, so too they resonated through the debate about the police power as well; the question of liberal *peace* is always already a question of liberal *police*. I shall close this chapter with a few comments on this dimension of the police problem, but do so also to clear the way for a more extended engagement with the police idea in the chapters that follow.

Police discourse in this period was developing in response to shifts in the underlying political economy of liberal order: on the one hand, the question of making the poor work – and thus making the working class – intensified with the rise of an increasingly liberal and industrial commercial order; on the other hand, the police problem of orderliness revolved around a number of concerns over the disorderly. Although at the heart of this double-sided problem of work and (dis)order was the place of an emerging proletariat in a civil society of liberty and civility, the question of the manly virtue needed for controlling 'unmanly' habits was also prevalent.[110] It was noted in the previous chapter that order and property are conjoined in the concept of propriety, and here we should note that 'propriety' also runs through eighteenth-century liberal thought: Part I of Smith's *Theory of Moral Sentiments* is on propriety, which he uses to help explain the importance of sympathy in the moral order. As it does so, propriety connotes 'decency' as well as property as the bridge between individuals and the social world.[111] The *Oxford English Dictionary* notes that as well as 'belonging to oneself', 'owned as property' and 'that which is one's own', 'proper' also connotes 'conformity with social ethics' and 'becoming decent, decorous, respectable, genteel and correct'. In this way, questions of decency and respectability fold into the police concept: propriety becomes a key issue of police power. In the mid-eighteenth century William Blackstone defined 'public police' as involving the citizens conforming to 'the rules of propriety' and being 'decent, industrious, and inoffensive in their respective stations'.[112] The point is that within this realm of decency lies the norm of manliness and assumptions about the (in)appropriateness of forms of behaviour associated with civic virtue.

This reinforced a set of assumptions about the gendered nature of the police function. One set of essays on police history and masculinity illustrates the extent to which the various police models of the eighteenth century'demonstrate a deep and abiding connection between masculine identity and community control through policing'.[113] This meant that debates about the reform of police which took place in the late eighteenth century focused heavily on the idea of policing as masculine citizen-soldiering and sought to replicate the masculine ideal of the militiaman. 'The importance of the citizen-soldier in the eighteenth century', writes Matthew McCormack, means that 'a particular form of militarism has always had a place in the English police tradition', and this overlap between the police power and the war power needs to be understood through the 'strain of martial masculinity within the cherished ideal of the citizen-constable itself'.[114] Police power, as the ordering of the urban environment, was understood as an expression of this strain of martial masculinity. At the same time, however, and as a result of the inherent connection between police and the city, the fact that questions of effeminacy, the 'effeminizing' effect of luxury and related issues such as decency and disorderliness were essentially questions of urban order meant that they were automatically subject to the police power.[115]

Hence effeminacy and luxury appear as a problem of order through-out the police schemes of the late eighteenth century. John Brown, for example, ends the text which had placed effeminacy at the heart of disorder with a compliment to 'the salutary Effects of a new Kind of Police, established by a useful Magistrate in the City of London', and this reference to a police solution to the problem was far from isolated.[116] Leading police reformer Henry Fielding comments in his *Enquiry into the Causes of the Late Increase of Robbers*, a tract which was to shape police discourse for half a century if not more, on the 'vast Torrent of Luxury which of late Years hath poured itself into this Nation'. The country, according to Fielding, is in danger of replicating Rome: 'from virtuous Industry to Wealth, from Wealth to Luxury; from Luxury to Impatience of Discipline and Corruption of Morals down to total Degeneracy and

Loss of Virtue'. Just a few years earlier Fielding had also written about the danger of effeminacy in *The Female Husband*.[117] Cesare Beccaria, that great liberal jurist and thinker said by many to be founder of what later became known as 'criminology', commented in his lectures on police science in 1768 that all of his reasoning ultimately culminated in an answer to the question of luxury,[118] and the new liberal police science that was emerging at the end of the eighteenth century reflected this. William Godschall, for example, begins his *General Plan of Police* by pointing to the problems of luxury and immorality generated by commerce.[119]

We might say that the haunting power of effeminacy was so strong that as a threat to 'order' it had to be a police matter. Hence the enemies identified above, the pirate, the communist, the anarchist, the colonial rebel, along with all the figures whose unstable gender identity appears disorderly, turn out to be the creatures most subject to the police power. In other words, effeminacy as a fundamental problematic of the liberal war power thus turns out to be part of the fundamental problematic of liberal police. Perhaps they are the same problematic. And perhaps the key to that problematic lies in one of the phrases that appears on the very first page of Ferguson's *Essay on the History of Civil Society*: outlining the progress of man, Ferguson suggests that just as 'the individual advances from infancy to manhood' so the species advances 'from rudeness to civilization'. Into the dialectic of war power and police power enters a new term, one which will build on, play off and reinforce these terms, but which will also in the process transform them: civilisation.

Chapter 4

THE POLICE OF CIVILISATION:
WAR AS CIVILISING OFFENSIVE

═══════

What they could do with round here is a good war. What else can
you expect with peace running wild all over the place? You know
what the trouble with peace is? No organization. And when do
you get organization? In war … How many horses have they got
in this town? How many young men? Nobody knows! They
haven't bothered to count 'em! That's peace for you! I've been in
places where they haven't had a war for seventy years and you
know what? The people haven't even been given names! They
don't know who they are! It takes war to fix that. In war, everyone
registers, everyone's name's on a list. Their shoes are stacked, their
corn's in the bag, you count it all up – cattle, men, *Et cetera* – and
you take it away! That's the story: no war, no order!

Brecht, *Mother Courage* (1939)

Civilisation is back. The 'war on terror' is said be about many things:
'freedom, democracy, and free enterprise', as the US National Security
Strategy of 2002 puts it. Or, as found in other quarters, 'values', 'civil
society', 'the rule of law', 'way of life', even the return of 'real men' as we
saw in the previous chapter. A regular item on such lists is 'civilisation'.
This view is found far and wide and in a variety of discursive forms.
According to the National Security Strategy, 'the war on terror is not a
clash of civilizations', but 'the allies of terror are the enemies of civilization'. This attempt to distance the strategy from the more politically
awkward 'clash of civilisations' thesis merely underlines the claim that it
is still 'civilisation' that is ultimately at stake. We are living, suggests the
Strategy, 'in an age when the enemies of civilization openly and actively
seek the world's most destructive technologies'.[1] This is the view that

was very quickly asserted by President Bush during the early stages of the war. In an Address to a Joint Session of Congress and the American People on 20 September 2001, Bush commented that the war was not America's fight; rather, 'this is civilization's fight'. Hence America was not fighting alone, because 'the civilized world is rallying to America's side'. Likewise, Colin Powell described the attacks on the World Trade Center as an 'assault on civilization' and the purpose of the war as the defeat of those 'attacking civilization'.[2] One finds similar comments made elsewhere: the German Chancellor called 9/11 a 'declaration of war against all of civilization', and the former New York Mayor commented that 'you're either with civilization or the terrorists'. Elsewhere one finds publications such as the one called *Defending Civilization* by the American Council of Trustees and Alumni and published as part of their 'Defense of Civilization Fund' (2002).[3] The list of examples could go on and on.

Civilisation is back, then, and can be found at the heart of geopolitics, in the acquiescence of various powers to the ideology that underpins this geopolitics, and is therefore at the centre of a new stage in the permanent global war of accumulation.

One way of grappling with this return is to point to the fact that, read in terms of international law, it appears to be a rather embarrassing anachronism. International law was for a long time driven by the idea of civilisation as its 'standard', but while a 'standard of civilisation' may have made sense in the nineteenth century when racial differences between 'civilisation' and its 'others' were at the forefront of European thought, it is widely said to make no sense now, in these 'postcolonial' days. As Gerrit Gong suggests, 'given the contemporary consensus that all countries are now to be considered "civilized", the distinction between "civilized" and "uncivilized" has declined in relevance'.[4] The colonial legacy betrayed by 'civilisation' as a category means that anti-colonial movements and postcolonial states argued long and hard through the second half of the twentieth century that states should not be discriminated against on the basis of some standard of 'civilisation' rooted in the heyday of imperialism, and succeeded in having this recognised by the United Nations. The outcome was that textbooks and international organisations gradually desisted from suggesting that the idea of civilisation was the foundation stone for international law. Lauterpacht, for example, challenged the idea in his *Recognition in International Law* of 1947, and the International Law Commission slowly stopped referring to 'civilised countries'.[5] This shift was supported by the body of critical international legal theory and Third World approaches to international law that we discussed in Chapter 2.

One way of dealing with the current return of 'civilisation', then, is to show that it is indeed a rather embarrassing anachronism, harking back to a time when the category was one of colonialism's most powerful ideological tools and one of the many binary oppositions on which colonial violence was based: good/evil, West/East, modern/primitive, and so on.[6]

Yet to dismiss the return of civilisation as an ideological anachronism or a form of Western hypocrisy would be to close ourselves off from some of the interesting political issues at stake. For a start, the idea of 'civilisation' never quite disappeared. Rather, it appeared to get incorporated into other ideas. On the one hand, 'internationally recognized human rights have become very much like a new international "standard of civilization"', notes Jack Donnelly. On the other hand, rather than being 'uncivilised', countries are now considered 'unglobalised' or just 'undemocratic'.[7] Thus in one sense 'civilisation' did not disappear, but became subsumed under other ideas that became central to international law and ordering.

To refer to 'law and ordering' is to signal a turn in our attention towards the police power. James Scott has noted that 'uncivilised' is often code for those outside the reach of the state,[8] which is to say: beyond police. As we saw in the Introduction, many of the actions historically understood under the category 'war' are now being discussed through the idea of 'police', with a whole range of documents, texts and thinkers claiming that war and police are now dynamically linked. I suggested there that despite this growing consensus connecting war and police there has been a marked unwillingness to think through precisely what the connection means. 'Police' is still rather narrowly defined in terms of law enforcement, and thus the focus has been really on the question of how a rather mundane 'military model' and 'criminological model' might be brought together, or whether criminology and international relations might be synthesised in some way. As I pointed out, this involves a seriously impoverished concept of police, ignoring the rich history of the police power in the fabrication of social order. Chapters 1 to 3 have touched on this, but thinking about the police idea in relation to civilisation highlights this rich history. The argument here therefore seeks to connect the concept of civilisation to the logic of police power by pointing to the role of 'civilisation-as-police', and thus 'police-as-civilisation', in the fabrication of international order. It does so by turning to the question of police in a conceptual history designed to make sense of the original emergence of 'civilisation' as a category of police power.

In his account of civilisation as an imperial idea, Brett Bowden comments that civilisation 'is a concept that is used to both describe and shape reality'.[9] I argue that this power to shape reality – to fabricate order – stems from civilisation's historical roots in the police power. Further-more, I suggest that this helps explain why these terms have once more come to the fore. In the context of the liberal dream of global capitalism and world order organised through a 'war on terror', the logic of 'civilisa-tion' and the growing importance of 'police' turn out to be supremely apt. This chapter and the two which follow therefore seek to connect war and police in a way which has only been touched on in previous chapters. Here, I argue that we can make sense of the return of civilisation by tracing it as an idea back to the original police science as a science of administration, security and order. The argument is then developed through an account of air power and international police in Chapters 5 and 6.

CIVILISATION: LAW

The use of 'civilisation' in the 'war on terror' hints at a long history of the term in international law. It also proposes a rather obvious and crude political distancing from the major enemy in this war. This combination can be seen in a brief outline of the importance of civilisation in international law as it emerged in the nineteenth century. Gong suggests that the roots of 'civilisation' as a standard in international law are documented by two historical records: on the one hand, the nineteenth-century treaties signed between European and non-European countries, and, on the other hand, the legal texts written by the leading inter-national lawyers of the era.[10] In fact, there was a third dimension, namely liberal political thought more generally.

In an essay in the *London and Westminster Review* in 1836, John Stuart Mill comments that 'civilisation' has a 'double meaning', both of which play heavily on the idea that we noted in Chapter 2 to be central to the liberal war on waste: improvement.

It sometimes stands for human improvement in general, and sometimes for certain kinds of improvement in particular. We are accustomed to call a country more civilized if we think it more improved; more eminent in the best characteristics of Man and Society; farther advanced in the road to perfection; happier, nobler, wiser. But in another sense it stands for that kind of improvement only, which distinguishes a wealthy and powerful nation from savages and barbarians.[11]

The concept thus concerns a level of productive life and a degree of cultural sophistication, and it is these features that generate the possibility of international comparison. Hence, in a later essay on international disputes in 1859, Mill comes back to the idea:

There is a great difference ... between the case in which the nations concerned are of the same, or something like the same, degree of civilization, and that in which one of the parties to the situation is of a high, and the other of a very low, grade of social improvement. To suppose that the same international customs, and the same rules of international morality, can obtain between one civilized nation and another, and between civilized nations and barbarians, is a grave error.[12]

Mill's comments are just one example of the liberal distinction between civilised and barbarian forms of society. Such ideas came to figure in legal documents and fed into the wider narrative of liberal internationalism that underpinned nineteenth-century international law.[13] The connection lies once more in the links made within the liberal mind between peace and security, law and order, and civilisation: law, as the 'gentle civiliser of nations', brings peace, security and order. For international order to be secured, the 'uncivilised' communities and states have to be policed through the introduction of Western law and administration. 'Civilisation' thereby connected international law not just with assumptions about peace and security, but also with the political economy of human labour and free trade, liberal political institutions and certain standards of bourgeois conduct. In so doing it became the main criterion by which the place and status of different human groups would be judged. The principle of opposition is the ordering principle of civilisation itself, as Terry Castle puts it, and the standard of 'civilisation' could thus be conceived only by reference to a diverse range of others – the 'primitive', 'savage', 'barbarian', 'pirate'[14] – understood as enemies: enemies of law, of order, of civilisation.[15] Those who fulfil the requirements of the standard are brought inside a circle of 'members', while those who do not conform are left 'outside'.

By the end of the nineteenth century the standard of 'civilisation' was being articulated in major Peace Conferences. The Hague conference of 1899 was called for and attended by those who regarded themselves as 'recognizing the solidarity which unites the members of the society of civilized nations',[16] while the 1907 conference was said to be based on 'the solidarity uniting the members of the society of civilized nations'. Key international lawyers confirmed this process in texts on the subject: T. J. Lawrence suggested that 'civilisation' rather than religion (Christianity) had become the test of entry into the international system,[17] and Oppenheim's major 1905 text defined international law as 'the body of customary and conventional rules which are considered legally binding by civilised States in their intercourse with each other'. Oppenheim went on to suggest that to be admitted into the 'Family of Nations' a state 'must, first, be a civilized State which is in contestant intercourse with members of the Family of Nations'.[18] By the time the League of Nations was being created those nations which, due to their lack of 'civilisation' could not be admitted fully into the international system (those 'inhabited by peoples not yet able to stand by themselves under the strenuous conditions of the modern world'), were in turn to be policed according to the principle: 'the well-being and development of such peoples form a sacred trust of civilization' (Article 22). This sacred trust would turn out to be fundamental to the process of accumulation.

To the extent that it was central to international law and accumulation, 'civilisation' was also central to colonial war. As Elias notes, 'it is not a little characteristic of the structure of Western society that the watchword of its colonizing movement is "civilization"'.[19] Article 6 of the Berlin Conference of February 1885, in which the imperial powers decided how they would carve up Africa, held that each of the powers should 'aim at instructing the natives and bringing home to them the blessings of civilization'. As Charles Alexandrowicz points out:

A review of documents in the principal collections of African treaties … would reveal that the transfer of sovereign rights or titles by the African rulers to the protecting European Powers was either expressly or implicitly connected to the duty of civilization, *i.e.,* the task of the transferee to assist African communities in achieving a higher level of civilization before they re-entered the family of nations as equal sovereign entities.[20]

This combined power of law and war meant that by the end of the nineteenth century the logic of 'civilisation' could shed its European and Christian dimensions: the entry of the US into 'international society' broke the European stranglehold and the inclusion of non-Christian but nonetheless imperial powers such as Japan meant that what had in the eighteenth and early nineteenth centuries been understood as the 'law of Christian nations' or the 'public law of Europe' had by the end of the nineteenth century become redefined as the international law of civilised nations.[21] In other words, what was of ultimate importance for 'civilisation' was not European Christianity but the exercise of the war power in the process of systematic colonisation.

The idea of civilisation in international law, then, is widely accepted to be a product of nineteenth-century developments in the concept of civilisation and the widening of the net of international law. There was widespread agreement that the general principles of law and war were those recognised by civilised nations, with implicit or explicit assumptions about the rule of law, respect for fundamental liberties, the right to property, and the possibility of diplomatic exchange and communication. Within this, the distinction between 'civilised' and 'uncivilised' was simply assumed necessary, and so the standard of civilisation helped establish a taxonomy through which states could be granted legal personality in international society.[22] This was to become central to the idea of international order, and this itself reminds us that there is more to the term 'civilisation' than the focus on nineteenth-century international law allows, as we shall now see.

CIVILISATION: POLICE

'Civilisation' seems to us like such an old word. This impression is in part achieved by its root in *civil*, from *civilis*, connected to the Latin 'citizen'. 'Civil' was thus used from the fourteenth century onwards, connected to 'civility' and 'civilise', and morphing into 'civil society' in the seventeenth century. But 'civilisation' in fact came into the language only very recently, in the second half of the eighteenth century.[23] The reason why it came into the language at this time is important for the argument here.

In France, the first recorded use of the term would appear to be in the Marquis de Mirabeau's *L'Ami des hommes ou Traité de la population*, first published in 1757. From then on, writers increasingly came to use the term in the sense used by Mirabeau: first, to refer to the *process* through which humanity emerged from barbarity and, second, as a *state* of society, of which various examples might then be found.[24] In so doing it built on much older terms such as the participle *civilisé* (civilised) and the verb *civiliser* (to civilise), together taking us back to the idea of refinement and its cultivation. Lucien Febvre suggests that from 1765 the term becomes increasingly naturalised and forces its way into the *Dictionnaire de l'Academié* in 1798.[25]

One of its main themes seems to have been modes of behaviour. Prior to the emergence of 'civilisation', concepts such as *politesse* or *civilité* were used to express the self-image of the European aristocracy. *Civilisé* was, like *cultivé, poli* or *policé,* one of the terms by which the courtly elite designated the specific quality of their behaviour, refinement and social manners in contrast to the lower orders.[26] In its emergence in the second half of the eighteenth century, however, 'civilisation' was very closely associated with rising social movements challenging the power of this aristocracy. Elias comments that 'the French bourgeoisie – politically active, at least partly eager for reform, and even, for a short period, revolutionary – remained strongly bound to the courtly tradition in its behaviour and its affect-molding even after the edifice of the old regime had been demolished'.[27] In terms of social origins then, the concept of *civilisation* developed in France within the opposition movement in the second half of the eighteenth century; the 'civilising process' became a project of the bourgeois class. The French concept of *'civilisation'* reflects the rising importance of the bourgeoisie in that country, becoming a key instrument in dealing with internal conflict and for articulating a vision of a new world. For this vision, terms such as *civilité* were a little too static.[28] At the same time, however, in the work of Quesnay and the physiocrats, the idea emerged that society and the economy have their own laws which are never fully manageable by rulers, and thus that 'enlightened' administration should govern in accordance with the laws of political economy. As Eric Cheyfitz notes, the distinction between civilisation and its 'other' is one of the fundamental fictions of the history of private property.[29]

This had an exact parallel in England, where 'civilisation' also proved to be a crucial ideological tool of a rising industrial class and its key thinkers. As with the French, the English 'civilise' and 'civilised' are much older than 'civilisation', which again appears for the first time in the same period as in France. The *Oxford English Dictionary* (*OED*) lists as one of the earliest written usages an entry by Boswell in his *Life of Johnson*, in which Boswell reports a visit to Johnson in 1772, finding the latter preparing a new edition of his *Dictionary*: 'On Monday, March 23, I found him busy, preparing a fourth edition of his folio Dictionary ... He would not admit *civilization*, but only *civility*. With great deference to him, I thought *civilization*, from *to civilize*, better in the sense opposed to *barbarity*, than *civility*'.[30] Boswell was picking up on the new word that was then coming to the fore. The fact that Boswell thought 'civilisation' worth entering as distinct from 'civility' suggests a reasonably well-established difference between 'civility', in the sense of manners and politeness, and 'civilisation', as the opposite of barbarity. Resisting the modern, Johnson preferred the older 'civility' but Boswell, as a Scotsman with legal training, was perhaps trying to identify a term which captured the French concern for manners (civility) with the Scottish commitment to Civil Law (the *OED* notes one meaning of the term as being the assimilation of common law to civil law), and the transformation of the Scottish people from clansmen and cattle ranchers to merchants and bankers.[31] That it is unlikely that Boswell was doing little more than picking up a term that was already in use is suggested by the use of the term in, for example, Adam Ferguson's *Essay on the History of Civil Society* (1767) which, as we saw in the previous chapter, opens with a comment on the advance 'from rudeness to civilization' and which then uses this advance to elaborate on the history of civil society through the rest of the book. 'Civilisation' also appears in *Ash's English Dictionary* in 1775 and Adam Smith felt comfortable making use of the term in the *Wealth of Nations*, published in 1776.[32]

It is therefore clear that the term is a product of the second half of the eighteenth century and has a variety of senses. First, the sense that it is somehow equivalent to 'civility', drawing together various dimensions of the ideas of *civilised* and *civilising*, including politeness in manners;

second, the sense of a *condition*, a stage in history beyond barbarism and savagery; and, third, the sense of a *process*.[33] This idea of process is important here, for it marks civilisation not merely as a state or a set of manners, but as an action to be actively carried out; indeed, an action to be carried out *politically*. Hence Webster's *American Dictionary of the English Language*, published in 1828, has as its first entry for 'civilisation': 'the *act* of civilizing'. The term thus enters the rhetoric of power as a *political mission* (eventually, of course, becoming 'the civilising mission') or declaration of political intent. This was a period of profound conceptual innovation and transformation, not least in the way that a significant number of concepts became invested with connotations of historical change. In both France and England a large number of nouns ending as *-ation* were formed from verbs ending as *-iser*: *centralisation, democratisation, fraternisation, nationalisation, utilisation* and, of course, *industrialisation*. Taking on board the fact that words ending as '*-ation*' also suggest the presence of an agent, it is clear that the agency behind the process transcended the individual, especially the idea of the individual implicit in the older aristocratic notion of *civilisé*.[34] In other words, we can see behind the idea of 'civilisation' a new historically emerging collective agency carrying out a historical process. In its origins, then, civilisation's central connotation might be thought of in terms of a nineteenth-century 'standard' (legal, cultural or otherwise), but the term in fact connoted a distinctly political project borne out of the bourgeois reform movements of the second half of the eighteenth century. Herein lies the term's essentially new – essentially *modern* – dimension (and thereby connecting it to 'modernisation'), referring to the process of generating a specific stage of social development charact- erised by private property, money, commerce and trade. 'Civilisation' thereby became associated with a certain vision of humanity and order, useful as a criteria in political judgement, not least in defending the civilised order from its monstrous other, the savage/barbarian, but useful more than anything else as the basis of bourgeois rule. It became nothing less than a key concept of bourgeois ideology; a new fetish for the ruling class.[35]

Yet there is a further dimension to the term about which little is said but which is far more revealing: police. 'Throughout the whole of the seventeenth century', Febvre notes, 'French authors classified people according to a hierarchy which was both vague and very specific'.

At the lowest level there were the *sauvages*. A bit higher on the scale, but without much distinction being made between the two, there come the *barbares*. After which, passing on from the first stage, we come to the people who possess *civilité*, *politesse* and finally, good *police*.[36]

As 'civilisation' takes its place within the political lexicon, one of the key words from which it develops, and which functions more or less as its midwife, is 'police'. Febvre notes that 'in his essay *De la félicité publique* and in his work on *Considérations sur le sort des homes dans les différentes époques de l'histoire*, the first volume of which appeared in Amsterdam in 1772, Father Jean de Chastellux uses the word *police* a great deal but never, so it appears, *civilisation*'.[37] Indeed, Febvre's attempt to identify the first use of the term in France shows that many of the assumed first usages of civilisation turn out to have been references to police; his finding has been confirmed by Elias. For example, although Turgot is widely assumed to have been the first to use 'civilisation', the appearance of the term in his work was the responsibility of later editors. Turgot does not use the word 'civilisation', says Febvre. 'He does not even use the verb *civiliser*, or the participle *civilisé*, which was then in current use'. Rather: 'he always keeps to *police* and to *policé*'. Likewise, Febvre continues, people often think that the word first appears in Boulanger's *Antiquité dévoilée par ses usages* (1766). Yet the appearance of the word 'civilisation' in that text was placed there by Holbach, who edited the work after Boulanger's death in 1759 (the *Antiquité dévoilée par ses usages* being a posthumous work). Of the *Recherches sur l'origine du despotisme oriental* (1761), also sometimes suggested as containing the first use, '*civilisé* does appear in it, but fairly infrequently; *civilisation* never does; *police* and *policé* are the usual terms'.[38] In the *Encyclopédie*, published between 1751 and 1772, police appears, but not civilisation. In the work of some writers 'civilisation' really does replace 'police'. Writing of Mirabeau's use of the term, Benveniste says that 'for Mirabeau "civilisation" is the process of what had been up until his time called "police" in French'. That is, it refers to 'an act tending to make man and society more *policé* [orderly]'.[39] In the work of others, however, there is an oscillation between the two terms: Voltaire, in The *Philosophy of History* (1766), shifts from *policé* to *civilisé* and back again, and at one point writes of peoples becoming 'united into a civilized [*civilises*], polished [*polices*], industrious body'.[40] As Febvre notes, Voltaire still requires the two words. We might add that Ferguson retains the use of 'polished' as a synonym for 'civilised' and adds an explanatory etymological point: 'The term polished, if we may judge from its etymology, originally referred to the state of nations in respect to their laws and government. In its later applications, it refers no less to their proficiency in the liberal and mechanical arts, in literature, and in commerce'.[41]

The historical picture is thus a little complicated, and hence the connection between civilisation and police is easily missed.[42] Although in both France and England the verb *civiliser*/civilise and the participle *civilisé*/civilised take us back to the idea of refinement and its cultivation, whereas *policé* is derived from the Greek *polis*, *politeia* and gives us *politie* and *police*, there is no doubt that what was at stake in 'civilisation' as it emerges was very much connected to what was at stake in 'police'. And so, as much as police gives rise to civilisation, the former continues to permeate the latter, circulating around it and through it.

On the one hand, the tendency was such that by the end of the century two words were no longer necessary for some people. Volney in *Éclaircissements sur les États-Unis*, in 1803, could write that:

> By *civilisation* we should understand an assembly of men in a town, that is to say an enclosure of dwellings equipped with a common defence system to protect themselves from pillage from outside and disorder within ... The assembly implied the concepts of voluntary consent by the members, maintenance of their natural right to security, personal freedom and property: ... thus *civilisation* is nothing other than a social condition for the preservation and protection of persons and property etc.[43]

This is civilisation as police, yet no longer articulated as police. The substance of 'civilisation' has assimilated all the substance of the word 'police'. Likewise, in a text such as Adam Ferguson's *Principles of Moral and Political Science*, civilisation connotes the basic ideas associated with police: 'peace and good order', 'security of the person and property', 'good order and justice'.[44] Yet just as civilisation could never fully lose its connections with *politesse* or *civilité*, so it could never lose its links to police. Thus, 'in spite of all, *policé* resisted', notes Febvre, adding that 'then there was *police* lying behind it which was a considerable nuisance to the innovators'.

What about *civilisé*? They were tempted in fact to extend its meaning; but *policé* put up a struggle and showed itself to be still very robust. In order to overcome its resistance and express the new concept which was at that time taking shape in people's minds, in order to give to *civilisé* a new force and new areas of meaning, in order to make of it a new word and not just something that was a successor to *civil*, *poli* and even, partly, *policé*, it was necessary to create behind the participle and behind the verb the word *'civilisation'*.[45]

And so, on the other hand, the connections between the two terms could never quite be fully broken. Just as *civilisé* was often used synonymously with words like *cultivé*, *poli*, or *policé* to designate certain social manners, so civilisation and police were often used synonymously in the same way to designate a certain kind of order. For example, just as one of the lists in Guizot's *Dictionary of Synonyms* runs *Poli*, *Policé*, *Civilisé*, so he also continues to include 'police' as one of the fundamental elements of civilisation.[46]

Behind this affinity lie a number of assumptions. First is the belief that there are always people in need of 'polishing', those who lack the necessary 'polish'. Necessary, that is, for an orderly – *well-policed* – society. Second is the idea that left to themselves some people will fall (back) into the state of barbarism or savagery. And third is the assumption that this is a group process: polishing, avoiding barbarism or savagery, is a task of the group.[47] This set of assumptions applies to the barbarians and savages outside the domestic frame, but applies also to the members of the population who lack the necessary 'polish', who are close to or might fall into a state of barbarism or savagery, and who therefore need to be worked on by a group which is already civilised by definition, namely the bourgeois class. Those who require polishing – the disorderly, lawless and thus uncivilised poor – are those who must be most obviously subject to the police power. 'To polish was to civilize individuals, to polish their manners and language', writes Starobinski. Both the literal and the figurative senses of 'polish' evoke ideas of order and thus the discipline and law necessary for an orderly society. 'The intermediate link in this chain of associations was provided by the verb *policer*, which applied to groups of individuals or to nations: "*Policer*": to make laws and regulations (*règlements de police*) for preserving the public tranquillity'.[48]

Thus the word 'police' worked alongside civility and politeness in the development of 'civilisation'. As the new term develops, the power contained within the principle of police will come to play a role in the idea of civilisation as a process and a political project. By the beginning of the nineteenth century 'civilisation' possessed a range of meanings, including, not least, a reference to habits and practices regarded as 'cultural'. Ideas were evolving in such a way as to confer superiority not merely on peoples equipped with good police, but on peoples said to be more generally rich in bourgeois art, philosophy and literature.[49] Culture and civilisation would become joined together in the minds of those thinkers and publicists for whom good order goes hand-in-hand with manners and refinement, art and literature, philosophy and science. Yet cultural practices are but one dimension of social ordering, and thus Febvre is right to argue that 'at the top of the great ladder whose bottom rungs were occupied by savagery and whose middle rungs were occupied by barbarity, "*civilisation*" took its place quite naturally at the same point where '*police*' had reigned supreme before it'.[50] For all its novelty around civilisation vis-à-vis civilise and civility, the rising bourgeois movement and liberal ideology could not forego some notion of police.

In this vision of social order and political ordering, those who are most made subject to the police power form the threat to civilisation. They are the ones which the whole history of liberalism from hereon will come to describe as most in need of the *discipline* of civilisation and thus *disciplining into* civilisation.[51] To the extent that 'civilisation' was configured as a war over manners, property and culture – a war, that is, over order itself – it could never quite relinquish the idea of police. To coin a phrase in the shadow of Walter Benjamin, we might say that there is no document of civilisation that is not also a document of police. Civilisation was and is never just about values such as 'civility'. Rather, it captured and continues to capture the meaning at the very heart of the police power: the fabrication of social order.

CIVILISATION: OFFENSIVE

If we accept the original meaning of police and the emergence of civilisation from this concept, then the function of civilisation as a standard in nineteenth-century international law becomes much clearer: the fabrication of *international* order. We might say that whereas police had been the principle of social order, so 'civilisation' as an international idea extended this principle geopolitically. Or, to put it another way, civilisation implicitly held on to its original police remit and extended it to the international realm, which is how it became a principal ordering category of international power. The oft-repeated criticisms of the standard of 'civilisation' – that it was never easy to define, that putting it into practice involves a complex and often indefinable set of apparatuses, and that once this complex set of apparatuses is stripped back it often worked as a rather blunt instrument – miss the fact that these very same criticisms are made of the police idea.

Civilisation, like police, generates and uses a range of mechanisms of political administration to shape human subjectivity and order civil society. Internationally, this has been a means of ordering global society around a certain conception of good order. Such order is the systematic colonisation of the world by capital.

> The bourgeoisie ... compels all nations, on pain of extinction, to adopt the bourgeois mode of production; it compels them to introduce what it calls civilization into their midst, ie., to become bourgeois themselves. In one word, it creates a world after its own image.[52]

As Marx and Engels sought to show, the project of introducing 'civilisation' to all nations is fundamental to the nature of capital.[53] The fabrication of an international bourgeois order was a project of global scope, requiring the permanent exercise of organised violence. In this way civilisation could very easily come to function as a key principle around which the war power and the police power could coalesce.

Here, however, the concept of violence once again complicates the concept of peace. As we saw in Chapter 1, one of the implications of the work of Elias and others is that the 'civilising process' implies the elimination of violence from the social order.[54] For those invested in this word, civilisation connotes peace rather than war. Plenty of examples of this can be found in the liberal tradition: Condorcet, for example, in his *Vie de Voltaire* (1789) comments that 'the more civilization spreads across the earth, the more we shall see war and conquest disappear in the same way as slavery and want'.[55] Each of Smith's uses of 'civilisation' in the *Wealth of Nations* refers to the peace and security involved in its production, and the same link with peace can be seen in Ferguson's *Principles of Moral and Political Science*, as noted above, or, a little later, in Mill's suggestion that a people is civilised when 'the arrangements of society … are sufficiently perfect to maintain peace'.[56] The savagery of the savage and barbarity of the barbarian are to be superseded by the *pacific* world of civilisation; the pirate replaced by police.[57]

In contrast to the standard liberal claim, we might cite a rather astute observation about the foundations of government in India, made in 1883 by James Fitzjames Stephens, that liberal who 'made a career of bringing out the implicit and uneasy assumptions of his brethren'.[58] 'The English in India', he said, 'are the representatives of a belligerent civilization'. The phrase, he added 'is epigrammatic', yet strictly true. After all, 'the English in India are the representatives of peace compelled by force'.[59] Stephens here grasps the point not only of English power in India, but of all acts of power carried out under the banner of civilisation: these are acts of peace, compelled by force. Stephens understood that the peace of civilisation needs to be read as legitimised violence and coded war. Or as we might put it in terms developed in Chapter 1: 'civilisation' could thus carry out the work of pacification that we saw was so intimately connected to the idea of police. Civilisation demands pacification. And as Elias has shown, this process involves the *transformation* rather than elimination of violence. On the surface, civilisation is founded on the eradication of all that is considered 'barbaric', 'irrational' and 'uncivilised'.[60] But this leaves an ongoing and always unresolved tension between civilisation and violence. General Bugeaud, for example, overseer of the French pacification of Algeria in the nineteenth century, could claim that the process of pacification is founded on 'the ideas of civilisation' without ever feeling the need to explain how the violence meted out on the Algerians might be understood as 'civilised'; he knew his audience would understand exactly what he meant.[61] As Marx puts it, 'the civilization and justice of bourgeois order comes out in its lurid light whenever the slaves and drudges of that order rise against their masters. Then this civilization and justice stand forth as undisguised savagery and lawless revenge'.[62] 'Civilization-mongers', as Engels calls them,[63] are never far from dropping bombs on defenceless cities, as we shall see in the next chapter.

This is why rather than speak of the civilising *process*, we might be better off speaking of the civilising *offensive*,[64] an idea which points to the fact that 'civilisation' *presupposes* violence and aggression against those considered 'uncivilised'. Indeed, 'civilisation' could be conceived only by reference to perceived enemies and adversaries against which wars must be fought. As Cristina Rojas puts it, the very process that made 'civilisation' such a key element of Western self-consciousness was the very same process that authorised violence in the name of civilisation; far from being opposites, civilisation and violence are inter-connected parts of a single economy, involving conquest of the barbarian lesser breeds abroad and repression of the barbarian lower orders at home, fought and pacified in the name of bourgeois security.[65]

The monopoly over the means of violence that is fundamental to the fabrication of social order is the core of the police power. Although such a formal monopoly over the means of violence does not exist in the international realm – which is the very reason why so many people have found it difficult to develop the concept of 'international police', to which we turn in the following two chapters – the violence through which this realm has been structured is obvious. It has traditionally been cast under the label 'war'. But the exercise of this violence is nonetheless frequently thought of as carrying out the project of civilisation and has more than anything sought to order the international world. Thus whatever might be new about the 'war on terror' within the wider framework of a debate about 'new wars', the insistence that it is a war of/for civilisation comes straight out of a much earlier age: in 1798, as Napoleon sends his troops off for the pacification of Egypt, he shouts to them, 'Soldiers, you are undertaking a conquest with incalculable consequences for civilization'.[66] To say that police and war coalesce around the project of civilisation is to say nothing other than violence has remained intrinsic to the process in question.

The following two chapters pursue this further still, through a consideration of air power and the idea of international police, but for the moment we can suggest that declaring the 'war on terror' to be a war of and for civilisation is rather telling, for it reveals that the war power has long been a rationale for the imposition of international order and the police power has long been a wide-ranging exercise in pacification. The 'war on terror' is thus the violent fabrication of world order in exactly the way that the original police power was the violent fabrication of social order. The war on terror, as international ordering, is a form of police; civilisation writ large.

Chapter 5

AIR POWER AS POLICE POWER I

═══════

The military angle is secondary; it is the police side that matters.
I know you dislike that word ... but it is the only one which sums
up our task.

Colonel Mathieu, in *The Battle of Algiers*
(dir. Gillo Pontecorvo, 1966)[1]

Walt Disney's political credentials are well known: using scab labour to
produce *Dumbo*, retelling the history of colonialism through the myth of
Pocahontas, appearing at the House Un-American Activities Committee
informing on 'security threats', being the only Hollywood celebrity to
receive Nazi film-maker Leni Riefenstahl, and being himself received
by Mussolini. Less well known amid this political posturing and
ideological work is a cartoon film released by the company in 1943 called
Victory Through Air Power. Based on a book of the same title written by
Major Alexander P. De Seversky published a year before and selling in
the hundreds of thousands through the Book-of-the-Month Club, the
film opens with an old newsreel clip of leading air power theorist Billy
Mitchell outlining the doctrine of strategic bombing which was by then
all the rage. Following the dedication of the film to Mitchell, the film
then covers the history of airplanes, moving quickly to their use in battle
and superiority to warships, and to the bombing of the Japanese octopus
('think of Japan as a great octopus', Seversky had suggested in his book).
The imperial tentacles of the Japanese octopus throttle various parts of
the globe, but the film ends with Japan being bombed into ruins ('we
have no alternative but to attack the tentacles one by one', Seversky had
added) and climaxes with the bombers transforming into one of the
symbols of sovereignty and American state power, the eagle, which then
claws the Japanese octopus to death. At the climax of the battle 'America

the Beautiful' can be heard and the film ends with 'Victory Though Air Power' running across the screen in large letters. The meaning of the film was abundantly clear: air power means that 'the job of annihilation … can be carried out more efficiently', for 'when the skies over a nation are captured, everything below lies at the mercy of the enemy's air weapons'.[2]

Disney's film was unavailable for decades, yet in 2004 it was repackaged as part of a two-set edition of propaganda films made by the company, of which *Victory Through Air Power* constituted the whole of the second disc along with some bonus material. It was a remarkably timely year to issue a sixty-year-old propaganda film on air power, because by 2004 the civilising offensive known as the 'war on terror' had taken a decidedly air-centric turn. When the 'war on terror' was officially started on 7 October 2001, it quickly became clear that this was to be a bombing war. During the first week alone B1 and B52 bombers dropped on Afghanistan some 500 GPS-guided bombs, 1,000 Mk-82 'dumb bombs' (that is, unguided bombs) and 50 Combined Effects Munitions (CEM, or 'cluster bomb', a weapon which releases hundreds of submunitions over a wide area). Over a thousand more cluster bombs were used by the end of 2001, by which point Fuel-Air Explosives (FAEs: 'thermobaric' bombs producing an overpressure of 427 pounds psi and a temperature of 2,500 to 3,000 degrees Centigrade, generating an impact that has been compared to the effect of a tactical nuclear weapon but without the radiation) were also being used along with 15,000-lb BLU-82 slurry bombs, known as 'daisy cutters', roughly the size of a small car and dropped from the back of a cargo plane from high altitude carrying over 12,000 pounds of a chemical 'slurry' formed of ammonium nitrate, aluminium powder and polystyrene. In Iraq, in the first month alone some 1,500 cluster bombs were dropped on the country in an attempt to 'shock and awe' the population, and over the following three months a further 10,000 were dropped by the US and just over 2,000 by the UK.[3] This air war continued in Pakistan, Yemen and elsewhere, and anyone who reads the newspapers will also be aware of the proliferation of the use of drones, an issue to which I will turn later in this chapter. The war on terror is nothing if not a war from the air.

We live in a world made by air power.[4] Looking back over just the last half-century we see the use of aircraft in Vietnam by the US and by the French before them, the bombing used by the British in Malaya,

Aden and Oman, by Portugal in Angola and Mozambique during the 1960s, by the French in Algeria, by white Rhodesia against Black resistance in the 1970s, by South Africa against the South West African Peoples Organization in the 1970s, across Latin America, by the Somoza in its attempt to crush the Sandinistas, to say nothing of the Soviets in Afghanistan or Israel's extensive and systematic use of air power against the Palestinians, as well as more recent forays such as that by the French in Mali in 2013. We really do live in a world shaped by air power.

In thinking about how the world has been shaped in this way, the hold of WWII on the political imagination is a strong one. Even those seeking to grasp the *longue durée* of air power usually go back to WWII and no further.[5] Caren Kaplan, for example, links national security discourse after 11 September 2001 to the rise of a 'national security of air power' during WWII, and John Dower similarly considers the strategic bombing of the twenty-first century in terms of terror bombing as a standard procedure of WWII; Andreas Huyssen has also noted that opposition to the air war in the 'war on terror' looks back to the air war over Europe 60 years previously.[6] But the trouble with going back to WWII is that this tends to encourage people to think of air power either in purely military and usually quite conservative terms, such as the impact of air power on military strategy, or purely ethical and usually quite liberal terms, such as the role of bombing as/in 'just war'. As Derek Gregory points out, 'there is a long history of assuming that air war is, by its very nature, virtuous'.[7] This is the reason why bombing features heavily in liberal 'just war' theory – bombing, we are told, is a way of 'making it easier to be good'[8] – and why the bombing of German and Japanese cities towards the end of WWII figures so large in the debates. I want to start, however, by tracing what Gregory calls the 'lines of descent'[9] beyond WWII and back to the 1920s.

Why the 1920s? In 2009 the US Air University published a document on air power as a politically viable, legitimising and flexible option for the United States, adding that in future conflicts as well as in Iraq the strategy should be to appropriate the air methods developed in the colonial context of the 1920s. That is, the document claims that 'the British RAF air policing of Iraq in the 1920s was a COIN [counter-insurgency] mission in the truest sense'.[10] This built on previous work, such as: an Air Power Research Institute report (published in 1986 but reprinted three times since) which noted that the history of the British air force between the wars offers the important lesson 'that air power can be shaped in creative ways to achieve political results', on the grounds that 'the objective of most air control operations was long-term political stability, pacification, and administration';[11] reports in the 1990s on 'British air control' as a 'model for the application of air power in contemporary low-intensity conflict';[12] and a 2006 Department of Defense Report on Iraqi 'tribes' which pointed to the historical example of the British success in their use of force in Iraq. The last of these Reports claims that 'the 1920 Revolt [in Iraq] collapsed when British decisiveness in countering it became apparent. The British successfully conveyed that they were the superior force, or the superior tribe', and this was achieved through air power: 'enabled largely by air power, the British were able to stay in Iraq – with minimal resources – through its independence in 1932 and beyond'.[13] These are just some of many such documents in which the world's leading military power has recently sought to learn some lessons from colonial practices, especially British colonial practices, of the 1920s.[14] Its leading ally has done much the same: in 2011 the UK's Joint Services Command and Staff College published an extensive 'Research Guide' on 'Air Policing during the Inter-War Years'.[15]

My aim, however, is not so much to make a historical point about the first 'airminded' period,[16] but to help lay down some of the groundwork for thinking of air power as police power. Building on the argument from the previous chapter, in which we started to explore the idea of war as a civilising project, and thus as a project of police, in this chapter I want to think through what is generally regarded as a quintessentially 'military' mode of action in terms of the logic of police. The analysis of a particular moment in twentieth-century air war in the first part of the chapter is intended to open a debate in the rest of the chapter about how we might use the concept of police power to grasp more recent developments in aerial technology, namely drones. Chapter 6 opens the debate further by taking up the idea of air power in terms of 'international police'. The two chapters together are intended to show the extent to which the police power and war power operate in tandem: if there is a victory to be had by the state and capital, it is victory through air power.

BOMBED INTO ORDER

In 1918 the British released two Reports on the idea that 'in the next war the existence of the British Empire will depend primarily on its air force'. 'The Royal Air Force is an Imperial service', it was claimed and, as a consequence, what was needed was an imperial air force to 'be the first line of defence of the British Empire'.[17] Plans along these lines had already been made in 1914 when Winston Churchill, then First Lord of the Admiralty, commissioned a report on the possible use of air power in Somaliland following the use of aircraft in the campaigns in Arabia, South-West and East Africa during WWI.[18] In March 1919 British planes bombed those rebelling against martial law in Egypt, and the Royal Air Force (RAF) was also used to suppress uprisings in Punjab, Yemen, Palestine and Mesopotamia; in the longest operation, lasting one and a half months from mid-November 1919, in Punjab, somewhere between 2.5 and 7 tons of bombs were dropped on the Mahsud and Wazir tribal groups. In Afghanistan in 1919 air raids were carried out on Kabul, Jalalabad and Dakka, and in Somaliland in 1920. But the real shift occurs in Iraq, a land rich in untapped resources and a geopolitical space offering a secure route to India if brought under control. A major revolt through the summer of 1920 and running into early 1921 led to Churchill assembling over 40 military and civilian experts at a conference in Cairo to determine the policy for the region. Troop numbers were to be reduced and replaced by subsidies paid to indigenous rulers, and the apparently contradictory aim of maintaining order while removing troops was to be resolved through the development and application of air power. A paper from the Air Staff proposed that 'the efficacy of the Royal Air Force as an independent arm should be put to proof by the transference to it of primary responsibility for the maintenance of order in some area of the Middle East, preferably Mesopotamia'.[19] As a number of historians have pointed out, it is no exaggeration to say that the main institution in both the creation of Iraq and in the subsequent exercise of state power in the region was the air force.[20] It was in Iraq 'that the British would rigorously practice, if never perfect, the technology of bombardment as a permanent method of colonial administration and surveillance and there that they would fully theorise the value of air power as an independent arm of the military'.[21]

Yet this was far from being a peculiarly British practice, for it was understood and applied by every colonising state from the moment when Lieutenant Giulio Cavotti of the Italian army leaned out of his monoplane and dropped a hand-held bomb on Tagiura on 1 November 1911. As well as the air power used by the British in Iraq and elsewhere, the same power was used by Italy in Libya for many years after Cavotti dropped his bomb there, by France in Morocco and Syria (they even referred to 'colonial bombing', for which they developed a fighter-bomber called *Type Coloniale* for the same purpose), and by the US in Mexico, the Dominican Republic and Nicaragua.[22] Air power and strategic bombing were, in effect, developed as the colonial state's main weapon of pacification between the two World Wars. Systematic colonisation from the end of WWI was without doubt an 'aerially enforced' process: 'liberal empire in the sky', as Priya Satia puts it.[23]

This colonial exercise of air power and aerial exercise of colonial power has tended to be treated as a marginal note to the history of strategic bombing. It's a 'small wars' affair, mere counterinsurgency, if one reads the military histories,[24] or 'a low-cost method of suppressing native discontent', if one reads the international histories.[25] But we need to be clear about what air power was doing, not least because what it was doing then might tell us something about air power now. For air power in fact turns out to consist not just of bombing the enemy as a military strategy, but as a key mechanism of order-building. Far from being understood in terms of *military* strategy, air power and strategic bombing were considered by the liberal democracies of the time as an ordering mechanism: a 'swift agent of government', in the words of Sir John Maffey when Governor-General of the Sudan.[26] 'If we use our Air Force wisely and humanely, such outcry as there is will cease and air action will be regarded as a normal and suitable weapon for enforcing the just demands of government', commented the Commanding Air Officer in India in 1923.[27] One can see this in the various concepts which came and went to capture what was being done through air power: 'air substitution'; 'control without occupation'; 'police bombing'. These eventually morph into the term which gets used much more widely and which then has a history of its own: air police. Thus when Air Commodore Lionel Charlton arrived in Baghdad in February 1923 as a senior air officer and he came across the injured in a bombing campaign, he 'was aghast to learn on further enquiry that an air bomb in Iraq was, more or less, the equivalent of a police truncheon at home'.[28] And it is precisely this concept of 'air police' that tends to be sidelined in the main work on air power and strategic bombing, which treats it as either a footnote to domestic police politics or as a prelude to the major air battles of 1939 to 1945. In fact, as we shall see, air police was a universal feature of colonial domination.[29]

The real extent to which air power has from its inception been structured around the police concept can be seen in its regurgitation of the terms of classical police doctrine: 'preventive police', 'security', 'civilisation' and 'order'. Far from being 'purely a war of destruction', as Carl Schmitt puts it,[30] air power has been central to the *construction* of order. The concept that had been at the heart of the fabrication of bourgeois order – police – came to be centrally employed in the colonial context and achieved through air power. We might flesh this out by pointing to several dimensions of air power as police power in the colonial context.

The first, most obvious, is that the central practice involved, bombing, was explicitly meant to crush any rebellion against colonial rule and cut off the possibility of resistance. There is little reason to say much about this. Not only is it a fairly obvious feature of air power, it also relies heavily on a concept of police as purely 'reactive' to disorder when in fact the argument here seeks to work with a police concept that sees police power as creative and productive.

The second dimension concerns the use of air power to deny tribesmen subsistence outside the political economy being imposed within the colonial order. A report from Air Vice-Marshal Sir John Salmond, following a 1922 mission to India to spread the gospel of air control following its application to Iraq, noted that:

> the real weight of air action lies in the daily interruption of normal life which it can inflict … It can knock the roofs of huts about and prevent their repair, a considerable inconvenience in winter time. It can seriously interfere with ploughing or harvesting – a vital matter; or burn up the stores of fuel laboriously piled up and garnered for the winter; by attack on livestock, which is the main form of capital and source of wealth to the less settled tribes, it can impose in effect a considerable fine, or seriously interfere with the actual food source of the tribe – and in the end the tribesman finds it is much the best to obey.[31]

Salmond's view paralleled the instructions of a'Confidential Document 22', a Royal Air Force manual titled'Operations'(dated 1922 and known as'CD 22'):'the force in the field must first be attacked and destroyed. This should then be followed up by continuous bombing of his capital and subsequently the surrounding villages, crops and live stock'. The manual went on to refer to factories and railway junctions as legitimate targets.[32] This idea found its way into official doctrine and semi-official professional journals such as *Royal Air Force Quarterly*:

> air operations are not planned to spread death and suffering, but to wear down the tribesman's morale [and] dislocate his normal life … If desirable, small practice bombs are first dropped to give a final opportunity of escape to safety. Bombing is then regulated according to requirements to keep the villages empty and the tribesmen from attending to their crops, cattle and daily wants … The tribesman, driven from his village which contains all his needs, finds the burden of his existence increasing daily; he is deprived of his normal shelter; stripped of his usual amenities; and interrupted in his sleep; his flocks are scattered … Shelters or stores of grain and fuel may be bombed; crops may be destroyed.[33]

In dispersing or killing flocks, preventing tribesmen from entering their fields, obstructing them from ploughing when in the fields, interrupting harvesting during the most important periods, and denying access to springs and rivers for water, air power was used specifically to destroy modes of subsistence that might have enabled indigenous peoples to survive outside the new regime of accumulation being imposed on them. This is strategic bombing as systematic colonisation: air power as primitive accumulation.

Third, as part of the process of primitive accumulation'air control' also figured as a form of tax collection, with bombing used in order to ensure that tribes either paid their taxes or as punishment for failing to do so.[34] Sir Percival Phillips, writing in the *Daily Mail* in 1922, claimed that'whatever the government may say to the contrary, rule by bomb in Mesopotamia has as one of its underlying motives the collection of taxes from turbulent Arabs'.[35] The broader picture here requires a reminder of the centrality of taxation as a technique of state power and a mechanism for proletarianisation and commercialisation. One of the key figures in the British colonisation of Africa, Sir Harry Johnston, laid down the principles of colonial taxation in 1896:

> Given abundance of cheap native labour, the financial security of the Protectorate is established ... All that needs to be done is for the Administration to act as friends of both sides, and to introduce the Native labourer to the European capitalist. A gentle insistence that the Native should contribute his fair share to the revenue of the country by paying his tax is all that is necessary on our part to ensure his taking a share in life's labour which no human being should avoid.[36]

Hence the first thing that many colonising states did was to impose heavy taxes. In part this was said to be used to cover the costs of the 'civilising process' involved in building railways, roads and bridges, but the tax was also meant to teach indigenous peoples the value of work, since the easiest way to pay it was either to find or grow some kind of cash crop to sell, to work for wages or to send one's children to work for wages. This view that wage-labour could be produced via a new tax regime, which would in turn also help monetise the economy – the French called it the *impôt moralisateur* (the 'moralising tax') – came to permeate the colonial mind.[37]

Reflecting on a long career in colonial administration, Sir Frederick Lugard claimed that taxation, paid in cash, was 'a means of promoting the recognition of individual labour and responsibility' which is otherwise destroyed by the system of forced labour and slavery. The creation of free wage-labour through the abolition of slavery and the 'emancipation of the peasantry' also 'marks the recognition of the principle that each individual in proportion to his means has an obligation to the State, to which he owes security for life and property, and his increased wealth – due to fair wages for his labour'. It likewise has an 'educative' effect with 'the habits of work it inculcates', 'curbing lawlessness ... and stimulating industry'. Being paid in cash meant the circulation of currency and thus the monetisation of the economy.[38] It also taught the colonised an important lesson about the power of this new colonial state which now governed them. In other words, if 'the fiscal policy of the colonial state ... violated the moral economy of the subsistence ethic',[39] it did so through the taxation process and the implications of this process: the need to work for wages and the destruction of a long-standing moral economy of rights to various means of subsistence. As Sir Percy Girouard put it in 1913, speaking of his own long experience in exercising colonial power:

> We consider that the only natural and automatic method of securing a constant labour supply is to ensure that there will be competition among labourers for hire and not among employers for labourers; such competition can be brought about only by a rise in the cost of living for the native, and this can be produced only by an increase in the tax.[40]

The introduction of such tax regimes (which had to be a direct tax, such as hut tax, poll tax, head tax, wife tax or land tax, in order to better force the people to work as wage-labourers, to grow cash crops and thereby to extend commercialisation) is one of the secrets of primitive accumulation,[41] constituting indigenous peoples as productive wage-labourers and active economic subjects in a monetised economy. Taxation is thus a classic police operation – tax collection itself was usually a police duty in the colonies[42] – and air power was central to this process.

Refusal to pay taxes was therefore one of the most common forms of resistance, and understood by the colonial state as rebellion. And as rebellion, it was seen as a form of warfare. Tribes were thus bombed for their refusal to pay taxes or even for refusing to have crops inspected for revenue purposes. In turn, however, the collection of taxes was often presented as part of a wider attempt to crush rebellion and lawlessness and thus win the war, even in areas that were largely pacified. For example, 'in the autumn of 1923, the authorities attempted to collect taxes in the Samawa qadha for the first time for many years', writes Peter Sluglett. 'There was no suggestion that there had been any serious unruliness or disorder in the area', and the people living there were, according to official reports, 'exceptionally poor'. Yet a recommendation came through that 'punitive action' should be taken for non-payment of taxes.[43] A letter from the Ministry of Interior to the local administrators stressed that they should be 'careful not to impose collection of revenue as the main condition since if it is found necessary to bomb them it must be for the defiance of Government orders and not to increase the exchequer'.[44] When this bombing operation had finished, one local administrator, J. B. Glubb, wrote to Air Headquarters that 'it is regrettable but it appears almost inevitable that aerial action should be associated with the payment of taxes'.[45] Such punitive air strikes were often carried out only after air power had been used to convince the colonial subjects to pay their taxes by dropping propaganda leaflets from the air, or further leaflets warning them to flee their villages in advance of a bombing attack.

A fourth dimension is air power's use as a means of surveillance. What one writer in the *Naval Review* called air power's 'ocular demonstration of power'[46] worked both ways, in that the aircraft were meant to see as well as be seen. Lord Thompson, air secretary in 1924, spoke of the bomber's 'all-seeing power', and other reports spoke in the same terms: 'from the ground every inhabitant of a village is under the impression that the occupant of an aeroplane is actually looking at *him* ... establishing the impression that all their movements are being watched and reported'.[47] From the very birth of air power it was clear that the aircraft could and would be a crucial instrument of surveillance, allowing a vantage point while simultaneously denying that position to others.[48]

As a consequence, and thus fifth, 'a dominant use for the aeroplane has been a mode of knowledge capture'.[49] As we saw in the previous chapter, Article 22 of the Covenant of the League of Nations held that the 'sacred trust of civilisation' required 'the well-being and development' of the colonised under the 'tutelage' of the civilised nations. This meant an intensification of the political administration of the colonies and air power was central to this process, being used to develop censuses, land surveys and for general information-gathering. In the case of the UK, for example, an Air Survey Committee was established in 1920 to help realise the potential of air power for new practices of surveying and surveillance, as photography and data-gathering from the air helped finesse the cartographic and knowledge enterprise, and an entire discipline of aerial photography was invented.[50] On the one hand, this concerned accumulation: aerial surveys could overcome 'the most serious obstacles which had hitherto delayed the development of many of the natural resources of the Dominions and Colonies'.[51] One lecture to the Royal Society of Arts in 1928 noted air power's central importance in 'bringing into production those tracts of land which now lay idle' and the ensuing discussion centred on the role of air photography in the 'economic development' of the colonies.[52] On the other hand, this was also pure counter-insurgency, as aerial surveys showed the houses, the streets and the alleys of villages and towns, thereby enabling them to be better managed and policed.[53] The French replicated these practices in Morocco and Syria.[54] If the state is a knowledge-machine and the war of accumulation dependent on the knowledge in question, then air power was crucial to both.

In carrying out these functions air power was intended to transform the political subjectivity of the colonised. A sixth point, then, is that air power was a mechanism for bringing about 'a change of heart' in the colonial subject, as it was put by Air Commodore C. F. A. Portal in a lecture on 'policing the empire'. He went on: 'the object of all coercive police action is to bring about a change in the temper or intention of the person or body of persons who are disturbing the peace'.[55] Thus air power was to have an impact on the political conduct of the colonised, consolidating their acquiescence to the new order. One report on forest management from 1926 claimed that identifying by air which tracts of land would be suitable for clearance and restoration would 'go far to leaving the land in the most productive condition to which it can be brought' and so encourage the indigenous people to 'gradually learn more settled habits'.[56]

Central to the promotion of air power was its definition as an explicitly moral instrument of control, and it was often argued by air power theorists that air policing achieved its results *not* by inflicting heavy casualties, but through the 'moral effect' it could have on the population, and planes sometimes made attacks solely in order to have such an effect.[57] The idea of the 'moral' effect slipped into the more military-sounding concept of 'morale', which was then becoming a popular term (and which resonates for us now in its updated version, 'shock and awe'). That the meaning of such nebulous notions shifts according to what is seen as operationally possible or politically expedient is one thing, as Omissi notes, but we might also note that 'moral effect', and thus 'morale' and 'shock and awe', almost always returns to the disruption of human life caused by bombing.[58] One Air Staff Memorandum from 1922 argued that 'air action must rely for its effect less on material damage than on the effect on the tribal morale of constant liability to attack and the consequent continuing dislocation of daily life'.[59]

This idea points us back to the conjunction of violence and moral force characteristic of police power as a civilising process. Part of this lay purely in air power as a *way of communicating*.[60] This communicative bombing contains a logic of domination, with the subordinate and foreign Other being made to recognise their subordination to the technical, military and political superiority of the force behind the bombing, such that 'the vast technocapital of air power had power far beyond physical destruction; its mere appearance was a form of power'.[61] Moreover, its mere appearance as a form of *civilised* power was itself to have a *civilising effect*: air power was 'intended to keep order and gradually to reconcile hostile tribes to a civilized rule', noted one Cabinet memo in 1921;[62] 'air is the greatest civilising influence these countries have ever known', commented Trenchard in 1925; the aim and object of air policing 'is not the destruction of tribes but should be a policy of civilization', commented the Acting Governor General of Baluchistan in 1930. Air power was thus an important moment in the civilising offensive. Unsurprisingly, this offensive adopted the classic police concept: prevention.[63] 'Air methods are, in short, the reverse of the old punitive column', claims Trenchard: 'our policy is one of prevention'.[64] Such prevention works only when the subjects have accepted the 'peace' imposed upon them and become 'civilised' – that is, show a general acceptance of the order being created. To bomb is to exercise one's civilisation; to be bombed is to experience civilisation.

Seventh: colonial air power was a means of working around as well as through law, especially international law and the ethical principles which supposedly underpin it. This was a period when most liberal states were falling over each other in the rush to declare that the bombing of civilians was the mark of an uncivilised, savage enemy and should thus be illegal. As late as 1938 the British Prime Minister Neville Chamberlain was insisting that 'it is against international law to bomb civilians as such and to make deliberate attacks upon civilian populations', and the US Senate passed a resolution condemning 'the inhuman bombing of civilian populations'; a year later President Roosevelt described the same act as 'inhuman barbarism'.[65] This was consistent with a tradition within international law which had held that 'the unarmed citizen is to be spared in person, property, and honor', a claim from Article 22 of the US Lieber Code of 1863 which found its way either as an exact phrase or as a similar phrase into the Geneva Convention of 1864, the Brussels Conference of 1874, and various pieces of domestic legislation in Europe and Russia. Bombing cities was something that barbarian nations might do and which warmongering fascist dictatorships did do – it was generally felt 'that bombing cities had a special place in the heart of fascists' and the bombing of Guernica crystallised many of the fears connected with the aerial attack on undefended civilians[66] – but was in theory not something civilised and peace-seeking democracies would or should do. Yet what of the bombing in the colonies? Surely it was clear that 'civilised' nations were bombing civilians? 'What are the laws in this kind of cricket?' asked Chief Commissioner of the Frontier Province, Sir John Maffrey, in 1923, concerning police bombing in India.[67] The answer: none.

'The rules of International Law apply only to warfare between civilised nations … They do not apply in wars with uncivilised States and tribes', noted the *British Manual of Military Law*.[68] The fact that colonial peoples lacked legal personality in international law meant that such wars were often not treated as 'wars' at all, as we have noted, and this fact was reflected in international law. Thus, the War of the Riff, for example, one of the most significant 'revolts' against a colonial power during the period in question, 'was beyond the purview of mainstream international law in 1925', notes Nathaniel Berman. 'No major French, American, or British international law journal published an article about this war'.[69] Indeed, when consulted by the French Human Rights League about this 'conflict', leading international lawyer Georges Scelle claimed that 'legally, one cannot even say that there is a war'.[70] The point here is that this position was reinforced by framing such 'operations' as exercises of the police power, and air power was situated within this frame. At the Peace Conference held at The Hague in 1923 and designed to create a 62-article 'Rules for Aerial Warfare' prohibiting aerial bombardment of civilians, the agreement was that this applied between civilised nations but made no difference to the use of bombing *as a technology of police power*. At a later conference in Geneva in 1933, the leading powers sought once more to establish that the bombing of civilians be outlawed, yet the British delegation still felt comfortable proposing that while bombing in general should indeed be outlawed, the exception should be bombing 'for police purposes in certain outlying regions'.[71] As Colonel Phillip Meilinger of the US Naval War College has put it, Britain was 'in the awkward position of advocating a prohibition on the bombing of her enemies, but not on her own subjects'.[72] Bombing civilians was from a *police* perspective entirely acceptable.

All of which explains why, when Syria protested against the French bombing of the country in 1925, the *American Journal of International Law* noted that 'France … looks upon the activity of her forces as police measures outside of international law'.[73] It also explains why, in the war against Nicaraguan resistance fighters led by Augusto Sandino, the rules of war were said not to apply since the US was fighting 'bandits'.[74] But note that it also goes some way to explaining why, during the same period, the state was willing to use air power as police power domestically too, during intense periods of the class war and the race war: for police purposes, air power could be used against striking workers and rebellious blacks, as well as refractory colonial subjects.[75]

Taken together, these dimensions point to something fundamental about air power: its use not to attack enemy states or to defend the state from enemy attacks but, rather, to the creation of a new geopolitical system being developed between the wars. It suggests that to understand properly the geopolitical role of air power, we need to grasp it conceptually as police power and central to the process of primitive accumulation and systematic colonisation. Air power, as police power, was at the heart of the fabrication of social order.

In this context it is telling that this set of processes was understood, together, as part of the logic of security and fundamental to pacification. In *The Reformation of War* (1923), one of the most significant works of strategic thinking in Britain, leading military theorist J. F. C. Fuller discusses air power as essential not just for the police of Iraq, but 'for the major police work of the Empire', pointing to the problem of 'internal security' and the maintenance of 'law and order' in the Empire and flirting with the idea of the 'police-soldier' and the 'police-army'.[76] He hesitates about these things because he wants to hold on to a very traditional conception of war, but then concedes that these are achievable if the air force is used 'as every police force should be used, namely, to pacify, and not to obliterate'.[77] The distinction is important: 'the British Empire has not been built upon obliteration but upon pacification'.[78] Pacification here is once again understood as a building process: the fabrication of new order, not the destruction of old. His point is that if the logic of police is to pacify, then aerial power falls within this remit, and the idea was not specific to Fuller. In a long debate over the efficiency and economy of air power which took place in the House of Lords in April 1930, Viscount Plumer commented that most parts of the Empire 'have been and are being consolidated and pacified by a constant daily association and contact with the air force'. Lord Lloyd spoke in the same debate about the need to 'civilise and pacify' the people in the Empire, reiterating what we know from previous chapters: civilisation demands pacification.[79] In a lecture to the RAF Staff College in 1936, Wing Commander Robert Saundby, an officer who served in Iraq in the 1920s and then later as a pilot in Bomber Command during WWII, emphasised that the purpose of air control was 'to support the political authorities in their tasks of pacification or administration'.[80] He reiterated the point later as Air Chief Marshal and knight of the realm in a book on the history of air power: 'During the ten years of control in Iraq ... a standard of internal and external security, higher than the country had known for centuries', was maintained by what he calls 'genuine pacification',[81] and Air Commodore L. E. O. Charlton talked about air power as the 'pacification of truculent tribesmen'.[82] As police power – and thus a key technology of security – air power became central to the whole process of pacification as order-construction.[83]

What I am suggesting, then, is that a form of technology which has been understood too readily and too easily in 'military' terms is better understood through the lens of police power. This is not 'war-becoming-police' and neither is it the idea that war is being *reduced* to police. Neither is it a 'small wars' affair. My argument is that understood in terms of the fabrication of order this particular technology has always needed to be understood through a war–police nexus. Let me have a stab at strengthening this argument by briefly using it to try to make sense of perhaps the fundamental issue in contemporary air power: drones; and conversely, to use the contemporary development of drone technology to help restate my argument.

VICTORY THROUGH AIR POWER I: THE DRONE

As is well known, the air power used in the 'war on terror' has increasingly incorporated and operated drone technology. The US Department of Defense's Unmanned Aerial Vehicle (UAV) inventory increased more than 40-fold between 2002 and 2010, from 167 to 7,000.[84] Between 2001 and 2008 the hours of surveillance coverage for US Central Command encompassing Iraq, Afghanistan, Pakistan and Yemen rose by 1,431 per cent as a result of the developing drone technology; in 2010 the US Air Force projected that the combined flight hours of all its drones would exceed 250,000 hours, exceeding in one year the total number of hours from 1995 to 2007,[85] while in the UK the Reaper UAV reached a landmark figure of 20,000 flying hours in 2011.[86] At the same time, news about drones is now constant, as more and more states operate them.

This technology has had a significant impact on thinking about war in a number of ways, which I separate here for purely analytical purposes.

First, the unmanned nature of drones means that they are regarded as a new step in the technology of military 'distancing'. What has been described as the 'impersonalisation' of war[87] seems to be perfected with the drone, the ultimate 'action-at-a-distance' weapon.[88] Second, this impersonal and remote decision-making means that the drone appears to have brought about a certain 'risk-transfer' in warfare and thus transformed the idea of war as involving some kind of reciprocal risk. With the drone it would appear that the superior technology means that only one side is likely to suffer large numbers of casualties. Third, drones occupy a key place in debates about the new virtuous war. The long history of assuming that air war is by its very nature virtuous and that bombing is a way of making it easier for war to be just, has come to the fore again in the exercise of unmanned technology: 'at the heart of virtuous war is the technical capability and ethical imperative to threaten and, if necessary, actualise violence from a distance ... *with no or minimal casualties*'.[89] Drones, in this view, are a more ethical form of killing by virtue of their technological sophistication;[90] that their power is being fully realised in what for liberals is one of the most virtuous wars ever should not surprise. Fourth, the sophisticated technology of the drone allows for targeted killings, what amount to assassinations, in a manner completely distinct from the 'classical' age of war. Fifth, the drone has facilitated the killing of large numbers of non-combatants and civilians. Sixth, the drone has been described as especially useful given the nature of modern war, especially the war on terror, as involving a fight against clandestine insurgent groups.

What might we make of such claims? One thing to note is that barring a few minor changes in vocabulary and subtlety, these same points were all made about air power in the 1920s. The use of air power in the colonies in the 1920s was described as making it easier for the colonising powers to be just; was understood as allowing a new form of military 'distancing'; shattered the idea of war as involving some kind of reciprocal risk; involved targeted killings; saw the killing of large numbers of non-combatants and civilians; and, finally, was said to be necessary because of the nature of the fight against clandestine insurgent groups. Looked at in terms of the way air power was used between the wars, drone warfare looks rather like colonial warfare of the 1920s.

One implication of this is that seen in the longer historical perspective of air power, the drone is not as new or as revolutionary as many would like to claim. But might this not imply something else: that drone warfare might be better understood as a continuation of air power as police power?

Pursuing this possible implication takes us to one further point about drones: that they now control the skies not just in the lands of Afghanistan, Iraq and Pakistan but the whole planet, and not just in 'war zones' but in 'civilian areas'. The 50 or so sovereign powers that now operate drones do so domestically as much as they do for 'international' purposes. Thus one finds that they now fly over cities engaged in a whole plethora of policing operations, from managing emergencies, spying on foreign drug cartels, fighting crime, conducting border control operations and general surveillance. In one case in the US drones were used to look for missing cows.[91] In the US, following a 2003 decision by the Federal Aviation Authority to grant license to UAVs to fly over American civilian airspace, more and more American states now work with drones. A Congressional Research Service Report noted in 2010 that 'recent UAV modification is part of an ongoing push by some policymakers and CBP [Customs and Border Protection] to both expand CBP's UAV resources and open domestic airspace for UAV operations',[92] and the use of drones by CBP is part of the wider attempt at integrating drones into national airspace as part of the project of 'homeland security'. Thus in February 2012 President Obama signed off a Bill that requires the Federal Aviation Administration to develop the full integration of drones into US airspace by 2015.[93] In the UK a number of police forces have trialled the use of drones, over 120 companies have been given 'blanket permission' to fly small drones within the UK for surveillance purposes, and the UK ASTRAEA programme aims to 'enable the routine use of UAS (Unmanned Aircraft Systems) in all classes of airspace without the need for restrictive or specialised conditions of operation'.[94]

One of the fastest increases in applications to fly drones has come from universities.[95]

Hence the major criticism: this is air power technology designed for war but being used in civilian spaces for police purposes, and so it is yet another step in the 'militarisation of policing' and 'policization of the military'. My argument, however, is that air power has *always been police power*. We therefore need to read the drone not as a new form of military technology that is somehow being allowed to sneak into civilian spaces for police purposes but, rather, as a continuation of the police logic inherent in air power since its inception. The fact that the drone has come of age in the 'war on terror' reinforces this fact, given that, as I have already suggested, the war in question is a police action par excellence.

Drones need to be understood first and foremost as a technology of police power. Despite the publicity surrounding them, the vast majority of drones are *not* sophisticated bombing or killing machines but are in fact small and unarmed models used primarily for surveillance – hence one of their key developing features is that they are disposable, highlighted by the smaller and smaller UAVs, dropped from aircraft, carried in a backpack and fired into the air by hand, catapult or slingshot.[96] Their main function is not to bomb or assassinate but to gather and construct knowledge. This explains the surveillance-oriented names for almost all the different drones – Global Hawk, Dragon Eye, Desert Hawk, Gorgon Stare, Watchkeeper – and also goes some way to explaining why they are spoken of by the state less as killing machines and more in terms of a range of other abilities, such as recognising and categorising humans and human-made objects, identifying movements, interpreting footprints, and distinguishing different kinds of tracks on the earth's surface. It is also the reason why most drone 'strikes', in which weapons are used, are nonetheless described as 'police actions'.

There is, however, an even more significant point to be made about this question of a supposedly 'military' technology seeping into 'civilian' space. We need to understand that from the wider historical perspective of air power there are no civilian areas and there are no civilians; which is one way of saying that from the wider historical perspective of air power the only logic is police logic. As soon as air power was created one central issue was: what does this do to civilian space? The answer, essentially, was: it destroys it. And in destroying civilian space, it simultaneously destroys the concept of the civilian. Let me make this point through a more historical lens before returning to the question of drones.

The idea that with air power the civilian is threatened was one of the most significant themes of the air power literature of the 1920s. This came wrapped up in a debate about the impact of war in the city. The image of what one air power strategist called the coming 'City of the Dead'[97] can be found in more or less every major text on air power published between the wars. (The more recent work on 'place annihilation', 'urbicide', 'planned destruction of the city', 'dead cities', 'cities under siege' all really need to be traced back to this first body of work on air power.[98]) In *The Command of the Air* by Giulio Douhet, first published in 1921, expanded in 1927, and widely regarded as the foundational text on air power, the art of aerial warfare is the art of destroying cities, of attacking civilians and of terrorising the population. The invention of air power means that 'war is no longer a clash between armies, but is a clash between nations, between whole populations'. War will therefore 'be waged essentially against the unarmed populations of the cities and great industrial centres'.[99] Although debate still rumbles about the precise extent of Douhet's influence,[100] air doctrine in general 'followed Douhet not merely in its broad emphasis on strategic bombing, but also through most of the finer ramifications of his philosophy',[101] and most notably in terms of the targeting of cities. A few examples will suffice.

In 1923 J. F. C. Fuller, who shared with Douhet a penchant for fascist authority – a fact which is not without some interesting implications but which I can only note in passing here[102] – 'peeped beneath the veil of future war' and envisaged 'great cities, such as London ... attacked from the air'. 'Picture, if you can, what the result will be: London for several days will be one vast raving Bedlam, the hospitals will be stormed, traffic will cease, the homeless will shriek for help, the city will be in pandemonium'.[103] In similar fashion, J. M. Spaight, a senior official in Britain's Air Ministry, one of the country's most influential international lawyers and a leading air power theorist, commented in his *Air Power and War Rights* (1924) that because air power can 'strike straight at the heart of the enemy state', it is 'unlikely in the extreme that belligerents will be satisfied with a right to bombard for purely military purposes only'. Rather:

The object of their attack will be moral, psychological, and political rather than military; the aim will be so to disorganise and disturb the life and business of the enemy community as to make it impossible for the enemy State to continue to resist, and at the same time to create in the enemy population as a whole a feeling of depression and hopelessness.[104]

Writing as an international lawyer sensitive to the arguments against bombing of unprotected civilians that had been building since the end of WWI, Spaight was nonetheless adamant: 'let there be no mistake about it – the cities will be bombed, whatever rule is laid down'.[105]

In *Paris: or the Future of War* (1925) Liddell Hart reiterates the theme. Crushing a population's morale by 'dislocating their normal life' would be the means to a decisive victory, which would come from destroying a nation's 'nerve-system'. The city is the Achilles heel of the state (hence the title of his book: the future of war lies in finding the enemy's weakest point, just as Paris found the heel of Achilles). 'Imagine for a moment London, Manchester, Birmingham, and half a dozen other great centres simultaneously attacked, the business localities and Fleet Street wrecked, Whitehall a heap of ruins, the slum districts maddened into the impulse to break loose and maraud, the railways cut, factories destroyed'.[106] Likewise, in a series of essays published in the *Saturday Evening Post* between December 1924 and March 1925, Billy Mitchell sought to challenge what he saw as the prevailing consensus among US political and military elites: that the US was not the kind of society that would intentionally bomb civilians. Eventually published in extended form as *Winged Defense*, and selling close to 5,000 copies in the first year of publication, Mitchell makes the same point: 'Air forces will attack centers of production of all kinds, means of transportation, agricultural areas, ports and shipping'.[107]

Even the idea of precision bombing, cultivated by the US in the 1930s, made the same point about the attack on cities and killing of civilians: first, because 'precision bombing' was never far from the bombing of 'targets of opportunity', and targets of opportunity were so numerous that it was hard to distinguish 'precision' from 'area bombing'; second, because the problem with 'precision targets' is that 'they are hard to hit', as one US Commander noted in 1943;[108] and third, because any 'precision bomb' that missed its intended target could still be described as successfully waging war on enemy morale. 'Precision bombing' thereby continued the same line pursued by the air power theorists, in that it assumed that factories, refineries, shipyards, dockyards and other installations where the machinery of war was produced were legitimate targets and thus so too were the workers within them.[109]

Thus by the end of WWII it was clear that 'modern war [had] become war to the death against cities'.[110] Now, it would appear that a war to the death against cities meant that killing civilians was a military necessity. The point of this body of work was to recognise and justify 'the cruel necessity of killing not only non-combatants but people innocent of any complicity', as Salmond put it in 1924.[111] And so one common interpretation is that air power increased the risk that civilians would be killed. 'Because no person or space or institution or form of labor was finally dissociable from a nation's war effort, entire cities and all citizens [were] considered legitimate targets for indiscriminate aerial bombings', notes Paul Saint-Amour. Or as Stephen Budiansky puts it, 'the classic air-power theorists had never quailed at the notion of killing citizens'.[112] These are important observations, yet there is a sense in which they miss the real point, which is that the inhabitants of the city are, in effect, *no longer* 'citizens' or 'civilians' or 'non-combatants'. To put that another way: the major implication of the invention of air power was not that civilians and non-combatants might be targeted and might suffer in larger numbers than ever before. Rather, the implication was that the distinction between combatant and non-combatant, between soldier and civilian, disappeared. The language used in the air power literature, from 'strategic bombing' to 'morale bombing', from attacking 'vital centres' to bombarding 'economic infrastructures', from smashing 'commercial hubs' to destroying 'communications networks', points to the simple fact that the inhabitants of the networks and infrastructures, the hubs and centres, the industrial fabric and commercial activities, are *all part of the war machine* and are therefore *no longer civilians.* 'There will be no distinction any longer between soldiers and civilians', Douhet states. 'The civilian and the fighting man are now merged in one', Charlton adds.[113]

The major powers fought against accepting this for some time. Or at least, fought against accepting this for their classic doctrine of war as a battle between militarily industrialised nation-states – there was little in the way of either moral or legal restriction on bombing civilians in colonial territories, as we have seen. But eventually, in the course of

WWII, they conceded the point. By July 1945 an official US intelligence review of strategic air power could openly state that 'the entire population of Japan is a proper Military Target', adding, in capitalised letters for effect, that 'THERE ARE NO CIVILIANS IN JAPAN'.[114] This view has been maintained ever since: 'There are no innocent civilians', says US General Curtis LeMay.[115] Recent air power literature confirms this, which is why so much of it still keeps insisting that 'Douhet was right', that 'the prophecies of Giulio Douhet and other air power visionaries appear realized', and that we could do worse than share a 'cognac with Douhet'.[116] Thus Colonel John Warden III, perhaps the leading US air power strategist in the last 25 years, confirms the idea that because 'the enemy functions as a system' air power must be used to 'neutralize' urban centres and smash industrial production.[117]

To reiterate: with air power there is no clear categorical boundary between combatants and non-combatants. Killing workers in the factories is a necessity and killing unarmed men, women, children, the sick and the elderly is acceptable, because in one way or another everyone was and is a combatant.[118] (It is this expansion of the concept of the fighting body that helps explain how air power could bring a new word into the English language: 'overkill'.) And here we should make a point that will not be a surprise given the argument in Chapters 1 and 2: international law did nothing to stop this happening.[119]

I am arguing, then, that contra claims made at both ends of the political spectrum that recent air attacks reveal 'the increasing meaninglessness of the word "civilian"' (Alan Dershowitz) or that they mean we might be 'witnessing … the death of the idea of the civilian' (Derek Gregory),[120] it has to be said that any meaningful concept of 'the civilian' was *destroyed with the very invention of air power*. To put that another way, the distinction between combatant and non-combatant that 'has been recognized as the fundamental principle on which the entire notion of "humanity in warfare" rests'[121] became meaningless once air power was created.[122]

Let me push this point about the death of the civilian even further, in light of the fact that those in power still insist on telling us how much they wish to minimise the killing of 'non-combatants' and that the whole discourse of the 'war on terror' includes extensive discussion of 'civilian deaths'. For what the realisation of air power in the 'war on terror' actually reveals is that the status of 'civilian' is in fact now only possible on death. After one air attack in Afghanistan in February 2002, in which three men scavenging for scrap metal were killed but none of whom it later transpired had links to Al Qaeda or even any interest in Islamic politics, the Pentagon's statement was: 'we're convinced that it was an appropriate target … [although] we do not yet know exactly who it was'.[123] The only logic that can underpin the idea that even though the state does not know who a person is they are still an appropriate target is one which presupposes that there are no innocent civilians. And with every human being an appropriate target while alive, one might be formally acknowledged as 'civilian' only by being killed. As Joseph Pugliese points out, the only way for human beings to reclaim the status of 'civilians' is *retrospectively*.[124] One is only a non-combatant – that is, one is only categorised as not a threat to the war power – when one is dead; this is the historical shift that gives real meaning to the phrase 'death of the civilian'. What all of this means is that the argument about the use of drone technology over what some would still like to call 'civilian spaces' is redundant. Not only are there no 'civilian spaces', but the implication of the argument just made is that the only real 'civilian space' will be, in effect, the City of the Dead.

Paul Virilio has argued that 'to say that the City and War go hand in glove is a euphemism', and goes on to suggest that 'the city, the polis, is constitutive of the form of conflict called WAR, just as war is itself constitutive of the political form called the CITY'.[125] Air power would seem to exemplify his point. Drone technology is thus nothing less than the realisation of the City – and, in effect, *everywhere* – as a permanent war zone; this is the 'everywhere war', as Derek Gregory calls it.[126] Yet if we are to follow through on the argument concerning air power as *police* power then we must also take on board Foucault's comment that the City has always been the 'space' of police.[127] On this basis we witness the opening up of the real potential of drone technology: ubiquitous and permanent police power exercised over the territory. 'Unmanned aircraft have just revolutionized our ability to provide a constant stare against our enemy', said a senior US military official. 'Using the all-seeing eye, you will find out who is important in a network, where they live, where they get their support from, where their friends are'.[128] The UK Ministry of Defence calls the drone 'a persistent intelligence-gathering capability',[129] and the US military now likes to think of air power in terms of 'predictive battlespace awareness'. Much as this might be important geopolitically, with drones being capable of maintaining non-stop surveillance of vast swathes of land and sea for so long as the technology and fuel supplies allow, it is also nothing less than the state's dream of a perpetual police presence across its own territory.[130] Like air power technology in general, the drone serves as *both plane and possibility*,[131] and what becomes possible with the drone is precisely this absolute and perpetual presence. Hence the language with which drones are defended is the same language long used in defending police power: 'it gives us a good opportunity to have an eye up there … a surveilling eye to help us do the things we need to do, honestly, to keep people safe'.[132] This is nothing less than a permanent police presence for the reproduction of order – air power as the *everywhere police* – in which the exercise of violence is an ever-present possibility.

Drones have been described as the perfect technology of democratic warfare, combining as they do a certain utilitarian character with an appealing 'risk-transfer'.[133] On this view, drones constitute a perfect technology of liberal war. But we should be thinking of them equally as the perfect technology of liberal police: on the one hand, we have *power projection* – 'the ability to project power from the air and space to influence the behaviour of people or the course of events' – as *police projection*.[134] On the other hand, we have 'air occupation',[135] in the form of a permanent police presence in the skies. One might want to say that the City has become a war zone subject to absolute police power. But then one might also want to say that the City has become a police zone subject to absolute war power. One would be making the same point either way.

When in 1943 Disney sought to popularise the idea of 'victory through air power' the company probably had little idea just quite what this victory might mean beyond the defeat of Japan. But if there is a victory through air power to be had on the part of the state it is the victory of perpetual police, a conquering power anywhere and everywhere, tied to the dream of purging the world of anything disorderly. To complete this victory, the war power would need to invent its major companion: the 'no-fly zone'.

Chapter 6

AIR POWER AS POLICE POWER II

=====

'Postwar' means Nothing.
What fools called 'peace' simply meant moving away from the front.
Fools defended peace by supporting the armed wing of money.

Wu Ming, 54 (2002)

What is a no-fly zone? Formally, a no-fly zone is a prohibition on flying in order to call a halt to hostilities in the region, usually enacted in aid of a group or groups which might otherwise suffer violence. When the Libyan civil war broke out in early 2011 one of the first demands made by several political actors of varying political persuasions was for a no-fly zone. The debate surrounding this continued until the passing of the United Nations Security Council Resolution 1973, on 17 March 2011, imposing a no-fly zone over the country. This was one in a growing line of no-fly zones imposed for 'humanitarian reasons' by the 'international community'. The 'humanitarian reasons' are important, since although within the Security Council the case was made by major military states such as the US, UK and France, the decision had wider support from those progressives and radicals who have insisted on an international 'responsibility to protect' or to intervene in support of democratic resistance movements. In having a 'military' and a 'humanitarian' rationale, the no-fly zone appears to be a form of geopolitical action with widespread appeal. This was the case in Libya, has been the case in the debate about a no-fly zone in Syria in 2013, and was true of previous no-fly zones such as have been imposed over Iraq (in 1991, expanded in 1996 and lasting until the US-led invasion of the country in 2003) and Bosnia (in 1992–5).

Yet is 'military intervention', 'humanitarianism' or even, for that matter, 'military humanism',[1] the best way of thinking about the no-fly zone? In this chapter I take a long circuitous route through the conjunction of war, law and space in order to situate the no-fly zone within the wider frame of air power as police power.

The conjunction of war, law and space has been central to some important developments in critical and political geography since the end of the Cold War and during the 'war on terror', some of which we have already encountered in the previous chapter. One group of political geographers has pointed to the 'imaginative geographies' that have been employed during the war on terror,[2] and military geography has explored the way military operations rework space and 'surround us, are always with us'.[3] But there is something odd about much of this work, in that it rarely considers the space of air space. There is little in the 'geopolitical imagi-nation of the state'[4] about what we might call the 'imagi-nation' of air space, and in the recent articulation of the idea of 'imaginative geographies' there is little imagining of the geography of air power aside from a brief comment on the verticality of maps showing bombing campaigns. 'Military geography' likewise offers fleeting references to spy planes and satellites, but the analysis remains firmly on the ground: the 'castles and bastles, forts and ports, depots and silos'[5] which occupy the material and cultural landscape get plenty of attention, but the space of the sky gets very little. This same absence affects otherwise insightful analyses in which war, law and space come together, from the concrete analyses of 'mastering space' combining international political economy with critical geography, to the abstractions of 'nomospheric investigations'.[6] There is also an absence of any analysis of the 'other space' of air in the creative thinking about questions of space and power in work by Foucault and inspired by Foucault.[7]

In other words, the 'territorial trap'[8] of thinking about space two-dimensionally would seem to be one into which many are still falling.[9] Moreover, when the space of air has been considered, for example in the now considerable number of texts on borders, globalisation and the ambiguities of territory, it is usually in terms of the ease and speed with which travellers and commodities can fly. This is presented as evidence of time–space compression within radical geographical thinking or time–space instantiation from within social theory, but little else. And mention of 'time–space compression' and 'time–space instantiation' is a reminder that neither David Harvey nor Anthony Giddens has much to say about the space of air other than the fact that technological changes have made air transport easier and thus our imaginations (a little) wider.

Yet as we have seen in the previous chapter, if we are to understand the police power then a consideration of the politics of air space is essential. In this light, there is an important body of work within critical geography that has grappled with some of the general issues concerning air power, including work by Caren Kaplan, Peter Adey, Derek Gregory, Alison Williams and Eyal Weizman,[10] and in some cases this has dealt directly with the question of the no-fly zone. This body of work, which overlaps with work on the same subject in law[11] and strategic studies,[12] has made a substantial contribution to our understanding of war, law and space and I build here on some of it. However, the central concepts used to analyse the no-fly zone remain centred on sovereignty and territory, framing the zones in terms of categories such as 'territorial integrity', 'vertical geopolitics', a 'crisis in aerial sovereignty', 'politics of verticality', 'techno-geopolitics', 'techno-territoriality'.[13] Here I argue that to understand the no-fly zone we need more than 'sovereignty' and 'territoriality', and more than just a critical interrogation of war and space. Rather, we need to situate the no-fly zone within a much longer and wider historical debate about 'international police' and, in particular, the central space in which this police operates. Doing so will help us reinforce the argument started in the previous chapter concerning air power as police power, but will also enable us to grapple with the concept of 'international police' in terms of the wider arguments that have been developing in this book. As we noted in previous chapters, the 'space' of police has historically been the City. The 'space' of *international* police, however, is the air, and like all spaces of police – the city included – it is shot through with questions of war and law. At the very least, the no-fly zone needs to be understood as one of the manifestations of this international police problematic. But pushed to its logical conclusion, the no-fly zone needs to be understood in terms of the potential for the exercise of the police power in pursuit of the violent constitution of order.

'CUJUS EST SOLUM'; OR, POLICE POWER REACHES
ALL THE WAY TO HEAVEN

What is a no-fly zone, then? This question really cannot be answered without addressing a prior question: who owns the sky? This question, however, raises some complicated historical and conceptual issues.

In their classic texts on English law, both Chief Justice Edward Coke and William Blackstone comment on two cases in 1598 and 1610 involving English landowners successfully suing their neighbours for building houses that overhung the line of their own properties. For Coke, the building of a balcony which extends over the line of a neighbouring property is impermissible, for 'the earth hath in law a great extent upwards, not only of water as hath been said, but of ayre and all things even up to heaven'. For Blackstone the cases show that 'land hath also, in its legal signification, an indefinite extent, upwards as well as downwards ... therefore no man may erect any building, or the like, to overhang another's land ... The word "land" includes not only the face of the earth, but everything under it, or over it'. [14] As Coke notes and Blackstone repeats, a property in land meant that one owned the air directly above it, and this was the basis of the doctrine *Cujus est solum ejus est usque ad coelum*: 'whoever owns the land owns it up to the sky', or 'whoever owns the soil, it is theirs all the way up to Heaven'.

The principle *cujus est solum*, as it became known, remained firmly established all the way through the centuries.[15] It took a jolt with the emergence of air balloons first flown in France in 1783 which, as well as generating a debate about their military potential, also generated heated legal debate about whether the flight of a person in an air balloon constituted a trespass on the property beneath. This led to the first air laws, introduced in the form of police regulations.[16] But the principle *cujus est solum* otherwise seems to have remained intact until the twentieth century. In a book called *Air Sovereignty*, published in 1910, J. F. Lycklama a Nijeholt found that the principle *cujus est solum* appeared in some form or another in the key legal treaties of most states, that it had the support of many a legal scholar, and that the few legal cases there had been across Europe also held to that view.[17] The French Civil Code, for example, held that 'the ownership of the soil carries the ownership of whatsoever is above and beneath it', while the German Civil Code of 1900 included the principle that 'the right of an owner of a piece of land extends to the space above the surface'. So when Louis Blériot flew across the English Channel in 1909 and pilots started flying at 20,000 feet in 1913, lawyers were still trying to make sense of the legal implications by discussing Coke and Blackstone, and by citing cases dealing with disputes over balconies and tree branches. Yet as the technology of air power progressed, that situation changed. For although initially the concern remained with individual property rights, it became a matter of state sovereignty and territorial control once the military implications of the new technology became clear.

States first began to develop formulations which allowed for commercial flying over space that was owned as property by individuals by limiting the height at which individuals might claim an interest. Thus the German Civil Code of 1900 just cited also included the claim that the right of the owner did not 'forbid interference which takes place at such a height or depth that he has no interest in its prevention'. Likewise the Swiss Civil Code of 1907 held that although 'the ownership of the soil implies the ownership of all that is above and below the surface', it does so only 'to such a height and depth respectively as the owner may require'. But what about the state's rights? Does a *state* have the sovereign right to cordon off its air space as property? Legal opinion at the time was clear. Aside from the technical issue that if individuals genuinely claimed sole right over the air space above their property then air power could not be developed, it was also thought that 'by giving such a right to a landowner, the State says that it considers itself sovereign over the airspace'.[19] A 1910 conference held in Paris to consider flight regulation saw most states claiming absolute vertical sovereignty in precisely this way.

This then generated a new and far more telling question: if the state controlled the airspace above its territory, could other states travel across or through that same space? In a world in which aviation had truly gripped the cultural, military, political and legal imaginations, this was regarded as a question of fundamental importance. The question took legal and political theory back three centuries to the debate about the 'free seas' (and is the reason we speak of 'aeronautics' and why so much of the vocabulary of the air replicates that of the sea: pilots, ports, stewards and so on). There are two ways of understanding the 'aerial ocean', as French lawyer André Blachère put it in 1911: 'On the one side is the sovereignty of the State – integral and egotistical – on the other side the still imprecise rights of the international community'.[20] Blachère's comment identifies the key issue concerning the legal status of air space in the earlier part of the twentieth century: on the one hand, an argument for freedom of the air; on the other hand, an argument for national sovereignty over that same air.

In the years prior to WWI international lawyers struggled to reconcile the principles of state sovereignty and the international freedom of the air. An International Juridical Congress for the Regulation of Aerial Locomotion held in Verona in 1910 resolved that, on the one hand, 'the atmosphere above the territory and territorial waters is to be considered territorial space subject to the sovereignty of the State', but also held that, on the other hand, 'in territorial space, the passage and circulation of airships should be free, except for regulations necessary to protect public and private interests'. A similar tension emerged from a congress of the Institute of International Law held the following year: 'International aerial circulation is free', the Institute argued, 'except for the right of the subjacent States to take certain measures to be determined, in view of their own security and that of the persons and property of their inhabitants'.[21] And similar positions with the same tensions emerged from meetings of the International Juridical Committee on Aviation held in Paris in 1912, Geneva in 1913 and Frankfurt in 1913. Thus the freedom of the air (as 'common property') was somehow limited by the security and sovereignty of the state over the air above its territory (as its own property), but no one knew just quite how or where or when. One solution was to slice the air space such that the state might claim right of sovereignty up to a certain number of feet that could in theory be made the state's property. This had the advantage of replicating the law of the ocean, which had divided the sea into a territorial zone surrounding the land and a further zone of 'international waters'. It thus satisfied the demand for both state sovereignty and the 'free air'. But this had some practical defects, concerning how to measure the distance and whether the distance that might now seem appropriate might come to seem less appropriate with the development of better technology. At which point, WWI broke out.

The outbreak of war temporarily put paid to the principle of the international freedom of the air. If before the war that principle had been both desirable and possible, a war which saw the first extensive military use of air power swept aside the claim for international freedom of the air.'The neo-Grotian claim, that air by its nature could not be possessed, virtually disappeared', notes Banner. 'As the nations of Europe battled for control of airspace, it was clear that air not only *could* be possessed but that it had to be possessed if a country hoped to defend itself against attack'.[22] Thus Article 1 of the Paris Convention of October 1919, also known as the Convention Relating to the Regulation of Aerial Navigation, opened as follows: 'The High Contracting parties recognise every Power has complete and exclusive sovereignty over the air space above its territory'. The International Commission for Air Navigation created by the Convention was meant to be a component part of the structures of international order created at the same conference, including the League of Nations, and disputes regarding the Convention were to be settled by the Permanent Court of International Justice. It meant that by the end of WWI the international order had settled on the principle that sovereign states had the right of eminent domain over their territory and thus the right to exclude foreign aircraft from the skies above the land. The principle underlying the system of air travel, and thus by extension the principle underlying the system of air power, was that a nation had complete control over its own air space.[23] This fundamental principle was confirmed in the 1944 Convention on International Civil Aviation held in Chicago, superseding the Paris Convention of 1919: the opening Article of the 1944 Convention held that 'every state has complete and exclusive sovereignty over the air space above its territory', and that other states may use this space only with that state's consent. International lawyers quickly confirmed the principle, claiming it as a fundamental tenet or well-recognised rule of international law.[24] The international agreement by the end of WWII was clear: sovereignty extended into the sky.

Nonetheless, at the end of WWII the central tension from decades before remained. On the one hand was the principle of sovereignty, extending above the state's territory on the ground and recognised in international law. Who owns and controls the sky? The simple answer was: the state, which owns and controls the ground below it. On the other hand was the rapidly developing technology of air power which seemed to offer new possibilities for capital, for transport and for international order, but which presupposed the ability to fly across and through the air above a state's territory. This tension was compounded by the fact that the ability to fly across and through the air had in 1945 been revealed as potentially the most destructive force ever created: the question of war – and, as we shall see, peace – was now nothing if not a battle to determine who controlled the space of the sky.

This tension was compounded yet further by the fact that even if sovereign ownership of the 'fly-zone' in the sky above the territory had been conceded, it was never quite clear what 'sky' actually meant. The vertical limit of state sovereignty was unsettled, and remains so: there is no agreed delineation between what might count as a state's territory and what might count as free outer space. As Dean Reinhardt shows, many articles were written on the subject in the 1950s, not only because the 'space age' was dawning but also because in 1956 the US had begun a programme of releasing unmanned high-altitude balloons. Designed ostensibly to conduct atmospheric research, the US Air Force was also launching similar balloons in intelligence-gathering operations, as well as using high-altitude aircraft for the same purpose, such as the Lockheed U-2 to fly missions over the Soviet Union. In one famous case, a U-2 flown by Gary Powers was brought down over the Soviet Union on 1 May 1960, raising once again the question of the territorial 'roof': just where did sovereignty stop? A fair number of air theorists and military strategists expressed the opinion that the US had not violated the sovereignty of the Soviet Union, citing a number of reasons: that 'air sovereignty' had not been defined; that sovereignty should be based on effective control but that this must by definition be lacking above a certain height; and that the formal boundary between sovereign 'air space' and non-sovereign 'outer space' is (and would remain) a 'never ending dispute' in international law.[25]

Committees of the United Nations would thereafter debate the exact height to which such sovereignty extends, and a convention seems to have emerged around the idea that a 'sovereign ceiling' of some sort exists, though no height has ever been agreed. Some claim that it should be the height at which an object enters into orbit and thus somewhere between 70 km and 160 km, itself quite a large span. The 'aeronautical ceiling theory' places the maximum altitude for aircraft at around 80 km, while space activities cannot be carried out below approximately 120 km, and so halving the distance would place the 'ceiling' at approximately 100 km above the earth's surface.[26] Others, such as the equatorial states which signed the Bogota Declaration of 1976, claim sovereignty up to the geostationary orbit, which is 36,000 km. Indeed, 'between 1957 and

1960 alone the proposals made ranged from 20 km to 1,500,000'.[27] What is agreed on is that despite the complex intertwinement of air law and space law, in the former the principle of sovereignty is paramount whereas in the latter 'effective control' and 'sovereignty' are impossible to effectuate. What this means is that when one hits 'outer space', 'free space' begins.[28] Significantly, according to the two key UN Treaties in this area, the *Treaty on Principles Governing the Activities of States in the Exploration and Use of Outer Space, including the Moon and Other Celestial Bodies* (1967), and the *Agreement Governing the Activities of States on the Moon and Other Celestial Bodies* (1979), 'outer space' is defined in international law as 'not subject to national appropriation by claim of sovereignty' and is thus 'the province of all mankind' or 'the common heritage of mankind', though these terms have never been defined. About this we might make two small observations. The first is that in terms of law and geopolitics it is recognised that a space exists somewhere *above territory* and *beyond sovereignty*. The existence of outer space means that sovereignty seems to end somewhere; though precisely where, nobody knows. The second observation is that the implication of the 1967 and 1979 Treaties is rather telling: the common heritage of mankind, beyond sovereignty, lies in outer space; in other words, the common heritage of mankind remains out of the reach of more or less the whole of mankind.

I will return to the question of sovereignty and space shortly, but for now we can note that the problem identified by political geographers remains: regardless of precisely where, vertically, sovereignty ends, surely any aerial military intervention infringes the logic of sovereignty? Surely the logic of such intervention requires other states to fly under the state's territorial roof, regardless of where that roof might be said to be? And surely this is nowhere clearer than in the no-fly zone, which not only allows aircraft of other states the right to fly but simultaneously denies a sovereign state the use of its own air space? Such questions are even more pressing when one realises that the legality of no-fly zones is muddy at best.[29] At worst, the legality is non-existent. Even the Secretary General of the UN considered the no-fly zones over Iraq to be illegal.[30] (In contrast to UN Security Council Resolutions 781 and 816, which prohibited flights over Bosnia and Herzegovina in 1992, Resolutions 678, 687 and 688 passed the year before authorised member states to use force in Iraq but did not specifically mention no-fly zones.) It is for these reasons that the no-fly zone is often seen as violating 'territorial integrity', as a 'crisis in aerial sovereignty' and as imposing a new form of 'techno-geopolitics' or 'techno-territoriality'. There is no doubt that these points are correct, for in denying a sovereign state the use of its own air space a no-fly zone deprives that state of a large measure of its territorial sovereignty. But there is a more telling point to be made.

Given that air space is considered territory and that the purpose of a no-fly zone is to restrict not only movement in the air space but also movement on the ground, the no-fly zone is a *de facto* occupation; the no-fly zone is a form of 'air occupation'. By undermining a state's borders, attacking a state's sovereignty and occupying the territory, the no-fly zone is an act of war. Liberal interventionists and pacifists like to deny this, citing humanitarian reasons for the introduction of the zones, but a comment by the US Secretary of Defense during the US intervention in Libya in 2011 is rather telling. 'Let's just call a spade a spade', said Robert Gates, the Secretary in question. 'A no-fly zone begins with an attack on Libya to destroy the air defenses'. The point concerned not just Libya, but no-fly zones in general. 'That's the way you do a no-fly zone. And then you can fly planes around the country and not worry about our guys being shot down. But that's the way it starts'.[31] In other words, the first act in a no-fly zone is the classic act of air power – a bombing campaign – to destroy the military capability of the state which in theory controls the territory of the 'zone' in question. The no-fly zone is thus clearly an act of war. And yet the fact that the no-fly zone is so widely treated as an act of humanitarian intervention and 'peacekeeping' rather than an act of war is heavily due to the fact that such zones are an exercise of *police power*; as we saw in the previous chapter, 'air occupation' is activated through and constituted as a *police zone*. Here the fact that the no-fly zone is a *prohibition* on flying is important.

The fact of 'prohibition' was more readily apparent from the no-fly zone's precursor, air interdiction. 'Air interdiction' took its name from a term that came into the language in the sixteenth century. An interdiction is a prohibition, and a military interdiction is the attempt to prohibit the enemy from engaging in the war, such as by cutting off weapons, food and information. Colonel John Warden III, who we cited in the previous chapter as a leading US air power strategist, makes the point that although 'the history of interdiction is as long, and nearly as important, as the history of battle', the 'advent of the airplane ... added a new dimension to this form of warfare'.[32] In military parlance 'interdiction' very quickly became 'air interdiction', defined as 'an effort on the part of air forces primarily … to deny an enemy materiel and human resources that it needs to carry on the war. The purpose of interdiction is simply to isolate the battlefield'.[33] The idea of 'air interdiction' came to the fore in the extensive air campaign carried out during the US war in Korea, and this fact is important for two reasons. First, it reinforces the point just made: that an air interdiction (and thus the no-fly zone) is never simply a prohibition on all flying but involves extensive bombing of targets within the zone by those imposing the prohibition. Second, and more important, is the term stressed by the US in describing its military 'intervention' and interdiction in Korea: it was a 'police action'.[34]

Now, on the one hand, this term was meant in the broadest sense of air power as police power that was developed through the process of colonisation in the 1920s: the police action in question involved extensive bombing combined with an attempt at a reconstitution of social order.[35] On the other hand, when the US described its air interdiction as a police action it was acting on what had been a key idea of liberal geopolitics for the previous 25 years, and to understand why we need to situate air power within the broader context of the liberal internationalism that developed in the twentieth century, before returning to the no-fly zone. We need to situate it, in other words, as part of the solution to what was once described as the problem of the twentieth century.

THE PROBLEM OF THE CENTURY … AND ITS SOLUTION: INTERNATIONAL POLICE

On 6 December 1904, in an address to the Senate and House of Representatives, the US President raised the Dominican Republic as an example of a more general problem of international disorder.

> In international law we have not advanced by any means as far as we have advanced in municipal law. There is as yet no judicial way of enforcing a right in international law. When one nation wrongs another or wrongs many others, there is no tribunal before which the wrongdoer can be brought. Either it is necessary supinely to

acquiesce in the wrong, and thus put a premium upon brutality and aggression, or else it is necessary for the aggrieved nation valiantly to stand up for its rights. Until some method is devised by which there shall be a degree of international control over offending nations, it would be a wicked thing for the most civilized powers, for those with most sense of international obligations and with keenest and most generous appreciation of the difference between right and wrong, to disarm. If the great civilized nations of the present day should completely disarm, the result would mean an immediate recrudescence of barbarism in one form or another. Under any circumstances a sufficient armament would have to be kept up to serve the purposes of international police ...

Therefore it follows that a self-respecting, just, and far-seeing nation should on the one hand endeavor by every means to aid in the development of the various movements which tend to provide substitutes for war, which tend to render nations in their actions toward one another, and indeed toward their own peoples, more responsive to the general sentiment of humane and civilized mankind; and on the other hand that it should keep prepared, while scrupulously avoiding wrongdoing itself, to repel any wrong, and in exceptional cases to take action which in a more advanced stage of international relations would come under the head of the exercise of the international police ...

Chronic wrongdoing, or an impotence which results in a general loosening of the ties of civilized society, may in America, as elsewhere, ultimately require intervention by some civilized nation, and in the Western Hemisphere the adherence of the United States to the Monroe Doctrine may force the United States, however reluctantly, in flagrant cases of such wrongdoing or impotence, to the exercise of an international police power.[36]

The speech by Theodore Roosevelt became known as the founding statement of the 'Roosevelt Corollary' to the Monroe Doctrine, and has been central to debates about international politics, intervention, imperial reach and the rise of American capital. Yet Roosevelt's 'corollary' needs further attention, for at the heart of a debate about war and order Roosevelt places the question of an international police power.

As James Holmes notes, most accounts of these issues content themselves with citing the Roosevelt Corollary and leaving it at that, as though the meaning of 'international police power' were self-evident.[37] Yet the concept, which appears in neither the original Monroe Doctrine nor the classical liberal tradition, is important. In making his announcements Roosevelt was declaring that not only the Dominican Republic, but also the rest of the Caribbean, Latin America and, by extension, the whole world, might be subject to some kind of 'international police'. Although the day after his speech Roosevelt was identified by the *London Chronicle* as 'Police Constable Roosevelt of the International Police' and by the *New York Times* as 'Policeman for the Hemisphere',[38] the idea had been coming for some time. In his first Annual Message in December 1901, for example, he commented that as 'wars between the great civilized powers … become less and less frequent', wars with uncivilised peoples impose on the civilised a 'regrettable but necessary international police duty'.[39] The 1904 speech was thus a restatement of a solution to a long-held problem: international order required the police power. The police power was to underpin the US shaping of the geopolitical sphere of the Americas and, potentially, the global order as a whole. At the same time, however, Roosevelt also refers to the internal policing of other states: 'I thought it for the interest of all the world that each part of the world should be prosperous and well policed'.[40] Just as America is to be well policed, so the world is to be well policed and each part of the world to be well policed; domestic order and global order rely on one another.

One of the reasons Roosevelt thought of such actions as a form of police power was because he saw them as part and parcel of an expansionist policy which applied both 'domestically' and 'internationally'. Thus, for example, he drew a parallel between US control of the Philippines and the Louisiana Purchase: 'The parallel between what Jefferson did with Louisiana and what is now being done in the Philippines is exact', in that in both cases the peoples being conquered were 'not fit or ready for self-government'. The actions were an attempt to bring order to those unfit for self-government and thus were simply a corollary to the operations of domestic police. The US was doing 'nothing but what a policeman has to do'.[41] Thus the pacification of states such as the Philippines could be equated with the pacification of the Indians, to the extent that they are one and the same process: the imposition of order on the world through the conjunction of war power and (international) police power.[42] In fact, this pacification through police has its roots in Roosevelt's understanding of the 'problem' posed by organised labour confronting capital.

It is notable that the fourth Annual Message begins with an account of the struggles between capital and labour. In other words, the speech only gets to the issue of international police by having first spoken of the problem of police power over organised labour, and this tells us something important: Roosevelt's idea of an international police power emerges from his interest in the policing of the class war. In the mid-1890s Roosevelt had been Police Commissioner for New York, which was at that point the greatest centre of organised and militant labour in the country. A burgeoning labour movement saw some 7,000 strikes between 1880 and 1900 including, during Roosevelt's tenure as Police Commissioner, strikes of garment workers, metal workers, express company workers, bookbinders, cab drivers, street cleaners and others, compounded by the rise of women's rights advocates and newly empowered blacks. The strikes and movements were indicative of the extent to which American cities were, in effect, spaces of civil war.[43] One feature of this urban warfare was a combined build-up of police authority, to the extent that 'the center of public life was occupied by a vast war machine [of] fortified police forces'.[44] This build-up intensified in the last quarter of the century: seven armouries were built in Manhattan between 1872 and the end of the century,[45] the National Guard called out to fight against the workers, and martial law declared.[46]

Roosevelt consciously built the idea of the war power into his conception of police power, drawing an exact analogy on the basis of 'peacekeeping': peace between nations (international peace) on the one hand and peace between capital and labour (industrial peace) on the other.[47] This drawing together of domestic and international peace saw Roosevelt describe police officers as 'soldiers on the field of battle' and the purpose of police power as an 'unending warfare against crime'.[48] On the desk in his Police Commissioner's office sat a tablet inscribed 'aggressive fighting for the right is the noblest sport the world affords',[49] and in several speeches and essays he articulated the view that 'the police service is military in character'. He constantly claimed that the principles which apply in the army apply equally to the police: 'keep before your minds the military service of the department', he said to his police officers, adding that the experience some of them had in the civil war would 'encourage the military virtues' and forge a police department ready to make 'war upon all criminals'.[50] This was an idea he held on to through the rest of his career. As he was to put it much later in a Presidential Address: 'the war we wage must be waged against misconduct, against wrongdoing wherever it is found'.[51] Finally, Roosevelt's immediate response to any disorder or rebellion was to call in the military and to describe it as a *police action*.[52]

This conception of the unity of the police power and the war power is what seeps into his corollary to the Monroe Doctrine, for it did not take a huge leap of imagination to turn this argument around: if the police is engaged in war, then acts of war – or at least acts which others might call 'war' – might be considered acts of police. In effect, the significance of Roosevelt's corollary lies in the way that he grafted the police power onto the Monroe Doctrine, thereby placing the logic of 'law and order' at the heart of colonial war and military intervention.[53]

In this light the observation made by Holmes and others needs to be reiterated: that underpinning Roosevelt's concept of *international police* is nothing less than the *original police science*.[54] For as much as Roosevelt's arguments and proposals might appear to be a repressive constabulary to enforce US interests – 'gunboat diplomacy' – it is also clear that in his mind the international police has a duty to *produce order* and *ensure civilisation*. Roosevelt's 'international police' is police power in the classical sense of the term, transposed onto the geopolitical realm as a means of confronting international disorder, subsuming the international war power under the concept of police. On this basis, the US and other civilised states have an obligation to engage in the fabrication of international order in exactly the same way that civilised states engage in the fabrication of social order at home.

We might also note in passing that in many other ways Roosevelt's beliefs and policies exemplify the features of liberalism which we have encountered in previous chapters. Four observations might be briefly made here. First, in the spirit of eighteenth-century liberalism he accepts military virtues as virtues, romanticises war and craves its excitement: he says that 'to condemn all war is just as logical as to condemn all business',[55] that 'this country needs a war'[56] and gives various speeches in which he speaks about war with a poetic enthusiasm.[57] Commentators ever since have noted how Roosevelt 'personally ... glorified in war, was thrilled by military history, and placed warlike qualities high in his scale of values',[58] a reflection, no doubt, of his well-known love of the 'strenuous life', of hunting and killing in the great outdoors.[59] Secondly, the 'manly man' of eighteenth-century liberalism is also present in Roosevelt's thinking, as is a concern over the effeminate degeneracy that might come anything remotely looking like actual peace.[60] Roosevelt is famous for talking about the need to 'speak softly and carry a big stick', but, notes Harvey Mansfield, 'when it came to the manly virtues, he actually spoke quite loudly',[61] and, in a resounding echo of eighteenth-century liberalism, Roosevelt argued throughout his life for 'virile virtues … which go to make up a race of statesmen and soldiers'.[62]

Third, Roosevelt's vision of how to manage war and disorder is founded on the dialectic of police and civilisation: it is a duty of civilised states to bring civilisation to the barbarous parts of the world, by force if necessary, because such expansion goes hand in hand with peace, not war. 'Every expansion of civilization makes for peace', Roosevelt claims. 'In other words, every expansion of a great civilized power means a victory for law [and] order'.[63] This use of 'civilisation as ideology' renders him as a major figure in liberal as well as American internationalism.[64] Finally, we might note that his arguments relied on and reiterated the idea of a liberal war on waste. The opening lines of Roosevelt's four-volume *The Winning of the West* hold that 'the spread of the English-speaking peoples over the world's waste spaces has been … the most striking feature in the world's history', and this spread is integrally related to war: 'Unless we were willing that the whole continent west of the Alleghanies should remain an unpeopled waste … war was inevitable'. Settling on Indian land, Roosevelt says, 'has no resemblance whatever to the forcible occupation of land already cultivated. The white settler has merely moved into an uninhabited waste'.[65] This theme he returns to time and again: 'As the world is now, with huge waste places still to fill up, and with much of the competition between the races reducing itself to … warfare'.[66] In these four ways Roosevelt thus adopted and reinforced some of the fundamental themes of liberal war power.

This historical excursus into Roosevelt's account of international police has taken us a long way from the question of no-fly zones, but it has been necessary. For Roosevelt's attempt to incorporate both the early police science and nineteenth-century police powers into a rethinking of international police is a profound moment in the history of war power and police power. Three themes emerge which remain at the heart of the debate in the century that follows.

First, the idea of international police would seem to be rooted in the process that becomes known as 'intervention' ('military', but then also 'humanitarian'). Felix Grob writes, 'The operations of the [US] marines in both Haiti and the Dominican Republic thus were in the nature of police measures. One hesitates to call such operations "war". "Intervention" surely was a more appropriate term'.[67] It is this process of 'intervention' that animates the debate among international lawyers of the period. Leading international lawyer William Edward Hall, writing in 1895 about the practice of military intervention, commented that 'regarded from the point of view of the state intruded upon it must always remain an act which, if not consented to, is an act of war. But from the point of view of the intervening power it is not a means of obtaining redress for a wrong done, but a measure of prevention or of police, undertaken sometimes for the express purpose of avoiding war'.[68]

Second, describing such interventions as 'police' is reinforced by the way that the police operation folds into the construction of actual 'police forces' in the country which is the object of the intervention. Thus, to take the Philippines as an example, Vic Hurley notes that 'the history of the American occupation and conquest of the Philippines is, in large measure, the history of the Philippine Constabulary'. In quantitative terms, the US created a security apparatus of 47,000 personnel, including Manila police, Manila sheriffs, constabulary officers, customs staff, prison officers and coast guard officers, which meant there was one 'security operative' for every 170 civilians.[69] Yet the issue was not just the sheer numbers of posts created for, as Alfred McCoy has shown at length, the US Army's application to municipal administration of its own military science and history of police powers 'created something of a revolution in policing'.[70] One reason was because the revolution appropriated the broader police concept and thus extended to establishing work programmes, enforcing laws against vagrancy, tax collection, road building, harbour improvements, the promotion of commerce, street cleaning, education programmes, and providing health clinics. Andrew Birtle makes the point directly in describing the 'pacification of the Philippines' by the new police powers as a project of 'social engineering designed to reshape the subject society'.[71] This pattern continued elsewhere, and it is no exaggeration to say that the establishment of a broad police power for the fabrication of social order and the security of private property has been a central facet of 'interventions' across the globe.[72]

Third, 'international policing' became a way of referring to the relations between states themselves within the wider geopolitical order. The militarily and industrially developed states still required a certain kind of action which held them together under the rubric of 'international order' and 'international peace', and this was also often being referred to when people spoke of 'international police': Roosevelt's desire to be able to 'enforce a right in international law' was intended to apply 'when one nation wrongs another', and this was by definition meant to apply to civilised states more than anything else.

The tension between these three meanings of 'international police' was never worked out, and never could be worked out. But what unites them is the core concept of the police idea: 'order'. In this regard the work of international lawyer T. J. Lawrence in the late nineteenth and early twentieth centuries stands out. In his *Principles of International Law* he comments that 'in cases where a strong state or group of states finds itself obliged to undertake what are potentially measures of police against weak or barbarous powers, one or other of the means described above [reprisal, embargo, blockade] may be a useful alternative to war',[73] yet he also laments the fact that while in the domestic sphere 'the most pacific among us gladly pays a police-rate … in the Society of Nations there is … no common superior, and no international police-force'.[74] But what Lawrence saw was that although one cannot understand 'law' without recourse to the concept of *force*, the key concept for under-standing law is in fact *order*: 'the root-meaning of the English word *law* is, that which lies in due order, just as the Latin *jus*, in its sense of law, signifies "what is fitting, orderly and regular"'.[75] Law in this sense is the opposite of chaos. It is this that drives Lawrence's conception of international law, not least when writing about 'intervention': the white race which has produced international law and thus the grounds of intervention has, in effect, 'produced order from chaos'.[76] It is therefore a *process of ordering* that lies at the heart of international law, according to Lawrence. As Annelise Riles comments, Lawrence's work reveals an important focus, rare for an international lawyer, on the idiom of order,[77] and this underpinned his idea of international police too: a mechanism for order between states, but also the order of those states considered by the international society of civilised states to be failed states, failing states, rogue states, criminal states, terrorist states, and more. Thus, in contrast to the wrangling over the precise meaning of 'international policing', Lawrence recognised that if the heart of law is order and the heart of order is police, then the logic of international police is the fabrication of international order.

Despite this, Lawrence was in not much of a better position than Roosevelt in grasping the possibilities of international police. What was needed was a wholesale shift in technological capability, one which returns us to the argument in the previous chapter and which will allow us eventually to return to the question of the no-fly zone: air power. Put bluntly, the new technology of air power provided everything that was needed to refine the concept of 'international police'. By the end of the 1920s, amid debates about some kind of 'league to enforce peace' or 'league of nations', and the emergence of an 'outlawry-of-war' move-ment,[78] the scene was set for air power to be presented to the world as the foundation of international police and thus, in a roundabout way, as the solution to the problem of the century. This is where Lord Davies's work, *The Problem of the Twentieth Century*, first published in 1930, becomes important.

Liberal politician, active supporter of the League of Nations and founder of the League of Free Nations, for Davies the problem of the twentieth century is the 'spirit of insecurity' and the need for a lasting peace. Since insecurity is the national experience of international disorder, and a breach of one nation's security by another is, in effect, a hostile act likely to result in a state of war, the solution to insecurity coincides with the solution of how to achieve peace: police. Since security in general requires police, so the solution to the problem of war in the twentieth century, and thus the foundation of international order and peace, becomes clear: 'international police'.[79]

Over some 800 pages Davies then seeks to 'gauge the policing require-ments of the world'.[80] Such requirements depend on good national police forces. But while domestic constabularies are 'ready to aid the civil authority in repressing disorder' by constantly 'curbing the animosities of individuals, restraining the propensities of evil-doers, compelling the appearance of criminals at the bar of justice and executing the decrees of municipal law', the international police 'stand guard over the treasure-house of civilisation, sternly suppressing breaches of the peace [and] deterring the would-be aggressor from the crime of war'.[81] The crime of breaching the peace and undermining law and order domestically is thus matched by the 'crime' of war: disorder and war mirror each other. Hence

despite the focus on the problem of international order, Davies returns
to the fabrication of domestic order and its key issue: wage-labour. 'In
many countries a succession of strikes, lock-outs and economic
upheavals have taken place in which a war mentality has been allowed
free play. The speeches of the protagonists leave no doubt on this point.
They abound with warlike metaphors'. Moreover, the events and
processes of international affairs 'tend to reappear in the industrial
warfare between labour and capital'.[82] The 'war on disorder' once again
functions as code for 'class war'. Thus the 'reign of law' and peaceful order
requires police, internationally as well as domestically, and Davies
reinforces this idea by underpinning it with an analogy between
municipal and international law held up by authorities such as Grotius.[83]

Davies's book was a major contribution to a proliferation of proposals
for international police between the wars. This was the heyday of the
new 'liberal internationalism'. Taking its cue from John Hobson's *Towards
International Government* (1915) and Philip Noel Baker's *Disarmament*
(1926),[84] liberalism in the 1930s developed an internationalist strand that
was distinct from and explicitly opposed to socialist internationalism.
This filtered into textbooks, such as Clyde Eagleton's *International
Government* (1932) and Frederick L. Schuman's *International Politics*
(1933, but reprinted in revised form several times), and into liberal
opinion more generally, as the *Manchester Guardian* and *The Economist*
both came to offer support for the idea. And at the heart of this liberal
internationalism was a belief in air power and the logic of police. Rather
than advocate the abolition of air power as a technology of war, this
liberal internationalism incorporated the bomber into its own politics
by adopting air power as a force for police.[85] The airplane 'will become
the decisive weapon of the future', Davies claims, due to 'the unique
position of aircraft as a policing agency'. The 'chariots of the air' will come
to play 'a decisive part' in establishing peace: 'the potentialities of the air,
when they are developed for policing purposes, are so immeasurable
that the strength of this arm may be increased rather than diminished'.
At which point Davies refers back to one of the key concepts of the 1920s
air power: 'control without occupation'.[86]

The same argument, give or take a few minor differences, can be
found in a whole host of other publications, including Baker's
Disarmament, J. M. Spaight's *An International Air Force* (1932), James H.
Ashton's *International Police Force* (1932) and, following the resolution

passed by the Labour Party at its 1933 Annual Conference calling for an international police force, a pamphlet by Clement Attlee called *An International Police Force* (1934). Attlee articulates the central contradiction:'Particularly in connection with the growing appreciation of the menace to civilisation inherent in air warfare there has emerged the idea that the dominant weapon to-day, the Air Force, should be reserved to a supernational authority for the preservation of peace'. That is, the weapon of war – 'the weapon of air is the bomb' – is to be a weapon of peace by being at the heart of an international police force.[87] Attlee's argument was published by The New Commonwealth Society, established by Davies in 1932, which also published a series of pamphlets following a series of lectures on the topic, including *Why a World Police is Inevitable* (1934, reprinted in 1937); *The Relations Between Disarmament and the Establishment of an International Police Force* (1935); *A Plan for the Organisation of a European Air Service* (1935); *The First Stage in International Policing* (1935); *An International Police Board* (1935); *Military Force or Air Police* (1935); *Theory and Practice of International Policing* (1935); *The Functions of an International Air Police* (1936); and General Allenby's lecture and then pamphlet called *World Police for World Peace* (1936).[88] Other publications include two chapters on an 'international air police force' in the collectively authored volume *Challenge to Death* (1934), W. Bryn Thomas's *An International Police Force* (1936), Lord Davies's much shorter follow-up to his own earlier book, *Nearing the Abyss* (1936) on a European Air Police Force, and Squadron-Leader E. J. Kingston-McCloughry's *Winged Warfare: Air Problems of Peace and War* (1937).[89] Major conferences were being increasingly held on the subject, such as the one in London in 1935 organised by the British League of Nations Union on 'The Problem of the Air', including sessions on an international police force. The British Labour Party manifesto of 1935 also proposed 'the creation of an international air police'.[90] So common was the issue that by the end of the decade Gallup was running opinion polls asking people whether they favoured an International Police Force. A British historical drama documentary was produced called *The Conquest of the Air* (1940) which treated air power as largely civil and essentially peaceful, and *Fortune Magazine* ran a whole issue on 'Air Power as World Power' in March 1941.[91] 'It became fashionable to speak of an "International Police Force"', as one history of the United Nations puts it, adding that 'the abbreviation "IPF" was

used as if it were as generally known as "UN" is today'.[92] This was also a
time when extensive moves were afoot to develop an international
criminal police, or at least to extend the idea of policing such that it
might function across national boundaries, with the development of an
International Criminal Police Commission (ICPC) which would
eventually morph into Interpol.[93]

The intensity of the debate about international police through air
power did not subside through WWII; indeed, in many ways it intensified. 'It is believed that air power ... makes possible the development
of an international police', as Quincy Wright put it in an Editorial for the
American Journal of International Law in 1943.[94] Again, a sample of books
will suffice. In William Bishop's *Winged Peace*, world order requires world
government, world government requires world police, and world police
requires air power. International aviation will enable us to 'police the
world', though when Bishop speaks of a 'properly policed air' he very
quickly adds: 'policed, that is, in the military sense'.[95] This is also the
impulse behind Allan Michie's *Keep the Peace Through Air Power*, in which
'the use of airplanes by the RAF to impose effective control over
disturbers of the peace in the years from 1922 onwards' offers nothing
less than a new 'sword of justice' for a 'long-range police power'.[96] This
'world police force' is not just about 'immediate bombing' but *forms order*
by transforming subjects. 'The object of all coercive police action is to
bring about a change in the temper, or intention of the person or body
of persons who are disturbing the peace. In other words, we want a
change of heart'.[97] Both Michie and Bishop were following in the steps
of Ely Culbertson's *Total Peace* published the previous year, in which an
extensive design for a world police was presented,[98] and we should also
recall from the previous chapter that Seversky's *Victory Through Air Power*
was published in 1942. The key themes of these books were reiterated
in J. M. Spaight's *Bombing Vindicated* in 1944, in which the 'police bomber'
saves civilisation.[99] The year 1944 also saw Brazilian Ambassador J. F. de
Barros Pimentel's *The International Police: The Use of Force in the Structure
of Peace*, James T. Shotwell's *The Great Decision* (the 'decision' in question
partly involving using the airplane as a force for international peace and
police) and Julia E. Johnsen's compilation of essays by figures such as
Quincy Wright and Lord David Davies, run together as though they
were a single text, called *International Police Force*. The following year saw
Eugene E. Wilson's *Air Power for Peace*.[100] Before his death in 1944 Lord

Davies produced a short book on 'the seven pillars of peace' in which Hobbes, Kant and Sir Robert Peel are brought together in an argument for an international police force founded on air power, and one finds the idea being raised and discussed in diverse places in the last two years of the war: in books such as Laski's *Reflections on the Revolution of Our Time* (1943), in reports from within the aviation industry such as the memorandum by aeronautical engineer T. P. Wright called *The Organization of an Airforce for International Policing* (1943), and in the series of meetings held by the Chatham House 'Aviation Group' through 1943.[101]

The theme also permeates popular culture. In 1943, the year Walt Disney issued *Victory Through Air Power*, two essays by Culbertson appeared in *Reader's Digest* outlining the arguments in his *Total Peace* book, and *Time Magazine* ran an article on 'International Police' in which it claimed that the idea of an international aerial police power had 'captured the public mind'. In 1944 the journal *Popular Science* ran an article by Volta Torrey called 'Will Airborne Police Enforce World Peace?', citing Major General F. A. M. Browning, Commander of Britain's first airborne division, to the view that 'the day will most assuredly come when airborne armoured forces will control the world, and the inhuman, though at present inevitable, bombing of women and children, inherent in strategic bombing, will be a barbaric relic of the past', and the June 1945 issue of *Fortune* magazine ran a survey and found that 'the people are sold on peace through air power'.[102] Gill Robb Wilson, writing in the *New York Herald Tribune* in April 1945, spoke of 'future global air power upon which American security will rest'.[103] All of which might explain why, at the Dumbarton Oaks Conference in August 1944 to discuss postwar peace, 'air power' and 'international police' were commonplace terms and usually spoken of in the same breath. That conference is known for the emergence of the 'four policemen' which would institute the new world order, but F. D. Roosevelt had also charged his Joint Chiefs of Staff to plan for an international police force and at various points the US Senate discussed the development of an international air force as the basis of peace.[104]

This historical account has been necessarily terse, but hopefully the point is clear: by the close of WWII it was widely held that a new liberal international order could be achieved only through an international police. What was at stake by the end of WWII, then, was nothing less than what we might call an attempt at global pacification through air power.[105] There were four main implications of this solution to the problem of the century that remain with us. First, the logic of *international police* could legitimately override the logic of *national sovereignty*. Second, this meant that liberal internationalism was always already a form of liberal *militarism*, as Edgerton reminds us.[106] Third, this militarism would masquerade as an ideology of peace to be conducted under the process of international police. And fourth, what would count as 'international police' was dependent – conceptually, strategically, geopolitically, legally and technologically – on the nature and existence of air power. I am suggesting that the no-fly zone needs to be understood as part of this long trajectory of air power as police power.

VICTORY THROUGH AIR POWER II: THE NO-FLY ZONE

If the legality of the no-fly zone is muddy, then, it is because its roots lie in police, and thus come with all the legal muddiness of police powers.[107] This is also why the guiding principle of such zones is *order* rather than *law*. The no-fly zone, in other words, is a form of police power for the building of international order, a technology for coercively compelling states to behave in certain ways; an exercise of war power without a declaration of war. This idea that international police might be realised through air power presupposes that sovereignty must give way to order, and holds in reserve the possibility that however much a sovereign entity might resist intervention in the name of order, the requirements of international peace (that is, police) demand it.

Of course, the astute reader will know full well that in one sense 'international police' is meaningless, which is why the scholarship on the topic is remarkably varied, covering police forces working across different nations, comparison of such forces, state collaboration over crime, the international activities of organs such as the CIA or FBI, UN peacekeeping, the control of postcolonial orders, military intervention, humanitarian intervention, military-humanitarian intervention, the use of military power in aid of civil government, and often a combination of two or more of these.[108] The tensions between these different conceptions of 'international police' lie at the heart of a profound instability in the idea.

One can see this profound instability in various 'future world order' models and 'world peace' projects, which invariably follow the same pattern: principles are proposed around which mankind should organise for peace (such as minimising violence, maximising well-being, realising human rights, maintaining ecological stability), to be realised through an international governance structure (such as a World Assembly, a Central Coordinating Council, a World Grievance System, a World Economic System, World Economic Planning, a World Disarmament Service and, of course, World Security Forces). Despite the various titles of such projects, the operational drive is almost always 'world order' rather than 'world government' or 'world federation', and hence the issue ultimately turns on the police idea: the move is towards 'an imposed and policed peace', such that 'the World Security Forces would try to operate as a police force rather than as an army'.[109] Yet we are rarely told what this police would actually do; it is assumed that we know what 'international police' would do because we already know what 'police' does. The 'domestic analogy' – that we need to think of international peace, security and order as somehow analogous with domestic peace, security and order – is thus to all intents and purposes a police analogy.[110] But as is often commented, the domestic analogy stands or falls on the question of the monopoly over the means of violence. Raymond Aron puts the point as well as anyone: 'So long as humanity has not achieved unification into a universal state, an *essential* difference will exist between internal politics and foreign politics. The former tends to reserve the monopoly of violence to those wielding legitimate authority, the latter accepts the plurality of centers of armed force'.[111] Translated into the terms of war and police, this means: in internal politics there is the army and the police, but internationally there can be only pluralities, since the exercise of the means of violence is assumed to presuppose some kind of sovereign body.

This concern that the domestic analogy both stands and falls on the police idea is at the heart of the profound instability in the concept of international police and this instability is why, despite decades of writing on the subject, a critical examination of the international police power encounters nothing essential at all. Like police power in general, it is formless and intangible, and yet it has an all-pervasive, ghostly presence.[112] The no-fly zone needs to be understood as a manifestation of this ghostly presence, a rare moment in which the intangible becomes briefly tangible. But note: its intangibility as international *police power* becomes tangible in the form of the war powers of *sovereign states imposing the zone*.

Danilo Zolo once suggested that any 'police operation' carried out by a supranational organ claiming a monopoly of force is destined to take on all the connotations of war,[113] and we have already noted that the no-fly zone is an act of war. But, conversely, we might say that any 'war operation' carried out by a supranational organ claiming a monopoly of force is destined to take on all the connotations of police, and this too applies to the no-fly zone. Here, the no-fly zone needs to be understood as running alongside and as part of the increased use of drones: when in March 2011 the UN declared a no-fly zone over Libya, it was pretty quickly followed by the use of drones in the region. For if the drone needs to be seen as the perfect technology of police power, then the no-fly zone needs to be understood as a fundamental tool in this same power, a key political technology for the fabrication of order. The no-fly zone might be the manifestation of international police, but this is by virtue of its role alongside drones in offering the possibility of occupying and controlling the air perpetually and universally. 'A writer in a German military review predicted [in 1784] that the first nation to occupy and control the air would be in a position to impose *Universal-monarchie*, which was the eighteenth century's way of saying global dominance'.[114] The combined power of drones and no-fly zones means that this imposition has more or less arrived. This was the point foreseen by the very first air theorists, including Billy Mitchell's claim that the nation which controls the air 'may be able to control the whole world more easily than a nation has controlled a continent in the past', a step towards 'world dominion',[115] Major Seversky writing about the 'global command of the air',[116] and Alan Cobham's suggestion that 'the nation that controls the air will control the earth'.[117]

Yet this argument has a further twist. One of the problems in trying to understand no-fly zones solely through the lens of 'territorial integrity', 'aerial sovereignty' and related terms, is that these treat the no-fly zone as simply an issue in international relations. In one sense this is not surprising, since it is the no-fly zones over places such as Bosnia and Libya that get media attention. But this sidelines the remarkable fact that no-fly zones are used far more extensively on the domestic front. No-fly zones were declared over the US after the attacks on 11 September 2001, but they are now enacted for a whole host of events in that country: for major political summits (such as the NATO summit in Chicago in 2012), for major sporting events, during Presidential visits to towns and cities, during the transportation of hazardous substances, over disaster zones (such as the one declared for Mayflower, Arkansas, in April 2013 following an oil spillage there, and which is managed by ExxonMobil), during police hunts for missing children. A no-fly zone was even declared over the area in which Chelsea Clinton's wedding took place. Such temporary zones – in June 2011 alone the US Federal Aviation Authority announced at least 40 temporary no-fly zones, the details of which it has since removed from its website – need to be connected to the Air Defence Identification Zone (ADIZ), established in 2003 to restrict air traffic around Washington (a circle of 30 miles radius with Reagan Washington National Airport at the centre), the status of which was changed in February 2009 from a 'Temporary Flight Restriction' to a permanent 'Special Flight Rules Area' (SFRA). The permanence of the SFRA over Washington is matched by the permanence of other zones elsewhere: over the houses of ex-Presidents, over nuclear plants, over airports.

In the UK a similar practice has emerged, with no-fly zones put in place over London and the south-east of England during 2012 (not only for the Olympics, but also for other sporting events such as the Wimbledon tennis tournaments), and over the Farne Islands (a once temporary no-fly zone which has now become permanent). Thus, while debate was taking place in June 2013 about the possible introduction of a no-fly zone over Syria, no-fly zones were declared for Belfast for the G8 summit being held there and for Hertfordshire for the meeting of the Bilderberg Group being held in Watford.

The beauty of such zones for the state lies in being able to embrace a key functionality of police power: on the one hand, a permanent police presence over/in some zones; on the other hand, the possibility of other zones being introduced with immediate effect, on a temporary basis, subject to change with very little notice, and very easily made permanent.

It is impossible for us not to connect the increased use of no-fly zones domestically with the increased use of drones on the same front. Together, drones and the no-fly zone transform the space of power: the realisation not so much of *international* police, but of *perpetual* police, a general police power engaged permanently in the reproduction of order. *Universal-monarchie* always begins with the pacification of the population at home. Far from being a crisis in aerial sovereignty, the no-fly zone is in this context the perfect accompaniment for the drone as the realisation of a universal liberal police power. Victory through air power, over and over again. But then: who are the defeated?

US General John M. Shalikashvili once commented that 'it is one thing to say that you are going to enforce a no-fly zone over Bosnia or Iraq; it is quite another to explain why'.[118] The question becomes even more pressing when no-fly zones are used domestically. For the answer as to *why* they are used lies in the sign under which the war power and the police power operate: the sign of security.

Chapter 7

UNDER THE SIGN OF SECURITY: TRAUMA, TERROR, RESILIENCE

I tried to be as prepared as much as was possible, that I thought
possible. I prepared myself. There was no counsel. Not that I
would term, not any. I could look, listen, sensing what I might ...
the thing to separate us from my fellows
who we were
I may speak of security, perhaps of securitys, the security, that
security, security.

James Kelman, Translated Accounts (2001)

The extent to which the war power seeps into our everyday thoughts
and routines has been well documented. As everything and everywhere
becomes a security zone, so the war power finds a way of threading itself
through our lives. We know plenty about the militarised nature of toys
and games, about fashion as military chic,[1] about cars designed as combat-
ready flexible fortresses[2] and of urban spaces secured as war zones.[3]
More than anything, our everyday language and thus our being and
thinking is weighed down by war power: we talk in everyday terms of
launching a blistering attack, continuing fallout, receiving flak, of 'press-
gangs' (originating from the collective noun for a group of sailors who
forced men into the navy), 'headhunters' (originally from the desire to
decapitate the enemy King), 'blockbusters' (originally a large bomb used
to demolish a number of buildings simultaneously), 'pickets' (originally
the term for a group of soldiers placed in advance of the rest of the troops),
'freelancers' (originally a medieval mercenary) and 'raids' (originally a
military expedition on horseback or a hostile and predatory incursion of
mounted men). Workplaces are now filled to the brim with 'strategic
thinking' (originally from the Greek *strategos*, meaning a 'general' or

'military commander', which in turn comes from *stratos*, meaning 'army') about this, that and the other.[4] More than anything, perhaps, we are constantly faced with a society that seems to be struggling under the weight of 'trauma'.

This weight has partly come about through the ways in which war has been discussed. At some point in the future, note the editors of one collection of essays on the trauma of war, historians looking back at the wars of the 1980s, 1990s and early twenty-first century will notice 'trauma projects' appearing amid all the military and humanitarian interventions that now take place.[5] But such projects are evidence of the much wider extent to which the idea of trauma is now deeply engrained in our political, cultural and intellectual universe. What in the seventeenth century was a surgeon's term to describe a physical wound, transformed in the nineteenth century to include psychic ailments comparable to shock, morphed into 'shell shock' and 'nervous trauma' by the end of WWI, and from there eventually became a psychiatric category now used to describe experience of war, genocide and catastrophe. The history of the category could be described as moving from the idea of physical damage to the mental health system and on to the social management of major disasters.[6] From there, however, trauma has become the discourse through which virtually all suffering is expressed: 'That was really traumatic!' is now thought to be an appropriate response to any event that would once have been described as 'rather unpleasant' or 'quite difficult'.

When categories and concepts take on an increasing appearance of being the 'natural' categories through which we are encouraged to think, critical theory needs to be on the alert. Such is the case with trauma. In this closing chapter I want to ask what the proliferation of trauma-talk might be doing, ideologically and politically. This proliferation of trauma-talk is connected to the idea that we live in an 'age of anxiety'. A glance at any security text, from the most mundane government pronouncement to the most sophisticated literature within academic 'security studies', reveals that through the politics of security runs a political imagination of fear and anxiety.[7] Connecting this imagination with the question of trauma, I suggest that the management of trauma and anxiety has become a way of mediating the demands of the war power as it operates under the sign of security. The war *of* security and *for* security is a war that functions *through* security. This is a war the permanence and universality of which has been established to match the permanence and universality of our supposed desire for security. This closing chapter therefore seeks to understand the emergence of a hypertrophied concept of trauma and the proliferation of discourses of anxiety as ideological mechanisms deployed by the war power in the name of security. This deployment manifests itself in terms of the key political category of our times: resilience. I want to suggest that the language of trauma and anxiety, and the training in resilience that we are now required to undertake in order to deal with what we are told is the coming trauma, is a means of policing us as subjects in the permanent exercise of the war power: the war on terror, the war of security and the war for accumulation.

ANXIETY: RESILIENCE

We live, apparently, in anxious times. Judging by material available in bookshops, the idea of an 'age of anxiety' would appear to have become part of our cultural common sense, being used to think through questions of crime (*Fear of Crime: Critical Voices in an Age of Anxiety*, 2008); conspiracy theory (*The Age of Anxiety: Conspiracy Theory and the Human Sciences*, 2001); corporate management (*Global Firms and Emerging Markets in an Age of Anxiety*, 2004); parenting (*Perfect Madness: Motherhood in the Age of Anxiety*, 2005; *Worried all the Time: Overparenting in an Age of Anxiety and How to Stop It*, 2003); religions of all sorts (*Hope Against Darkness: The Transforming Vision of St Francis in an Age of Anxiety*, 2002; *For Our Age of Anxiety: Sermons from the Sermon on the Mount*, 2009; *Ancient Wisdom for an Age of Anxiety*, 2007); language (*At War with Diversity: US Language Policy in an Age of Anxiety*, 2000); drugs (*The Age of Anxiety: A History of America's Turbulent Affair with Tranquilizers*, 2009; *A Social History of the Minor Tranquilizers: The Quest for Small Comfort in the Age of Anxiety*, 1991); new age claptrap (*The Road Less Travelled: Spiritual Growth in an Age of Anxiety*, 1997); sex (*Mindblowing Sex in the Real World: Hot Tips for Doing It in the Age of Anxiety*, 1995); food and drink (*Consuming Passions: Cooking and Eating in an Age of Anxiety*, 1998); and just plain old hope (*Hope in the Age of Anxiety*, 2009). This list could go on, taking in the various tomes on 'status anxiety', 'middle-class anxiety', 'millennial anxiety', the 'anxiety of influence', and, apropos of the argument in Chapter 3, 'anxious masculinity'. Symptomatically, one also finds accounts of the 'war on terror' called *The Age of Anxiety* (2005).[8]

'In Western intellectual history, the concept of anxiety seems to have acquired a certain epistemological cache', notes Sianne Ngai, with the concept 'stretching across knowledge formations and disciplinary vocabularies'.[9] This cache has in part been achieved by the Diagnostic and Statistical Manual of Mental Disorders (DSM), the American Psychiatric Association's list of mental disorders and how to diagnose them. The first edition of DSM in 1952 ran to 129 pages and contained just 106 diagnostic 'disorders'. The second edition was published in 1968, with 134 pages and 182 categories. DSM-III, in 1980, was 494 pages long and contained 265 categories. DSM-IV, from 1994, had 886 pages and 297 diagnostic categories. Part of the increase in size and proliferation of categories has been because disorder has been defined according to forms of behaviour and used to define clinical categories. For example, being a bit nervous or shy is a symptom of an underlying condition, which then becomes a clinical category, such as social phobia, which is the term used as an explanation of what the manual calls 'social anxiety disorder'. Some of what it says about social anxiety concerns specific conditions, such as Parkinson's disease or disfigurement, but the term is also intended to capture fear or anxiety about one or more social situations in which the person is exposed to scrutiny by others, such as being observed or performing; fear that one will be negatively evaluated; and fear of situations which might provoke anxiety. DSM-IV then adds further detail on what it calls 'Generalized Anxiety Disorder (GAD)', which includes excessive anxiety and worry about two or more domains such as family, health, finances and school/work difficulties; excessive anxiety on more days than not for three months or more; anxiety showing symptoms such as restlessness, edginess, muscle tension; anxiety associated with behaviours such as avoidance of situations in which a negative outcome could occur, or marked time and effort preparing for situations in which a negative outcome could occur, or procrastination due to worries, or seeking reassurance due to worries.

On the basis of the DSM it might actually be impossible to be human and avoid being diagnosed with a treatable mental disorder connected with anxiety. This would be consistent with the fact that, according to the World Health Organization, anxiety has emerged as the most prevalent mental health problem across the globe, and a UK report, *Working Our Way to Better Mental Health* (2008), estimates anxiety and associated mental health disorders are responsible for a major part of sickness at work.[10] Thus one finds anxiety articulated as a problem just about everywhere one looks. The Agoraphobia Society started life in the UK over 30 years ago with a fairly specific remit, dealing with agoraphobia; it later extended this remit and became the National Phobics Society, with the remit extended along the lines of the change of name, and has since renamed itself Anxiety UK.

In this regard we might pay heed to Franz Neumann's comment on the role of anxiety as one of the cornerstones of the political mobilisation of fear under fascism.[11] But one of Neumann's insights was to grasp that anxiety could play a similar role in the formation of liberal political subjectivity, one which therefore opened the door to liberalism's authoritarian mobilisations and manoeuvres. After all, was 'the anxiety of freedom' not the cornerstone of the kind of liberal subject announced with the birth of liberal politics?[12] Might not that anxiety of freedom be intensified even further in a historical period defined as the 'age of anxiety' but which is also an age of intensified (neo-)liberalism and in which liberalism's violent and authoritarian core is clear for all to see? And how might this connect to the fact that the age has also made clear the extent to which security is liberalism's core idea? If we accept that an anxiety of insecurity underpins the politics of security, and we understand the war power under the sign of security, then might we not think of the 'age of anxiety' in terms of the deployment of anxiety in a permanent security war?

One way to consider this is through the concept of 'resilience'. In the aftermath of the bombs in London in July 2005 the British Prime Minister spoke of 'the stoicism and resilience of the people of London', and the Deputy Assistant Commissioner of the Metropolitan Police assured viewers that the emergency services 'had sufficient resilience to cope'.[13] Their use of the term was significant, for 'resilience' has very quickly become the new fetish of the liberal state. The word falls easily from the mouths of politicians, state departments of all kinds fund research into it, urban planners are now obliged to take it into consideration, disaster recovery systems compelled to plan it into their preparations, and academics are falling over themselves to conduct research on it.

Resilience stems from the idea of a system (the term originates in ecological thought), which gives a certain scientific weight to ideas such as 'preparedness' and 'prevention' and, as Claudia Aradau and Rens van Munster point out, 'smoothly combines meanings derived from physiology (the capacity of material to return to a previous state), psychology (the capacity of an individual to return to normal after a traumatic event), ecology (the capacity of systems to continue funct-ioning and renew themselves after a disruptive event) and informatics (the capacity of a system to keep on functioning despite anomalies and design flaws)'.[14] The central meaning is the capacity of a system to return to a previous state, to recover from a shock, or to bounce back after a crisis or trauma. Thus, for example, a 2008 OECD document on state-building, styled 'from fragility to resilience', defines the latter as 'the ability to cope with changes in capacity, effectiveness or legitimacy. These changes can be driven by shocks … or through long-term erosions (or increases) in capacity, effectiveness or legitimacy'.[15] As well as offering a succinct definition, this OECD document also reveals what is at stake and why the concept has become so appealing: rather than speak of fragility and its (negative) associations, we should be speaking of resilience and its (positive) connotations.

The first thing to note is the impact this is having on the concept of security. The *National Security Strategy of the United States of America* (2002), published as a major statement of US strategy following the attacks on the World Trade Center, mentions 'resilience' just once. In contrast, five years later the *National Strategy for Homeland Security* (2007) is almost obsessed with the idea. The document outlines the need for 'structural and operational resilience of … critical infrastructure and key resources', but resilience is also planned for 'the system as a whole' and even for 'the American spirit', with the overall aim to 'disrupt the enemy's plans and diminish the impact of future disasters through measures that enhance the resilience of our economy and critical infrastructure before an incident occurs'.[16] By the tenth anniversary of the attacks, President Obama could publicly declare that 'these past 10 years tell a story of our resilience'.[17]

The UK's *National Security Strategy* published a year after the US *Strategy for Homeland Security*, notes that 'since 2001, the Government has mounted a sustained effort to improve the resilience of the United Kingdom'. The document goes on to talk about the resilience of the armed forces, of police and of the British people, of 'human and social resilience' and of 'community resilience'. Yet more than anything, the document is focused on preparing for future attacks: 'We will work with owners or operators to protect critical sites and essential services; with business to improve resilience'. It outlines a 'programme of work to improve resilience' at national, regional and local level, and across 'government, the emergency services, the private sector, and the third sector'.[18]

Such claims have created the rationale for state institutions and personnel to be reorganised and retrained. This includes, for example, the resilience training offered to armed forces: the US now has CSF2, which stands for 'Comprehensive Soldier and Family Fitness', a programme designed to push the fitness of US army personnel, their families and friends, and, in a roundabout way, the citizenry. The original strap line of the programme was 'Strong Minds, Strong Bodies', but this was changed in 2012 to 'Building Resilience, Enhancing Performance', and in the same year the programme as a whole underwent substantial rethinking and restructuring around the idea of resilience. As a consequence, CSF2 offers a Performance and Resilience Enhancement Program (CSF2-PREP), run by Master Resilience Trainers and consisting of various aspects such as Universal Resilience Training and Institutional Resilience Training. More advanced Comprehensive Resilience Models include Building Resilience for the Male Spouse, Building Your Teen's Resilience and Dynamics of Socially Resilient Teams. The programme publishes *CSF2 Quarterly*, which runs 'Resilience Tips', and the website even offers a Global Assessment Tool for individuals to assess their resilience. Other evidence of the way in which resilience has seeped through state power would be the creation of units such as 'UK Resilience' based in the UK Cabinet Office, through resilience training as a means of developing a military ethos in British schoolchildren,[19] new techniques designed to predict violent behaviour among soldiers and to stop them from 'snapping' by increasing their 'resiliency',[20] right down to the fact that sniffer dogs now receive resilience training.[21]

What both the US and the UK strategy documents reveal is the extent to which resilience, which emerged from under the sign of security, is subsuming and surpassing the logic of security itself. The demand of security and for security is somehow no longer enough. Thus whenever one hears the call 'security', one now also finds the demand of 'resilience'. For example, much was made about the security measures enacted for the London Olympics of 2012, but the relevant body of the London

Organizing Committee was not a 'Security' section but a 'Security and Resilience' section, working with a 'London Resilience Team' whose task it was to 'deliver Olympic Resilience in London'. It is as though the state is fast becoming exhausted by its own logic of security and wants a newer concept, something better and bolder: enter 'resilience'.

Yet as well as being newer, better and bolder, resilience is also more imaginative. The state now assumes that one of its key tasks is to imagine the worst-case scenario, the coming catastrophe, the crisis-to-come, the looming war attack, the emergency that could happen, might happen and probably will happen, all in order to be better prepared.[22] In the US and UK security strategies just cited, a future attack of some (unstated) sort is assumed to be going to happen, and even if a terror attack is prevented a disaster of some other sort is assumed bound to happen at some time. Preparedness, prevention, planning and preemption have therefore become core ideas surrounding resilience. Resilience both engages and encourages a culture of preparedness, in such a way that the logic of security in the form of preparation for a terrorist attack folds into a much broader logic of security in the form of preparation for an unknown disaster (hence the 'readiness campaigns' run via websites such as Ready.gov). But the real power of this culture lies in the idea of a coming *political* disaster striking at the very heart of the war power. Although the 'terror' attack and the 'natural' disaster are often brought together – the forest fire raises the possibility of terrorist arson, a new strain of flu raises the possibility of bioterrorism, and so on – taken together they are intensely future-oriented. They thereby come to shape behaviour beyond stocking up on duct-tape, batteries, tinned food and bottles of water, for they orient us towards a future event beyond our control and about which we must be anxious, but which we must be prepared to take under our control by being trained to withstand and bounce back from.

Resilience is nothing if not an apprehension of the future, but a future imagined as disaster/attack and then, more importantly, recovery from the disaster/attack. In this task resilience plays heavily on its origins in systems thinking, explicitly linking security with urban planning, civil contingency measures, public health, financial institutions, corporate risk and the environment in a way that had previously been incredibly hard for the state to do. Thus a Department for International Development publication on *Defining Disaster Resilience* (2011) finds that disaster resilience stretches across the whole social and political fabric, while a UN document on disaster management suggests that to be fully achieved a policy of resilience requires 'a consideration *of almost every physical phenomenon on the planet*'.[23] One way that such a diverse range of things used to be grasped together was under the rubric of the police power, in the original meaning of the term within the first police science. But the liberal state now finds itself unable or unwilling to openly describe such measures as 'police'. Hence it has had to develop other categories. Security has been one such category; resilience is now another.

Moreover, the presupposition of permanent threat – to the war power, to the social order, to human being – demands a constant reimagining of the myriad ways in which the threat might be realised. Resilience thereby comes to be a fundamental mechanism for policing the imagination. 'Imagination is not a gift usually associated with bureaucracies', noted the official *9/11 Commission Report* in 2004, which then went on to suggest that what the state needed was a means of connecting state bureaucracy with the political imagination.[24] 'Resilience' is the concept that facilitates that connection, nothing less than the attempted colonisation of the political imagination by the state.

Seen in this light, the administration of anxiety is a means of preparing us for the next attack in the permanent war on terror, the attack we are told time and again is bound to come – how many times does a politician, police chief or security intellectual tell us that 'an attack is highly likely', even just after (or *especially* just after) a supposed victory in the war? – and which could be and probably will be worse than the last attack and might even be worse than anything we can imagine, all of which enables an acceptance of the ubiquity of the war power, the purported endlessness of the 'war on terror' and the permanence of the security preparations carried out in its name. 'Resilience' appears to fulfil a large part of this role. 'War is no longer in its execution, but in its preparation', says Paul Virilio,[25] and in such preparation the war power subsumes the imagination of the future. No political imagination except an imagination of attack and recovery; no political future except an infinite preparation for war.

What war is this? It is easy to think that the war in question is the 'war on terror', and of course in one sense it obviously is. But type 'resilience' into the website of the International Monetary Fund and the search reveals that almost 2,000 IMF documents contain some reference to the term; 'resilient' generates another 1,730 hits.[26] 'Resilience' or 'resilient' appear in the title of 53 documents. All of these documents have been published since 2008. Separating these into two broad types gives a group of texts in which resilience and disaster go hand in hand – for example, *Sendai: A Tale of Natural Disaster, Resilience and Recovery* (2010) – and a second, far larger group, in which resilience is something that needs nurturing or building: *Enhancing Resilience to Shocks and Fostering Inclusive Growth* (2012), *Latin America Needs to Build Resilience and Flexibility* (2012), *Building Up Resilience in Low-Income Countries* (2012), and so on. Running through the texts is one core assumption: that the global financial system needs to become resilient, that national and regional economies need to build resilience, and that 'sustained adjustment' is a means of developing this resilience. Relatedly, the World Economic Forum now speaks about 'systemic financial resilience'. The World Bank also has a 'Social Resilience and Climate Change' Group which has published a series of pieces on 'social resilience' as a means of fighting poverty and overcoming the weaknesses of fragile states, and in conjunction with the UN, the World Bank has come up with the novel idea that resilience is now the means for 'growing the wealth of the poor'.[27] The beauty of the idea that resilience is what the world's poor need is that it turns out to be something that the world's poor already inherently possess; all they require is a little training in how to realise it. Hence the motif of building, nurturing and developing that runs through so much of the IMF literature.

It is clear that resilience has registered with these organisations as a means of further pursuing an explicitly neoliberal agenda. Not only is resilience increasingly coming to replace security in political discourse, then, but it is doing so by simultaneously becoming one of the key ideological tropes underpinning the war of accumulation. If security is being subsumed under the idea of resilience, and security is the supreme concept of bourgeois society, then resilience is, in effect, becoming the supreme concept under which accumulation is being organised. This is why as well as becoming the official means by which the world's poor are to move out of poverty, resilience is also becoming central to corporate restructuring, with 'organisational resilience' trumpeted and defended by the 'International Consortium for Organizational Resilience' (which runs a range of courses offering 'certification' in various aspects of resilience). Likewise, state officials very quickly resort to the theme as a mechanism for undermining anti-austerity actions.[28] This consolidation of the centrality of 'resilience' to political discourse thus reunites state and capital by foregrounding a politics of anticipation.

Yet resilience has also expanded to straddle the subjective as well as the objective, and so systemic, organisational and political resilience is connected to *personal* resilience. Hence the theme of resilience as a personal attribute now dominates self-help books: *The Resilience Factor: 7 Keys to Finding Your Inner Strength and Overcoming Life's Hurdles* (2003); *The Power of Resilience: Achieving Balance, Confidence, and Personal Strength in Your Life* (2004); *Resilience: Bounce Back from Whatever Life Throws at You* (2010); *Find Your Power: A Toolkit for Resilience and Positive Change* (2010); *Building Resilience in Children and Teens* (2011); *Resilience: Teach Yourself How to Survive and Thrive in Any Situation* (2012); *Resilience: The Science of Mastering Life's Greatest Challenges* (2012). This list of books could go on and on and the longer it went on the more obvious would be the fact that they have all been published in the twenty-first century. It is here that one finds the relationship between the economic development of liberal subjectivity and the political development of resilient citizenship.

Marx long ago spelt out the ways in which bourgeois society, rooted objectively in capitalism's need and desire for permanent change and constant revolutionising of production, is a system of everlasting uncertainty; capital both generates and thrives on the anxiety that lies at the core of bourgeois subjectivity. The intensification of this aspect of class society, repackaged by politicians and employers as an inevitable fact of contemporary labour and exacerbated by the anxiety associated with the rise of consumerism, a decline of trust in public institutions and private corporations, and a collapse in pension schemes, has been compounded by this articulation of resilience as personal as well as systemic. Resilience comes to form the basis of *subjectively* dealing with the uncertainty and instability of contemporary capital as well as the insecurity of the national security state and a condition of permanent war, as the administration of anxiety becomes part of the wider emotional administration within the corporations and organisations of capitalism.[29] As Pat O'Malley puts it, 'resilience does not seek only to render individuals able to "bounce back" … an essentially reactive model'. Rather, 'it aims to create subjects capable of adapting to, and exploiting to their advantage, situations of radical uncertainty'.[30] Good subjects will 'survive and thrive in any situation': they will 'achieve balance' across the several insecure and part-time jobs they have, 'overcome life's hurdles' such as facing retirement without a pension to speak of, and just 'bounce back' from whatever life throws, whether it be cuts to benefits, wage freezes or global economic meltdown. This is war-preparation and self-help conjoined – the policing of the resilient subject for the war power – which also coincides with the socio-economic fabrication of resilient yet flexible labour. Political subjectivity is nothing if not a training in resilience as the new technology of the self: a training to withstand whatever crisis capital undergoes and whatever political measures the state carries out to save it. And one needs to stress here the *training* that is at stake, for although some individuals, communities, states or societies might be conceived of as more resilient than others, none might ever be conceived of as fully resilient. Resilience is always a work in progress, a training in how to manage one's place in the accumulation wars as well as the security wars.

This in turn explains two notable developments during the same period. First is the growth of political 'happiness agendas' and official 'happiness indices'. Resilience is central not only to the self-help industry, but also to the wider 'happiness studies' now being peddled by politicians and academic disciplines such as psychology and economics.[31] The *Journal of Happiness Studies* was launched in 2000 and has gradually increased its interest in resilience. 'Resilience is very, very important' says Richard Layard, a leading figure of the new 'Action for Happiness' movement and now a British Lord for his work in the field. What might improve a nation's happiness score? For Layard, it is 'a programme in schools to build resilience among children'.[32] Happiness is to become part of our resilience training; resilience is to be learnt as part of our happiness training.

Second, and more broadly, it is for this reason that the psy-disciplines have been central to the growth of 'resilience'.[33] Major groups such as the American Psychological Association have been central to the 'happy resilient citizen' agenda. The APA launched a major 'Road to Resilience' campaign in 2002 explicitly in order to link the attacks on 11 September 2001 with 'the hardships that define all of our lives, anytime that people are struggling with an event in their communities'. 'It became clear that these events helped to open a window to self discovery for many', said Jan Peterson, assistant executive director of public relations in APA's

Practice Directorate. 'People were interested in learning more about themselves – and in particular, how to become more resilient'. The APA launched a 'multi-media approach', with a free tool kit including '10 ways to build resilience', a documentary video *Aftermath: The Road to Resilience* with three 'overarching messages' ('resilience can be learned'; 'resilience is a journey, not an event or single turning point'; 'there is no prescribed timeline for the road to resilience'), special phases of the campaign including 'Resilience for Kids and Teens', and resilience workshops for journalists.[34] The main theme to emerge is how individuals, communities and organisations might 'bounce back' from any attacks, setbacks or challenges.[35] A leading article called 'Providing Direction on The Road to Resilience' by Russ Newman, executive director at the APA, published in *Behavioral Health Management* in July 2003 to publicise the campaign, has been made available on websites run by and for business management.[36] The APA has pursued this to such an extent that resilience has become one of the guiding principles of what is regarded as psychological health.

All of which is to say that resilience now nestles alongside anxiety as part of the jargon of authenticity.[37] Superficially, such jargon is full of 'recognition' for the complexities of human experience and human beings as sensuous and therefore suffering beings. 'The need to lend a voice to suffering is a condition of all truth', notes Adorno.[38] But whether this should be understood as anxiety (or trauma, as we shall see) is doubtful, for the way it is presented merely encourages the naturalisation of an anxious subjectivity mobilised for capital and the state. If, as Franco Fornari once put it, 'war could be seen as an attempt at therapy',[39] the success of this therapeutic desire within the war power is heavily dependent on an aspect of the police power: the policing of the self. Our anxiety as subjects, as workers, as citizens preparing to be damaged by the war to come, becomes subsumed under a structure of self-policing. This is police power at its most profound, shaping subjectivity and fabricating order through psy-experts here, there and everywhere: counsellors in police departments, therapists in the workplace, psychologists in the media and analysts in the cultural field, all offering advice on our anxieties, coaching us in our resilience and thus, in a roundabout way, functioning as technologies of security and the war power. As a consequence, it achieves the ultimate police dream: closing down alternative possibilities. We can be individually anxious about the state of the world and about what might happen but our response must be resilience-training, not political struggle. We are permitted to be collectively anxious and structurally resilient; we are not permitted to be mobilised politically.

RESILIENCE: TRAUMA; OR, THIS IS NOT A CONCLUSION

Towards the end of an essay on anxiety published in 1926, Freud explores the relationship between anxiety and danger. He suggests that we can distinguish realistic anxiety centred on known danger and neurotic anxiety centred on unknown danger. In this context, he introduces the concept of trauma: danger conjures up feelings of helplessness and Freud suggests that a situation of helplessness that has been actually experienced is a traumatic situation. He therefore ends his comments with a dialectical triad that runs: 'anxiety-danger-helplessness (trauma)'.[40] Since we have been speaking politically about anxiety, what might we make of the connection with trauma?

A few years before that essay, Freud published *Beyond the Pleasure Principle* (1920). Early in that text he writes about the lack of any analysis of war neuroses, which had been a major issue during and in the aftermath of WWI. 'Shell shock' is that war's emblematic psychiatric disorder, but by 1916 the term 'shell shock' was being used as a synonym for 'war neuroses'.

Now, the first DSM (DSM-I, 1952) contained a category known as 'gross stress reaction', picking up on the experience of soldiers in WWII and trying to move beyond 'shell shock' and 'war neuroses'. DSM-II, however, published in 1968, no longer had a listing for any kind of psychiatric disorder produced by war. Rather, it was suggested that the symptoms formerly understood under 'gross stress reaction' should be reclassified under 'adjustment reaction to adult life'. This meant that war veterans returning from Vietnam after 1968 were being assessed using a diagnostic nomenclature that did not appear to have any terminology specific to war-related trauma. Vietnam veteran groups gradually mobilised around and against this, since they believed that the experiences of returnees were either not being properly recognised or appreciated by the authorities. Or where they were recognised, it was not through the right prism – of war. The issue was finally resolved in 1980 with the *invention*, as Allan Young puts it, of 'post traumatic stress disorder' (PTSD). In other words, the fate of the category 'trauma' was tied to the history of warfare, and one can't understand PTSD without grasping it in the context of America's attempt to understand Vietnam and its own role (and 'traumatic' defeat) in that war. That is, we need to recognise that PTSD was a *politically driven psychiatric diagnosis*.[41]

One of the outcomes of the struggles over PTSD was that as a label it meant abandoning the term 'neurosis' in dealing with the experiences of the people in question. Didier Fassin and Richard Rechtman point out that this was a huge conceptual shift with profound political implications, because it meant jettisoning the tradition of suspicion that had always surrounded the idea of trauma and which had been captured with the label 'neuroses'. This suspicion had its roots in the class politics of the terminology in question, because despite its long history in the English language 'trauma' only really came into its own as a category in the nineteenth century, and it did so as a means of interpellating workers on railways who were thought to be malingering after an accident. In the early twentieth century it was then used for interpellating working-class soldiers thought to be malingering after war experience. The original 'trauma' victims were 'the workforce in a rapidly expanding industrial society and cannon fodder for its great international conflicts'.[42] In other words, the term 'trauma' was originally applied to what were thought to be the malingerers and shirkers of the working class, although at that point the term was not being used with any sympathy.

The withdrawal of the neurotic paradigm and the end of the crusade to discover fraud or malingering had a major impact, since not only was trauma no longer a mark of malingering or cowardice, it was also now something that could be grasped and sympathised with. That this eventually occurred through the struggle for recognition of the trauma suffered by Vietnam veterans was crucial, since it meant that if American soldiers could be understood as genuine victims of trauma, then the implication was that the perpetrators of violence and atrocities could be counted among its victims. Indeed, as it agitated for changes to DSM-III the Vietnam Veterans Working Group argued that the symptoms of Vietnam compensation victims were very similar to those of the victims of what is widely said to be the most politically significant trauma of a century of traumas: the concentration camp survivors. And when not invoking the holocaust, the comparison was made with victims of other mass historical atrocities, such as the slave trade or Hiroshima. In the

American context, classing perpetrators as victims was a move that satisfied both pacifists and supporters of the war because it meant that the war could be denounced by both sides and without directly condemning those who fought in it. In terms of healing and unifying a nation seriously divided by the war, not least given the historical moment in which more and more atrocities committed by American troops were being uncovered, the importance of the step taken in shifting the language of trauma perhaps can't be overstated, for it generated the all-encompassing categories of 'survivor' and 'trauma-victim'.[43] This transformation of Vietnam veterans from agents of genocide into victims of trauma was assisted by mass cultural production, which took on a decidedly 'post-traumatic' coloration.

Understood outside the American context and in terms of the wider political and cultural shifts, we might say that by re-presenting trauma through a narrative of victimhood, psychiatry has played a crucial role in helping the war power conceal the trauma that the war power itself produces; experiences and memories understood as trauma come to play a central role in the reassertion of political authority.[44] Depoliticising a highly charged situation, 'trauma' replaces politics with a concept of psychic wounding, to be managed by the individual and the state.

From here on, psychiatry would treat the war experience as a 'microcosm of trauma',[45] so that 'war zones' are now always already understood through the language of the traumatic: 'Iraqis are being traumatized every day'; 'within five years of the falling of the regime, all Iraqis will be traumatized'; and so on.[46] This trauma talk is also now incorporated into what passes as 'postwar' (hence war crimes tribunals and truth and reconciliation commissions are often mapped out as a working through of the trauma of the war),[47] what passes as 'terrorism' ('trauma and terrorism' are now so frequently placed together and assumed to go together that handbooks are published on the topic),[48] and what passes as 'peace talk' (leading figures in 'peace research' now insist that the 'underlying *problem* is *trauma* ... of both victims and perpetrators').[49]

Yet as we have seen in previous chapters, one of the features of 'contemporary' war is that the war zone is now global. The whole social order is understood to be the ground of war, and there is no 'frontline' or 'battlefield' in any meaningful sense of the term; the 'everywhere war', as Derek Gregory calls it.[50] And so trauma has moved away from the battlefield and into every walk of life. Not only has this made PTSD virtually indistinguishable from combinations of already established disorders such as depression, panic disorder and, of course, generalised anxiety disorder, it has also enabled the consciousness of trauma to penetrate all areas of social life and be applied to human experience in general.[51] Thus 'traumatic memory' has become a way of unravelling people's experiences even when they do not think of themselves as traumatised. Bruno Bettelheim, for example, writes of concentration camp survivors who 'often do quite well in life' and who appear 'symptom-free', but adds that this is only 'as far as appearances go'. So they must be placed under the sign of security: 'their life is in some essential respects ... full of inner insecurity' which 'they usually manage to hide'. Bettelheim knows this because 'the trauma [is] so horrendous' that real 'integration' requires 'acceptance of how severely one has been traumatized'.[52] At the same time, the term 'distant traumatic effects' is now widely used to describe people traumatised through a medium, the most common being TV, and 'tele-suffering' is a term used to describe suffering 'at a distance' in the form of 'secondary traumatisation' but captures the fact that it is thought to occur through watching the TV. This was something that became crucial to the supposedly mass traumatisation following 9/11, when it was simply taken for granted that the trauma-effect might apply to anyone who watched the event on television, thereby implicating us all, once again, as victims of this event and enmeshing us into the war power that was then said to be going to help us overcome it.

The extent to which it would be hard to overestimate the plasticity, power and apparently universal applicability of the concept is illustrated by the fact with which we began this chapter: that 'that was really traumatic!' has become a common way of describing a whole gamut of ultimately rather mundane experiences.[53] It is on this basis that traumatology has taken off, not least in the explosion of 'trauma-lit', 'trauma-drama' in general and the 'misery memoir' in particular,[54] and 'trauma tourism'.[55] Encouraged by specialist organisations such as the International Society for Traumatic Stress Studies (founded: 1985) and specialist outlets such as the *Journal of Traumatic Stress* (first volume: 1988), trauma talk has become everyday; Frank Furedi has revealed the proliferation of trauma talk in British newspapers, from just under 500 citations in 1994 to several thousand by the early twenty-first century,[56] and UNICEF now regularly reports on the huge numbers of children that it claims are psychologically traumatised. As a number of scholars have noted, a therapeutic ethos pervades public discourse in general and policy-making in particular, and a new 'therapeutic security paradigm' pervades the international scene.[57] The category 'trauma' has been central to this process: the state's appeal to trauma and related emotions is invoked as a way of authenticating suffering and thus validating the political claims made in response to that suffering. Trauma, we might say, has become part of the jargon of contemporary liberal authenticity. But then might it not also be so in a way similar to the relationship between anxiety and resilience, one which we have seen is organised through and with the war power, the police power?

In a discussion in 2003 Jacques Derrida asked a pertinent question: 'imagine that the Americans and, through them, the entire world, had been told: what has just happened, the spectacular destruction of two towers ... is an awful thing, a terrible crime, a pain without measure, but it's all over, it won't happen again, there will never again be anything as awful as or more awful than that'. Mourning would be possible, selves could be remade, pages would be turned, and a line could be drawn under the event. But as Derrida suggests, the traumatism which followed, like all traumatism, 'is produced by the *future*, by the *to come*, by the threat of the worst *to come*, rather than by an aggression that is "over and done with"'.[58] Derrida's suggestion runs counter to the common trope of 'trauma and/as memory', an approach which encourages us to think of trauma in terms of a 'remaking of the self' in the light of the past, as 'unclaimed experience', as the 'redemptive authority of history', as 'forgetfulness and forgiveness', as 'struggles over representations of the past', as 'remember suffering'.[59] This is especially the case following 9/11, an event which is presented to us as *the* collective trauma of our time: 'these are the days after', as one character puts it in Don DeLillo's novel *Falling Man*, 'everything now is measured by after'.[60] But the assumption that memory liberates is too easy. Indeed, when articulated in terms of the nation, the claim that memory liberates might equally be thought of as a form of containment.[61] The 'national healing' of a national trauma is too easily rendered a gesture of foreclosure. That is, it becomes a form of reconciliation, a distinctly conservative mode of politics.[62]

In contrast, Derrida's suggestion helps us read trauma in terms of the danger of the terror *to come*, or which *might* be to come. The trauma is the trauma of a future which is unknowable but imaginable, and *imaginable as traumatic*. Less 'the days after' and more 'the days before': the 'wound' of trauma is less the wound of the past and much more, to paraphrase Derrida, a wound which remains open in our terror of the danger that we imagine lies ahead, our anxiety of what we think might happen and which we are encouraged to imagine as being worse than anything that has ever taken place.

In this light, the issue is not the remaking of the self in the light of past trauma but the *making of the self in preparation for the trauma to come*. And that making of the self is how political subjectivity now comes to be policed: endlessly, just like the war power itself. The imagination of danger and the anxiety of terror is the contemporary psychopolitical ground of trauma politics. If the catastrophe must be imagined and the worst-case scenario considered so that contingency plans, emergency measures and, more than anything, the security arrangements be put in place for the war power to be preserved, then trauma is central to this preparation. To put that another way: if 'society must be defended', as we are now all fond of saying with Foucauldian irony (albeit with rather different levels of irony, depending on our politics), then it must be defended more than anything from its future traumas. Trauma has become a means of organising the subject of (in)security within a state of permanent war and thus, in a sense, within the war power itself.

This is where trauma connects to the growth of resilience as a political concept.[63] If resilience has come to the fore in the context of an anxious political psyche engaged in a permanent war of security and accumulation, we might add that it has done so for a social order and international system understanding itself as traumatised and preparing for more trauma to come. 'Resilience training' represents a general preparation for events defined in advance as traumatic. The biological and psychological frailty implied in the concept of trauma has to be somehow compensated for in advance by the strength and endurance implied in the concept of resilience. To be a viable political subject now means planning one's resilience to withstand the trauma-to-come.[64] Hence when the APA launched its 'Road to Resilience' campaign in 2002 it was explicitly designed to link 9/11 as a *traumatic* event with the more everyday hardships for which it believed people must prepare. Elsewhere one finds that resilience workshops are conducted in centres specialising in trauma.[65]

By pairing trauma with resilience, the subject's personal anxieties become bound up with the political dangers facing the nation; the trauma is individual and collective, and so the resilience training is the training in and of liberal subjects within the war power. The fabrication of liberal subjectivity and its martial defence are thereby achieved in one and the same moment. In this way the trauma-resilience couplet, and the therapeutic turn in general, are central to the way in which we now become subject to the logic of war, police and accumulation, and the way in which the war power and the police power are subsumed under the sign of security. The outcome is nothing less than the resilience of the war power itself.

'We have become waiting-machines', Henri Barbusse said of soldiers preparing for battle in WWI.[66] A century later, we have become preparation-machines. In the eyes of the state, being a preparation-machine is now what makes us an authentic citizen. 'Authentic' in the sense of the term as it is derived from the Greek *autos*, meaning self, and *hentes*, meaning prepared,[67] but also in the sense that it renders us part of the machinery of a state that is itself in constant war-preparation. And this preparation of the self for the war power forecloses political action, depriving us of the possibility of engaging in political acts beyond those determined by the state and carried out under the sign of security. We can prepare to be traumatised, we can undertake resilience training in preparation for the trauma-to-come, and we can obtain some therapy to help us cope with all the anxieties that this anticipation and preparation brings, but we must not challenge the preparation-machine politically, for to do so would be to challenge the war power and the police power in its entirety. Thus although the spreading use of the word 'trauma' might appear as an important interpretive magnification that marks contemporary critical thinking, that very fact is, as Geoffrey Hartman notes, 'probably a reaction to the absence of something more collectively defining'.[68]

The new jargon of authenticity renders obsolete the key categories of critical theory and seeks to replace them with the key tropes of contemporary bourgeois thought, the tropes determined and desired by the state, by capital, by the war power, by the police power. The idea of trauma replaces the idea of alienation and the war power rolls on, never stopping, never resting, never sleeping, on and on. The idea of anxiety replaces the idea of exploitation and the police power rolls on, across the workers and across their unions, on and on, over their rights and over their jobs, on and on, always rising, always consuming, always devouring. The prospect of resilience replaces the possibility of revolution and the war-police rolls on and on, on and on, and all the time capital changes, capital grows, capital wins.[69]

NOTES

A few internet sources have been used in the writing of this book. Publishers have a tendency to want to replicate the whole url when such references are made, for example: 'http://www.mod.uk/DefenceInternet/DefenceNews/ EquipmentAndLogistics/RafReaperReaches20000HoursOverAfghanistan.htm (accessed 25 December 2012)'. Aside from being extremely ugly, such citations do not really suit the purpose for which references are meant to be given. The provision of a url on an actual internet page is useful as the reader merely has to click on the link to connect to the reference, but I doubt that anyone reading a book ever sits down and types out the whole url provided in such a reference. I have therefore limited the number of urls provided in these notes to either the more obscure ones or to those which are simple to read and copy. Unless otherwise stated, all references to US Presidential speeches or comments are taken from the Presidential Papers internet resource http://www.presidency. ucsb.edu, which is the standard resource for official statements, speeches and discussions.

INTRODUCTION

1. Rupert Smith, *The Utility of Force: The Art of War in the Modern World* (London: Penguin, 2006), pp. 1, 2.
2. Anthony H. Cordesman, *The Lessons and Non-Lessons of the Air and Missile Campaign in Kosovo* (Washington, DC: Centre for Strategic and International Studies, 2003), p. 59.
3. Ray Odierno cited in Steven Lee Myers and Thom Shanker, 'General Works to Salvage Iraq Legacy', *New York Times*, 24 March 2010.
4. Michael Sherry, *In the Shadow of War: The United States since the 1930s* (New Haven: Yale University Press, 1995), p. 461.
5. John Mueller, 'War Has Almost Ceased to Exist: An Assessment', *Political Science Quarterly*, Vol. 124, No. 2, 2009, pp. 297–321.
6. Herfried Munkler, *The New Wars* (2002), trans. Patrick Camiller (Cambridge: Polity, 2005), pp. 3–4.

7. Chris Hables Gray, *Postmodern War: The New Politics of Conflict* (London: Guilford Press, 1997), p. 3.

8. Alain Badiou, 'Fragments of a Public Journal on the American War against Iraq', 26 February 2003, in *Polemics*, trans. Steve Corcoran (London: Verso, 2006), pp. 39–41; Antonio Negri and Eric Alliez, 'Peace and War' (2002), in Antonio Negri, *Empire and Beyond*, trans. Ed Emery (Cambridge: Polity, 2008), pp. 54–6.

9. Giorgio Agamben, *State of Exception* (2003), trans. Kevin Attell (Chicago: University of Chicago Press, 2005), p. 22.

10. Slavoj Žižek, in 'About War and the Missing Center in Politics: Sabine Reul and Thomas Deichmann talk to philosopher Slavoj Žižek', *Eurozine*, 15 March 2002, pp. 1–8, p. 8.

11. Slavoj Žižek, *Welcome to the Desert of the Real: Five Essays on September 11 and Related Dates* (London: Verso, 2002), pp. 93–4.

12. Ulrich Beck, 'The Silence of Words: On Terror and War', *Security Dialogue*, Vol. 34, No. 3, 2003, pp. 255–67, p. 256; Daniel Ross, *Violent Democracy* (Cambridge: Cambridge University Press, 2004), p. 12; Rey Chow, *The Age of the World Target: Self-Referentiality in War, Theory and Comparative Work* (Durham: Duke University Press, 2006), p. 34; Gopal Balakrishnan, *Antagonistics: Capitalism and Power in an Age of War* (London: Verso, 2009), p. 104; François Debrix, *Tabloid Terror: War, Culture, and Geopolitics* (London: Routledge, 2008), p. 97.

13. Oliver Richmond, *Peace in International Relations* (London: Routledge, 2008), p. 5.

14. Fritz Grob, *The Relativity of War and Peace: A Study in Law, History, and Politics* (New Haven: Yale University Press, 1949); Quincy Wright, 'When Does War Exist?', *American Journal of International Law*, Vol. 26, 1932, pp. 362–8, p. 363; Carl Schmitt, 'The Turn to the Discriminating Concept of War' (1937), trans. Timothy Nunan, in Carl Schmitt, *Writings on War* (Cambridge: Polity, 2011), pp. 31, 32; Georg Schwarzenberger, 'Jus Pacis Ac Belli? Prolegomena to a Sociology of International Law', *American Journal of International Law*, Vol. 37, No. 3, 1943, pp. 460–79; Philip C. Jessup, 'Should International Law Recognize an Intermediate Status between Peace and War?', *American Journal of International Law*, Vol. 48, No. 1, 1954, pp. 98–103.

15. Elihu Lauterpacht, 'The Legal Irrelevance of the "State of War"', *American Society of International Law, Proceedings*, Vol. 62, 1968, pp. 58–67, p. 59.

16. John Frederick Maurice, *Hostilities Without Declaration of War* (London: HMSO, 1883); Grob, *Relativity of War and Peace*, p. 203; Jessup, 'Should International Law Recognize', p. 99.

17. Mark Neocleous, *Critique of Security* (Edinburgh: Edinburgh University Press, 2008), pp. 46–59, 114–17.

18. C. Wright Mills, *The Power Elite* (New York: Oxford University Press, 1956), pp. 198, 222. Also see Jean Bethke Elshtain, *Meditations on Modern Political Thought: Masculine/Feminine Themes from Luther to Arendt* (University Park, PA: Pennsylvania State University Press, 1992), p. 122.
19. Philip Anthony Towle, *Pilots and Rebels: The Use of Aircraft in Unconventional Warfare 1918–1988* (London: Brassey's, 1989), p. 1. Nelson Maldonado-Torres has recently reiterated the account of European modernity since 1492 as the history of bourgeois society constituted as a social order of war – *Against War: Views from the Underside of Modernity* (Durham: Duke University Press, 2008).
20. Ian Hernon, *Britain's Forgotten Wars: Colonial Campaigns of the 19th Century* (Stroud: Sutton Publishing, 2003), p. 3.
21. For attempts along these lines which I have benefited from reading, see Tarak Barkawi, *Globalization and War* (Lanham: Rowman and Littlefield, 2006); Randy Martin, *An Empire of Indifference: American War and the Financial Logic of Risk Management* (Durham: Duke University Press, 2007); Michael McKinley, *Economic Globalisation as Religious War: Tragic Convergence* (Abingdon: Routledge, 2007); Christian Parenti, 'Planet America: The Revolution in Military Affairs as Fantasy and Fetish', in Ashley Dawson and Malini Johar Schueller (eds), *Exceptional State: Contemporary US Culture and the New Imperialism* (Durham: Duke University Press, 2007); Peter Alexander Meyer, *Civic War and the Corruption of the Citizen* (Chicago: University of Chicago Press, 2008); Tarik Kochi, *The Other's War: Recognition and the Violence of Ethics* (London: Birkbeck Law Press, 2009); Tiqqun, *Introduction to Civil War* (2009), trans. Alexander R. Galloway and Jason E. Smith (Los Angeles: Semiotext(e), 2011); Tiqqun, *This is Not a Program* (2009), trans. Joshua David Jordan (Los Angeles: Semiotext(e), 2011).
22. Frederick Engels, 'Speech at Elberfeld', 8 February, 1845, in Karl Marx and Frederick Engels, *Collected Works, Vol. 4* (London: Lawrence and Wishart, 1975), p. 248.
23. Frederick Engels, *The Condition of the Working Class in England* (1845), in Karl Marx and Frederick Engels, *Collected Works, Vol. 4* (London: Lawrence and Wishart, 1975), pp. 329, 331, 554, 502, 512.
24. Karl Marx, 'The June Revolution', in *Neue Rheinische Zeitung*, 29 June 1848, in Karl Marx and Frederick Engels, *Collected Works, Vol. 7* (London: Lawrence and Wishart, 1977), p. 147.
25. Karl Marx, *Capital: A Critique of Political Economy, Vol. 1* (1867), trans. Ben Fowkes (Harmondsworth: Penguin, 1976), pp. 409, 412–13.
26. Karl Marx and Frederick Engels, *The Manifesto of the Communist Party* (1848), in Karl Marx and Frederick Engels, *Collected Works, Vol. 6* (London: Lawrence and Wishart, 1984), pp. 477–519, p. 495.

27. Sinisa Malesevic, *The Sociology of War and Violence* (Cambridge: Cambridge University Press, 2010), p. 22.

28. See my 'The Political Economy of the Dead: Marx's Vampires', *History of Political Thought*, Vol. 24, No. 4, 2003, pp. 668–84, and, at further length, *The Monstrous and the Dead: Burke, Marx, Fascism* (Cardiff: University of Wales Press, 2005).

29. Marx, *Capital, Vol. 1*, p. 916.

30. Michael Dillon and Julian Reid, *The Liberal Way of War: Killing to Make Life* (London: Routledge, 2009). Also see Tarak Barkawi, *Globalization and War* (Lanham: Rowman and Littlefield, 2006); Domenico Losurdo, *Liberalism: A Counter-History* (2006), trans. Gregory Elliott (London: Verso, 2011).

31. Michel Foucault, *'Society Must Be Defended': Lectures at the Collège de France, 1975–76*, trans. David Macey (London: Allen Lane, 2003), pp. 15–16, 46–8, 50–1. Also see *Discipline and Punish: The Birth of the Prison* (1975), trans. Alan Sheridan (London: Penguin, 1977), p. 168; *The History of Sexuality: An Introduction* (1976), trans. Robert Hurley (London: Penguin, 1979), p. 93.

32. Carl von Clausewitz, *On War* (1832), trans. Michael Howard and Peter Paret (Princeton, NJ: Princeton University Press, 1976), p. 149, 605.

33. In the 'Declaration' he writes of war being the seed of life, the basis of rebirth, of manly courage and the need for war, his own happiness in war, of war as 'true salvation', while in the letters he writes of looking forward to the forthcoming 'great battle' (the battle of Jena) 'with joy as I would to my own wedding day'. See Carl von Clausewitz, 'Political Declaration' (1812), in *Historical and Political Writings*, ed. and trans. Peter Paret and Danial Moran (Princeton, NJ: Princeton University Press, 1992), pp. 290–1, 293; Letters to Countess von Bruhl, 18 September 1806 and 12 October 1806, both cited in Anatol Rapoport, 'Introduction', to Clausewitz, *On War* (1832), (Harmondsworth: Penguin, 1968), pp. 22, 416n6.

34. US Army and Marine Corps, *Counterinsurgency Field Manual*. US Army Field Manual No. 3-24/Marine Corps Warfighting Publication No. 3-33.5, 2006, Sects. 6-95, 7-26. Department of Defense and Department of Justice, *Memorandum of Understanding between Department of Defense and Department of Justice on Operations Other than War and Law Enforcement*, 20 April 1994, Sect. I, Pt. B.

35. Headquarters, Department of the Army, *Law and Order Operations*, ATTP, 3-39.10 (FM 19-10), Washington, DC, 20 June 2011.

36. Just a sample: Max Boot, *The Savage Wars of Peace: Small Wars and the Rise of American Power* (New York: Basic Books, 2002), pp. xx, 350; Rachel Bronson, 'When Soldiers Become Cops', *Foreign Affairs*, Vol. 81, No. 6, 2002, pp. 122–32; Howard Caygill, 'Perpetual Police: Kosovo and the Elision of Military Violence', *European Journal of Social Theory*, Vol. 4, No. 1, 2003, pp. 73–80; Graham Day and Christopher Freeman, 'Policekeeping is the

Key: Rebuilding the Internal Security Architecture of Postwar Iraq', *International Affairs*,Vol. 79, No. 2, 2003, pp. 299–313; Simon Cooper,'Perpetual War within the State of Exception', *Arena Journal*, 21, 2003–4, pp. 99–126; Kimberly Zisk Marten, *Enforcing the Peace: Learning from the Imperial Past* (NewYork: Columbia University Press, 2004), pp. 104–14; Michael Ignatieff, *Empire Lite: Nation-Building in Bosnia, Kosovo and Afghanistan* (London: Vintage, 2003), p. 79; Klaus Mladek, 'Exception Rules: Contemporary Political Theory and the Police', in Klaus Mladek (ed.), *Police Forces: A Cultural History of an Institution* (Basingstoke: Palgrave, 2007), p. 231; Nick Mansfield, *Theorizing War: From Hobbes to Badiou* (Basingstoke: Palgrave Macmillan, 2008), p. 5; Christian Olsson, 'Military Interventions and Concept of the Political', in Didier Bigo and Anastassia Tsoukala (eds), *Terror, Insecurity and Liberty: Illiberal States and Liberal Regimes after 9/11* (London: Routledge, 2008), pp. 146–77, p. 155; James Salt and M. L. R. Smith,'Reconciling Policing and Military Objectives: Can Clausewitzian Theory Assist the Police Use of Force in the United Kingdom?', *Democracy and Security*,Vol. 4, No. 3, 2008, pp. 221–44; Colin S. Gray, *Sheriff: America's Defense of the New World Order* (Lexington, KY: University of Kentucky Press, 2009).

37. Just a few examples:Thomas M. Franck and Faiza Patel,'UN Police Action in Lieu of War: "The Old Order Changeth"', *American Journal of International Law*,Vol. 85, No. 1, 1991, pp. 63–74; Peter Andreas,'The Rise of the American Crimefare State', *World Policy Journal*,Vol. 14, No. 3, 1997, pp. 37–45; Peter Andreas and Richard Price,'From War Fighting to Crime Fighting:Transforming the American National Security State', *International Studies Review*, Vol. 3, No. 3, 2001, pp. 31–52; Nathaniel Berman, 'Privileging Combat? Contemporary Conflict and the Legal Construction of War', *Columbia Journal of Transnational Law*,Vol. 43, No. 1, 2004, pp. 1–71; Alice Hills, *Future War in Cities: Rethinking a Liberal Dilemma* (London: Frank Cass, 2004); David Kennedy, *The Dark Sides of Virtue: Reassessing International Humanitarianism* (Princeton, NJ: Princeton University Press, 2004), p. 262; Peter Andreas and Ethan Nadelman, *Policing the Globe: Criminalization and Crime Control in International Relations* Oxford: Oxford University Press, 2006); David Kennedy, *Of War and Law* (Princeton, NJ: Princeton University Press, 2006), pp. 122–3; Jonathan Simon, *Governing Through Crime* (Oxford: Oxford University Press, 2007), p. 280; Robert Chesney and Jack Goldsmith,'Terrorism and the Convergence of Criminal and Military Detention Models', *Stanford Law Review*, Vol. 60, 2008, pp. 1079–133; Dominic Corva,'Neoliberal Globalization and the War on Drugs: Transnationalizing Illiberal Governance in the Americas', *Political Geography*,Vol. 27, No. 2, 2008, pp. 176–93; Dario Melossi, *Controlling Crime, Controlling Society: Thinking about Crime in Europe and America* (Cambridge:

Polity, 2008), p. 248; Paul W. Kahn, *Political Theology: Four New Chapters on the Concept of Sovereignty* (New York: Columbia University Press, 2011), p. 15. Also see the special issue of *Policing and Society*, Vol. 19, No. 2, 2009, on the problems of war, police and 'peace-keeping'.

38. Alain Badiou, *Infinite Thought: Truth and the Return of Philosophy*, trans. Oliver Feltham and Justin Clemens (London: Continuum, 2003), pp. 153–5; Paul Virilio, 'Endo-colonization and the State-as-Destiny', in Paul Virilio and Sylvere Lotringer, *Pure War* (New York: Semiotext(e), 2008), p. 106; Giorgio Agamben, 'The Sovereign Police', in Brian Massumi (ed.), *The Politics of Everyday Fear* (Minneapolis: University of Minnesota Press, 1993), p. 61; Michael Hardt and Antonio Negri, *Empire* (Cambridge, MA: Harvard University Press, 2000), pp. 12–13, 39, 180, 181; Michael Hardt and Antonio Negri, *Multitude: War and Democracy in the Age of Empire* (New York: Penguin, 2004), p. 14.

39. Mark Neocleous, *The Fabrication of Social Order: A Critical Theory of Police Power* (London: Pluto Press, 2000), building on the argument concerning political administration in Neocleous, *Administering Civil Society: Towards a Theory of State Power* (Basingstoke: Macmillan, 1996).

40. Marc Raeff, *The Well-Ordered Police State: Social and Institutional Change Through Law in the Germanies and Russia, 1600–1800* (New Haven: Yale University Press, 1983).

41. Hence the rich but overlooked history of 'medical police' – see Neocleous, *Fabrication*, pp. 88–9, and the continuing argument about the body politic in Mark Neocleous, *Imagining the State* (Milton Keynes: Open University Press, 2003), pp. 8–38.

42. Michel Foucault, 'Omnes et Singulatim: Towards a Criticism of "Political Reason"', in S. McMurrin (ed.), *The Tanner Lectures on Human Values, Vol. II* (Cambridge: Cambridge University Press, 1981), p. 249; Michel Foucault, *The Birth of the Clinic: An Archaeology of Medical Perception* (1963), trans. Alan Sheridan (London: Routledge, 1973), p. 26.

43. Michel Foucault, *History of Madness* (1961), trans. Jonathan Murphy and Jean Khalfa (London: Routledge, 2006), p. 62, emphasis added.

44. See Neocleous, *Fabrication*, Chapters 3 and 4 on 'ordering insecurity', as developed further in Neocleous, *Critique of Security*.

45. Michel Foucault, *Security, Territory, Population: Lectures at the Collège de France, 1977–1978*, trans. Graham Burchell (Basingstoke: Palgrave, 2007); *The Birth of Biopolitics: Lectures at the Collège de France, 1978–1979*, trans. Graham Burchell (Basingstoke: Macmillan, 2008).

46. Michel Foucault, *Psychiatric Power: Lectures at the Collège de France, 1973–1974*, trans. Graham Burchell (Basingstoke: Palgrave, 2006), p. 7.

47. Foucault, *Security, Territory, Population*, p. 296. Also see pp. 110, 311–12, 314, 317.

48. One only has to consider for a moment what Foucault would have made of counter-insurgency theorist David Kilcullen's oft-cited claim that 'counterinsurgency is armed social work' to get a glimpse of the possibilities in the conjunction. See Kilcullen's '"Twenty-Eight Articles": Fundamentals of Company-level Counterinsurgency', *Military Review*, Vol. 86, No. 3, 2006, pp. 103–8, p. 107.

49. To give just a few examples: Franz-Ludwig Knemeyer, 'Polizei', *Economy and Society*, Vol. 9, No. 2, 1980, pp. 173–95; Keith Tribe, 'Cameralism and the Science of Government', *Journal of Modern History*, Vol. 56, 1984, pp. 263–84; Jeffrey Minson, *Genealogies of Morals: Nietzsche, Foucault, Donzelot and the Eccentricity of Ethics* (London: Macmillan, 1985); Mitchell Dean, *The Constitution of Poverty: Toward a Genealogy of Liberal Governance* (London: Routledge, 1991); Colin Gordon, 'Governmental Rationality: An Introduction', in Graham Burchell, Colin Gordon and Peter Miller (eds), *The Foucault Effect: Studies in Governmentality* (Hemel Hempstead: Harvester Wheatsheaf, 1991); Mitchell Dean, *Governmentality* (London; Sage, 1999); Pasquale Pasquino, 'Theatrum Politicum: The Genealogy of Capital – Police and the State of Prosperity', in Burchell, Gordon and Miller (eds), *Foucault Effect*; Markus Dubber, *The Police Power: Patriarchy and the Foundations of American Government* (New York: Columbia University Press, 2005); Markus Dubber and Mariana Valverde (eds), *The New Police Science: Police Powers in Comparative Perspective* (Stanford, CA: Stanford University Press, 2006).

50. Mitchell Dean, 'Military Intervention as "Police" Action?', in Dubber and Valverde (eds), *New Police Science*; Ron Levi and John Hagan, 'International Police', in Dubber and Valverde (eds), *New Police Science*; and William Walters, 'Deportation, Expulsion, and the International Police of Aliens', *Citizenship Studies*, Vol. 6, No. 3, 2002, pp. 265–92. It is worth noting that the second edition of Mitchell Dean, *Governmentality* (London: Sage, 2010) tries to develop the idea of police beyond the question of 'pastoral power' in the first edition and onto the international organisation of population. However, the discussion is somewhat limited (pp. 244–5).

51. One can register here two broad examples taking in some 15 published articles. In 2010 the journal *International Political Sociology* published an issue (Volume 4, Issue 2) with a special section stemming from a roundtable discussion exploring the relationship between Foucault and IR at the 2009 International Studies Association conference. The following year the journal *Geopolitics* published a special issue (Volume 16, Issue 2) on 'War beyond the Battlefield', with the title designed to signify an approach to war outside mainstream military and strategic studies. As explained by David Grondin in his opening paper, the authors seek to explore 'through a Foucauldian understanding' the spaces 'where the boundaries of war and politics collide', yet none utilises Foucault's account

of the police power – David Grondin, 'The Other Spaces of War: War beyond the Battlefield in the War on Terror', *Geopolitics*, Vol. 16, No. 2, 2011, pp. 253–79, p. 254.

As well as the 15 articles in the two journal issues, a sampler of the work using Foucault for IR and geopolitics, yet veering away from an engagement with 'police', would include Cynthia Weber, *Simulating Sovereignty: Intervention, the State and Symbolic Exchange* (Cambridge: Cambridge University Press, 1994); Jens Bartelson, *A Genealogy of Sovereignty* (Cambridge: Cambridge University Press, 1995); Kimberly Hutchings, 'Foucault and International Relations Theory', in Moya Lloyd and Andrew Thacker (eds), *The Impact of Michel Foucault on the Social Sciences and Humanities* (Basingstoke: Macmillan, 1997), pp. 102–27; Stuart Elden, 'The War of Races and the Constitution of the State: Foucault's *"Il faut defendre la société"* and the Politics of Calculation', *boundary 2*, Vol. 29, No. 1, 2002, pp. 125–51; Heriberto Cairo, 'The Field of Mars: Heterotopias of Territory and War, *Political Geography*, Vol. 23, No. 8, 2004, pp. 1009–36; Andrew Neal, 'Cutting Off the King's Head: Foucault's Society Must Be Defended and the Problem of Sovereignty', *Alternatives*, Vol. 29, No. 4, 2004, pp. 373–98; Julian Reid, 'War, Liberalism, and Modernity: The Biopolitical Provocations of "Empire"', *Cambridge Review of International Affairs*, Vol. 17, No. 1, 2004, pp. 63–79; Vivienne Jabri, 'Michel Foucault's Analytics of War: The Social, the International, and the Racial', *International Political Sociology*, Vol. 1, No. 1, 2007, pp. 67–81; Jan Selby, 'Engaging Foucault: Discourse, Liberal Governance and the Limits of Foucauldian IR', *International Relations*, Vol. 21, No. 3, 2007, pp. 324–45; Dillon and Reid, *Liberal Way of War*; Nicholas J. Kiersey, 'Scale, Security, and Political Economy: Debating the Biopolitics of the Global War on Terror', *New Political Science*, Vol. 31, No. 1, 2009, pp. 27–47; Anna Agathangelou, 'Bodies of Desire, Terror and the War in Eurasia: Impolite Disruptions of (Neo) Liberal Internationalism and the "New" Imperium', *Millennium: Journal of International Studies*, Vol. 38, No. 3, 2010, pp. 693–722; Brad Evans, 'Foucault's Legacy: Security, War and Violence in the 21st Century', *Security Dialogue*, Vol. 41, No. 4, 2010, pp. 413–33.

52. Dean, 'Military Intervention as "Police" Action?'
53. Neocleous, *Fabrication*, pp. 82, 92; Guillermina Seri, *Seguridad: Crime, Police Power, and Democracy in Argentina* (New York: Continuum, 2012), p. 105.
54. Foucault, *'Society Must Be Defended'*, p. 50. Also see Antonio Negri, *The Porcelain Workshop: For a New Grammar of Politics* (2006), trans. Noura Wedell (New York: Semiotext(e), 2008), p. 56.
55. Gilles Deleuze and Felix Guattari, *A Thousand Plateaus: Capitalism and Schizophrenia* (1980), trans. Brian Massumi (London: Athlone Press, 1987), pp. 421–2; Zainab Bahrani, *Rituals of War: The Body and Violence in Mesopotamia* (New York: Zone Books, 2008), p. 13.

56. Arther Ferrill, *The Origins of War: From the Stone Age to Alexander the Great* (London: Thames and Hudson, 1985), p. 11.

57. This argument coincides with one of the themes of the emerging field of 'critical war studies' which points to the 'truth' and 'order' that war itself creates. See Tarak Barkawi and Shane Brighton, 'Powers of War: Fighting, Knowledge, and Critique', *International Political Sociology*, Vol. 5, No. 2, 2011, pp. 126–43. In a slightly different form (Tarak Barkawi, 'From War to Security: Security Studies, the Wider Agenda, and the Fate of the Study of War', *Millennium: Journal of International Studies*, Vol. 39, No. 3, 2011, pp. 701–16) this has generated a debate about the relationship between 'critical security studies' and 'critical war studies'. Most of that debate seems to focus on the degree to which the study of war and the study of security are or should be (in)separable. Symptomatically, and so far as I can tell, no one in that debate wants to say anything about 'police'. 'Crime' and 'criminality' occasionally get a mention; 'police' never.

58. Zygmunt Bauman, *Legislators and Interpreters: On Modernity, Post-modernity and Intellectuals* (Cambridge: Polity Press, 1987), p. 85.

59. Theodor Adorno, *Minima Moralia: Reflections from Damaged Life* (1951), trans. E. F. N. Jephcott (London: Verso, 1978), p. 80.

60. Cited in Francis Steegmuller, *Flaubert and Madame Bovary: A Double Portrait* (1939), (New York: New York Review Books, 2005), p. 283.

CHAPTER 1

1. Details given on the Nobel Prize website at nobelprize.org.

2. Frédéric Mégret, 'From "Savages" to "Unlawful Combatants": A Post-colonial Look at International Humanitarian Law's "Other"', in Anne Orford (ed.), *International Law and its Others* (Cambridge: Cambridge University Press, 2006), p. 273.

3. It is perhaps encapsulated by the way Kant is treated in these fields. Liberalism, and thus many international lawyers, like to cite Kant's essay 'Perpetual Peace' as a key philosophical document outlining the liberal foundations of peace, yet usually omit the fact that the essay was published in October 1795, just one month after the military suppression of the revolt in Poland led by Tadeusz Kosciuszko and Poland's partition by Russia and Prussia, and about which Kant has nothing to say.

4. Hans Kelsen, *Law and Peace in International Relations: The Oliver Wendell Holmes Lectures, 1940–41* (Cambridge, MA: Harvard University Press, 1942), pp. 1, 11–12.

5. Peter Malanczuk, *Akehurst's Modern Introduction to International Law*, Seventh edition (London: Routledge, 1997), pp. 9, 11.

6. Benno Teschke, *The Myth of 1648: Class, Geopolitics and the Making of*

Modern International Relations (London: Verso, 2003). Also Stéphane Beaulac, *The Power of Language in the Making of International Law* (Leiden: Martinus Nijhoff, 2004).

7. David Kennedy, 'Primitive Legal Scholarship', *Harvard International Law Journal*, Vol. 27, No. 1, 1986, pp. 1–98, pp. 1–2. Also Kennedy, 'A New Stream of International Law Scholarship', *Wisconsin International Law Journal*, Vol. 7, No. 1, 1988–9, pp. 1–49; Nathaniel Berman, 'The Grotius Lecture Series II: In the Wake of Empire', *American University International Law Review*, Vol. 14, 1998–9, pp. 1521–54.

8. Malanczuk, *Akehurst's Modern Introduction*, pp. 12–14.

9. Julius Stone, *Human Law and Human Justice* (Sydney: Maitland Publications, 1965), p. 62; James Leslie Brierly, *The Law of Nations* (Oxford: Clarendon Press, 1955), p. 26; Paul Muldoon, 'Francisco De Vitoria and Humanitarian Intervention', *Journal of Military Ethics*, Vol. 5, No. 2, 2006, pp. 128–43.

10. Vitoria, 'On Civil Power' (c. 1528), in Vitoria, *Political Writings*, ed. Anthony Pagden and Jeremy Lawrance (Cambridge: Cambridge University Press, 1991), p. 40.

11. James Brown Scott, *The Spanish Origin of International Law: Francisco de Vitoria and his Law of Nations* (Oxford: Clarendon Press, 1934), pp. xvi, 280.

12. Vitoria, 'Letter to Miguel de Arcos', 8 November 1534, *Political Writings*, pp. 331, 332.

13. Vitoria, *De Indis*, in *Political Writings*, pp. 246, 250–1.

14. Vitoria, 'Letter to Miguel de Arcos', p. 333; *De Indis*, p. 251.

15. Cannibalism will come to be one of the central practices used in justifying colonisation and enslavement in the minds of the conquerors, and next to it Vitoria's reference to raw food seems a little odd. But it is important since, as we shall see in Chapter 2, for the colonisers the point of colonisation was 'improvement'. The consumption of raw food is thus symptomatic of the Indian failure to 'improve' the world – to transform nature according to human desire and ability. For Vitoria's general arguments on these issues, see *On Dietary Laws, Or Self-Restraint* (1537–8), in *Political Writings*, pp. 207–30.

16. On this term, see Robert F. Berkhofer, Jr., *The White Man's Indian: Images of the American Indian from Columbus to the Present* (New York: Vintage Books, 1979), pp. 3, 25; Irene Silverblatt, *Modern Inquisitions: Peru and the Colonial Origins of the Civilized World* (Durham: Duke University Press, 2004), pp. 26, 179, 190–3, 210.

17. Anghie, *Imperialism, Sovereignty and the Making of International Law*, pp. 15–22, 36–7.

18. See A. Pearce Higgins, 'International Law and the Outer World, 1450–1648', in J. Holland Rose, A. P. Newton and E. A. Benians (eds), *The Cambridge*

History of the British Empire (Cambridge: Cambridge University Press, 1960), p. 190; Donald R. Kelly, 'Law', in J. H. Burns (ed.), *The Cambridge History of Political Thought, 1450–1700* (Cambridge: Cambridge University Press, 1991), p. 86; Richard Waswo, 'The Formation of Natural Law to Justify Colonialism, 1539–1689', *New Literary History*, Vol. 27, No. 4, 1996, pp. 743–59, 745; Kathleen Davis, *Periodization and Sovereignty: How Ideas of Feudalism and Secularization Govern the Politics of Time* (Philadelphia: University of Pennsylvania Press, 2008), p. 40.

19. Vitoria, *De Indis*, pp. 278–80.
20. Marjorie Grice-Hutchinson, *Economic Thought in Spain: Selected Essays of Marjorie Grice-Hutchinson*, ed. Lawrence S. Moss and Christopher K. Ryan (Aldershot, Hants: Edward Elgar, 1993), pp. 126–42. Also Martii Koskenniemi, 'Empire and International Law: The Real Spanish Contribution', *University of Toronto Law Journal*, Vol. 61, No. 1, 2011, pp. 1–36, pp. 22, 25–6.
21. Robert A. Williams, *The American Indian in Western Legal Thought* (New York: Oxford University Press, 1990), p. 102.
22. Vitoria, *De Indis*, pp. 282–3.
23. Vitoria, *De Indis Relectio Posterior*, in *Political Writings*, p. 318.
24. Vitoria, *De Indis Relectio Posterior*, p. 321.
25. David Armitage, *The Ideological Origins of the British Empire* (Cambridge: Cambridge University Press, 2000), pp. 63–8; Ken MacMillan, *Sovereignty and Possession in the English New World: The Legal Foundations of Empire, 1576–1640* (Cambridge: Cambridge University Press, 2006), pp. 45–6; James Turner Johnson, *Ideology, Reason, and the Limitation of War: Religious and Secular Concepts, 1200–1740* (Princeton, NJ: Princeton University Press, 1975), pp. 158, 174; Williams, *American Indian*, pp. 165–73; 194–9; Pagden, *Spanish Imperialism*, p. 22; L. C. Green and Olive P. Dickason, *The Law of Nations and the New World* (Edmonton: University of Alberta Press, 1989), pp. 48–9, 195.
26. Onuma Yasuaki, 'Appendix: Eurocentrism in the History of International Law', in Onuma Yasuaki (ed.), *A Normative Approach to War: Peace, War, and Justice in Hugo Grotius* (Oxford: Clarendon Press, 1993), p. 375.
27. Arthur Nussbaum, *A Concise History of the Law of Nations* (New York: Methuen, 1961), pp. 74, 83, 296–306.
28. J. G. A. Pocock, *The Machiavellian Moment: Florentine Political Thought and the Atlantic Republican Tradition* (Princeton, NJ: Princeton University Press, 1975).
29. Mikael Hornqvist, *Machiavelli and Empire* (Cambridge: Cambridge University Press, 2004), pp. 61, 72, 74.
30. Niccolò Machiavelli, *The Prince* (1532), in *The Chief Works and Others*, Vol. 1, trans. Allan Gilbert (Durham: Duke University Press, 1989), p. 55.
31. Michael Dillon, 'Lethal Freedom: The Divine Violence of the Machiavellian

Moment', *Theory and Event,* Vol. 11, No. 2, 2008, pp. 1–21, p. 4.

32. Vitoria, *De Indis,* p. 283; *De Indis Relectio Posterior,* p. 319.

33. Vitoria, *De Indis Relectio Posterior,* p. 298.

34. Christine Bell, *On the Law of Peace: Peace Agreements and the Lex Pacificatoria* (Oxford: Oxford University Press, 2008), p. 86, building on Randall Lesaffer, 'Peace Treaties from Lodi to Westphalia', in Randall Lesaffer (ed.), *Peace Treaties and International Law in European History: From the Late Middle Ages to World War One* (Cambridge: Cambridge University Press, 2004), pp. 9–44.

35. Charles Tilly, 'Reflections on the History of European State-Making', in Charles Tilly (ed.), *The Formation of National States in Europe* (Princeton, NJ: Princeton University Press, 1975), p. 42.

36. Jean Bodin, *The Six Books of a Commonweale* (1576), ed. Kenneth Douglas McRae (Cambridge, MA: Harvard University Press, 1962), Bk. 5, Chap. V (pp. 598–9, 603); Giovanni Botero, *The Reason of State* (1589), trans. P. J. Waley and D. P. Waley (London: Routledge and Kegan Paul, 1956), Bk. 3, Chap. 3 (pp. 76–8).

37. Otto Brunner, *Land and Lordship: Structures of Governance in Medieval Austria* (1939; 4th edn 1959), trans. Howard Kaminsky and James Van Horn Melton (Philadelphia: University of Pennsylvania Press, 1992), pp. 16–17.

38. Marc Bloch, *Feudal Society, Vol. 2: Social Classes and Political Obligation* (1940), trans. L. A. Manyon (London: Routledge, 1961), pp. 410–11; Brunner, *Land and Lordship,* pp. 18, 33–4; Perry Anderson, *Lineages of the Absolutist State* (London: New Left Books, 1974), p. 31; Piet Strydom, *Discourse and Knowledge: The Making of Enlightenment Sociology* (Liverpool: Liverpool University Press, 2000), p. 96.

39. Brunner, *Land and Lordship,* pp. 28–30. Also see Otto Hintz, 'Military Organization and the Organization of the State' (1906), in Felix Gilbert (ed.), *The Historical Essays of Otto Hintz* (New York: Oxford University Press, 1975), pp. 180–215.

40. Frances A. Yates, *Astraea: The Imperial Theme in the Sixteenth Century* (London: Routledge and Kegan Paul, 1975), pp. 133–4, 210; Ralph Bauer, *The Cultural Geography of Colonial American Literature: Empire, Travel, Modernity* (Cambridge: Cambridge University Press, 2003), p. 44.

41. James Hutton, *Themes of Peace in Renaissance Poetry* (Ithaca: Cornell University Press, 1984), p. 19.

42. Ben Lowe, *Imagining Peace: A History of Early English Pacifist Ideas* (Pennsylvania: Pennsylvania State University Press, 1997). Also see Georges Duby, *The Legend of Bouvines: War, Religion and Culture in the Middle Ages* (1973), trans. Catherine Tihanyi (Cambridge: Polity Press, 1990), p. 59; J. R. Hale, *War and Society in Renaissance Europe 1450–1620*

(London: Fontana, 1985), pp. 40–1; Anthony Adolf, *Peace: A World History* (Cambridge: Polity, 2009), pp. 103–18; John Gittings, *The Glorious Art of Peace: From the Iliad to Iraq* (Oxford: Oxford University Press, 2012), pp. 98–122.

43. Ben Lowe, 'The Role of Peace in Elizabethan Military Strategy, 1572–1593: A Look at the Manuals', *Fides et Historia*, Vol. 24, No. 2, 1992, pp. 3–14.

44. Sir Henry Sumner Maine, *International Law: A Series of Lectures Delivered before the University of Cambridge, 1887* (London: John Murray, 1888), p. 8.

45. The first edition is called *The New Pollecye of War, wherein it is declared not only how the mooste cruell Tyraunt the great Turke maye be Ouercome*. The second edition is called *The True Defense of Peace, wherein it is declaredde the cause of all warres now a days, and how they maye be pacified*. For discussion, see Ben Lowe, 'War and the Commonwealth in Mid-Tudor England', *Sixteenth Century Journal*, Vol. 21, No. 2, 1990, pp. 171–92, pp. 186–9.

46. José A. Fernández, 'Erasmus on the Just War', *Journal of the History of Ideas*, Vol. 34, No. 2, 1973, pp. 209–26.

47. Erasmus, 'Letter to Martin Bucer', 11 November, 1527, in J. Huizinga, *Erasmus and the Age of Reformation* (1924) (London: Phoenix Press, 2002), pp. 288–92; Niccolò Machiavelli, *Discourses on the First Decade of Titus Livius* (1513–17), in *The Chief Works and Others, Vol. 1*, trans. Allan Gilbert (Durham: Duke University Press, 1989), pp. 224, 399. Note too his comment on Ancus, a man 'so gifted … that he could both enjoy peace and carry on war' (p. 245).

48. Gerardo Zampaglione, *The Idea of Peace in Antiquity* (1967), trans. Richard Dunn (Notre Dame: University of Notre Dame Press, 1973), p. 133. Also Stephen C. Neff, *War and the Law of Nations: A General History* (Cambridge: Cambridge University Press, 2005), p. 31.

49. Ali Parchami, *Hegemonic Peace and Empire: The Pax Romana, Britannica, and Americana*, (London: Routledge, 2009), pp. 15–17, 42, 62, 92–3.

50. Zampaglione, *Idea of Peace*, pp. 134, 135. Also Stefan Weinstock, 'Pax and the "Ara Pacis"', *Journal of Roman Studies*, Vol. 50, Nos. 1 and 2, 1960, pp. 44–58.

51. The first is from Antonio Negri, *Time for Revolution* (1997), trans. Matteo Mandarini (London: Continuum, 2003), pp. 122–3, the second from Michel Foucault, '*Society Must Be Defended*': *Lectures at the Collège de France, 1975–76*, trans. David Macey (London: Allen Lane, 2003), p. 51.

52. Thomas Hobbes, *Leviathan* (1651), ed. Richard Tuck (Cambridge: Cambridge University Press, 1991), p. 128.

53. Sir Frederick Pollock and Frederic William Maitland, *The History of English Law before the Time of Edward I, Vol. I* (1898) (Indianapolis: Liberty Fund, 2010), p. 55; also p. 502. It has been suggested that the Biblical prohibition

'Thou shalt not kill' only really began to be stressed as a prohibition between 1562 and 1648 – Robert Muchembled, *A History of Violence: From the End of the Middle Ages to the Present* (2008), trans. Jean Birrell (Cambridge: Polity, 2012), p. 14.

54. See Neff, *War and the Law of Nations*, pp. 78–81; James Q. Whitman, *The Verdict of Battle: The Law of Victory and the Making of Modern War* (Cambridge, MA: Harvard University Press, 2012), pp. 97–106.

55. Marx, Letter to Engels, 25 September 1857, in Karl Marx and Frederick Engels, *Collected Works, Vol. 40* (London: Lawrence and Wishart, 1983), p. 186; Michel Foucault, *Discipline and Punish: The Birth of the Prison* (1975), trans. Alan Sheridan (London: Penguin, 1977), pp. 168–9. Also see Max Weber, *Economy and Society*, ed. Guenther Roth and Claus Wittich (California: University of California Press, 1978), pp. 972, 981; Michael Mann, *The Sources of Social Power, Vol. I: A History of Power from the Beginning to AD 1760* (Cambridge: Cambridge University Press, 1986), pp. 146, 148, 278, 363.

56. Norbert Elias, *The Germans: Power Struggles and the Development of Habitus in the Nineteenth and Twentieth Centuries* (1989), trans. Eric Dunning and Stephen Mennell (New York: Columbia University Press, 1996), pp. 173, 174, 176. Also see Weber, *Economy and Society*, p. 972; Mann, *Sources of Social Power, Vol. I*, pp. 377, 383, 420, 437, 500, 510; Muchembled, *History of Violence*, pp. 83–91, 116, 122, 163, 219, 223.

57. Charles Townshend, *Britain's Civil Wars: Counterinsurgency in the Twentieth Century* (London: Faber and Faber, 1986), p. 16.

58. James C. Scott, *Domination and the Arts of Resistance: Hidden Transcripts* (New Haven: Yale University Press, 1990), p. 53; Bernd Greiner, *War Without Fronts: The USA in Vietnam* (2007), trans. Anne Wyburd and Victoria Fern (London: Bodley Head, 2009), p. 60.

59. George Orwell, 'Politics and the English Language' (1946), in *The Collected Essays, Journalism and Letters of George Orwell, Vol. IV*, ed. Sonia Orwell and Ian Angus (London: Secker and Warburg, 1968), p. 136.

60. King of France Henry IV, *The Kings Edict and Declaration Upon the Former Edicts of Pacification Published in Paris at the Parliament Held the XXV of Februarie, 1599, at Paris* (London: Thomas Man, 1599).

61. Cited in Tzvetan Todorov, *The Conquest of America* (New York: Harper-Perennial, 1984), p. 173.

62. Todorov, *Conquest*, p. 174. Compare J. H. Elliott: 'In 1573 Philip II promulgated a long set of ordinances … designed to regulate any further territorial expansion. The ordinances came late in the day, and new-style "pacification" often proved to be little more than a euphemism for old style "conquest"' – J. H. Elliott, *Empires of the Atlantic World: Britain and Spain in America 1492–1830* (New Haven: Yale University Press, 2006), p. 77.

63. Cited in Todorov, *Conquest*, pp. 173–4.
64. 'Pacification had to be productive', notes William Gibson of Vietnam – *The Perfect War: Technowar in Vietnam* (New York: Grove Books, 1986), p. 281.
65. Johnson, to his advisors, cited in Frank L. Jones, 'Blowtorch: Robert Komer and the Making of Vietnam Pacification Policy', *Parameters: US Army War College Quarterly*, Vol. 35, No. 3, 2005, pp. 103–18, p. 104. This was 'nation building', as Robert Komer put it in *Organization and Management of the 'New Model' Pacification Program – 1966–1969* (RAND, 7 May 1970), p. 120.
66. On pacification and the hunt, see Mark Neocleous, 'The Dream of Pacification: Accumulation, Class War and the Hunt', *Socialist Studies*, 2013.
67. Bernardo de Vargas Machuca, *Milicia Indiana* (1599), trans. Timothy F. Johnson, in Captain Bernardo de Vargas Machuca, *The Indian Militia and Description of the Indies* (Durham: Duke University Press, 2008), pp. 7, 26, 56, 77, 111, 116, 148, 155–8. Also see Bernardo de Vargas Machuca, *Defense and Discourse of the Western Conquests* (1603), trans. Timothy F. Johnson, in *Defending the Conquest: Bernardo de Vargas Machuca's Defense and Discourse of the Western Conquests*, ed. Kris Lane (University Park, PA: Pennsylvania State University Press, 2010), pp. 33, 40, 87, 89, 113, 114, 133, 134.
68. Foucault, 'Society', p. 50.
69. 'If God grants me life … the last thing that I would like to study would be the problem of war … There again I would have to cross into the problem of law'. Interview with André Bertin, 1983, published as 'What Our Present Is', *Foucault Live*, ed. Sylvère Lotringer (New York: Semiotext(e), 1996), p. 415.
70. James Brown Scott, *The Hague Peace Conferences of 1899 and 1907: A Series of Lectures Delivered before The Johns Hopkins University in the Year 1908* (Whitefish, MT: Kessinger Publishing, 1908), pp. 185, 740–1; Nussbaum, *Concise History*, pp. 73, 113; Wilhelm G. Grewe, *The Epochs of International Law* (1984), trans. Michael Byers (Berlin: Walter de Gruyter, 2000), pp. 7, 214–16.
71. Adam Smith, *Lectures on Jurisprudence*, ed. R. L. Meek, D. D. Raphael and P. G. Stein (Indianapolis: Liberty Fund, 1982), Report dated 1766, p. 397.
72. Giovanni Arrighi, *The Long Twentieth Century: Money, Power and the Origins of Our Times* (London: Verso, 2010), pp. 47, 159.
73. Richard Tuck, *The Rights of War and Peace: Political Thought and the International Order from Grotius to Kant* (Oxford: Oxford University Press, 1999), p. 79.
74. Tuck, *Rights of War*, p. 80.
75. See David Armitage, 'Introduction' to Huge Grotius, *The Free Sea* (Indianapolis: Liberty Fund, 2004); Karl Zemanek, 'Was Grotius Really in Favour of the Freedom of the Seas?', *Journal of the History of International Law*, Vol. 1, No. 1, 1999, pp. 48–60.
76. The book remained in manuscript until being discovered in 1864, when it

was realised that Grotius's *Mare Liberum*, which had been prepared for publication in 1608, was in fact Chapter XII of the longer manuscript. The Chapter had been prepared separately at the request of the East Indies Company. Much of Grotius's more famous *De Iure Belli ac Pacis* was developed from this earlier treatise on the law of prize and booty. See C. H. Alexandrowicz, *An Introduction to the History of the Law of Nations in the East Indies* (Oxford: Clarendon Press, 1967), p. 43; Richard Tuck, *Philosophy and Government 1572–1651* (Cambridge: Cambridge University Press, 1993), pp. 169–71. References here will be to Grotius, *Commentary on the Law of Prize and Booty*, ed. Martine Julia van Ittersum (Indianapolis: Liberty Fund, 2006). Hereafter *C* in the main text.

77. Alexandrowicz, *History of the Law of Nations in the East Indies*, pp. 41, 44.
78. See Mark Neocleous, *Imagining the State* (Milton Keynes: Open University Press, 2003), Chapter 3.
79. Eric Wilson, 'The VOC, Corporate Sovereignty and the Republican Sub-Text of *De iure praedae*', in Hans W. Blom (ed.), *Property, Piracy and Punishment: Hugo Grotius on War and Booty in De Iure Praedae – Concepts and Contexts* (Leiden: Brill, 2009), pp. 312–13.
80. Carl Schmitt, *The* Nomos *of the Earth in the International Law of the* Jus Publicum Europaeum (1950), trans. G. L. Ulmen (New York: Telos Press, 2003), p. 116.
81. On the sea as a key space in the formation of both capital and war, see Philip E. Steinberg, *The Social Construction of the Ocean* (Cambridge: Cambridge University Press, 2001).
82. See Stephen Buckle, *Natural Law and the Theory of Property: Grotius to Hume* (Oxford: Clarendon Press, 1991), p. 11.
83. Tuck, *Rights of War*, p. 92.
84. Keene, *Beyond the Anarchical Society*, p. 52.
85. Evgeny Pashukanis, 'International Law', entry in the three-volume *Encyclopaedia of State and Law* (1925–7), in Piers Beirne and Robert Sharlet (eds), *Pashukanis: Selected Writings* (London: Academic Press, 1980), p. 176.
86. Tuck, *Philosophy and Government*, pp. 196–7; Tuck, *Rights of War*, p. 95; Zemanek, 'Was Grotius Really in Favour of the Freedom of the Seas?'
87. Hugo Grotius, *The Rights of War and Peace*, ed. Richard Tuck (Indianapolis: Liberty Fund, 2005). Hereafter *RWP* in the main text.
88. Tuck, *Rights of War*, p. 104.
89. Georg Schwarzenberger, 'Jus Pacis Ac Belli? Prolegomena to a Sociology of International Law', *American Journal of International Law*, Vol. 37, No. 3, 1943, pp. 460–79, p. 461; Onuma Yasuaki, 'War', in Yasuaki, *A Normative Approach to War*, pp. 57–62.
90. Ellen Meiksins Wood, *Empire of Capital* (London: Verso, 2003), p. 69. Also here see Tuck, *Rights of War*, pp. 85, 89, 95, 103, 108; Nussbaum, *Concise*

History, p. 107; China Miéville, *Between Equal Rights: A Marxist Theory of International Law* (Leiden: Brill, 2005), p. 210; Eric Wilson, 'Making the World Safe for Holland: *De Indis* of Hugo Grotius and International Law as Geo-Culture', *Monash University Faculty of Law Legal Studies Research Paper* No. 2010/35, 2010; Eric Wilson, '"The Dangerous Classes": Hugo Grotius and Seventeenth-century Piracy as a Primitive Anti-systemic Movement', *The Journal of Philosophical Economics*, Vol. 4, No. 1, Special Issue 2010, pp. 146–83; Frédéric Gros, *States of Violence: An Essay on the End of War* (2006), trans. Krzysztof Fijalkowski and Michael Richardson (London: Seagull Books, 2010), pp. 236–7.

91. Whitman, *Verdict of Battle*, pp. 110–11.
92. E. H. Carr, *The Twenty Years' Crisis 1919–1939: An Introduction to the Study of International Relations* (1939), (Basingstoke: Palgrave, 2001), p. 162. Also see B. V. A. Roling, 'Jus Ad Bellum and the Grotian Heritage', in T. M. C. Asser Instituut (ed.), *International Law and the Grotian Heritage* (The Hague: T. M. C. Asser Instituut, 1985), p. 119.
93. Martine Julia van Ittersum, 'The Long Goodbye: Hugo Grotius' Justification of Dutch Expansion Overseas, 1615–1645', *History of European Ideas*, Vol. 36, No. 4, 2010, pp. 386–411, p. 388. Also Keene, *Beyond the Anarchical Society*, p. 3; Perry Miller, *The New England Mind, Vol. 1: The Seventeenth Century* (Boston: Beacon Press, 1939), pp. 99, 200, 461; Timothy George, 'War and Peace in the Puritan Tradition', *Church History*, Vol. 53, No. 4, 1984, pp. 492–503; Jill Lepore, *The Name of War: King Philip's War and the Origins of American Identity* (New York: Vintage, 1999), pp. 120–1.
94. Christopher Tomlins, *Freedom Bound: Law, Labor, and Civic Identity in Colonizing English America, 1580–1865* (Cambridge: Cambridge University Press, 2010), p. 155.
95. Despite starting from the premise that slavery is contrary to the state of nature, Grotius allows that humans can become slaves as a result of voluntary submission due to their own weaknesses, but also 'in Consequence of some Crime', and such 'crime' might be a 'publick Crime' committed by a 'whole People' in which case 'a Nation's Slavery is perpetual'– *RWP*, II. V. XXVII-XXXII, pp. 557–65, and III. VII. I, p. 1360.
96. Tuck, *Rights of War*, p. 195.
97. Robert Cover, 'Violence and the Word', *Yale Law Journal*, Vol. 95, No. 8, 1986, pp. 1601–29; Austin Sarat and Thomas R. Kearns, 'A Journey Through Forgetting: Toward a Jurisprudence of Violence', in Austin Sarat and Thomas R Kearns (eds), *The Fate of Law* (Ann Arbor: University of Michigan Press, 1991), p. 209; Austin Sarat and Thomas R. Kearns, 'Introduction', in Austin Sarat and Thomas R. Kearns (eds), *Law's Violence* (Ann Arbor: University of Michigan Press, 1995), p. 3; Peter Fitzpatrick, *Modernism and the Grounds of Law* (Cambridge: Cambridge University

Press, 2001), p. 77; Candace Vogler and Patchen Markell, 'Introduction: Violence, Redemption, and the Liberal Political Imagination', *Public Culture*, Vol. 15, No. 1, 2003, pp. 1–10; Nathaniel Berman, 'Privileging Combat? Contemporary Conflict and the Legal Construction of War', *Columbia Journal of Transnational Law*, Vol. 43, No. 1, 2004, pp. 1–71; David Kennedy, *Of War and Law* (Princeton, NJ: Princeton University Press, 2006).

98. Walter Benjamin, 'Critique of Violence' (1920–1), trans. Edmund Jephcott, in *Selected Writings, Vol. 1: 1913–1926*, ed. Marcus Bullock and Michael W. Jennings (Cambridge, MA: Belknap/Harvard, 1996), p. 240. Also here see Nicos Poulantzas, *State, Power, Socialism* (1978), trans. Patrick Camiller (London: New Left Books, 1978), p. 76.

99. Neocleous, *Critique of Security*, pp. 69–75.

100. Pashukanis, 'International Law', p. 169.

101. Kennedy, *Of War and Law*, pp. 2, 8, 116, 127; Chris af Johnick and Roger Normand, 'The Legitimation of Violence: A Critical History of the Laws of War', *Harvard International Law Journal*, Vol. 35, No. 1, 1994, pp. 49–95.

102. Thus, for example, Eyal Weizman writes of a new 'age of lawfare' and this tends to get repeated in the various works which have followed this line – 'Legislative Attack', *Theory, Culture and Society*, Vol. 27, No. 6, 2010, pp. 11–32, p. 16.

103. Kennedy, *Of War and Law*, p. 164; Gros, *States of Violence*, pp. 183–4; Nicholas Blomley, 'Law, Property, and the Geography of Violence: The Frontier, the Survey, and the Grid', *Annals of the Association of American Geographers*, Vol. 93, No. 1, 2003, pp. 121–41, pp. 129–33; Miéville, *Between Equal Rights*, p. 148.

104. Anthony Carty, 'Critical International Law: Recent Trends in the Theory of International Law', *European Journal of International Law*, Vol. 2, No. 1, 1991, pp. 66–96; Talal Asad, *On Suicide Bombing* (New York: Columbia University Press, 2007), p. 59.

CHAPTER 2

1. Karl Marx, *Capital: A Critique of Political Economy, Vol. 1* (1867), trans. B. Fowkes (Harmondsworth: Penguin, 1976), pp. 915–16. Hereafter *C1* in the main text.

2. Anthony Carty, *Was Ireland Conquered? International Law and the Irish Question* (London: Pluto Press, 1996), p. 5.

3. David Kennedy, 'International Law and the Nineteenth Century: History of an Illusion', *Nordic Journal of International Law*, Vol. 65, 1996, pp. 385–420, p. 397.

4. For example, Mohammed Bedjaoui, *Towards a New International Economic*

Order (New York: Holmes and Meier, 1979); B. S. Chimni, *International Law and World Order: A Critique of Contemporary Approaches* (1993), pp. 223–6; Anthony Anghie, '"The Heart of My Home": Colonialism, Environmental Damage, and the Nauru Case', *Harvard International Law Journal*, Vol. 34, No. 2, 1993, pp. 445–506.

5. Anthony Anghie, 'Francisco de Vitoria and the Colonial Origins of International Law', *Social and Legal Studies*, Vol. 5, No. 3, 1996, pp. 321–36; Siba N'Zatioula Grovogui, *Sovereigns, Quasi Sovereigns, and Africans: Race and Self-Determination in International Law* (Minneapolis: University of Minnesota Press, 1996); James Thuo Gathii, 'Neoliberalism, Colonialism and International Governance: Decentering the International Law of Governmental Legitimacy', *Michigan Law Review*, Vol. 8, 2000, pp. 1996–2055; Edward Keene, *Beyond the Anarchical Society: Grotius, Colonialism and Order in World Politics* (Cambridge: Cambridge University Press, 2002); B. S. Chimni, 'Third World Approaches to International Law: A Manifesto', in A. Anghie, B. Chimni, K. Mickelson and O. Okafor (eds), *The Third World and International Order: Law, Politics and Globalization* (Leiden: Brill, 2003); Paul Keal, *European Conquest and the Rights of Indigenous Peoples: The Moral Backwardness of International Society* (Cambridge: Cambridge University Press, 2003); Nathaniel Berman, '"The Appeals of the Orient": Colonized Desire and the War of the Riff', in Karen Knop (ed.), *Gender and Human Rights* (Oxford: Oxford University Press, 2004); Anthony Anghie, *Imperialism, Sovereignty and the Making of International Law* (Cambridge: Cambridge University Press, 2005); Balakrishnan Rajagopal, *International Law from Below: Development, Social Movements and Third World Resistance* (Cambridge: Cambridge University Press, 2005); China Miéville, *Between Equal Rights: A Marxist Theory of International Law* (Leiden: Brill, 2005); B. S. Chimni, 'An Outline of a Marxist Course on Public International Law', *Leiden Journal of International Law*, Vol. 17, 2004, pp. 1–30; Ugo Mattei and Laura Nader, *Plunder: When the Rule of Law is Illegal* (Oxford: Blackwell, 2008); Martii Koskenniemi, 'Empire and International Law: The Real Spanish Contribution', *University of Toronto Law Journal*, Vol. 61, No. 1, 2011, pp. 1–36.

6. Miéville, *Between Equal Rights*, pp. 169, 226; Grovogui, *Sovereigns, Quasi Sovereigns*, p. 3; Gathii, 'Neoliberalism, Colonialism', p. 2020. Hence Matthew Craven's suggestion that *decolonisation* had to simultaneously put into question the very basis on which international law itself had been constructed – Matthew Craven, *The Decolonization of International Law: State Succession and the Law of Treaties* (Oxford: Oxford University Press, 2007), p. 16.

7. Fleur Johns, Richard Joyce and Sundhya Pahuja, *Events: The Force of International Law* (London: Routledge, 2011).

8. Anne Orford, 'A Jurisprudence of the Limit', in Anne Orford (ed.), *International Law and its Others* (Cambridge: Cambridge University Press, 2006), pp. 4, 5.

9. Thus, for example, his essay '"The Heart of My Home": Colonialism, Environmental Damage, and the Nauru Case', *Harvard International Law Journal*, Vol. 34, No. 2, 1993, pp. 445–506, highlights dispossession and self-determination rather than accumulation.

10. Anghie, *Imperialism, Sovereignty*; Miéville, *Between Equal Rights*; p. 207; Boaventura de Sousa Santos, 'Beyond Neoliberal Governance: The World Social Forum as Subaltern Cosmopolitan Politics and Legality', in Boaventura de Sousa Santos and César A. Rodriguez-Garavito (eds), *Law and Globalization from Below: Towards a Cosmopolitan Legality* (Cambridge: Cambridge University Press, 2005), p. 40.

11. Susan Marks (ed.), *International Law on the Left: Re-examining Marxist Legacies* (Cambridge: Cambridge University Press, 2008).

12. Anthony Carty, 'Marxism and International Law: Perspectives for the American (Twenty-first) Century', in Marks (ed.), *International Law*, p. 184, citing David Harvey, *The New Imperialism* (Oxford: Oxford University Press, 2003), p. 144.

13. Martti Koskenniemi, 'What Should International Lawyers Learn from Karl Marx?', *Leiden Journal of International Law* , Vol. 17, 2004, pp. 229–46, and reprinted in Marks (ed.), *International Law*, pp. 30–52; 'Empire and International Law: The Real Spanish Contribution', *University of Toronto Law Journal*, Vol. 61, No. 1, 2011, pp. 1–36.

14. B. S. Chimni, *International Law and World Order: A Critique of Contemporary Approaches* (1993), pp. 224, 295.

15. Chimni, 'Outline of a Marxist Course', since reprinted in Marks (ed.), *International Law*; B. S. Chimni, 'Prolegomena to a Class Approach to International Law', *European Journal of International Law*, Vol. 21, No. 1, 2010, pp. 57–82.

16. The same might be said of B. S. Chimni, 'International Institutions Today: An Imperial Global State in the Making', *European Journal of International Law*, Vol. 15, No. 1, 2004, pp. 1–37, where 'accumulation' gets a brief mention but primitive accumulation none at all.

17. Chimni, 'Prolegomena', p. 67.

18. Susan Marks rightly points to the ways in which international law has helped shift the category 'exploitation' away from anything that resembles what Marx understood by the term, and that exploitation in Marx's sense 'goes largely unremarked in international law' – Marks, 'Exploitation as an International Legal Concept', in Marks (ed.), *International Law*, pp. 281–307. I remain unconvinced, however, about her belief that international law might recognise this and start to perceive the world as a structured

totality; that seems to me to be precisely what international law is unable to do, as I began to argue in the previous chapter and here continue to argue.

19. Karl Marx, *Capital: A Critique of Political Economy, Vol. 3* (1867), trans. David Fernach (Harmondsworth: Penguin, 1981), p. 927.
20. Edward Gibbon Wakefield, *A Letter from Sydney, the Principal Town of Australasia, Together with the 'Outline of a System of Colonization'* (London: Joseph Cross, 1829); Edward Gibbon Wakefield, *A View of the Art of Colonization* (London: John W. Parker, 1849).
21. Karl Marx, *Grundrisse*, trans. Martin Nicolaus (Harmondsworth: Penguin, 1973), p. 489.
22. Richard Halpern, *The Poetics of Primitive Accumulation: English Renaissance Culture and the Genealogy of Capital* (Ithaca: Cornell University Press, 1991), pp. 61–2.
23. Étienne Balibar, 'Reflections on *Gewalt*', *Historical Materialism*, Vol. 17, 2009, pp. 99–125, p. 109.
24. Rosa Luxemburg, *The Accumulation of Capital* (1913), trans. Agnes Schwarzschild (London: Routledge, 2003), p. 349.
25. Marx, *Grundrisse*, p. 506n.
26. Richard H. Cox, *Locke on War and Peace* (Oxford: Clarendon Press, 1960); James Turner Johnson, *Ideology, Reason, and the Limitation of War: Religious and Secular Concepts, 1200–1740* (Princeton, NJ: Princeton University Press, 1975), pp. 232–40. For a differing and more compelling position, see Richard Tuck's placing of Locke in a longer history of liberal arguments justifying war, in *The Rights of War and Peace: Political Thought and the International Order from Grotius to Kant* (Oxford: Oxford University Press, 1999), on which I build in this chapter.
27. Oliver Richmond, *Peace in International Relations* (London: Routledge, 2008), pp. 23, 24, 37.
28. See Herman Lebovics, 'The Uses of America in Locke's Second Treatise of Government', *Journal of the History of Ideas*, Vol. 77, No. 4, 1986, pp. 567–81; James Tully, *An Approach to Political Philosophy: Locke in Contexts* (Cambridge: Cambridge University Press, 1993); Bhikhu Parekh, 'Liberalism and Colonialism', in Jan Nederveen Pieterse and Bhikhu Parekh (eds), *The Decolonization of Imagination: Culture, Knowledge and Power* (London: Zed Books, 1995); Barbara Arneil, *John Locke and America: The Defence of English Colonialism* (Oxford: Clarendon Press, 1996); Duncan Ivison, 'Locke, Liberalism and Empire', in Peter R. Ansty (ed.), *The Philosophy of John Locke: New Perspectives* (London: Routledge, 2003); David Armitage, 'John Locke, Carolina, and the *Two Treatises of Government*', *Political Theory*, Vol. 32, No. 5, 2004, pp. 602–27; Vicki Hsueh, 'Cultivating and Challenging the Common: Lockean Property, Indigenous

Traditionalisms, and the Problem of Exclusion', *Contemporary Political Theory*, Vol. 5, 2006, pp. 193–214.

29. See Uday Singh Mehta, *Liberalism and Empire: A Study in Nineteenth-Century British Liberal Thought* (Chicago: University of Chicago Press, 1999); Nicholas B. Dirks, *The Scandal of Empire: India and the Creation of Imperial Britain* (Cambridge, MA: Harvard University Press, 2006); Jennifer Pitts, *A Turn to Empire: The Rise of Imperial Liberalism in Britain and France* (Princeton, NJ: Princeton University Press, 2006); Domenico Losurdo, *Liberalism: A Counter-History* (2006), trans. Gregory Elliott (London: Verso, 2011).

30. John Locke, 'Some Considerations of the Lowering of Interest and Raising the Value of Money' (1691), in *The Works of John Locke, Vol. 5* (London: J. Johnson, 1801), p. 21.

31. Ellen Meiksins Wood, *Empire of Capital* (London: Verso, 2003), p. 98.

32. Zygmunt Bauman, *Modernity and Ambivalence* (Cambridge: Polity Press, 1991), p. 15.

33. Respectively: C. B. Macpherson, 'Editor's Introduction', in John Locke, *Second Treatise of Government* (Indianapolis: Hackett, 1980); John Dunn, *The Political Thought of John Locke* (Cambridge: Cambridge University Press, 1969).

34. John Locke, *Two Treatises*, ed. Peter Laslett (Cambridge: Cambridge University Press, 1988), II, sects. 14, 48, 103, 108. Hereafter *TT* in the main text.

35. Sarah Irving, *Natural Science and the Origins of the British Empire* (London: Pickering and Chatto, 2008), pp. 109 114, 126, 132.

36. Locke was well aware that native American Indians were far from being quite in the condition described in his state of nature, since many reports from America commented on the forms of Indian government, the skills exercised by the Indians, the extent to which they cultivated the land, and even the various ways in which they taught the colonialists how best to operate with land and local crops. This discussion is beyond the scope of my argument here, but see Arneil, *John Locke*, pp. 33, 41.

37. 'The Bahamas trade will turn to account if you meddle not with planting … If other men will plant there (I mean the Bahamas) hinder them not, they improve our province. But I would neither have you nor my Lord Shaftesbury engage in it' – Sir Peter Colleton to Locke, May 1673, cited in Maurice Cranston, *John Locke: A Biography* (Oxford: Oxford University Press, 1957), p. 156. Locke followed the advice and later sold the stock at a profit.

38. John Locke, *Some Thoughts Concerning Education* (1693), ed. John William Adamson (Mineola, NY: Dover, 2007), p. 91.

39. Lady Masham, in a letter to Jean le Clerc, in 1704/5, cited in Cranston, *John Locke*, p. 426.

40. Parekh, 'Liberalism and Colonialism', p. 84.
41. Neal Wood, *John Locke and Agrarian Capitalism* (Berkeley: University of California Press, 1984), p. 51; Neil Wood, *The Politics of Locke's Philosophy: A Social Study of 'An Essay Concerning Human Understanding'* (Berkeley: University of California Press, 1983), p. 74.
42. 'A Consideration of the Cause in Question before the Lords touching Depopulation', 5 July 1607, in Joan Thirsk and J. P. Cooper (eds), *Seventeenth-Century Economic Documents* (Oxford: Clarendon Press, 1972), p. 109.
43. Francis Bacon, *The Advancement of Learning* (1605), ed. G. W. Kitchen (1973), p. 68.
44. Paul Slack, *From Reformation to Improvement: Public Welfare in Early Modern England* (Oxford: Clarendon Press, 1999), p. 96n89.
45. Joan Thirsk, 'Seventeenth-Century Agriculture and Social Change', in Joan Thirsk (ed.), *Land, Church and People: Essays Presented to Professor H. P. R. Finberg* (Reading: Museum of English Rural Life, 1970), p. 167.
46. See Peter Harrison, '"Fill the Earth and Subdue It": Biblical Warrants for Colonization in Seventeenth Century England', *Journal of Religious History*, Vol. 29, No. 1, 2005, pp. 3–24.
47. Mark Girouard, *The English Town* (New Haven: Yale University Press, 1990), p. 86.
48. Wood, *John Locke*, p. 58; Ken MacMillan, *Sovereignty and Possession in the English New World: The Legal Foundations of Empire, 1576–1640* (Cambridge: Cambridge University Press, 2006), p. 12.
49. Sarah Tarlow, *The Archaeology of Improvement in Britain, 1750–1850* (Cambridge: Cambridge University Press, 2007), pp. 12–14.
50. Raymond Williams, *Keywords* (London: Fontana, 1976), p. 133. Also see Tania Murray Li, *The Will to Improve: Governmentality, Development, and the Practice of Politics* (Durham: Duke University Press, 2007); Alan Houston, *Benjamin Franklin and the Politics of Improvement* (New Haven: Yale University Press, 2008), p. 12. For some comparison in the Irish context, see Stuart McLean, *The Event and Its Terrors: Ireland, Famine, Modernity* (Stanford, CA: Stanford University Press, 2004), p. 68; James Livesey, *Civil Society and Empire: Ireland and Scotland in the Eighteenth-Century Atlantic World* (New Haven: Yale University Press, 2009), pp. 57–60, 77–84.
51. Ellen Meiksins Wood, 'Locke Against Democracy: Consent, Representation and Suffrage in the *Two Treatises*', *History of Political Thought*, Vol. 13, No. 4, 1992, pp. 657–89, p. 682.
52. William Blackstone, *Commentaries on the Laws of England, Vol. 2: Of the Right of Things* (1766) (Chicago: University of Chicago Press, 1979), pp. 32, 34.
53. Samuel Hartlib, *London's Charitie Stilling the Poore Orphan's Cry* (1649),

cited in George H. Sabine, 'Introduction' to *The Works of Gerrard Winstanley* (Ithaca: Cornell University Press, 1941), p. 14.

54. Timothy Nourse, *Campania Fóelix, or, a Discourse of the Benefits and Improvements of Husbandry* (London, 1700), pp. 15, 93; also pp. 98, 102; Adam Moore, *Bread for the Poor, And Advancement of the English Nation. Promised by Enclosure of the Wastes and Common Grounds of England* (London: R. & W. Leybourn, 1653), p. 30.

55. Pseudonismus, *A Vindication of the Considerations concerning Common Fields* (1656), in Thirsk and Cooper (eds), *Seventeenth-Century Economic Documents*, p. 144.

56. Anon., 'Waste Land's Improvement' (1653), in Thirsk and Cooper (eds), *Seventeenth-Century Economic Documents*, p. 136.

57. Gervase Markham, *The English Husbandman* (1613), cited in Andrew McRae, *God Speed the Plough: The Representation of Agrarian England, 1500–1660* (Cambridge: Cambridge University Press, 1996), p. 168.

58. John Bellers, *Proposals for a Profitable Imploying of the Poor*, in A. Ruth Fry, *John Bellers, 1654–1725: Quaker, Economist and Social Reformer* (London: Cassell, 1935), p. 128.

59. Joyce Oldham Appleby, *Economic Thought and Ideology in Seventeenth-Century England* (Princeton, NJ: Princeton University Press, 1978), p. 154. The whole climax of the logic of improvement and waste is reached when Jeremy Bentham suggests lowering by ten years the age at which the poor should be forced to start work (from fourteen years to four), on the following grounds: 'Ten years, ten precious years, may be looked upon in the existing state of things as the waste period of human life, the period lost to industry … Ten precious years in which nothing is done! Nothing for Industry! Nothing for improvement!' – Jeremy Bentham, *Manuscripts on Pauper Management*, cited by Gertrude Himmelfarb, 'Bentham's Utopia', in her *Marriage and Morals Among the Victorians, and Other Essays* (London: Faber and Faber, 1986), p. 130.

60. R. H. Tawney, *The Agrarian Problem in the Sixteenth Century* (New York: Burt Franklin, 1912), p. 244.

61. E. P. Thompson, *Customs in Common* (London: Penguin, 1993), pp. 135–6; Joan Thirsk, 'The Common Fields', *Past and Present*, 29, 1964, pp. 3–25, p. 4; Tawney, *Agrarian Problem*, pp. 238–9; J. D. Chalmers, 'Enclosure and Labour Supply in the Industrial Revolution', *Economic History Review*, Vol. 5, No. 3, 1953, pp. 319–43, pp. 333, 335, 336.

62. Tawney, *Agrarian Problem*, pp. 237, 243. Also see Barrington Moore, Jr., *Social Origins of Dictatorship and Democracy: Lord and Peasant in the Making of the Modern World* (London: Allen Lane, 1967), p. 29; David Graeber, *Debt: The First 5,000 Years* (New York: Melville House Publishing, 2012), pp. 232, 345.

63. Jacques Le Goff, *Time, Work, and Culture in the Middle Ages*, trans. Arthur Goldhammer (Chicago: University of Chicago Press, 1980), pp. xiii, 51–2.
64. See Mark Neocleous, *The Fabrication of Social Order: A Critical Theory of Police Power* (London: Pluto Press, 2000), pp. 39, 84; Zsuzsa Gille, *From the Cult of Waste to the Trash Heap of History: The Politics of Waste in Postsocialist Hungary* (Bloomington: Indiana University Press, 2001), p. 23; John Scanlan, *On Garbage* (London: Reaktion Books, 2005), p. 22.
65. Sidney Webb and Beatrice Webb, *English Local Government, Vol. 4: Statutory Authorities for Special Purposes* (London: Longmans, 1922), pp. 235, 348; T. A. Critchley, *A History of Police in England and Wales 900–1966* (London: Constable, 1967), pp. 25, 27. Also see David G. Barrie, *Police in the Age of Improvement: Police Development and the Civic Tradition in Scotland, 1775–1865* (Cullompton: Willan, 2008).
66. The fence plays a key role in Locke's *Second Treatise*, playing on the idea of security, liberty and property. For Locke, the law is meant 'to determine the Rights, and fence the Properties of those that live under it'. 'The Reason why Men enter into Society, is the preservation of their Property; and … that there may be Laws made, and Rules set as Guards and Fences to the Properties of all the Members of the Society'. The doctrine that the people can create a new legislative body if the existing legislature have broken their trust 'is the best fence against Rebellion' – Locke, *TT*, II, sects. 93, 136, 226.
67. Karl Marx, 'Economic and Philosophic Manuscripts of 1844', in Karl Marx and Frederick Engels, *Collected Works, Vol. 3* (London: Lawrence and Wishart, 1975), pp. 268–9. On these aspects of the fence, see William Cronon, *Changes in the Land: Indians, Colonists, and the Ecology of New England* (New York: Hill and Wang, 1983), p. 130; Eric Cheyfitz, *The Poetics of Imperialism: Translation and Colonization from* The Tempest *to* Tarzan (Philadelphia: University of Pennsylvania Press, 1997), p. 56; Patricia Seed, *Ceremonies of Possession in Europe's Conquest of the New World, 1492–1640* (Cambridge: Cambridge University Press, 1995), pp. 24–5, 38; John Hanson Mitchell, *Trespassing: An Inquiry into the Private Ownership of Land* (Reading, MA: Addison-Wesley, 1998), pp. 24–5, 79–85.
68. Roger B. Manning, *Village Revolts: Social Protest and Popular Disturbances in England, 1509–1640* (Oxford: Clarendon Press, 1988), p. 27.
69. Karl Marx, 'Debates on the Law on Thefts of Wood' (1842), in Karl Marx and Frederick Engels, *Collected Works, Vol. 1* (London: Lawrence and Wishart, 1975), p. 230; Marx, *Capital, Vol. 1*, pp. 915–16.
70. Roger Williams, *The Hireling Ministry None of Christs, or A Discourse Touching the Propagating the Gospel of Jesus Christ* (London, 1652), p. 13.
71. Thomas Hobbes, *Leviathan* (1651), ed. Richard Tuck (Cambridge: Cambridge University Press, 1991), p. 239.

72. William Bradford, *History of Plymouth Plantation* (1620–47), (Boston: Little, Brown and Co., 1856), p. 24.

73. This particular claim is in an essay, 'Virginia's Verger', cited in Robert F. Berkhofer, Jr., *The White Man's Indian: Images of the American Indian from Columbus to the Present* (New York: Vintage Books, 1979), p. 21.

74. Stephen Greenblatt, *Marvellous Possessions: The Wonder of the New World* (Chicago: University of Chicago Press, 1991), p. 68.

75. John Winthrop, 'General Observations for the Plantation of New England' (1629), in *Winthrop Papers Vol. II: 1623–1630* (Massachusetts: Historical Society, 1931), pp. 112–13, 120.

76. George Percy, 'A Discourse of the Plantation of the Southern Colonie in Virginia (1606–7), in Peter Mancall (ed.), *Envisioning America: English Plans for the Colonization of North America, 1580–1640* (Boston: Bedford/St Martin's, 1995), p. 123.

77. Richard Eburne, *A Plain Pathway to Plantations* (1624), ed. Louis B. Wright (Cornell University Press, 1962), pp. 50, 64; Bellers, *Proposals for a Profitable Imploying*, p. 128; William Symonds, *Virginia: A Sermon Preached at White-Chapel* (London: Theatrum Orbis Terrarum, 1609), p. 15; Robert Cushman, *Reasons and Considerations Touching the Lawfulness of Removing Out of England into the Parts of America* (1621), in Alexander Young (ed.), *Chronicles of the Pilgrim Fathers of the Colony of Plymouth From 1602 to 1625* (Boston: Charles C. Little and James Brown, 1844), pp. 243–4; William Strachey, *The Historie of Travaile into Virginia Britannia* (1612), (London: Hakluyt Society, 1849), p. 19; Richard Hakluyt, *A Discourse Concerning Western Planting* (1584), ed. Charles Deane (Cambridge: Press of John Wilson and Son, 1877), p. 154.

78. Christopher Hill, *Liberty Against the Law: Some Seventeenth-Century Controversies* (Harmondsworth: Penguin, 1996), p. 156.

79. See Francis Jennings, *The Invasion of America: Indians, Colonialism, and the Cant of Conquest* (New York. W. W. Norton, 1976), p. 78; Wilcomb E. Washburn, 'The Moral and Legal Justifications for Dispossessing the Indians', in James Morton Smith (ed.), *Seventeenth-Century America: Essays in Colonial History* (Westport, CT: Greenwood Press, 1959), p. 23; Cronon, *Changes in the Land*, pp. 63, 77; Gesa Mackenthun, *Metaphors of Dispossession: American Beginnings and the Translation of Empire, 1492–1637* (Norman: University of Oklahoma Press, 1997), pp. 267–8. Martha Finch has connected this discourse of improvement with a 'theology of the body' in colonial America – see *Dissenting Bodies: Corporealities in Early New England* (New York: Columbia University Press, 2010), pp. 88–90.

80. Thus as Stuart Banner has shown, waste was a central category in 'the possession of the Pacific'. 'In fulfilling the work of colonization we are fulfilling one of our appointed tasks', claimed Henry Sewell in the

Legislative Council of New Zealand in 1862, namely 'to bring the waste places of the earth into cultivation, to improve and people them'. Another settler, Maria Atkinson, claimed that the indigenous peoples held their 'wide uncultivated wastes … in communistic style'. Others identified waste with immorality: 'chastity, decency, and thrift cannot exist amidst the waste, filth, and moral contamination', noted one Minister. Summing up the issue as it pertains to New Zealand, Banner shows the extent to which land not under cultivation was described in 'the telling phrase used officially throughout the century, "waste land"'. 'An antipathy to waste ran deep', he adds. And the same issue is found across the Pacific: in Hawaii, 'large tracts of land lie waste', it was said in 1844; in British Columbia 'land is to be regarded as waste, and applicable to the purposes of colonization', it was said in 1846; in Vancouver 'we might justify our occupation … by the fact that of all the land lying waste without prospect of improvement', it was noted in 1868. All cited in Stuart Banner, *Possessing the Pacific: Land, Settlers, and Indigenous People from Australia to Alaska* (Cambridge, MA: Harvard University Press, 2007), pp. 87–9, 93, 94, 135, 206, 222.

81. Christopher Tomlins, *Freedom Bound: Law, Labor, and Civic Identity in Colonizing English America, 1580–1865* (Cambridge: Cambridge University Press, 2010), p. 99.
82. Locke, *Thoughts Concerning Education*, p. 152.
83. Hugo Grotius, *The Truth of the Christian Religion* (1622), as per the first Latin edition in 1627, trans. John Clarke (Edinburgh, 1819), Book II, Sect XIV (p. 107).
84. See Tuck, *Rights of War and Peace*, pp. 105–7; Paul Keal, *European Conquest and the Rights of Indigenous Peoples: The Moral Backwardness of International Society* (Cambridge: Cambridge University Press, 2003), p. 95.
85. The constant recourse to God by Locke, Grotius and these other writers is a reminder of the 'militant religiousness' (Adorno and Horkheimer) of the age, an age in which the 'battle cries' of the 'Church militant' made Puritanism 'one of the fathers of modern military discipline' (Weber), or the extent to which the military revolution of the time coincided with the rise of 'Protestant militancy' (Walzer). Theodor W. Adorno and Max Horkheimer, *Dialectic of Enlightenment* (1944), trans. John Cumming (London: Verso, 1979), p. 19; Max Weber, *The Protestant Ethic and the Spirit of Capitalism* (1920–1), trans. Talcott Parsons (London: George Allen and Unwin, 1930), pp. 99, 235n81; Michael Walzer, *The Revolution of the Saints: A Study in the Origins of Radical Politics* (New York: Atheneum, 1968), pp. 270–1, 277–8.
86. Emer De Vattel, *The Law of Nations: Or Principles of the Law of Nature, Applied to the Conduct and Affairs of Nations and Sovereigns* (1758), ed. Joseph Chitty (Philadelphia: T. & J. W. Johnson, 1853), Book III, Chap. XIII,

sect. 193. Hereafter *LN* in the main text.

87. Onuma Yasuaki, 'Appendix: Eurocentrism in the History of International Law', in Onuma Yasuaki (ed.), *A Normative Approach to War: Peace, War, and Justice in Hugo Grotius* (Oxford: Clarendon Press, 1993), p. 380.

88. A. John Simmons, 'Locke and the Right to Punish', *Philosophy and Public Affairs*, Vol. 20, No. 4, 1991, pp. 311–49.

89. Samuel Pufendorf, *De Jure Naturae et Gentium, Vol. II* (1672), trans. C. H. and W. A. Oldfather (New York: Oceana Publications, 1964), II.V.3, p. 269.

90. The centrality of Locke's account of the 'absolute power' inherent in slavery has been reinforced by the discovery among the papers of Shaftesbury that in 'The Fundamental Constitutions of Carolina' the article which held that 'every freeman of Carolina shall have absolute power and authority over his negro slaves' originally held that every freeman should have 'absolute authority'. Locke added the 'power and' to the 1669 manuscript. See Armitage, 'John Locke, Carolina' p. 609, and John Locke, *The Fundamental Constitutions of South Carolina* (1669), in John Locke, *Political Essays*, ed. Mark Goldie (Cambridge: Cambridge University Press, 1997), p. 180.

91. Dunn, *Political Thought of John Locke*, p. 172; Richard Ashcraft, *Revolutionary Politics and Locke's Two Treatises of Government* (Princeton, NJ: Princeton University Press, 1986), pp. 330–2; Wayne Glausser, 'Three Approaches to Locke and the Slave Trade', *Journal of the History of Ideas*, Vol. 51, No. 2, 1990, pp. 199–216, p. 209; Tully, *An Approach to Political Philosophy*, p. 142; Ross Harrison, *Hobbes, Locke, and Confusion's Masterpiece: An Examination of Seventeenth-Century Political Philosophy* (Cambridge: Cambridge University Press, 2003), p. 146.

92. Michel Foucault, *Discipline and Punish: The Birth of the Prison* (1975), trans. Alan Sheridan (London: Penguin, 1977), pp. 50–1.

93. Martin Seliger, *The Liberal Politics of John Locke* (London: George Allen and Unwin, 1968), pp. 114–15.

94. Aristotle, *The Politics*, 1255b, in *The Politics* and *The Constitution of Athens*, ed. Stephen Everson (Cambridge: Cambridge University Press, 1996), p. 19; Justinian's *Institutes*, trans. Peter Birks and Grant McLeod (New York: Cornell University Press, 1987), I.3.2 (p. 39).

95. This is the point made by Peter Laslett on the basis of comments from 'The Instructions to Governor Nicholson of Virginia', which Locke helped draft in 1698. See his footnote to section 24 of the *Second Treatise*. James Farr has also suggested that Locke's theory of slavery is not only consistent with his theory of natural rights but is probably *necessary* given his theory of just war – '"So Vile and Miserable and Estate": The Problem of Slavery in Locke's Political Thought', *Political Theory*, Vol. 14, No. 2, 1986, pp. 263–89, p. 273.

96. Hobbes, *Leviathan*, p. 219; Algernon Sidney, *Discourses Concerning Government* [written during the exclusion crisis but published in 1698], ed. Thomas G. West (Indianapolis: Liberty Fund, 1996), pp. 519, 522.
97. Arneil, *John Locke and America*, p. 88; Cranston, *John Locke*, pp. 399–448; Vicki Hsueh, *Hybrid Constitutions: Challenging Legacies of Law, Privilege, and Culture in Colonial America* (Durham: Duke University Press, 2010), p. 70.
98. Orlando Patterson, *The Sociology of Slavery: An Analysis of the Origins, Development and Structure of Negro Slave Society in Jamaica* (Cranbury, NJ: Associated University Presses, 1967), pp. 266–7; Richard S. Dunn, *Sugar and Slaves: The Rise of the Planter Class in the English West Indies, 1624–1713* (London: Jonathan Cape, 1973), pp. 256–62; Jerome S. Handler, 'Freedmen and Slaves in the Barbados Militia', *Journal of Caribbean History*, Vol. 19, No. 1, 1984, pp. 1–25; Sally E. Hadden, *Slave Patrols: Law and Violence in Virginia and the Carolinas* (Cambridge, MA: Harvard University Press, 2003), pp. 12–14; Robin Blackburn, *The Making of New World Slavery: From the Baroque to the Modern, 1492–1800* (London: Verso, 1997), p. 264.
99. Herbert A. Johnson and Nancy Travis Wolfe, *History of Criminal Justice* (Cincinnati, OH: Anderson Publishing, 1996), pp. 79, 81.
100. Karen Ordahl Kupperman, *Settling with the Indians: The Meeting of English and Indian Cultures in America, 1580–1640* (London: J. M. Dent, 1980), p. 55.
101. See Robert J. Steinfeld, *The Invention of Free Labor: The Employment Relation in English and American Law and Culture, 1350–1750* (Chapel Hill: University of North Carolina Press, 1991). That we forget this is a reminder of how easily we have become accustomed to thinking in terms of strict categorisations of the historical forms of labour – usually 'slave', 'serf' and 'wage-labourer', but also sometimes 'free' versus 'coerced' – when in fact various forms and degrees of coerced and yet contractual labour existed in Western industrialised nations as late as the late nineteenth century and in the colonies well into the twentieth century. Even in 1957 the 'Abolition of Forced Labour Convention' was needed to 'provide that wages shall be paid regularly and prohibit methods of payment which deprive the worker of a genuine possibility of terminating his employment', on the grounds that this was close to becoming 'analogous to slavery' – Office of the United Nations High Commissioner for Human Rights, 'Abolition of Forced Labour Convention', 1957. In a more recent work, Robert J. Steinfeld has also pointed out the extent to which our binary opposition between free and coerced labour is a product of the Scottish and Continental Enlightenments – *Coercion, Contract, and Free Labor in the Nineteenth Century* (Cambridge: Cambridge University Press, 2001).
102. Available as 'An Essay on the Poor Law' in Locke, *Political Essays*.
103. Manning, *Village Revolts*, pp. 23, 27, 31.

104. Constantine George Caffentzis, *Clipped Coins, Abused Words, and Civil Government: John Locke's Philosophy of Money* (New York: Autonomedia, 1989), p. 69. Also see Elizabeth Frazer and Kimberly Hutchings, 'Politics, Violence and Revolutionary Virtue: Reflections on Locke and Sorel', *Thesis Eleven*, 97, 2009, pp. 46–63.

105. This claim is now so common that I will avoid providing a list of references, but for a useful analysis of the attempts to argue about the (il)legality of the war in Iraq, within a broader theoretical frame which touches on the issues in this chapter, see Robert Knox, 'Marxism, International Law, and Political Strategy', *Leiden Journal of International Law*, Vol. 22, No. 3, 2009, pp. 413–36.

106. Derek Gregory, *The Colonial Present* (Oxford: Blackwell, 2004).

107. I am here paraphrasing and extending a comment made by Massimo De Angelis, *The Beginning of History: Value Struggles and Global Capital* (London: Pluto Press, 2007), p. 134.

108. Karl Marx, *Theories of Surplus Value, Vol. III* (London: Lawrence and Wishart, 1972), p. 272.

109. Marx, *Grundrisse*, p. 460.

110. Marx, *Capital, Vol. 3*, p. 354.

111. Luxemburg, *Accumulation of Capital*, pp. 345, 348–51.

112. Étienne Balibar, 'The Basic Concepts of Historical Materialism', in Louis Althusser and Étienne Balibar, *Reading Capital* (1968), trans. Ben Brewster (London: New Left Books, 1970), p. 279.

113. Werner Bonefeld, 'Primitive Accumulation and Capitalist Accumulation: Notes on Social Constitution and Expropriation', *Science and Society*, Vol. 75, No. 3, 2011, pp. 379–99, p. 379. Also Werner Bonefeld, 'The Permanence of Primitive Accumulation: Commodity Fetishism and Social Constitution', *The Commoner*, 2, 2001; Balibar, 'Reflections on *Gewalt*', pp. 111–12.

114. Michael Perelman, *The Invention of Capitalism: Classical Political Economy and the Secret History of Primitive Accumulation* (Durham: Duke University Press, 2000), pp. 28–9, 33–4. Also see Sandro Mezzadra, 'The Topicality of Prehistory: A New reading of Marx's Analysis of "So-called Primitive Accumulation"', *Rethinking Marxism*, Vol. 23, No. 3, 2011, pp. 302–21; Gavin Walker, 'Primitive Accumulation and the Formation of Difference: On Marx and Schmitt', *Rethinking Marxism*, Vol. 23, No. 3, 2011, pp. 384–404.

115. Midnight Notes Collective, 'The New Enclosures' (1990), reprinted in Midnight Notes, *Midnight Oil: Work, Energy, War, 1973–1992* (New York: Autonomedia, 1992), p. 318; De Angelis, *Beginning of History*, pp. 135–42.

116. GRAIN, *Iraq's New Patent Law: A Declaration of War Against Farmers* (Barcelona, Spain: GRAIN, October 2004), pp. 1–2.

117. Retort, *Afflicted Powers: Capital and Spectacle in a New Age of War* (London:

Verso, 2005). For an application of the concept to NAFTA and other free trade agreements, see James McCarthy, 'Privatizing Conditions of Production: Trade Agreements as Neoliberal Environmental Governance', in Nik Heynen et al. (eds), *Neoliberal Environments: False Promises and Unnatural Consequences* (Abindgon: Routledge, 2007).

118. Harvey, *New Imperialism*, pp. 144–5. Also see Harvey, *A Brief History of Neoliberalism* (Oxford: Oxford University Press, 2005) and *The Enigma of Capital: And the Crises of Capitalism* (London: Profile Books, 2010), pp. 48–9, 58. Harvey's reformulation has had an impact on recent political geography – see Jim Glassman, 'Primitive Accumulation, Accumulation by Dispossession, Accumulation by "Extra-economic" Means', *Progress in Human Geography*, Vol. 30, No. 5, 2006, pp. 608–25.

119. Vandana Shiva, *Biopiracy: The Plunder of Nature and Knowledge* (Boston, MA: South End Press, 1997); Ugo Mattei and Laura Nader, *Plunder: When the Rule of Law is Illegal* (Oxford: Blackwell, 2008); Laura Westra, *Globalization, Violence and World Governance* (Leiden: Brill, 2001).

120. These two comments are from Westra, *Globalization, Violence*, p. 48, and Joan Fitzpatrick, 'Speaking Law to Power: The War against Terrorism and Human Rights', *European Journal of International Law*, Vol. 14, No. 2, 2003, pp. 241–64.

121. Evgeny Pashukanis, 'International Law' (1925–7), reprinted in Piers Beirne and Robert Sharlet (eds), *Pashukanis: Selected Writings* (London: Academic Press, 1980), pp. 169, 172.

CHAPTER 3

1. Peggy Noonan, 'Welcome Back, Duke: From the Ashes of Sept., 11, Arise the Manly Virtues', *Wall Street Journal*, 12 October 2011. Noonan had a history of seeking to overcome the political problems of weak and effeminate men. A former aide of Ronald Reagan, Noonan was central to the transformation of George H. W. Bush from an effete and unmanly wimp during his time as Vice-President into 'his own man' as President, having written what became known as 'The Speech', delivered by Bush on 18 August 1988 at the Republican National Convention and now regarded as a key moment in his Presidential career. The central unifying theme of the speech was war. Bush talked about his life 'lived in the shadow of war', defined himself as 'a man who sees life in terms of … missions defined and missions completed', talked about his time as a torpedo bomber pilot and in the CIA, played on the tough life of a Texan hardman, and described his future Presidency as the completion of the mission started by the hyper-masculine Reagan in 1980. The military invasion of Panama early in his Presidency completed this transformation.

2. For these, see Stephen J. Ducat, *The Wimp Factor: Gender Gaps, Holy Wars, and the Politics of Anxious Masculinity* (Boston: Beacon Press, 2004), pp. 227–31, and Susan Faludi, *The Terror Dream: What 9/11 Revealed about America* (London: Atlantic Books, 2008), p. 21.

3. Such claims about manliness took on a new resonance as the pictures of the torture of prisoners at Abu Ghraib and elsewhere became known, for one of the notable features was how much the torture involved the use of women's underwear, as if the US state wanted not only to destroy minds and bodies in the prisons, but to do so both with and through emasculating and effeminising those they wanted to destroy. The film *Standard Operating Procedure* made by Errol Morris about the conditions in the prisons includes the observation that although basic amenities and commodities were in short supply, women's panties were always available.

4. These from George W. Bush, cited in Bob Woodward, *Bush at War* (New York: Simon and Schuster, 2002), p. 38.

5. 'Your man has got cojones', Bush said to Alistair Campbell, cited in Bob Woodward, *Plan of Attack* (New York: Simon and Schuster, 2004), p. 178.

6. David Halberstam, in a Preface dated 1 December 2001, in *War in a Time of Peace: Bush, Clinton, and the Generals* (London: Bloomsbury, 2003), p. 7.

7. Harvey C. Mansfield, *Manliness* (New Haven: Yale University Press, 2006).

8. David Cameron, 'PM's Speech at Munich Security Conference', 5 February 2011.

9. Martin van Creveld, 'A New World is Coming', *Newsday*, 30 September 2001, cited in Faludi, *Terror Dream*, p. 21.

10. Cathy Young, 'Feminism's Slide since September 11', *Boston Globe*, 16 September 2002.

11. On Vietnam, see Susan Jeffords, *The Remasculinization of America: Gender and the Vietnam War* (Bloomington: Indiana University Press, 1989). For the post-2001 reassertion of the issue, see Transnational Feminists, 'Transnational Feminist Practices Against War', in Susan Hawthorne and Bronwyn Winter (eds), *After Shock: September 11, 2001: Global Feminist Perspectives* (Vancouver: Raincoast Books, 2003), p. 85; Iris Marion Young, 'The Logic of Masculinist Protection: Reflections on the Current Security State', *Signs: Journal of Women in Culture and Society*, Vol. 29, No. 1, 2003, pp. 1–25; Zillah Eisenstein, *Sexual Decoys: Gender, Race and War in Imperial Democracy* (London: Zed Books, 2007); Faludi, *Terror Dream*; Bonnie Mann, 'The Gender Apparatus: Torture and National Manhood in the US "War on Terror"', *Radical Philosophy*, 168, 2011, pp. 22–32.

12. The literature on this is now vast. As well as the works cited in the previous note, see Betty Reardon, *Sexism and War System* (New York: Teachers College Press, 1985); Genevieve Lloyd, 'Selfhood, War and Masculinity', in Carole Pateman and Elisabeth Grosz (eds), *Feminist Challenges: Social*

and Political Theory (London: Allen and Unwin, 1986), pp. 63–76; Carol Cohn, 'Sex and Death in the Rational World of Defense Intellectuals', *Signs: Journal of Women in Culture and Society*, Vol. 12, No. 4, 1987, pp. 687–718; Barbara Ehrenreich, 'Foreword', to Klaus Theweleit, *Male Fantasies, Vol. 1: Women, Floods, Bodies, History* (1977), trans. Stephen Conway (Cambridge: Polity Press, 1987); Jean Bethke Elshtain, *Women and War* (Brighton: Harvester Press, 1987); Miriam Cooke and Angela Woollacott (eds), *Gendering War Talk* (Princeton, NJ: Princeton University Press, 1993); Cynthia Enloe, *The Morning After: Sexual Politics At the End of the Cold War* (Berkeley: University of California Press, 1993); Dana D. Nelson, *National Manhood: Capitalist Citizenship and the Imagined Fraternity of White Men* (Durham: Duke University Press, 1998); Joanna Bourke, *An Intimate History of Killing: Face-to-Face Killing in Twentieth-Century Warfare* (London: Granta, 2000); Cynthia Enloe, *Maneuvers: The International Politics of Militarizing Women's Lives* (Berkeley: University of California Press, 2000); Joshua S. Goldstein, *War and Gender* (Cambridge: Cambridge University Press, 2001); Charlotte Hooper, *Manly States: Masculinities, International Relations, and Gender Politics* (New York: Columbia University Press, 2001); Carol Burke, *Camp All-American, Hanoi Jane, and the High-And-Tight: Gender, Folklore, and Changing Military Culture* (Boston: Beacon Press, 2004); Sandra Whitworth, *Men, Militarism and UN Peacekeeping: A Gendered Analysis* (Boulder, CO: Lynne Rienner, 2004); Aaron Belkin, *Bring Me Men: Military Masculinity and the Benign Façade of American Empire, 1898–2001* (London: Hurst, 2012).

13. Joseph A. Schumpeter, *Capitalism, Socialism, and Democracy* (New York: Harper and Brothers, 1942), pp. 128, 129. And note Carl Schmitt's comment that 'the bourgeois … wants to be spared bravery and exempted from the danger of violent death'– *The Concept of the Political* (1932), trans. George Schwab (Chicago: University of Chicago Press, 1996), pp. 62–3. The supposed link between commerce and peace has also become part of the myth peddled about religion's supposed importance to peace – see, for example, John D. Brewer, Gareth I. Higgins and Francis Teeney, 'Religion and Peacemaking: A Conceptualization', *Sociology*, Vol. 44, No. 6, 2010, pp. 1019–37.

14. Michael Howard, *War and the Liberal Conscience* (Oxford: Oxford University Press, 1978), p. 20.

15. John R. Oneal and Bruce M. Russett, 'The Classical Liberals Were Right: Democracy, Interdependence, and Conflict, 1950–1985', *International Studies Quarterly*, Vol. 41, No. 2, 1997, pp. 267–94, p. 268.

16. Immanuel Kant, 'Perpetual Peace' (1795), in *Kant: Political Writings*, ed. Hans Reiss (Cambridge: Cambridge University Press, 1991), p. 114.

17. Antony Adolf, *Peace: A World History* (Cambridge: Polity, 2009), p. 164;

Michael W. Doyle, *Ways of War and Peace: Realism, Liberalism, and Socialism* (New York: Norton, 1997), pp. 230–1; Anthony Howe, 'Free Trade and Global Order: The Rise and Fall of a Victorian Vision', in Duncan Bell (ed.), *Victorian Visions of Global Order: Empire and International Relations in Nineteenth-Century Political Thought* (Cambridge: Cambridge University Press, 2007), p. 27.

18. Oliver Richmond, *Peace in International Relations* (London: Routledge, 2008), p. 23.
19. James T. Shotwell, *War as an Instrument of National Policy* (New York: Harcourt, Brace and Co., 1929), p. 30.
20. Michael Mousseau, Havard Hegre and John R. Oneal, 'How the Wealth of Nations Conditions the Liberal Peace', *European Journal of International Relations*, Vol. 9, No. 2, 2003, pp. 277–314.
21. F. A. Von Hayek, *Law, Legislation and Liberty, Vol. 2: The Mirage of Social Justice* (London: Routledge, 1979), p. 109.
22. Robert Gilpin, *The Political Economy of International Relations* (Princeton, NJ: Princeton University Press, 1987), pp. 27, 31.
23. Michael Mandelbaum, *The Ideas that Conquered the World: Peace, Democracy and Free Markets in the Twenty-First Century* (New York: Public Affairs, 2004), p. 37. Also see Craig N. Murphy, *International Organization and Industrial Change: Global Governance since 1850* (Cambridge: Polity Press, 1994), p. 18.
24. Oliver Richmond, 'The Problem of Peace: Understanding the "Liberal Peace"', *Conflict, Security and Development*, Vol. 6, No. 3, 2006, pp. 291–314.
25. Mikkel Vedby Rasmussen, *The West, Civil Society and the Construction of Peace* (Basingstoke: Palgrave, 2003), pp. 8, 12–13, 41, 42; John MacMillan, *On Liberal Peace: Democracy, War and the International Order* (London: I. B. Tauris, 1998), pp. 56–61.
26. Mark V. Kauppi and Paul R. Viotti, *The Worldly Philosophers: World Politics in Western Thought* (New York: Lexington Books, 1992), p. 205.
27. Doyle, *Ways of War*, a point noted by Edwin Van der Haar, 'The Liberal Divide over Trade, Peace and War', *International Relations*, Vol. 24, No. 2, 2010, pp. 132–54, p. 143.
28. For example, the material by Adam Smith in Brown, Nardin and Rengger's widely used text *International Relations and Political Thought* has a few pages from Smith on commercial treatises and a few on the division of labour but nothing from his copious comments on war and the importance of the military spirit. See entries from Smith in Chris Brown, Terry Nardin and Nicholas Rengger (eds), *International Relations in Political Thought* (Cambridge: Cambridge University Press, 2002), pp. 410–15, 532–4.
29. David Long, *Towards a New Liberal Internationalism: The International*

Theory of J. A. Hobson (Cambridge: Cambridge University Press, 1996), p. 176; Edwin Van de Haar, *Classical Liberalism and International Relations Theory* (Basingstoke: Palgrave, 2009), pp. 1–3, 70; Van der Haar, 'Liberal Divide'; Bruce Buchan, 'Civilization, Sovereignty and War: The Scottish Enlightenment and International Relations', *International Relations*, Vol. 20, No. 2, 2006, pp. 175–92.

30. The observation has been made by a number of writers on the history of ideas. See Donald Winch, *Adam Smith's Politics: An Essay in Historiographic Revision* (Cambridge: Cambridge University Press, 1978), p. 104; Christopher J. Berry, *The Idea of Luxury: A Conceptual and Historical Investigation* (Cambridge: Cambridge University Press, 1994), pp. 169–70; Robert A. Manzer, 'The Promise of Peace? Hume and Smith on the Effects of Commerce on War and Peace', *Hume Studies*, Vol. 22, No. 2, 1996, pp. 369–82, pp. 375–6; Andrew Wyatt-Walter, 'Adam Smith and the Liberal Tradition in International Relations', *Review of International Studies*, Vol. 22, 1996, pp. 5–28; Arthur Herman, *The Scottish Enlightenment: The Scots Invention of the Modern World* (London: Fourth Estate, 2003), pp. 214–15; Bruce Buchan, 'Enlightened Histories: Civilization, War and the Scottish Enlightenment', *The European Legacy*, Vol. 10, No. 2, 2005, pp. 177–92; Istvan Hont, *Jealousy of Trade: International Competition and the Nation-State in Historical Perspective* (Cambridge, MA: Harvard University Press, 2005), pp. 6–8, 298; John Robertson, *The Scottish Enlightenment and the Militia Issue* (Edinburgh: John Donald Publishers, 2009); Van der Haar, 'Liberal Divide', p. 142; Van der Haar, *Classical Liberalism*, pp. 62–3.

31. J. G. A. Pocock, *Virtue, Commerce, and History* (Cambridge: Cambridge University Press, 1985), p. 114.

32. Adam Ferguson, *An Essay on the History of Civil Society* (1767), ed. Duncan Forbes (Edinburgh: Edinburgh University Press, 1966), p. 225. Hereafter *E* in the main text.

33. As well as Robertson, *Scottish Enlightenment*, see J. R. Western, *The English Militia in the Eighteenth Century: The Story of a Political Issue 1660–1802* (London: Routledge and Kegan Paul, 1965); Lois G. Schwoerer, *'No Standing Armies!': The Antiarmy Ideology in Seventeenth-Century England* (Baltimore: Johns Hopkins University Press, 1974).

34. Adam Ferguson, *Reflections Previous to the Establishment of a Militia* (London: R. and J. Dodsley, 1756), pp. 57.

35. Ferguson, *Reflections*, pp. 3, 12, 15, 25, 30.

36. Adam Ferguson, Letter to John Macpherson, 9 February 1797, in *The Correspondence of Adam Ferguson, Vol. 2: 1781–1816*, ed. Vincenzo Merolle (London: William Pickering, 1995), p. 412.

37. Duncan Forbes, 'Introduction' to Ferguson, *Essay*, p. xxxiv; David Kettler, *The Social and Political Thought of Adam Ferguson* (Columbus: Ohio State

University Press, 1965); Robertson, *Scottish Enlightenment*, pp. 121, 201–2; Richard B. Sher, 'Adam Ferguson, Adam Smith, and the Problem of National Defense', *Journal of Modern History*, Vol. 61, No. 2, 1989, pp. 240–68; Fania Oz-Salzberger, *Translating the Enlightenment: Scottish Civic Discourse in Eighteenth-Century Germany* (Oxford: Oxford University Press, 1995), p. 109; Andreas Kalyvas and Ira Katznelson, 'Adam Ferguson Returns: Liberalism Through a Glass, Darkly' *Political Theory*, Vol. 26, No. 2, 1998, pp. 173–97; Lisa Hill, *The Passionate Society: The Social, Political and Moral Thought of Adam Ferguson* (Dordrecht: Springer, 2006), pp. 177–81, 217–19; Rosalind Carr, 'The Gentleman and the Soldier: Patriotic Masculinities in Eighteenth-Century Scotland', *Journal of Scottish Historical Studies*, Vol. 28, No. 2, 2008, pp. 102–21.

38. Jonathan I. Israel, *Democratic Enlightenment: Philosophy, Revolution, and Human Rights, 1750–1790* (Oxford: Oxford University Press, 2012), pp. 245–6.

39. Kettler, *Social and Political Thought*, p. 90.

40. Kettler, *Social and Political Thought*, pp. 45, 69n5; Oz-Salzberger, *Translating*, p. 94.

41. Adam Ferguson, *A Sermon Preached in the Ersh Language to His Majesty's First Highland Regiment of Foot, At their Cantonment at Camberwell, on the 19th Day of December, 1745* (London: A. Millar, 1746).

42. Adam Ferguson, Letter to John Macpherson, 26 June 1796, in *Correspondence, Vol. 2*, p. 399.

43. Adam Ferguson, Letter to John Macpherson, 31 December 1798, in *Correspondence, Vol. 2*, p. 447.

44. Adam Ferguson, 'Of the Separation of Departments, Professions and Tasks Resulting from the Progress of Arts and Society', in *The Unpublished Essays of Adam Ferguson, Vol. Two*, ed. Winifrid Philip (London: W. E. Philip, 1986), pp. 92–103; 'Of Statesmen and Warriours', in *The Unpublished Essays of Adam Ferguson, Vol. Three*, ed. Winifrid Philip (London: W. E. Philip, 1986), pp. 4–36.

45. Adam Smith, *Lectures on Jurisprudence*, ed. R. L. Meek, D. D. Raphael and P. G. Stein (Indianapolis: Liberty Fund, 1982), p. 7; Adam Smith, *An Inquiry into the Nature and Causes of the Wealth of Nations*, ed. R. H. Campbell, A. S. Skinner and W. B. Todd (Indianapolis: Liberty Fund, 1979), p. 689. Hereafter *LJ* and *WN* in the main text.

46. See Ian Simpson Ross, *The Life of Adam Smith* (Oxford: Oxford University Press, 1995), p. 141.

47. Ferguson, Letter to Smith, 18 April 1776, in *The Correspondence of Adam Smith*, ed. Ernest Campbell Mossner and Ian Simpson Ross (Indianapolis: Liberty Press, 1987), pp. 193–4.

48. Smith, Letter to Andreas Holt, 26 October 1780, in *Correspondence*, p. 251.

49. Smith, Letter to Gilbert Elliott, 7 September 1757, in *Correspondence*, pp. 21–2.
50. Adam Smith, *The Theory of Moral Sentiments* (1759), ed. D. D. Raphael and A. L. Mackie (Indianapolis: Liberty Fund, 1982), p. 236. Hereafter *TMS* in the main text.
51. Forbes, 'Introduction', p. xviii.
52. Edmund Burke, 'Letter I: On the Overtures of Peace' (1796), in *The Writings and Speeches of the Right Honourable Edmund Burke, Vol. 5* (New York: J. F. Taylor, 1901), p. 240.
53. [Rev. John Brown], *An Estimate of the Manners and Principles of the Times* (London: L. Davis and C. Reymers, 1757), pp. 29, 67, 82, 89, 91, 181.
54. Michael B. Young, *James IV and I and the History of Homosexuality* (Basingstoke: Macmillan, 2000), pp. 5–6, 77–8, 85–7.
55. *The Secret History of the Reigns of K. Charles II and K. James II* (1690), cited in Rachel Weil, 'Sometimes a Scepter is Only a Scepter: Pornography and Politics in Restoration England', in Lynn Hunt (ed.), *The Invention of Pornography: Obscenity and the Origins of Modernity, 1500–1800* (New York: Zone Books, 1993), p. 143; G. S. Rousseau, 'The Pursuit of Homosexuality in the Eighteenth Century: "Utterly Confused Category" and/or Rich Repository', in Robert Purks Maccubbin (ed.), *'Tis Nature's Fault: Unauthorized Sexuality during the Eighteenth Century* (Cambridge: Cambridge University Press, 1987), p. 152.
56. *The Levellers* (1745; first published in 1703), in *Mundus Foppensis and The Levellers* (Los Angeles: William Andrews Clark Memorial Library, 1988), p. 419.
57. Hence, for example, a pamphlet from 1691 suggesting that the declining masculinity of men was due to urbanisation, the influence of French culture and the demilitarised world of 'peacetime', was called *Mundus Foppensis: or, The Fop Displayed*. In *Mundus Foppensis and The Levellers* (Los Angeles: William Andrews Clark Memorial Library, 1988). For a discussion, see Philip Carter, *Men and the Emergence of Polite Society, Britain 1660–1800* (Harlow: Pearson, 2001), pp. 137–44, 152–6. For the molly, see Rictor Norton, *Mother Clap's Molly House: The Gay Subculture in England 1700–1830* (London: GMP Publishing, 1992), pp. 101, 103–4, 126–7.
58. 'Effeminacy did not always imply sodomy. But sodomy did imply effeminacy' – Michael B. Young, *King James VI and I and the History of Homosexuality* (Basingstoke: Macmillan, 2000), p. 70. Likewise: 'Effeminacy became the historical hallmark of the culturally marked sodomite' – Theo van der Meer, 'Sodomy and the Pursuit of a Third Sex in the Early Modern Period', in Gilbert Herdt (ed.), *Third Sex, Third Gender: Beyond Sexual Dimorphism in Culture and History* (New York: Zone Books, 1994), p. 149.

59. Although the terms 'heterosexual' and 'homosexual' are nineteenth-century inventions, appearing in the mid-1800s and only after then coming to be seen as defining a whole class of human beings, around 1700 in north-western Europe a new figure emerged onto the cultural landscape: a male understood as desiring sexual relations with other males (adult and equal rather than younger and passive) and identified by what seemed to be a certain effeminacy in manners and behaviour. Prior to this, however, the effeminate man was often associated with an excessive heterosexuality, to the extent that he preferred the company of women so much that he used perfume, cosmetics and jewellery, and seemed to prefer sensual rather than martial pleasures. See Randolph Trumbach, 'Erotic Fantasy and Male Libertinism in Enlightenment England', in Lynn Hunt (ed.), *The Invention of Pornography: Obscenity and the Origins of Modernity, 1500–1800* (New York: Zone Books, 1993), pp. 255–6; Randolph Trumbach, *Sex and the Gender Revolution, Vol. 1: Heterosexuality and the Third Gender in Enlightenment London* (Chicago: University of Chicago Press, 1998), pp. 3–22; Christopher E. Forth, *Masculinity in the Modern West: Gender, Civilization and the Body* (Basingstoke: Palgrave, 2008), pp. 32–3. For Parisian 'assemblies' of homosexuals, see Michel Rey, 'Parisian Homosexuals Create a Lifestyle, 1700–1750: The Police Archives', in Purks Maccubbin (ed.), *'Tis Nature's Fault*, pp. 179–91.

60. There is a huge body of work on this. See Susan Kingsley Kent, *Gender and Power in Britain, 1640–1990* (London: Routledge, 1990), p. 82; Mark E. Kann, *On the Man Question: Gender and Civic Virtue in America* (Philadelphia: Temple University Press, 1991), pp. 65–6, 93, 178; Michele Cohen, *Fashioning Masculinity: National Identity and Language in the Eighteenth Century* (London: Routledge, 1996); Philip Carter, 'An "Effeminate" or "Efficient" Nation? Masculinity and Eighteenth-century Social Documentary', *Textual Practice*, Vol. 11, No. 3, 1997, pp. 429–43; Julie Ellison, *Catos' Tears and the Making of Anglo-American Emotion* (Chicago: University of Chicago Press, 1999); Stefan Dudink, 'Masculinity, Effeminacy, Time: Conceptual Change in the Dutch Age of Democratic Revolutions', in Stefan Dudink, Karen Hageman and John Tosh (eds), *Masculinities in Politics and War: Gendering Modern History* (Manchester: Manchester University Press, 2004), pp. 77–95; Thomas A. King, *The Gendering of Men, 1600–1750, Vol. I: The English Phallus* (Madison, WI: University of Wisconsin Press, 2004), pp. 112–13, 180, 232–3; Karen Harvey, 'The History of Masculinity, circa 1650–1800', *Journal of British Studies*, Vol. 44, No. 2, 2005, pp. 296–312; Matthew McCormack, *The Independent Man: Citizenship and Gender Politics in Georgian England* (Manchester: Manchester University Press, 2005), pp. 75, 208–10; Andrew Wells, 'Masculinity and its Other in Eighteenth-Century Racial Thought',

in Heather Ellis and Jessica Meyer (eds), *Masculinity and the Other: Historical Perspectives* (Newcastle upon Tyne: Cambridge Scholars Publishing, 2009), pp. 85–113. The extent of this concern is illustrated by its place in the humour of the period, as illustrated by Vic Gatrell, who also notes that the disapproval implicit in the satire around effeminacy 'was linked to martial failure' and 'peaked in periods of military danger' – Vic Gatrell, *City of Laughter: Sex and Satire in Eighteenth-Century London* (New York: Walker and Co., 2006), p. 354.

61. John Locke, *Some Thoughts Concerning Education* (1693), ed. John William Adamson (Mineola, NY: Dover, 2007), p. 89; also see pp. 50–1.

62. Lord Shaftesbury, *Characteristicks of Men, Manners, Opinions, Times* (1711; new edition 1732), (Indianapolis: Liberty Fund, 2001), Vol. II, pp. 16, 35, 88.

63. Kathleen Wilson, *The Sense of the People: Politics, Culture and Imperialism in England, 1715–1785* (Cambridge: Cambridge University Press, 1995), p. 188.

64. John Barrell, *The Birth of Pandora and the Division of Knowledge* (Basingstoke: Macmillan, 1992), pp. 67, 82.

65. Gerardo Zampaglione, *The Idea of Peace in Antiquity* (1967), trans. Richard Dunn (Notre Dame: University of Notre Dame Press, 1973), p. 132; Linda Dowling, *Hellenism and Homosexuality in Victorian Oxford* (Ithaca: Cornell University Press, 1994), p. 8; Deirdre N. McCloskey, *The Bourgeois Virtues: Ethics for an Age of Commerce* (Chicago: University of Chicago Press, 2006), p. 201; Todd W. Reeser, *Moderating Masculinity in Early Modern Culture* (Chapel Hill: University of North Carolina Department of Romance Languages, 2006).

66. Pocock, *Virtue, Commerce, and History*, p. 79.

67. See Niccolò Machiavelli, *The Art of War* (1521), Preface. R. Claire Snyder, *Citizen-Soldiers and Manly Warriors: Military Service and Gender in the Civic Republican Tradition* (Lanham: Rowman and Littlefield, 1999), p. 19.

68. Hannah Fenichel Pitkin, *Fortune is a Woman: Gender and Politics in the Thought of Niccolò Machiavelli* (Berkeley: University of California Press, 1984), p. 25.

69. See Hont, *Jealousy of Trade*, pp. 9, 185, and note his comment (p. 296) that 'The writer who reintroduced into the debate of the 1760s the Machiavellian themes of growth and decay, virtue and corruption, was Adam Ferguson'. Also see Hill, *Passionate Society*, pp. 126–7, 181; Quentin Skinner, 'The Republican Ideal of Political Liberty', in Gisela Bock, Quentin Skinner and Maurizio Viroli (eds), *Machiavelli and Republicanism* (Cambridge: Cambridge University Press, 1990), p. 303; J. G. A. Pocock, *Barbarism and Religion, Vol. II: Narratives of Civil Government* (Cambridge: Cambridge University Press, 1999), p. 330, and *Barbarism and Religion, Vol. III: The First Decline and Fall* (Cambridge: Cambridge University Press, 2003), pp. 400–3.

70. David Hume, 'Of Refinement in the Arts' (1752) in *Essays: Moral, Political and Literary*, ed. Eugene F. Miller (Indianapolis: Liberty Fund, 1985), p. 268. On first publication the essay was titled 'On Luxury'; it was changed to the new title in 1760. It should be noted that Hume somewhat bucks the trend for this concern over effeminacy being traced here, suggesting that the luxury and refinement facilitated by commercial society need not necessarily lead to emasculation and effeminacy (pp. 274–5). For Hume, the problem of effeminacy exists in places such as Italy not because of commercial society and its arts and luxuries, but because the Italians have historically relied too heavily on mercenaries. What this does confirm, however, is that the problem of effeminacy is one of military organisation and not solely commerce and arts.

71. Maxine Berg and Elizabeth Eger, 'The Rise and Fall of the Luxury Debates', in Maxine Berg and Elizabeth Eger (eds), *Luxury in the Eighteenth Century: Debates, Desires, and Delectable Goods* (Basingstoke: Palgrave Macmillan, 2003), p. 7.

72. Berry, *Idea of Luxury*, p. 142. The theme is also pursued in Donald Winch, *Riches and Poverty: An Intellectual History of Political Economy in Britain, 1750–1834* (Cambridge: Cambridge University Press, 1996), and for French thought, see Anoush Fraser Terjanian, *Commerce and its Discontents in Eighteenth-Century French Political Thought* (Cambridge: Cambridge University Press, 2013). James Raven has shown the extent to which the 'luxury debate' ran through the press of the eighteenth century – 'Defending Conduct and Property: The London Press and the Luxury Debate', in John Brewer and Susan Staves (eds), *Early Modern Conceptions of Property* (London: Routledge, 1996), pp. 301–19.

73. Till Wahnbaeck, *Luxury and Public Happiness: Political Economy in the Italian Enlightenment* (Oxford: Clarendon Press, 2004), pp. 16–17.

74. Shaftesbury, *Characteristicks*, Vol. III, p. 16; Vol. I, pp. 193, 195.

75. John Millar, *The Origin of the Distinction of Ranks* (1771), ed. Aaron Garrett (Indianapolis: Liberty Fund, 2006), p. 152.

76. John Millar, *An Historical View of the English Government: From the Settlement of the Saxons in Britain to the Revolution in 1688, in Four Volumes* (1787, revised edition 1803), (Indianapolis: Liberty Fund, 2006), pp. 20, 69, 142, 359, 374, 405 (citing Smith).

77. William Russell, *The History of Europe, Part II: From the Peace of Westphalia, in 1648, to the Peace of Paris, in 1763* (1786) (New York: Harper and Brothers, 1839), p. 468.

78. Jean-Jacques Rousseau, *A Discourse on the Moral Effects of the Arts and Sciences* (1750), and *A Discourse on the Origin of Inequality* (1755), in Jean-Jacques Rousseau, *The Social Contract and Discourses*, ed. G. D. H. Cole (London: J. M. Dent, 1973), pp. 19, 52.

79. Robert B. Shoemaker, *Gender in English Society: The Emergence of Separate Spheres?* (London: Longman, 1998), p. 278.

80. Oz-Salzberger, *Translating*, p. 115.

81. G. J. Barker-Benfield, *The Culture of Sensibility: Sex and Society in Eighteenth-Century Britain* (Chicago: University of Chicago Press, 1992), p. 140; Stewart Justman, *The Autonomous Male of Adam Smith* (Norman: University of Oklahoma Press, 1993).

82. See 'Early Draft of Part of the *Wealth of Nations*' (1763), Appendix to Smith, *Lectures*, p. 563.

83. Henry Home, Lord Kames, *Sketches of the History of Man* (1774), ed. James A. Harris (Indianapolis: Liberty Fund, 2007), Book II, p. 493. This comment is in fact from the first edition, listed in this edition as an additional footnote.

84. Kames, *Sketches*, Book I, pp. 205, 322; Book II, pp. 390–4, 421–5, 493–5, 509, 520.

85. Kames, *Sketches*, Book II, pp. 401–2.

86. Kames, *Sketches*, Book II, pp. 409–10, 412, 493, 494.

87. George Turnbull, *Observations upon Liberal Education* (1742), ed. Terrence O. Moore, Jr. (Indianapolis: Liberty Fund, 2003), pp. 13, 26, 36, 38, 45, 53, 106, 158, 221, 231, 279, 294, 297–8, 303, 413, 421.

88. W[illiam] T[hornton], *The Counterpoise, Being Thoughts on a Militia and a Standing Army* (London: John Swan, 1753), pp. 24, 31–2.

89. Millar, *Origin*, pp. 241–2.

90. Millar, *Historical View*, pp. 20, 358, 751–2, 832.

91. Gordon S. Wood, *The Creation of the American Republic, 1776–1787* (New York: W. W. Norton and Co., 1972), p. 52.

92. John Adams, diary entry, 22 August 1770, in *The Works of John Adams, Vol. II* (Boston: Charles C. Little and James Brown, 1856), p. 250. Elsewhere in his diary he notes the danger of dronish and indolent effeminacy – diary entry 3 January 1759, in *Works, Vol. II*, pp. 59, 60. This repeats a diary entry from 1759, in *The Works of John Adams, Vol. I* (Boston: Little, Brown and Co., 1856), p. 45.

93. John Adams, letter of summer 1777, in *Works, Vol. I*, p. 267.

94. Wood, *Creation of the American Republic*, p. 418.

95. Cited in Wood, *Creation of the American Republic*, p. 418.

96. Dana D. Nelson, *National Manhood: Capitalist Citizenship and the Imagined Fraternity of White Men* (Durham: Duke University Press, 1998).

97. Edward Gibbon, *The Decline and Fall of the Roman Empire* (1776–89), (London: Dent, 1910): *Volume Two*, pp. 112n2, 135, 155, 215, 217; *Volume Five*, pp. 118, 129, 365, 545; *Volume Six*, p. 343.

98. Thomas Paine, *Rights of Man* (1791), in *Rights of Man, Common Sense and Other Political Writings*, ed. Mark Philp (Oxford: Oxford University Press, 1995), p. 145.

99. Mary Wollstonecraft, *A Vindication of the Rights of Women* (1792), in Mary Wollstonecraft, *Political Writings*, ed. Janet Todd (Oxford: Oxford University Press, 1994), p. 226. She later comments that too many sons are educated in 'the accomplishments of gentlemen' rather than 'the virtues of a man', and thus 'become vain and effeminate' (p. 242).

100. Immanuel Kant, *The Critique of Judgement* (1790), trans. James Creed Meredith (Oxford: Clarendon Press, 1952), p. 113.

101. The reader will note here the influence of Jacques Derrida, *Politics of Friendship* (1994), trans. George Collins (London: Verso, 1997), pp. 155–6. But for different ways of dealing with the same theme, see Norman F. Dixon, *On the Psychology of Military Incompetence* (London: Futura Publications, 1979), p. 208; Marjorie Garber, *Vested Interests: Cross-Dressing and Cultural Anxiety* (New York: HarperCollins, 1993), pp. 32, 139. On the same theme, and an essay that is worth returning to time and again for anyone who works with security intellectuals, is Carol Cohn, 'Sex and Death'.

102. Michel Foucault, *History of Sexuality: An Introduction* (1976), trans. Robert Hurley (Harmondsworth: Penguin, 1979). Also see Lee Edleman, *Homographesis: Essays in Gay Literary and Cultural Theory* (London: Routledge, 1994), p. 50; Leo Braudy, *From Chivalry to Terrorism: War and the Changing Nature of Masculinity* (New York: Alfred A. Knopf, 2003), p. 252. For an account of this process in Argentina's dirty war, see Diana Taylor, *Disappearing Acts: Spectacles of Gender and Nationalism in Argentina's 'Dirty War'* (Durham: Duke University Press, 1997), pp. 9, 16, 40, 249.

103. J. M. Barrie, *Peter Pan* (London: Penguin, 2004), p. 80.

104. On communism and sexuality, see Mark Neocleous, *Critique of Security* (Edinburgh: Edinburgh University Press, 2008), Chapter 4. For the 'unmanliness' of anarchism, see Carl Smith, *Urban Disorder and the Shape of Belief: The Great Chicago Fire, The Haymarket Bomb, and the Model Town of Pullman* (Chicago: University of Chicago Press, 2007), pp. 155–66. For the effeminate colonial rebel subject, see Mrinalini Sinha, *Colonial Masculinity: The 'Manly Englishman' and the 'Effeminate Bengali' in the Late Nineteenth Century* (Manchester: Manchester University Press, 1995), and John Marriott, *The Other Empire: Metropolis, India and Progress in the Colonial Imagination* (Manchester: Manchester University Press, 2003).

105. Shaftesbury, *Characteristicks*, Vol. III, p. 113.

106. Edward Mead Earle, 'Adam Smith, Alexander Hamilton, Friedrich List: The Economic Foundations of Military Power', in Peter Paret (ed.), *Makers of Modern Strategy: From Machiavelli to the Nuclear Age* (Oxford: Oxford University Press, 1990), pp. 222, 226; Howe, 'Free Trade and Global Order'; Winch, *Adam Smith's Politics*, p. 104.

107. Neocleous, *Critique of Security*, pp. 11–38.

108. Michael J. Shapiro, *Reading 'Adam Smith': Desire, History and Value* (London: Sage, 1993), p. 15.
109. Mark Neocleous, *The Fabrication of Social Order: A Critical Theory of Police Power* (London: Pluto Press, 2000), and Neocleous, *Critique of Security*.
110. Francis Dodsworth, 'Masculinity as Governance: Police, Public Service and the Embodiment of Authority, c. 1700–1850', in Matthew McCormack (ed.), *Public Men: Political Masculinities in Modern Britain* (Basingstoke: Palgrave, 2007), pp. 33–53.
111. Lois Peters Agnew, *Outward, Visible Propriety: Stoic Philosophy and Eighteenth-Century British Rhetorics* (Columbia, SC: University of South Carolina Press, 2008), pp. 108–33.
112. William Blackstone, *Commentaries on the Laws of England, Vol. 4: Of Public Wrongs* (1769), (Chicago: University of Chicago Press, 1979), p. 162.
113. Susan Broomhall and David G. Barrie, 'Introduction', in David G. Barrie and Susan Broomhall (eds), *A History of Police and Masculinities 1700–2010* (London: Routledge, 2012), p. 6.
114. Matthew McCormack, '"A Species of Civil Soldier": Masculinity, Policing and the Military in 1780s England', in Barrie and Broomhall (eds), *History of Police*, p. 68. Also see Susan Broomhall and David G. Barrie, 'Changing of the Guard: Governance, Policing, Masculinity, and Class in the Porteous Affair and Walter Scott's *Heart of Midlothian*', *Parergon*, Vol. 28, No. 1, 2011, pp. 65–90.
115. David Garrioch, 'The Paternal Government of Men: The Self-image and Action of the Paris Police in the Eighteenth Century', in Barrie and Broomhall (eds), *History of Police*, pp. 38, 46.
116. Brown, *Estimate*, p. 219.
117. Henry Fielding, *An Enquiry into the Causes of the Late Increase of Robbers* (1751), in *An Enquiry into the Causes of the Late Increase of Robbers and Related Writings*, ed. Malvin R. Zirker (Middletown, CT: Wesleyan University Press, 1988), pp. 74, 77; Henry Fielding, *The Female Husband* (1746), in *The Female Husband, and Other Writings*, ed. Claude E. Jones (Liverpool: Liverpool University Press, 1960), p. 38.
118. Cited in Wahnbaeck, *Luxury and Public Happiness*, p. 2.
119. William Man. Godschall, *A General Plan of Parochial and Provincial Police. With Instructions to Overseers and Constables, for better regulating their respective Parishes* (London: T. Payne and Sons, 1787), p. vii.

CHAPTER 4

1. *The National Security Strategy of the United States of America* (Washington, DC, September 2002), pp. vi, 31, 15.
2. President Bush, 'Address to a Joint Session of Congress and the American

People', 20 September 2001; also see, for example,'Speech at the Air Force Academy Graduation', 2 June 2004; Colin Powell, interviewed on NBC, *Today Show*, 12 September 2001; Colin Powell, 'Remarks to the Press', 14 September 2001.

3. Chancellor Schröder, 'Policy Statement by Chancellor Schröder', 19 September 2001; Rudolph Giuliani,'Opening Remarks to the UN General Assembly', 1 October 2001; American Council of Trustees and Alumni, *Defending Civilization: How Our Universities are Failing America and What Can be Done about It* (New York, 2001; revised and expanded February 2002).

4. Gerrit W. Gong, *The Standard of 'Civilization' in International Society* (Oxford: Clarendon Press, 1984), p. 69.

5. H. Lauterpacht, *Recognition in International Law* (Cambridge: Cambridge University Press, 1947), p. 31; Gong, *Standard of 'Civilization'*, p. 90.

6. Marina A. Llorent,'Civilization versus Barbarism', in John Collins and Ross Glover (eds), *Collateral Language: A User's Guide to America's New War* (New York: New York University Press, 2002); Mark B. Salter, *Barbarians and Civilization in International Relations* (London: Pluto Press, 2002); Brett Bowden, *The Empire of Civilization: The Evolution of an Imperial Idea* (Chicago: University of Chicago Press, 2009); Robbie Shilliam,'Civilization and the Poetics of Slavery', *Thesis Eleven*, 108, 2012, pp. 99–117.

7. Jack Donnelly, 'Human Rights: A New Standard of Civilization?', *International Affairs*,Vol. 74, No. 1, 1998, pp. 1–24, pp. 1, 16; David P. Fidler, 'A Kinder, Gentler System of Capitulations? International Law, Structural Adjustment Policies, and the Standard of Liberal, Globalized Civilization', *Texas International Law Journal*, Vol. 35, No. 3, 2000, pp. 389–413; Christopher Hobson,'Democracy as Civilization', *Global Society*,Vol. 22, No. 1, 2008, pp. 75–95.

8. James C. Scott, *The Art of Not Being Governed: An Anarchist History of Upland Southeast Asia* (New Haven:Yale University Press, 2009), p. 105.

9. Bowden, *Empire of Civilization*, p. 8. Also see Thomas C. Patterson, *Inventing Western Civilization* (New York: Monthly Review Press, 1997), p. 27.

10. Gong, *Standard of 'Civilization'*, p. 25.

11. John Stuart Mill,'On Civilization', *London and Westminster Review* (1836), in *The Collected Works of John Stuart Mill,Vol. XVIII* (Toronto: University of Toronto Press, 1977), p. 119.

12. John Stuart Mill,'A Few Words on Non-Intervention', *Fraser's Magazine* (1859), in *The Collected Works of John Stuart Mill, Vol. XXI* (Toronto: University of Toronto Press, 1984), p. 118.

13. Martii Koskenniemi, *The Gentle Civilizer of Nations: The Rise and Fall of International Law 1870–1960* (Cambridge: Cambridge University Press, 2001), p. 176; Georg Schwarzenberger, 'The Standard of Civilisation in

International Law', *Current Legal Problems 1955*, Vol. 8, 1955, pp. 212–34.

14. With the rise of the discourse of civilisation the ocean could now be understood as the space of anti-civilisation. As Philip E. Steinberg shows, state-sponsored ships were understood as the sole bastion of society on the ocean, as symbolised by the flag. Ships not flying a national flag were not of *a* land, and thus *the* land, but were *of the sea*. Since 'civilisation' was understood in terms of the rules of territorial statehood, ships not flying a flag were piratical. From this point on, piracy, as an attack against the state system itself, could be understood in international law as a crime against *civilisation* – Philip E. Steinberg, *The Social Construction of the Ocean* (Cambridge: Cambridge University Press, 2001), pp. 131–2.

15. Terry Castle, *Masquerade and Civilization: The Carnivalesque in Eighteenth-Century English Culture and Fiction* (London: Methuen, 1986), p. 78. Also George W. Stocking, *Victorian Anthropology* (New York: The Free Press, 1987), pp. 30–6; Silvia Federici, 'The God That Never Failed: The Origins and Crises of Western Civilization', in Silvia Federici (ed.), *Enduring Western Civilization: The Construction of the Concept of Western Civilization and Its "Others"* (Westport, CT: Praeger, 1995), p. 65; Robert J. C. Young, *Colonial Desire: Hybridity in Theory, Culture and Race* (London: Routledge, 1995), pp. 32, 994–5.

16. *Convention for the Pacific Settlement of International Disputes* (Hague I) and *Convention Respecting the Laws and Customs of War and Land* (Hague IV). Also see James Brown Scott (ed.), *Texts of the Peace Conferences at The Hague, 1899 and 1907* (Boston: Ginn and Co., 1908), pp. 23, 203–4.

17. T. J. Lawrence, *International Problems and Hague Conferences* (London: J. M. Dent and Co., 1908), pp. 32–5. 'It would, for instance, be absurd to expect the Sultan of Morocco to establish a Prize Court, or to require the dwarfs of the central African forest to receive a permanent diplomatic mission' – T. J. Lawrence, *The Principles of International law*, 3rd edn (Boston: D. C. Heath, 1905), p. 58.

18. L. Oppenheim, *International Law: A Treatise, Vol. 1: Peace* (London: Longmans, Green and Co., 1905), pp. 3, 31.

19. Nobert Elias, *The Civilizing Process, Vol. 2: State Formation and Civilization* (1939), trans. Edmund Jephcott (Oxford: Basil Blackwell, 1978), p. 313.

20. Charles H. Alexandrowicz, 'The Juridical Expression of the Sacred Trust of Civilization', *American Journal of International Law*, Vol. 65, No. 1, 1971, pp. 149–59, p. 154.

21. Gong, *Standard of 'Civilization'*, pp. 5, 15, 23, 54, 164; Robert W. Tucker, *The Inequality of Nations* (London: Martin Robertson, 1977), p. 9.

22. Georg Schwarzenberger, *A Manual of International Law*, 6th edn (Abingdon: Professional Books, 1976), p. 84; Gong, *Standard of 'Civilization'*, p. 73.

23. Lucien Febvre, '*Civilisation*: Evolution of a Word and a Group of Ideas' (1930), in Peter Burke (ed.), *A New Kind of History: From the Writings of Febvre*, trans. K. Folca (London: Routledge and Kegan Paul, 1973), p. 220; Raymond Williams, *Keywords* (London: Fontana, 1976), p. 48.

24. Emile Benveniste, 'Civilization: A Contribution to the History of the Word' (1954), in Benveniste, *Problems in General Linguistics*, trans. Mary Elizabeth Meek (Coral Gables, FL: University of Miami Press, 1971), pp. 290–1.

25. Febvre, '*Civilisation*', pp. 222–3.

26. Nobert Elias, *The Civilizing Process, Vol. 1: The History of Manners* (1939), trans. Edmund Jephcott (Oxford: Basil Blackwell, 1978), p. 39.

27. Elias, *Civilizing Process, Vol. 1*, p. 49.

28. Elias, *Civilizing Process, Vol. 1*, pp. 38, 49, 103; Benveniste, 'Civilization', pp. 289–92.

29. Eric Cheyfitz, 'Savage Law: The Plot Against American Indians in *Johnson and Graham's Lessee* v. *M'Intosh* and *The Pioneers*', in Amy Kaplan and Donald E. Pease (eds), *Cultures of United States Imperialism* (Durham: Duke University Press, 1993), p. 116.

30. James Boswell, *The Life of Samuel Johnson* (London: Wordsworth, 1999), p. 331.

31. Benveniste, 'Civilization', p. 293; George C. Caffentzis, 'On the Scottish Origins of "Civilization"', in Federici (ed.), *Enduring Western Civilization*, p. 32.

32. Adam Smith, *An Inquiry into the Nature and Causes of the Wealth of Nations* (1776), ed. R. H. Campbell, A. S. Skinner and W. B. Todd (Indianapolis: Liberty Fund, 1979), pp. 706–8. Benveniste, 'Civilization', p. 294, talks of 'the free use of the word' by Smith, but this is too strong a claim: Smith uses the term 'civilization' just three times, compared to a much wider use of 'civilized'. For wider background to the Scottish context, see Anthony Pagden, 'The "Defence of Civilization" in Eighteenth-Century Social Theory', *History of the Human Sciences*, Vol. 1, No. 1, 1988, pp. 33–45.

33. R. G. Collingwood, *The New Leviathan, or Man, Society, Civilization and Barbarism* (Oxford: Clarendon Press, 1942), p. 286.

34. Elias, *Civilizing Process, Vol. 1*, pp. 44, 47, 104; Zygmunt Bauman, *Legislators and Interpreters: On Modernity, Post-modernity and Intellectuals* (Cambridge: Polity Press, 1987), pp. 89–90; Jean Starobinski, *Blessings in Disguise; or, The Morality of Evil*, trans. Arthur Goldhammer (Cambridge, MA: Harvard University Press, 1993), p. 2; Olivia Smith, *The Politics of Language 1791–1819* (Oxford: Clarendon Press, 1984), p. vii.

35. See Horkheimer's comment along these lines in discussion in 1956 with Theodor Adorno, published as 'Towards a New Manifesto?', trans. Rodney Livingstone, *New Left Review*, 65, 2010, pp, 33–61, p. 33.

36. Febvre, '*Civilisation*', p. 225.

37. Febvre, *'Civilisation'*, p. 223.
38. Febvre, *'Civilisation'*, p. 221–3; also Elias, *Civilizing Process, Vol. 1*, p. 39.
39. Benveniste, *'Civilization'*, p. 291.
40. Voltaire, *The Philosophy of History* (New York: Philosophical Library, 1965), pp. 31, 40, 89.
41. Adam Ferguson, *An Essay on the History of Civil Society* (1767), ed. Duncan Forbes (Edinburgh: Edinburgh University Press, 1966), pp. 200, 205.
42. The otherwise impressive work of Bowden and Pagden on the idea and ideal of civilisation makes only single passing references to police. See Brett Bowden, 'The Ideal of Civilisation: Its Origins and Socio-Political Character', *Critical Review of International Social and Political Philosophy*, Vol. 7, No. 1, 2004, pp. 25–50; Bowden, *Empire of Civilization*, p. 26; Pagden, 'The "Defence of Civilization"'.
43. Volney, *Éclaircissements sur les États-Unis* (1803), cited Febvre, *'Civilisation'*, p. 252n1.
44. Adam Ferguson, *Principles of Moral and Political Science, Vol. 1* (Edinburgh: W. Creech, 1792), pp. 207, 252, 304.
45. Febvre, *'Civilisation'*, p. 229.
46. Francois Guizot, *Dictionnaire Universel des Synonymes de la Langue Française, Sixième Édition* (Paris: La Librairie Académique, 1863), pp. 566–7. In 1828 Guizot wrote that 'for a long period, and in many countries, the word civilization has been in use'. However, his use of the phrase through the book which followed is highly anachronistic. Francois Guizot, *The History of Civilization in Europe* (1828), trans. William Hazlitt (London: Penguin, 1997), p. 14.
47. Zygmunt Bauman, 'On the Origins of Civilisation: A Historical Note', *Theory, Culture and Society*, Vol. 2, No. 3, 1985, pp. 7–14, p. 8.
48. Starobinski, *Blessings*, p. 15.
49. Febvre, *'Civilisation'*, p. 228.
50. Febvre, *'Civilisation'*, p. 232.
51. Mill, 'On Civilization', p. 122; F. A. Hayek, *Law, Legislation and Liberty, Vol. 3: The Political Order of a Free People* (London: Routledge, 1979), p. 163.
52. Karl Marx and Frederick Engels, *The Manifesto of the Communist Party* (1848), in *Collected Works of Karl Marx and Frederick Engels, Vol. 6* (London: Lawrence and Wishart, 1984), pp. 477–519, p. 488.
53. Karl Marx, 'The Future Results of British Rule in India' (1853), in Karl Marx and Frederick Engels, *Collected Works, Vol. 12* (London: Lawrence and Wishart, 1979), p. 221.
54. Bauman, *Legislators and Interpreters*, p. 91.
55. Cited in Febvre, *'Civilisation'*, p. 233.
56. Mill, 'On Civilization', p. 120.
57. Michel Foucault, 'Different Spaces' (1967), trans. Robert Hurley, in Michel

Foucault, *Aesthetics: The Essential Works, Vol. 2*, ed. James D. Faubion (London: Penguin, 1998), p. 185.

58. Uday Singh Mehta, *Liberalism and Empire: A Study in Nineteenth-Century British Liberal Thought* (Chicago: University of Chicago Press, 1999), p. 52.

59. James Fitzjames Stephen, 'Foundations of the Government of India', *The Nineteenth Century*, 80, 1883, pp. 541–68, p. 557.

60. Elias, *Civilizing Process, Vol. 1*, p. 48. Norbert Elias, *The Germans: Power Struggles and the Development of Habitus in the Nineteenth and Twentieth Centuries* (1989), trans. Eric Dunning and Stephen Mennell (New York: Columbia University Press, 1996), p. 173.

61. Thomas Bugeaud, *Mémoir sur notre établissement dans la province d'Oran par suite de la paix* (1837), translated as 'On Pacification' by A. M. Berrett, in Gérard Chaliand (ed.), *The Art of War in World History: From Antiquity to the Nuclear Age* (Berkeley: University of California Press, 1994), p. 746.

62. Karl Marx, *The Civil War in France* (1871), in Karl Marx and Frederick Engels, *Collected Works, Vol. 22* (London: Lawrence and Wishart, 1986), p. 348.

63. The term is from Frederick Engels, 'Persia-China', 22 May 1857, in Karl Marx and Frederick Engels, *Collected Works, Vol. 15* (London: Lawrence and Wishart, 1986), p. 281.

64. This phrase has been widely used by Dutch sociologists, as in 'beschavingsoffensief'. See Arthur Mitzman, 'The Civilizing Offensive: Mentalities, High Culture and Individual Psyches', *Journal of Social History*, Vol. 20, No. 4, 1987, pp. 663–87; K. Verrips, 'Noblemen, Farmers and Labourers: A Civilizing Offensive in a Dutch Village', *Netherlands Journal of Sociology*, Vol. 23, No. 1, 1987, pp. 3–16; Robert van Krieken, 'The Organization of the Soul: Elias and Foucault on Discipline and the Self', *Archives Européennes de Sociologie*, Vol. 31, No. 2, 1990, pp. 353–71; Robert van Krieken, 'The Barbarism of Civilization: Cultural Genocide and the "Stolen Generations"', *British Journal of Sociology*, Vol. 50, No. 2, 1999, pp. 297–315. One might also point here to a broader 'civilizational turn' in historical sociology – see S. N. Eisenstadt, 'The Civilizational Dimension in Sociological Analysis', *Thesis Eleven*, 62, 2000, pp. 1–21.

65. Cristina Rojas, *Civilization and Violence: Regimes of Representation in Nineteenth-Century Colombia* (Minneapolis: University of Minnesota Press, 2002), p. xiii. Also Federici, 'The God That Never Failed', p. 65; Stanley Diamond, *In Search of the Primitive: A Critique of Civilization* (New Brunswick, NJ: Transaction Books, 1974), p. 1; Ann Laura Stoler, *Race and the Education of Desire: Foucault's History of Sexuality and the Colonial Order of Things* (Durham: Duke University Press, 1995), p. 12; Nick Mansfield, *Theorizing War: From Hobbes to Badiou* (Basingstoke: Palgrave Macmillan, 2008), p. 46.

66. Cited in Elias, *Civilizing Process, Vol. 1*, pp. 49–50. The idea of civilisation, notes Alice Conklin, 'was manifest in Napoleon's decision to set off from France not only with troops, but with all the scientific and cultural apparatus … that the French had not deemed necessary for any European state they had conquered'. Thus a group of experts consisting of 'engineers, Islamicists, printers, natural scientists, artists, mathematicians, and astronomers, were all to study conditions in Egypt, then place their knowledge at the service of the invading generals', but also, most importantly, 'to bring the accumulated knowledge and skills of the West to the peoples of Egypt'. For Napoleon 'the work of civilization included, in addition to encouraging trade, introducing the printing press, the French language, education, medicine, preventive hygiene, and the arts, as well as applying the principles of rational administration to fiscal, judicial, and land reform' – Alice L. Conklin, *A Mission to Civilize: The Republican Idea of Empire in France and West Africa, 1895–1930* (Stanford, CA: Stanford University Press, 1997), pp. 17–18.

    The history books are replete with comments similar to Napoleon's. When in early 1887 the explorer Stanley was getting ready to go to Africa, as well as taking 510 Remington rifles with 100,000 rounds, 50 Winchester repeaters with 50,000 cartridges, 2 tons of gunpowder, 350,000 percussion caps and 30,000 Gatling cartridges, Stanley was also to take a new gun provided by Hiram Maxim, one which could shoot 600 rounds per minute compared to a maximum 200 rounds from any other machine gun. The gun, said Stanley, 'would be of valuable service in helping civilisation to overcome barbarism' – Stanley's comment was in *Globe*, 19 January 1887, cited in Frank McLynn, *Stanley: Sorcerer's Apprentice* (London: Constable, 1991), p. 146.

CHAPTER 5

1. Reminder: Gillo Pontecorvo's film *The Battle of Algiers* was shown to some 40 military and civilian experts at the Pentagon in 2003.
2. Major Alexander P. De Seversky, *Victory Through Air Power* (New York: Simon and Schuster, 1942), pp. 104, 335, 352. On the politics of tentacles note the following story: 'In mid-December 2003 I did an Internet search for the keywords 'Al Qaeda' + 'tentacles' and I got 242 hits. When I widened the search to 'terrorists' + 'tentacles' I got 13,900 hits' – Caren Kaplan, 'Mobility and War: The Cosmic View of US "Air Power"', *Environment and Planning A*, Vol. 38, 2006, pp. 395–407, p. 403.
3. For the early figures, see Human Rights Watch, *Off Target: The Conduct of the War and Civilian Casualties in Iraq* (New York: Human Rights Watch, 2003), pp. 6, 56–7, 134–6, and Carl Conetta, *Operation Enduring Freedom:*

Why a Higher Rate of Civilian Bombing Casualties, Project on Defense Alternatives Briefing Report No. 13, 18 January 2002, pp. 3–4. For ongoing updates, see http://www.longwarjournal.org/ and www.iraqbodycount.org.

4. Daniel Swift, 'Bomb Proof', *Financial Times*, 4 September 2010; Peter Adey, *Aerial Life: Spaces, Mobilities, Affects* (Chichester: Wiley-Blackwell, 2010), p. 6.

5. Peter Adey, Mark Whitehead and Alison J. Williams, 'Introduction: Air-target', *Theory, Culture and Society*, Vol. 28, Nos. 7–8, 2011, pp. 173–87, p. 176.

6. Kaplan, 'Mobility and War', p. 398; John Dower, *Cultures of War: Pearl Harbor, Hiroshima, 9-11, Iraq* (New York: Norton/New Press, 2010); Andreas Huyssen, 'Air War Legacies: From Dresden to Baghdad', *New German Critique*, 90, 2003, pp. 163–76.

7. Derek Gregory, 'From a View to a Kill: Drones and Late Modern War', *Theory, Culture and Society*, Vol. 28, Nos. 7–8, 2011, pp. 188–215, p. 205.

8. Ward Thomas, *The Ethics of Destruction: Norms and Force in International Relations* (Ithaca: Cornell University Press, 2001), p. 172.

9. Derek Gregory, 'Lines of Descent', *openDemocracy*, 8 November 2011.

10. Erik K. Rundquist, *Desert Talons: Historical Perspectives and Implications of Air Policing in the Middle East* (Maxwell Air Force Base, AL, 2009), pp. 3, 7, 51.

11. David J. Dean, *The Air Force Role in Low-Intensity Conflict* (Maxwell Air Force Base, AL: Air University Press, 1986), pp. 23, 25. Elsewhere the author, a Lieutenant Colonel, reports on Project Control Report PCR1 of 1954, in which the British use of air power in its colonies is cited as a model for Cold War campaigns. The managers of Project Control 'first encountered the idea of control by air while studying the techniques used by the British to control obstreperous tribes in the Middle East during the 1920s and 1930s. The British found that the use of air power to enforce their will in colonial areas was cheaper, more effective, and more politically appealing than the use of land forces'– Lieutenant Colonel David J. Dean, 'Project Control: Creative Strategic Thinking at Air University', *Air University Review*, July–August, 1984, p. 1.

12. Capt. David Willard Parsons, USAF, 'British Air Control: A Model for the Application of Air Power in Low-Intensity Conflict?', *Airpower Journal*, Summer 1994.

13. Lin Todd et al., *Iraq Tribal Study: Iraq Al-Anbar Governorate* (US Department of Defense, 2006), sect. 5–23.

14. In the RAF's *Air Power Review* in 2001, James Corum writes: 'In the 15 years that the United States has found itself involved in various peacekeeping and peace-enforcement operations … Air Force officers and air power theorists have looked at the RAF's colonial air control as a useful

model for the kind of military-occupation missions that the United States conducts today' – James S. Corum, 'Air Control: Reassessing the History', *RAF Air Power Review*, Vol. 4, No. 2, 2001, pp. 15–35, p. 16. A 2002 RAND report also observed that 'since the end of the Cold War, the air instrument has become America's weapon of first resort to handle nearly all varieties of contingencies from disaster relief to major theater wars' – Jeremy Shapiro, 'Introduction: The Price of Success', in Zalmay Khalilzad and Jeremy Shapiro (eds), *Strategic Appraisal: United States Air and Space Power in the 21st Century* (Santa Monica, CA: RAND, 2002), p. 1.

15. JSCSC in Partnership with Serco, *Research Guide Series: Air Policing during the Inter-War Years, 2011.*

16. See Stephen Kern, *The Culture of Time and Space, 1880–1918* (London: Weidenfeld and Nicolson, 1983), pp. 241–7; Laurence Goldstein, *The Flying Machine and Modern Literature* (Bloomington: Indiana University Press, 1986); Michael S. Sherry, *The Rise of American Air Power: The Creation of Armageddon* (New Haven: Yale University Press, 1987); Valentine Cunningham, *British Writers of the Thirties* (Oxford: Clarendon Press, 1988), p. 169; David Edgerton, *England and the Aeroplane: An Essay on a Militant and Technological Nation* (Basingstoke: Macmillan, 1991); Robert Wohl, *A Passion for Wings: Aviation and the Western Imagination, 1908–1918* (New Haven: Yale University Press, 1994); Robert Wohl, *The Spectacle of Flight: Aviation and the Western Imagination, 1920–1950* (New Haven: Yale University Press, 2005); Adey, *Aerial Life*, p. 26. Apropos of the argument in Chapter 3, we should note that one aspect of this airmindedness was a focus on the chivalrous flying ace, and one aspect of this was the ace's hypermasculinity: the flying ace was thought to be a figure who could purge the male spirit of the effeminacy brought about by the industrial age. See Linda R. Robertson, *The Dream of Civilized Warfare: World War I Flying Aces and the American Imagination* (Minneapolis: University of Minnesota Press, 2003), pp. xvii–xviii, 119, 169–71, 308–22, 375, 386–7.

17. Chief of the Air Staff, 'Review of Air Situation and Strategy for the Information of the Imperial War Cabinet', 27 June 1918, and 'Memorandum by the Chief of the Air Staff on Air-power Requirements of the Empire', 9 December 1918, reprinted as Appendix V and Appendix VII respectively of Major-General The Right Hon. Sir Frederick Sykes, *From Many Angles: An Autobiography* (London: George G. Harrap and Co., 1942), pp. 544, 554, 558; and see Sykes's comments on this at p. 260.

18. In a secret memorandum to the Cabinet, 20 March 1914, cited in David Killingray, '"A Swift Agent of Government": Air Power in British Colonial Africa, 1916–1939', *Journal of African History*, Vol. 25, No. 4, 1984, pp. 429–44, p. 429.

19. Cited in David Omissi, *Air Power and Colonial Control: The Royal Air Force 1919–1939* (Manchester: Manchester University Press, 1990), p. 25.

20. Toby Dodge, *Inventing Iraq: The Failure of Nation Building and a History Denied* (New York: Columbia University Press, 2003), p. 132; Omissi, *Air Power and Colonial Control*, pp. 34, 37; Charles Townshend, *When God Made Hell: The British Invasion of Mesopotamia and the Creation of Iraq, 1914–1921* (London: Faber and Faber, 2010), pp. xxi, 455.

21. Priya Satia, *Spies in Arabia: The Great War and the Cultural Foundations of Britain's Covert Empire in the Middle East* (Oxford: Oxford University Press, 2008), p. 240.

22. Lee Kennett, *A History of Strategic Bombing* (New York: Charles Scribner's Sons, 1982), p. 15; Lieutenant Colonel David J. Dean, 'Air Power in Small Wars: The British Air Control Experience', *Air University Review*, July–August 1983, pp. 1–8; Charles Townshend, '"Civilization and Frightfulness": Air Control in the Middle East Between the Wars', in Chris Wrigley (ed.), *Warfare, Diplomacy and Politics: Essays in Honour of A. J. P. Taylor* (London: Hamish Hamilton, 1986), p. 143; H. Bruce Franklin, *War Stars: The Superweapon and the American Imagination* (New York: Oxford University Press, 1988), pp. 86, 88; Philip Anthony Towle, *Pilots and Rebels: The Use of Aircraft in Unconventional Warfare 1918–1988* (London: Brassey's, 1989), pp. 1, 9–55; John Buckley, *Air Power in the Age of Total War* (London: UCL Press, 1999), p. 102; David Killingray, 'Guardians of Empire', in David Killingray and David Omissi (eds), *Guardians of Empire* (Manchester: Manchester University Press, 1999), p. 6; Sven Lindqvist, *A History of Bombing* (1999), trans. Linda Haverty Rugg (London: Granta, 2001), para. 4; James S. Corum and Wray R. Johnson, *Air Power in Small Wars: Fighting Insurgents and Terrorists* (Lawrence, KS: University Press of Kansas, 2003), pp. 76, 78; Beau Grosscup, *Strategic Terror: The Politics and Ethics of Aerial Bombardment* (London: Zed Books, 2006), p. 27; Peter Dye, 'Royal Air Force Operations in South-West Arabia 1917–1967', in Joel Hayward (ed.), *Air Power, Insurgency and the 'War on Terror'* (Cranwell: RAF Centre for Air Power Studies, 2009), pp. 47–8.

23. Satia, *Spies in Arabia*, p. 245.

24. The small wars thesis stems largely from Colonel C. E. Callwell, *Small Wars: Their Principles and Practice*, first published in 1896, revised several times thereafter, and widely cited in the literature. The book is, in effect, a history of colonial pacification campaigns. As if to reinforce this, the term later becomes attached to counter-revolutionary and anti-guerrilla warfare.

25. Mark Mazower, *Governing the World: The History of an Idea* (London: Allen Lane, 2012), pp. 78–9.

26. Cited in Killingray, '"A Swift Agent of Government"', p. 431.

27. Philip Game, the Commanding Air Officer in India, 18 October 1923, cited

Omissi, *Air Power and Colonial Control*, p, 150.

28. L. E. O. Charlton, *Charlton* (London: Faber and Faber, 1931), p. 271.

29. Omissi, *Air Power and Colonial Control*, pp. ix–x, 208. For the French'aerial police actions' case, see Charles Christienne and Pierre Lissarague, *A History of French Military Aviation* (1980), trans. Francis Kianka (Washington, DC: Smithsonian Institution Press, 1986), p. 234. Practice showed some differentiation based on race, with much tighter rules of engagement applied to operations against, for example, white dissidents in Ireland and South Africa compared to other parts of the British Empire – Roger Beaumont, *Might Backed by Right: The International Air Force Concept* (Westport, CT: Praeger, 2001), p. 38.

30. Carl Schmitt, *The* Nomos *of the Earth in the International Law of the* Jus Publicum Europaeum (1950), trans. G. L. Ulmen (New York: Telos Press, 2003), p. 317. On the limitations of Schmitt's thinking on air power, see Nasser Hussain, 'Air Power', in Stephen Legg (ed.), *Spatiality, Sovereignty and Carl Schmitt* (Abingdon: Routledge, 2011).

31. Air Staff Memorandum No. 16, 1924, cited in Major Michael A. Longoria, *A Historical View of Air Policing Doctrine: Lessons from the British Experience Between the Wars, 1919–1939* (Maxwell Air Force Base, AL: Air University Press, 1992), p. 32.

32. Air Ministry, *Royal Air Force Operations Manual*, 1922, cited in Neville Parton, 'Air Power and Insurgency: Early RAF Doctrine', in Hayward (ed.), *Air Power, Insurgency*, p. 34.

33. Squadron-Leader E. J. Kingston-McCloughry, 'Policing By Air', *Royal Air Force Quarterly* (1932), reprinted in E. J. Kingston-McCloughry, *Winged Warfare: Air Problems of Peace and War* (London: Jonathan Cape, 1937), pp. 202–4.

34. Dodge, *Inventing Iraq*, p. 133.

35. Cited in Jafna L. Cox, 'A Splendid Training Ground: The Importance to the Royal Air Force of its Role in Iraq, 1919–32', *Journal of Imperial and Commonwealth History*, Vol. 13, No. 2, 1985, pp. 157–84, p. 172.

36. Cited in Ioan Davies, *African Trade Unions* (Harmondsworth: Penguin, 1966), p. 35.

37. Mathew Forstater, 'Taxation and Primitive Accumulation: The Case of Colonial Africa', *Research in Political Economy*, 22, 2005, pp. 51–64; David Graeber, *Debt: The First 5,000 Years* (New York: Melville House Publishing, 2012), pp. 50–1.

38. Sir F. D. Lugard, *The Dual Mandate in British Tropical Africa* (1922) (Edinburgh: William Blackwood and Sons, 1929), pp. 234–5, 254–5; 'Lugard's Political Memoranda', in A. H. M. Kirk-Greene (ed.), *The Principles of Native Administration in Nigeria: Selected Documents 1900–1947* (London: Oxford University Press, 1965), pp. 118, 132.

39. James C. Scott, *The Moral Economy of the Peasant: Rebellion and Resistance in Southeast Asia* (New Haven: Yale University Press, 1976), p. 92.

40. Cited in Robert A. Manners, 'Land Use, Labor, and the Growth of Market Economy in Kipsigis Country', in Paul Bohanna and George Dalton (eds), *Markets in Africa* (Evanston, IL: Northwestern University Press, 1962), p. 497.

41. Karl Marx, *Capital: A Critique of Political Economy, Vol. 1* (1867), trans. Ben Fowkes (Harmondsworth: Penguin, 1976), pp. 238–9, 242.

42. Mike Brogden, 'An Act to Colonise the Internal Lands of the Island: Empire and the Origins of the Professional Police', *International Journal of the Sociology of Law*, Vol. 15, No. 2, 1987, pp. 179–208, p. 202.

43. Peter Sluglett, *Britain in Iraq, 1914–1932* (London: Ithaca Press, 1976), pp. 265–6.

44. Letter of 19 November 1923, cited in Sluglett, *Britain in Iraq*, p. 266.

45. Letter of 20 January 1924, cited in Sluglett, *Britain in Iraq*, p. 266.

46. Anon., 'Fiends of the Air', *Naval Review*, Vol. 11, No. 1, 1923, pp. 81–115, p. 90. I suspect the article is by J. F. C. Fuller since passages are identical to those in *The Reformation of War*, cited below in this chapter.

47. Air Staff Memorandum, 'On the Power of the Air Force and the Application of this Power to Hold and Police Mesopotamia', March 1920. Thompson cited in Satia, *Spies in Arabia*, p. 245.

48. Eyal Weizman, 'The Politics of Verticality', Part II, *openDemocracy*, April–May 2002; Eyal Weizman, 'Thanato-tactics', in Ryan Bishop, Gregory K. Clancey and John Phillips (eds), *The City as Target* (London: Routledge, 2012).

49. Adey, *Aerial Life*, p. 86.

50. See Dov Gavish, *A Survey of Palestine under the British Mandate, 1920–1948* (Abingdon, Oxon: Routledge, 2005); Tom Vanderbilt, *Survival City: Adventures among the Ruins of Atomic America* (Chicago: University of Chicago Press, 2002), p. 557.

51. Thomas Holland, 'Introduction', to Colonel H. L. Crosthwait, 'Air Survey and Empire Development', *Journal of the Royal Society of Arts*, Vol. 77, 28 December 1928, pp. 161–2, p. 162.

52. Colonel H. L. Crosthwait, 'Air Survey and Empire Development', *Journal of the Royal Society of Arts*, Vol. 77, 28 December 1928, pp. 162–75, p. 163.

53. Adey, *Aerial Life*, p. 91.

54. 'Observation provided information about the enemy. Oblique photographs were used to prepare for the progress of troops on the ground, and groups of photographs were often given to column leaders to supplement the still incomplete maps. The enemy's advantage in being familiar with the terrain was thus largely compensated for' – Christienne and Lissarague, *History of French Military Aviation*, p. 231.

55. Air Commodore C. F. A. Portal, 'Air Force Co-Operation in Policing the Empire', Lecture at RUSI, London, 17 February 1937, in Eugene M. Emme (ed.), *The Impact of Air Power* (Princeton, NJ: D. Van Nostrand Co., 1959), p. 357.

56. Cited in Adey, *Aerial Life*, p. 92.

57. Dodge, *Inventing Iraq*, p. 146; Omissi, *Air Power and Colonial Control*, p. 152; Christienne and Lissarague, *History of French Military Aviation*, p. 233.

58. This relationship between 'moral(e)' and the material effects of bombing was never quite defined, nor could it. Trenchard had several good attempts, famously stating on one occasion that 'at present the moral effect of bombing stands undoubtedly to the material effect in a proportion of 20 to 1' – cited in Tammy Davis Biddle, *Rhetoric and Reality in Air Warfare: The Evolution of British and American Ideas about Strategic Bombing, 1914–1945* (Princeton, NJ: Princeton University Press, 2002), p. 48. Biddle points out: 'it was a curious statement'. What emerged was the common view that 'the moral effect produced by a hostile aeroplane … is all out of proportion to the damage which it can inflict' (Trenchard again, from 1916). This idea, repeated in phrases either identical or more or less identical to it, and certainly just as curious, reverberates through the literature (see Biddle, *Rhetoric*, pp. 76–81, 93, 130–1, 134, 156, 196).

59. 'Aircraft in Frontier Warfare', 1922, cited in Biddle, *Rhetoric*, pp. 82–3.

60. The point is made by Gibson in relation to Vietnam, but has a more general claim too – James William Gibson, *The Perfect War: Technowar in Vietnam* (New York: Atlantic Monthly Press, 1986), p. 319; also pp. 97–8, 369.

61. Gibson, *Perfect War*, p. 322; also p. 327.

62. Cited in Charles Townshend, *Britain's Civil Wars: Counterinsurgency in the Twentieth Century* (London: Faber and Faber, 1986), p. 97.

63. See Mark Neocleous, *The Fabrication of Social Order: A Critical Theory of Police Power* (London: Pluto, 2000), pp. 46–7, 64–6.

64. Trenchard, Letter to *The Times* in April 1925, cited in Smith, *British Air Strategy between the Wars*, p. 30; The Governor General, C. E. Bruce, cited in Philip Anthony Towle, *Pilots and Rebels: The Use of Aircraft in Unconventional Warfare 1918–1988* (London: Brassey's, 1989), p. 44.

65. Chamberlain, speaking in the House of Commons, 21 June 1938 – *Hansard: House of Commons Debates*, 1938, Vol. 337, col. 937–8; Senate cited in George E. Hopkins, 'Bombing and the American Conscience During World War II', *Historian*, Vol. 28, No. 3, 1966, pp. 451–73; F. D. Roosevelt, 'An Appeal to Great Britain, France, Italy, Germany, and Poland to Refrain from Air Bombing of Civilians', 1 September 1939.

66. Sherry, *Rise of American Air Power*, p. 71. We are reminded of the bombing of Guernica by fascist states time and again in cultural analyses and political debate, but the bombing of Taguira, Ben Carich, Tetuan and

countless other towns and cities by liberal states goes remarkably unreported – see Ian Patterson, *Guernica and Total War* (London: Profile Books, 2007); Sven Lindqvist,'Guernica', in Bregje van Eekelen et al. (eds), *War on Words* (Santa Cruz, CA: New Pacific Press, 2004), pp. 76–7.

67. Cited in Omissi, *Air Power and Colonial Control*, p. 170.

68. War Office, *Manual of Military Law* (London: HMSO, 1914), p. 235.

69. Nathaniel Berman, '"The Appeals of the Orient": Colonized Desire and the War of the Riff', in Karen Knop (ed.), *Gender and Human Rights* (Oxford: Oxford University Press, 2004), p. 202.

70. 'Rapport de M. Georges Scelle', *Les Cahiers des Droits de l'homme*, 25, 1925, cited in Berman,'"The Appeals of the Orient"', p. 202.

71. See J. H. H. [pseudonym], '"Police" Bombing in Outlying Regions', *The Naval Review*, Vol. 21, No. 3, 1933, pp. 461–5, and J. M. Spaight, *Air Power in the Next War* (London: Geoffrey Bles, 1938), p. 65.

72. Phillip S. Meilinger, 'Clipping the Bomber's Wings: The Geneva Disarmament Conference and the Royal Air Force, 1932–1934', *War in History*, Vol. 6, No. 3, 1999, pp. 306–30, p. 323.

73. Quincy Wright, 'The Bombardment of Damascus', *American Journal of International Law*, Vol. 20, No. 2, 1926, pp. 263–80, p. 265. Also Lindqvist. *History of Bombing*, sect. 123.

74. Richard Grossman, '"Looks Suspicious": The US Marines Air Campaign against the Sandino Insurgents of Nicaragua 1927–1933', in Hayward (ed.), *Air Power, Insurgency and the 'War on Terror'*, pp. 89–90.

75. In Britain in December 1917 aircraft had been used to drop leaflets urging aeroplane engine workers in Coventry to end a strike. During the 1919 rail strike air force squadrons flew government dispatches across the country and liaised with police forces. In early 1920, during the debates about how air power might be used to quell industrial revolt in established regions of the Empire, draft papers on the subject also suggested that 'a limited amount of bombing' by the RAF within the UK itself might be sanctioned (cited in Omissi, *Air Power and Colonial Control*, p. 115). Churchill insisted the references to England and Ireland be removed and never referred to again, *at least in writing*, Omissi notes (p. 41). The Emergency Powers Act itself had been passed in 1920 to ensure that members of the armed forces, including airmen, could be used as volunteer strike breakers (which until then it was illegal for them to do). These possibilities came to the fore during the General Strike of 1926, understood by the ruling class *as war* ('this thing is a war', commented Liberal politician Sir John Simon to the House of Commons in May 1926, and other members of his class were queuing up to agree with him: 'this interminable series of strikes and lockouts looked remarkably like warfare'; 'we speak of this situation as a "general strike" much in the same

way as we speak of the last war as the "great war". Many more claims along these lines could be provided.) And so one finds that the coordinating body for the General Strike was established in the Air Ministry, and the air force itself was to be used to deliver anti-strike propaganda, either to newspapers or as leaflet drops on towns with a history of radicalism and working-class action. The air force also delivered government mail, supplied strike breakers on steam engines, underground trains and power stations, supplied the personnel for the arrest of key communists, to search roads, railways, canals and bridges, and in Ireland, where the aircraft were armed, to protect armoured cars from ambush.

In the US, during a coal strike in Matewan, West Virginia, from May 1920 through to August 1921, and following a period in which military officers believed that class war was a reality, the workers formed a 'citizens army' and faced not only armed troops but also airplanes armed with gas bombs and machine guns (led by the Commander of the First Provisional Air Brigade, Brigadier General Billy Mitchell). Coal company operators liaised with the local police force to enable commercial aircraft to drop homemade bombs filled with nails and metal fragments on the striking miners, and Mitchell said that the case illustrated the potential of air power in civil disturbances and strike action. In May 1921, the black areas of Tulsa, Oklahoma, were invaded by several thousand whites looting and burning. Armed blacks defended their homes but their resistance was overcome with the use of eight airplanes manned by police that dropped bombs on neighbourhoods that had earlier been drenched with petrol (killing between 150 and 200 black people, mostly women and children, and burning the ghetto to the ground). And we should be reminded too of the story behind the cover of this book, as I point out in my Acknowledgements.

On these points, see Edgerton, *England and the Aeroplane*, p. 47; Joan M Jensen, *Army Surveillance in America, 1775–1980* (New Haven: Yale University Press, 1991), pp. 143–4, 188–9; Clayton D. Laurie, 'The United States Army and the Return to Normalcy in Labor Dispute Interventions: The Case of the West Virginia Coal Mine Wars, 1920–21', *West Virginia History*, Vol. 50, 1991, pp. 1–24; John Spritzler, *The People as Enemy: The Leaders' Hidden Agenda in World War II* (Montreal: Black Rose Books, 2003), p. 61; Franklin, *War Stars*, p. 95. For the General Strike as warfare, see Samuel Hynes, *A War Imagined: The First World War and English Culture* (London: Bodley Head, 1990), pp. 409–11, and Susan Kingsley Kent, *Aftershocks: Politics and Trauma in Britain, 1918–1931* (Basingstoke: Palgrave, 2009), pp. 122–48. On the use of summary justice as a mechanism for policing the working class and the colonies, see Brogden, 'An Act to Colonise', p. 199, and Mike Brogden, 'The Emergence of the

Police: The Colonial Dimension', *British Journal of Criminology*, Vol. 27, No. 1, 1987, pp. 4–14.

76. J. F. C. Fuller, *The Reformation of War* (New York: E. P. Dutton and Co., 1923), pp. 200, 202, 205–6.

77. Fuller, *Reformation of War*, pp. 207–8; Anon., 'Fiends of the Air', p. 103.

78. Fuller, *Reformation of War*, pp. 207–8.

79. Viscount Plumer and Lord Lloyd, speaking in the House of Lords, 9 April 1930 – *Hansard: House of Lords Debates*, 1930, Vol. 77, col. 37–8.

80. Wing Commander Saundby, 'Small Wars with Particular Reference to Air Control in Undeveloped Countries', Lecture to RAF Staff College, Andover, England, June 1936, cited in Dean, *Air Force Role*, pp. 22–3.

81. Air Marshal Sir Robert Saundby, *Air Bombardment: The Story of its Development* (London: Chatto and Windus, 1961), p. 44.

82. L. E. O. Charlton, *The Menace of the Clouds* (London: William Hodge and Co., 1937), p. 14.

83. As well as the argument in Neocleous, *Fabrication*, and *Critique of Security* (Edinburgh: Edinburgh University Press, 2008), I am building here on my 'Security as Pacification', in Mark Neocleous and George S. Rigakos (eds), *Anti-Security* (Ottawa: Red Quill Press, 2011).

84. See *Rise of the Drones: Unmanned Systems and the Future of War*, Hearing Before the Subcommittee on National Security and Foreign Affairs, 23 March 2010 (Washington, DC: US Government Printing Office, 2011), pp. 2, 75; Jeremiah Gertler, *US Unmanned Aerial Systems* (Congressional Research Service Report 7-5700, 2012).

85. Nick Turse and Tom Engelhardt, *Terminator Planet: The First History of Drone Warfare, 2001–2050* (Dispatch Book, 2012), p. 37.

86. Ministry of Defence, 'RAF Reaper Reaches 20,000 Hours over Afghanistan', *MOD Defence News*, 8 April 2011.

87. John Keegan, *The Face of Battle* (Harmondsworth: Penguin, 1978), p. 326; Eric Hobsbawm, *Age of Extremes: The Short Twentieth Century* (London: Penguin, 1994), p. 50.

88. Medea Benjamin, *Drone Warfare: Killing by Remote Control* (London: Verso, 2013).

89. James Der Derian, *Virtuous War: Mapping the Military-Industrial-Media-Entertainment Network* (Boulder, CO: Westview Press, 2001), p. xv.

90. Bradley Jay Strawser, 'Moral Predators: The Duty to Employ Uninhabited Aerial Vehicles', *Journal of Military Ethics*, Vol. 9, No. 4, 2010, pp. 342–68.

91. Tyler Wall and Torin Monahan, 'Surveillance and Violence from Afar: The Politics of Drones and Liminal Security-scapes', *Theoretical Criminology*, Vol. 15, No. 3, 2011, pp. 239–54, p. 240; Benjamin, *Drone Warfare*, p. 78.

92. Chad C. Haddal and Jeremiah Gertler, *Homeland Security: Unmanned*

Aerial Vehicles and Border Surveillance (Congressional Research Service: Report for Congress, 7-5700, 8 July 2010), p. 1.

93. Benjamin, *Drone Warfare*, p. 75.
94. ASTRAEA homepage: http://www.astraea.aero/ (accessed 21 September 2012). Also see Chris Cole, *Drone Wars Briefing* (Oxford: Drone Wars UK, 2012), p. 26.
95. Jefferson Morley,'Drones Invade Campus', *Salon*, 1 May 2012.
96. Jonathan Franklin, 'US Unleashes New Drones in Afghanistan', *The Guardian*, 13 June 2012, p. 17; Tim Blackmore, *War X: Human Extensions in Battlespace* (Toronto: University of Toronto Press, 2005), pp. 130–1; P. W. Singer, *Wired for War: The Robotics Revolution and Conflict in the 21st Century* (New York: Penguin, 2009), pp. 116–20.
97. Air Commodore L. E. O. Charlton, *War Over England* (London: Longmans, Green and Co., 1936), p. 174.
98. For a sample, see Kenneth Hewitt,'Place Annihilation: Area Bombing and the Fate of Urban Places', *Annals of the Association of American Geographers* Vol. 73, No. 2, 1983, pp. 257–84; Kenneth Hewitt, 'The Social Space of Terror: Towards a Civil Interpretation of Total War', *Environment and Planning D: Society and Space*, Vol. 5, No. 4, 1987, pp. 445–74; Robert Bevan, *The Destruction of Memory: Architecture at War* (London: Reaktion Books, 2006); A. C. Grayling, *Among the Dead Cities: Is the Targeting of Civilians in War Ever Justified?* (London: Bloomsbury, 2007); Martin Coward, *Urbicide: The Politics of Urban Destruction* (London: Routledge, 2009); Stephen Graham, *Cities Under Siege: The New Military Urbanism* (London: Verso, 2010); Ryan Bishop, Gregory K. Clancey and John Phillips (eds), *The City as Target* (London: Routledge, 2012).
99. Giulio Douhet, *The Command of the Air* (1921; 2nd expanded edn 1927), ed. Air Marshal Brijesh Dhar Jayal (Dehradun: Natraj Publishers, 2003), pp. 11, 158, 223.
100. See, for example, Robert Higham, *The Military Intellectuals in Britain: 1918–1939* (New Brunswick, NJ: Rutgers University Press, 1966), pp. 195, 257–9; Barry D. Powers, *Strategy Without Slide-Rule: British Air Strategy 1914–1939* (London: Croom Helm, 1976), pp. 175–8; Kenneth Hewitt, 'Place Annihilation: Area Bombing and the Fate of Urban Places', *Annals of the Association of American Geographers* Vol. 73, No. 2, 1983, pp. 257–84, p. 278; Ronald Schaffer, *Wings of Judgment: American Bombing in World War II* (Oxford: Oxford University Press, 1985), pp. 20–5; Philip S. Meilinger,'The Historiography of Airpower: Theory and Doctrine', *Journal of Military History*, Vol. 64, No. 2, 2006, pp. 467–502; Azar Gat, *A History of Military Thought: From the Enlightenment to the Cold War* (Oxford: Oxford University Press, 2001), pp. 588–97; Beaumont, *Might Backed by Right*, p. 43; Biddle, *Rhetoric and Reality*, pp. 106–7, 136, 148; Mark Clodfelter, *Beneficial*

Bombing: The Progressive Foundations of American Air Power, 1917–1945
(Lincoln, NE: University of Nebraska Press, 2010), p. 64.

101. Bernard Brodie, *Strategy in the Missile Age* (Princeton, NJ: Princeton
     University Press, 1965), pp. 23, 73–4. Even Higham, who resists any
     suggestion of Douhet's influence, says that'faced with the same challenge,
     various people developed the same responses' (*Military Intellectuals in
     Britain*, p. 259).
102. The links between air power and fascism are complex and important.
     Douhet served as Mussolini's commissioner of aviation, Fuller and Liddell
     Hart both openly talked about the need for a fascist leadership in Britain,
     and plenty of others, such as Charles A. Lindbergh, pilot of the first trans-
     Atlantic flight in 1927, gravitated towards Nazi Germany in the 1930s. Yet
     the issue concerns more than just personal political alliances. As a form
     of reactionary modernism, fascism loved to toy with air power as one of
     the highest forms of technology. The Nazi regime was portrayed in Leni
     Riefenstahl's film *Triumph of the Will* by Hitler flying across Germany to
     different cities time and again, and at one point Hitler flies over
     Nuremburg in a plane which casts a crucifix shadow on the land. The
     Nazis developed the slogan 'we must become a nation of flyers', and
     sought to instill what Peter Fritzsche calls 'the Nazi discipline of
     airmindedness'. Mussolini loved to portray himself and be portrayed as
     an aviator, and once commented that'the pilot truly knows what it means
     "to govern"'.

     Moreover, historians have noted that aviators formed a dispropor-
     tionate element in the membership of the British Union of Fascists. Mosley
     himself had flown for the RFC during the war and helped form fascist
     flying clubs in 1934. The British air industry's trade paper, *The Aeroplane*,
     was quite openly pro-fascist and anti-Semitic. Likewise Lord Rothermere,
     whose newspaper *The Daily Mail* supported the rise of fascism during the
     early 1930s, formed the National League of Airmen and demanded an
     'air-dictator'.

     One reason for these links could be that reactionary modernism is
     focused on the politics of technology. But a further reason is the fact that
     destroying the distinction between civilian and fighter, between
     combatant and non-combatant, is the dream of fascism. As I have argued
     elsewhere, war constitutes the fascist universal, a translation of the
     principles of art for art's sake to war itself. Seeking the realisation of these
     principles in the cult of the fallen soldier, the myth of the war experience,
     the fetish for the military form as the ideal type of community, and the
     importance of what Mussolini called the 'trenchocracy', fascism
     universalises war in a way which means that all must be soldiers. And if
     all must be soldiers, there are no civilians. For fascism, air power therefore

helped break down any distinction between citizen and soldier, non-combatant and combatant.

On the other hand, we should note that easy as it is to associate fascism and air technology, the history of air power suggests that liberal democracies were far more creative about the use to which the technology could be put, as the argument in this chapter and the next suggest.

For these points, see Robert Skidelsky, *Oswald Mosley* (London: Macmillan, 1981), p. 320; Richard Griffiths, *Fellow Travellers of the Right: British Enthusiasts for Nazi Germany 1933–39* (Oxford: Oxford University Press, 1983), pp. 137–41; Peter Fritzsche, *A Nation of Flyers: German Aviation and the Popular Imagination* (Cambridge, MA: Harvard University Press, 1992), pp. 185–219; Gerald Silk, '"Il Primo Pilota": Mussolini, Fascist Aeronautical Symbolism, and Imperial Rome', in Cladio Lazzaro and Roger J. Crum (eds), *Donatello Among the Blackshirts: History and Modernity in the Visual Culture of Fascist Italy* (Ithaca: Cornell University Press, 2005), pp. 67–81; Wohl, *Spectacle of Flight*, pp. 49–197; Edgerton, *England and the Aeroplane*, pp. 48, 57; David Edgerton, *Warfare State: Britain, 1920–1970* (Cambridge: Cambridge University Press, 2006), p. 317. For a wider account in the context of the history of military thought, see Gat, *History of Military Thought*, pp. 521–642. For the liaison of British fiction and fascism via air power, see Cunningham, *British Writers of the Thirties*, pp. 186–90. The treatment of fascism as universal war can be found in Mark Neocleous, *Fascism* (Milton Keynes: Open University Press, 1997).

103. Fuller, *Reformation of War*, pp. 150, 152.
104. Spaight, *Air Power*, p. 239.
105. Spaight, *Air Power*, pp. 12, 259, emphasis added. This was an argument Spaight continued to make through a succession of books, such as *Pseudo-Security* (1928) and *Air Power and the Cities* (1930).
106. Captain B. H. Liddell Hart, *Paris, or The Future of War* (London: Kegan Paul, Trench, Trubner and Co., 1925), pp. 20, 35, 42–3, 47–8.
107. William Mitchell, *Winged Defense: The Development and Possibilities of Modern Air Power – Economic and Military* (New York: G. P. Putnam and Sons, 1925), p. 16.
108. Cited in Clodfelter, *Beneficial Bombing*, p. 130.
109. Dower, *Cultures of War*, p. 165.
110. Edward Mead Earle, an academic who served on the Advisory Committee on Bombardment, in his rethinking of Mahan – 'The Influence of Air Power Upon History', *Yale Review*, Vol. 35, No. 4, 1946, pp. 577–93. More broadly, see Sherry, *Rise of American Air Power*, p. 323.
111. Sir John Salmond, cited in Townshend, *Britain's Civil Wars*, p. 98.
112. Paul K. Saint-Amour, 'Air War Prophecy and Interwar Modernism', *Comparative Literature Studies*, Vol. 42, No. 2, 2005, pp. 130–61, p. 132;

Stephen Budiansky, *Air Power: From Kitty Hawk to Gulf War II* (London: Penguin, 2004), p. 285. The point is a common one: 'It might ... be said that war from the air, since launched in Europe's colonies early in the last century, has always been essentially directed against civilians' – Tom Engelhardt, *The American Way of War: How Bush's Wars Became Obama's* (Chicago: Haymarket Books, 2010), p. 74. Compare Dower, *Cultures of War*, p. 156: 'Modern war breeds its own cultures, and incinerating civilians is one of them'.

113. Douhet, *Command of the Air*, p. 14; Charlton, *Menace of the Clouds*, p. 23.

114. *Fifth Air Force Weekly Intelligence Review*, No. 86, 15–21 July 1945, cited in W. F. Craven and J. L. Cate (eds), *The Army Forces in World War II, Vol. V: The Pacific* (Chicago: University of Chicago Press, 1948), p. 696. 'Leaders of the USAAF knew exactly what they were doing, and civilian casualties were one of the explicit objectives of area incendiary bombing approved by both the USAAF and the Joint Chiefs of Staff' – Thomas R. Searle, '"It Made a Lot of Sense to Kill Skilled Workers": The Firebombing of Tokyo in March 1945', *Journal of Military History*, Vol. 66, No. 1, 2002, pp. 103–34, p. 114.

115. US General Curtis LeMay, speaking in an interview with Michael Sherry, cited in Sherry, *Rise of American Air Power*, p. 287.

116. John F. Jones, 'General Douhet Vindicated: Desert Storm 1991', *Naval War College Review*, 45, 1992, pp. 97–101; Daniel L. Byman and Matthew C. Waxman, 'Kosovo and the Great Air Power Debate', in Thomas G. Mahnken and Joseph A. Maiolo (eds), *Strategic Studies: A Reader* (London: Routledge, 2008), p. 156; Major M. V. 'Coyote' Smith, 'Cognac with Douhet', *Air and Space Power Journal*, 1 May 2001.

117. Warden, a leading member of the US Air Force's Air Staff Plans Directorate and a key figure behind the strategy for the first Gulf War, published *The Air Campaign* in 1988, which quickly became a standard text. The book outlines an approach based on identifying and then attacking the enemy's centre or centres of gravity. These were initially seen as either equipment, logistics, geography, personnel, or command and control, but this later developed into a 'Five Ring Model' in which states are said to be organised in five rings, with leadership the inner ring and the military forces the outer ring, with population, infrastructure and 'organic essentials' between them, each ring constituting a 'centre of gravity' which might be targeted. The implication is that the population, production and infrastructure might all need to be targeted, on the grounds that 'the enemy functions as a system'. For all its formulations and permutations, the theory is one which points to neutralising urban centres and smashing industrial production; in other words, to devastating civilian populations. See Colonel John Warden III, *The Air Campaign: Planning for Combat*

(Washington, DC: Pergamon-Brasseys, 1989), pp. 34, 54; 'The Enemy as a System', *Air Power Journal*, Vol. 9, No. 1, 1995, pp. 40–56.

118. Dower, *Cultures of War*, pp. 165–6.

119. Note the rather timid commentary in the *British Yearbook of International Law* in 1949: 'the distinction between members of the armed forces and civilians has, it is generally appreciated, been affected during the present century by … the development of aerial warfare'– Joyce A. C. Gutteridge, 'The Geneva Conventions of 1949', *British Yearbook of International Law*, Vol. 26, 1949, pp. 294–326, p. 319. Arthur 'Bomber' Harris, who in WWII contributed more than most to the killing of large numbers of 'non-combatants', puts it thus: 'International law can always be argued pro and con, but in this matter of the use of aircraft in war there is, it so happens, no international law at all'– Arthur C. Harris, *Bomber Offensive* (New York: Macmillan, 1947), p. 177.

120. Alan Dershowitz, '"Civilian Casualty"? That's a Gray Area', *Los Angeles Times*, 22 July 2006; Derek Gregory, 'Editorial', *Environment and Planning D: Society and Space*, Vol. 24, 2006, pp. 633–8, p. 633.

121. Karma Nabulsi, *Traditions of War: Occupation, Resistance, and the Law* (Oxford: Oxford University Press, 1999), p. 1, building on Geoffrey Best, *Humanity in Warfare: The Modern History of the International Law of Armed Conflicts* (London: Weidenfeld and Nicolson, 1980).

122. Richard Shelly Hartigan, *The Forgotten Victim: A History of the Civilian* (Chicago: Precedent Publishing, 1982), p. 119.

123. Pentagon spokeswoman Victoria Clarke, cited in John F. Burns, 'A Nation Challenged: The Manhunt', *New York Times*, 17 February 2002.

124. Joseph Pugliese, *State Violence and the Execution of Law: Biopolitical Caesurae of Torture, Black Sites, Drones* (London: Glasshouse, 2013), p. 199.

125. Paul Virilio, *Desert Screen: War at the Speed of Light* (London: Continuum, 2000), p. 5. Also Paul Virilio/Sylvere Lotringer, *Pure War* (1983), trans. Mark Polizzotti (Los Angeles: Semiotext(e), 2008).

126. Derek Gregory, 'The Everywhere War', *The Geographical Journal*, Vol. 177, No. 3, 2011, pp. 238–50.

127. Michel Foucault, 'Space, Knowledge, and Power' (1982), trans. Christian Hubert, in Paul Rabinow (ed.), *The Foucault Reader* (London: Penguin, 1984), pp. 239–56.

128. Cited in Julian E. Barnes, 'Military Refines a "Constant Stare against our Enemy"', *Los Angeles Times*, 2 November 2009.

129. Spokesman for the MoD, cited in Nick Hopkins, 'New Drones in Afghanistan to be Controlled from Britain', *Guardian*, 23 October 2012, p. 2.

130. See Neocleous, *Fabrication of Social Order*, Chapter 5.

131. The phrase is from Mihir Pandya's argument concerning the F-117 Stealth

airplane – 'The Cold War Present: The Logic of Defense Time', in John D. Kelly, Beatrice Jauregui, Sean T. Mitchell and Jeremy Walton (eds), *Anthropology and Global Counterinsurgency* (Chicago: University of Chicago Press, 2010), p. 143.

132. Miami-Dade Police Director James Loftus, 6 January 2011 – http://www.wsvn.com/news/articles/local/21003198189967/ (accessed 25 December 2012).
133. Frank Sauer and Niklas Schoring, 'Killer Drones: The "Silver Bullet" of Democratic Warfare', *Security Dialogue,* Vol. 43, No. 4, 2012, pp. 363–80.
134. The definition of air power just given comes from the fourth edition of the RAF's *Air and Space Power Doctrine*, published in 2009 (known as AP3000 and with roots in AP1300 first published in 1928) – Royal Air Force, *AP 3000, British Air and Space Power Doctrine*, 4th edn (London: Ministry of Defence, 2009), pp. 7, 14, 35, 44–5. On the document's history, see Group Captain Christopher Finn, 'British Thinking on Air Power – The Evolution of AP3000', *Air Power Review,* Vol. 12, No. 1, 2009, pp. 56–67.
135. The phrase is from the army document *StrikeStar 2025* describing the political potential of the drones – Bruce W. Carmichael et al. *StrikeStar 2025* (Research Paper Presented to Air Force 2025, August 1996), p. viii. But also see Weizman, 'Politics of Verticality'; Eyal Weizman, *Hollow Land: Israel's Architecture of Occupation* (London: Verso, 2007), p. 239; Alison J. Williams, 'A Crisis in Aerial Sovereignty? Considering the Implications of Recent Military Violations of National Airspace', *AREA,* Vol. 42, No. 1, 2010, pp. 51–9, p. 55; Adey, *Aerial Life*, p. 77.

CHAPTER 6

1. Noam Chomsky, *The New Military Humanism: Lessons from Kosovo* (Monroe, ME: Common Courage Press, 1999).
2. Luiza Bialasiewicz, David Campbell, Stuart Elden, Stephen Graham, Alex Jeffrey and Alison J. Williams, 'Performing Security: The Imaginative Geographies of Current US Strategy', *Political Geography,* Vol. 26, No. 4, pp. 405–22, p. 417.
3. Rachel Woodward, *Military Geographies* (Oxford: Blackwell, 2004). Lisa Parks, *Cultures in Orbit: Satellites and the Televisual* (Durham: Duke University Press, 2005), Chapter 3, offers an interesting account of satellites in the war in Bosnia but the claims made there remain firmly on the military role of the satellite and not air space in general.
4. Gearoid O Tuathail and Simon Dalby, 'Introduction: Rethinking Geopolitics: Towards a Critical Geopolitics', in Gearoid O Tuathail and Simon Dalby (eds), *Rethinking Geopolitics* (London: Routledge, 1998), p. 3.
5. Woodward, *Military Geographies*, p. 4.

6. John Agnew and Stuart Corbridge, *Mastering Space: Hegemony, Territory and International Political Economy* (London: Routledge, 1995), pp. 182–4; David Delaney, *The Spatial, The Legal and the Pragmatics of World-Making: Nomospheric Investigations* (London: Routledge, 2011).

7. Jeremy W. Crampton and Stuart Elden (eds), *Space, Knowledge and Power: Foucault and Geography* (Aldershot: Ashgate, 2007).

8. John Agnew, 'The Territorial Trap: The Geographical Assumptions of International Relations Theory', *Review of International Political Economy*, Vol. 1, No. 1, 1994, pp. 53–80.

9. 'The world of the international is flat', we are told in a special issue of *International Political Sociology* seeking to bring critical geography to bear on the limited spatial analyses of IR, and yet one can read the whole issue and come away still thinking the same – *International Political Sociology, Special Issue: Territorialities, Spaces, Geographies*, IPS Virtual Issue 2013.

10. For example, Caren Kaplan, 'Mobility and War: The Cosmic View of US "Air Power"', *Environment and Planning A*, Vol. 38, 2006, pp. 395–407; Peter Adey, *Aerial Life: Spaces, Mobilities, Affects* (Chichester, West Sussex: Wiley-Blackwell, 2010). The issue of *Theory, Culture and Society*, Vol. 28, Nos. 7–8, 2011 contains a range of materials, including an essay by Derek Gregory. For Gregory, see his pages at http://geographicalimaginations.com/, and also Derek Gregory, 'Lines of Descent', *openDemocracy*, 8 November 2011. Eyal Weizman, 'The Politics of Verticality', *openDemocracy*, April–May 2002, and the range of useful insights concerning aerial occupation in Eyal Weizman, *Hollow Land: Israel's Architecture of Occupation* (London: Verso, 2007). Stephen Graham has also highlighted the role of air power in his *Cities Under Siege: The New Military Urbanism* (London: Verso, 2010).

11. Timothy P. McIlmail, 'No-Fly Zones: The Imposition and Enforcement of Air Exclusion Regimes over Bosnia and Iraq', *Loyola of Los Angeles International and Comparative Law Review*, 17, 1994, pp. 35–83; Michael N. Schmitt, 'Clipped Wings: Effective and Legal No-fly Zone Rules of Engagement', *Loyola of Los Angeles International and Comparative Law Journal*, 20, 1997–8, pp. 727–89.

12. Alexander Benard, 'Lessons from Iraq and Bosnia on the Theory and Practice of No-fly Zones', *Journal of Strategic Studies*, Vol. 27, No. 3, 2004, pp. 454–78.

13. For examples, Stephen Graham, 'Vertical Geopolitics: Baghdad and After', *Antipode*, Vol. 36, No. 1, 2004, pp. 12–23; Alison Williams, 'Hakumat al Tayarrat: The Role of Air Power in the Enforcement of Iraq's Boundaries', *Geopolitics*, Vol. 12, No. 3, 2007, pp. 505–28; Alison J. Williams, 'A Crisis in Aerial Sovereignty? Considering the Implications of Recent Military Violations of National Airspace', *AREA*, Vol. 42, No. 1, 2010, pp. 51–9; Eyal Weizman, 'The Politics of Verticality', Part II, *openDemocracy*, April–May

2002; David L. Butler, 'Technogeopolitics and the Struggle for Control of the World's Air Routes, 1910–1928', *Political Geography,* Vol. 20, No. 5, 2001, pp. 635–58; Stuart Elden, 'Territorial Integrity and the War on Terror', *Environment and Planning A: Society and Space,* Vol. 37, No. 12, 2005, pp. 2083–2104; Adey, *Aerial Life,* pp. 77–8.

14. Sir Edward Coke, *The First Part of the Institutes of the Lawes of England* (London: Societie of Stationers, 1628), Chapter 1, Section 1; William Blackstone, *Commentaries on the Laws of England, Vol. 2: Of the Right of Things* (1766) (Chicago: University of Chicago Press, 1979), p. 18.

15. Yehuda Abramovitch, 'The Maxim "Cujus est solum ejus est usque ad coelum" as Applied in Aviation', *McGill Law Journal,* Vol. 8, No. 4, 1962, pp. 247–69; Stuart Banner, *Who Owns the Sky?: The Struggle to Control Airspace from the Wright Brothers On* (Cambridge, MA: Harvard University Press, 2008).

16. John Cobb Cooper, 'Roman Law and the Maxim *Cujus est solum* in International Air Law', *McGill Law Journal,* Vol. 1, No. 1, 1952, pp. 23–65, p. 25.

17. J. F. Lycklama a Nijeholt, *Air Sovereignty* (The Hague: Martinus Nijhoff, 1910), pp. 34–5, 40–2, 73–4.

18. Abramovitch, 'The Maxim "Cujus est solum"', p. 266; Banner, *Who Owns the Sky?,* pp. 110–15; G. S. Sachdeva, 'Sovereignty in the Air – A Legal Perspective', *Indian Journal of International Law,* Vol. 22, Nos. 3–4, 1982, pp. 396–421, pp. 396, 403.

19. Nijeholt, *Air Sovereignty,* p. 34.

20. André Blachère, *L'Air: Voie de Communication et le Droit* (1911), cited in Banner, *Who Owns the Sky?,* p. 56.

21. Both cited in Banner, *Who Owns the Sky?,* pp. 60–1. Also see Jean A. Martial, 'State Control of the Air Space Over the Territorial Sea and the Contiguous Zone', *Canadian Bar Review,* Vol. 30, 1952, pp. 245–63; Alan P. Dobson, *Peaceful Air Warfare: The United States, Britain, and the Politics of International Aviation* (Oxford: Clarendon Press, 1991), p. 6.

22. Banner, *Who Owns the Sky?,* p. 63; Sachdeva, 'Sovereignty in the Air', p. 410.

23. William Latey, 'The Law of the Air', *Transactions of the Grotius Society,* Vol. 7, 1921, pp. 73–87.

24. John C. Cooper, *The Right to Fly* (New York: Henry Holt and Co., 1947), pp. 24–8; Bin Cheng, 'Recent Developments in Air Law', *Current Legal Problems,* Vol. 9, 1956, pp. 208–34; Bin Cheng, 'From Air Law to Space Law', *Current Legal Problems,* Vol. 13, 1960, pp. 228–54.

25. Dean N. Reinhardt, *The Vertical Limit of State Sovereignty* (unpublished thesis, Institute of Air and Space Law, McGill University, June 2005), pp. 33–4; Robert F. A. Goedhart, *The Never Ending Dispute: Delimitation of Air Space and Outer Space* (Paris: Éditions Frontiers, 1996); Gbenga

Oduntan, 'The Never Ending Dispute: Legal Theories on the Spatial Demarcation Boundary Plane between Airspace and Outer Space', *Hertfordshire Law Journal*, Vol. 1, No. 2, 2003, pp. 64–84.

26. I. H. Ph. Diederiks-Verschoor, *An Introduction to Space Law* (The Hague: Kluwer Law International, 1999), p. 18.
27. Oduntan, 'Never Ending Dispute', p. 81.
28. Diederiks-Verschoor, *Introduction to Space Law*, pp. 3–4, 5–6, 17.
29. For example, McIlmail, 'No-Fly Zones', p. 83; Schmitt, 'Clipped Wings', pp. 736, 739; Adey, *Aerial Life*, p. 77.
30. 'They offer no legitimacy to countries sending their aircraft to attack Iraq', Boutros Boutros-Ghali said. 'Does that mean they are illegal?' he was asked. 'They are illegal', he replied. Interviewed by John Pilger, in *The New Rulers of the World* (London: Verso, 2003), p. 79.
31. Cited in David E. Sanger and Thom Shanker, 'Gates Warns of Risks of a No-Flight Zone', *New York Times*, 2 March 2011.
32. Colonel John Warden III, *The Air Campaign: Planning for Combat* (Washington, DC: Pergamon-Brasseys, 1989), p. 71.
33. General Jacob E. Smart, in *Air Interdiction in WWII, Korea, and Vietnam: An Interview with General Earle E. Partridge, General Jacob E. Smart and General John W. Vogt, Jr.* (Washington, DC: Office of Air Force History, 1986), p. 16.
34. See President Truman, 'President's News Conference', 29 June 1950.
35. This included establishing health care facilities, implementing water, sanitation and other public welfare utilities, constructing transport and communication systems, building orphanages and schools – Andrew J. Birtle, *US Army Counterinsurgency and Contingency Operations Doctrine 1942–1976* (Washington, DC: United States Army Center of Military History, 2006), p. 111.
36. Theodore Roosevelt, 'Fourth Annual Message', 6 December 1904.
37. James R. Holmes, *Theodore Roosevelt and World Order: Police Power in International Relations* (Washington, DC: Potomac Books, 2006), pp. 5, 103–4.
38. Both cited in Ron Levi and John Hagan, 'International Police', in Markus Dubber and Mariana Valverde (eds), *The New Police Science: Police Powers in Comparative Perspective* (Stanford, CA: Stanford University Press, 2006), p. 213.
39. Roosevelt, 'First Annual Message', 3 December 1901.
40. Theodore Roosevelt, Letter to Cecil Arthur Spring Rice, 13 June 1904, in *The Letters of Theodore Roosevelt, Vol. IV: The Square Deal, 1903–1905* (Cambridge, MA: Harvard University Press, 1951), p. 830.
41. Theodore Roosevelt, Letter to Edward Oliver Wolcott, 15 September 1900, in *The Letters of Theodore Roosevelt, Vol. II: The Years of Preparation, 1898–1900* (Cambridge, MA: Harvard University Press, 1951), pp. 1397–1405;

Theodore Roosevelt, Letter to Joseph Bucklin Bishop, 23 February 1904, in *The Letters of Theodore Roosevelt, Vol. IV: The Square Deal, 1903–1905* (Cambridge, MA: Harvard University Press, 1951), p. 734.

42. Holmes, *Theodore Roosevelt*, pp. 66, 211. At the same time, however, the fact that the Indian wars were still *wars* could never quite be forgotten, as Roosevelt would occasionally let slip, such as his comparison of Filipino resistance to the 'Indian wars', his frequent recourse to the language of 'race war' and his concern over 'race suicide' by the white race. See Roosevelt, 'First Annual Message', 3 December 1901; Theodore Roosevelt, Letter to Bessie Van Vorst, 18 October 1902, and Letter to James Wilson, 3 February 1903, in *The Letters of Theodore Roosevelt, Vol. III: The Square Deal, 1901–1903* (Cambridge, MA: Harvard University Press, 1951), p. 416.

43. Mary P. Ryan, *Civic Wars: Democracy and Public Life in the American City during the Nineteenth Century* (Berkeley: University of California Press, 1997), pp. 138, 139, 157, 180. On Roosevelt and the strikes, see Howard Lawrence Hurwitz, *Theodore Roosevelt and Labor in New York State, 1880–1900* (New York: Columbia, 1943), pp. 155, 163, 260; Holmes, *Theodore Roosevelt*, p. 37.

44. Ryan, *Civic Wars*, p. 180.

45. Lisa Keller, *Triumph of Order: Democracy and Public Space in New York and London* (New York: Columbia University Press, 2009), p. 199.

46. John K. Mahon, *History of the Militia and the National Guard* (New York: Macmillan, 1983), p. 112–22.

47. Theodore Roosevelt, 'Industrial Peace', Address at the Chamber of Commerce, New York, 11 November 1902, in *The Roosevelt Policy: Speeches, Letters and State Papers Relating to Corporate Wealth and Closely Allied Topics, Vol. 1* (New York: Current Literature Company, 1908), pp. 97–103; Roosevelt, 'International Peace', Address Before the Nobel Prize Committee, Christiana, Norway, 5 May 1910, in *The Works of Theodore Roosevelt, Vol. XVIII* (New York: Charles Scribner's Sons, 1925), pp. 410–11.

48. Theodore Roosevelt, Remarks made at Police Headquarters, New York, 16 July 1896, reprinted as 'The Commissioner's Advice to his Men', in *The Works of Theodore Roosevelt, Vol. XVI* (New York: Charles Scribner's Sons, 1925), pp. 301–2.

49. Cited in Frederick W. Marks, III, *Velvet on Iron: The Diplomacy of Theodore Roosevelt* (Lincoln: University of Nebraska Press, 1979), p. 92.

50. See Theodore Roosevelt, 'Administering the New York Police Force', *Atlantic Monthly*, September 1897, in *The Works of Theodore Roosevelt, Vol. XV* (New York: Charles Scribner's Sons, 1925), pp. 170, 173; 'Commissioner's Advice', pp. 301–2.

50. Theodore Roosevelt, 'Eighth Annual Message', 8 December 1908.

51. There is a story told about Roosevelt about the time when he was Civil

Service Commissioner in 1886, and therefore involved in selecting the Chief of Police. Among the questions asked concerned the option of calling out the National Guard in controlling strikers. The successful candidate, Peter Conlin, suggested 'grape and canister' might be used, and Roosevelt replied that order was to be kept at whatever cost: 'If it comes to shooting we shall shoot to hit. No blank cartridges or firing over the heads of anybody'. Roosevelt's comments are recorded in New York Protective Association, *Fourteenth Annual Convention on Labor Day, September 7, 1886*, cited in Hurwitz, *Theodore Roosevelt and Labor*, p. 157.

53. Holmes, *Theodore Roosevelt*, p. 3; Christopher Tomlins, 'Necessities of State: Police, Sovereignty, and the Constitution', *Journal of Policy History*, Vol. 20, No. 1, 2008, pp. 47–63, p. 60.

54. Holmes, *Theodore Roosevelt*, pp. 74, 101, 108; Levi and Hagan, 'International Police', pp. 213–14; Hurwitz, *Theodore Roosevelt and Labor*, p. 167.

55. Theodore Roosevelt, 'Expansion and Peace', *The Independent*, 21 December 1899, in *The Works of Theodore Roosevelt, Vol. XV* (New York: Charles Scribner's Sons, 1925), p. 284.

56. Letter to Henry Cabot Lodge, in *The Letters of Theodore Roosevelt, Vol. 1*, ed. Elting E. Morison (Cambridge, MA: Harvard University Press, 1951), p. 504.

57. In an oft-cited speech at the Naval War College in June 1897 in his role as assistant Secretary of the Navy he comments on the 'masterful races' as 'fighting races', 'an ignoble peace [being] worse than an unsuccessful war', and says that 'peace is a goddess only when she comes with sword girt on thigh' – Theodore Roosevelt, 'Naval War College Address', Newport, RI, 2 June 1897. As *Harper's Weekly* Editor Carl Schurz noted at the time, the speech was a 'panegyric on war', with Roosevelt's rather conventional words about peace contrasting starkly with the 'poetic enthusiasm' with which he speaks about war – Carl Schurz, 'Armed or Unarmed Peace', *Harper's Weekly*, 19 June 1897, in *Speeches, Correspondence and Political Papers of Carl Schurz, Vol. V*, ed. Frederic Bancroft (New York: G. P. Putnam's Sons, 1913), pp. 398–403.

58. Beale, *Theodore Roosevelt*, p. 48.

59. As one of Roosevelt's friends noted, 'he wants to be killing something all the time' – cited in Beale, *Theodore Roosevelt*, p. 49. Other commentators have noted that this love of hunting serves to naturalise the other forms of violence Roosevelt was keen to pursue – Richard Slotkin, *Gunfighter Nation: The Myth of the Frontier in Twentieth-Century America* (Norman: University of Oklahoma Press, 1998), p. 41.

60. Peace threatens the 'virile fighting qualities'; 'luxury-loving' and 'flabby' men lack the 'virile energy' and 'iron qualities' that 'go with true manhood'; 'a certain effeminacy of character' undermines national strength. See Theodore Roosevelt, 'The Manly Virtues and Practical Politics', *The Forum*,

July 1894, in *The Works of Theodore Roosevelt, Vol. XV* (New York: Charles
Scribner's Sons, 1925), p. 44; Theodore Roosevelt, 'Manhood and
Statehood', Address at the Quarter-centennial celebration of Statehood
in Colorado, Colorado Springs, 2 August 1901; 'National Duties', in *Works
of Theodore Roosevelt, Vol. XV*, pp. 325–6, 328–30; Theodore Roosevelt,
'Machine Politics', in *The Century*, November 1886, in *The Works of
Theodore Roosevelt, Vol. XV* (New York: Charles Scribner's Sons, 1925), p.
121. As Richard Hofstadter notes, 'manly' and 'masterful' are two of the
most common words in Roosevelt's language, and his commitment to the
'strenuous life' is part and parcel of the deep and abiding connection
between imperial politics and a cult of masculinity – Richard Hofstadter,
The American Political Tradition (New York: Vintage, 1948), p. 211. He
likewise castigated those 'whose cult is non-virility' – Letter to Henry
Cabot Lodge, 19 January 1896, in *Letters, Vol. 1*, p. 508. In a speech in April
1899, called 'The Strenuous Life', Roosevelt sought to define what it means
to be American and identify the threats to the nation. Under such diversity
of threats, from the proletariat through to the Spanish, Americans must
avoid sinking into 'scrambling commercialism, avoid concerning
themselves with only the daily wants of their bodies, and must not lose
their 'manly' qualities. The 'strenuous life' was thereby connected to a crisis
of masculinity at the turn of the century. As both the testing ground for
manly vigour and the crucible of military power, the frontier played a
defining part in liberal masculinity: the pacification of the 'Wild West' was
also the realisation of manly power – see Donald J. Mrozek, 'The Habit of
Victory: The American Military and the Cult of Manliness', in J. A. Mangan
and James Walvin (eds), *Manliness and Morality: Middle-class Masculinity
in Britain and America 1800–1940* (Manchester: Manchester University
Press, 1987), p. 226.

   This desire to characterise and enact a masculine power were part of
an attempt to forge a break from the image others had of him early in his
political career, captured in his nicknames of 'weakling', 'Jane-Dandy' and
'Punkin-Lily', being compared to Oscar Wilde, and 'accused of effeminacy',
as Gail Bederman puts it, in *Manliness and Civilization: A Cultural History
of Gender and Race in the United States, 1880–1917* (Chicago: University of
Chicago Press, 1995), p. 174. On these points more generally, also see
Ronald Takaki, *Iron Cages: Race and Culture in 19th-Century America*
(Oxford: Oxford University Press, 1990), p. 275; Mark E. Kann, *On the Man
Question: Gender and Civic Virtue in America* (Philadelphia: Temple
University Press, 1991), p. 203; Tom Lutz, *American Nervousness, 1903*
(Ithaca: Cornell University Press, 1991), pp. 63–4, 79–83; Kristin L.
Hoganson, *Fighting for American Manhood* (New Haven: Yale University
Press, 1998), pp. 143–5; Amy Kaplan, *The Anarchy of Empire in the Making*

of US Culture (Cambridge, MA: Harvard University Press, 2002), pp. 92–120; Warwick Anderson, *Colonial Pathologies: American Tropical Medicine, Race, and Hygiene in the Philippines* (Durham: Duke University Press, 2006), pp. 132–3.

61. Theodore Roosevelt, 'National Duties', Address at Minnesota State Fair, 2 September 1901, in *The Works of Theodore Roosevelt, Vol. XV* (New York: Charles Scribner's Sons, 1925), pp. 325–6, 328–30; Harvey C. Mansfield, *Manliness* (New Haven: Yale University Press, 2006), pp. 84, 97–8. One of Roosevelt's main aims was to rescue the idea of the warrior and reinstate it as a core feature of the myth of the West, and one of the people he most admired was William F. Cody, a Western scout and model for the 'Buffalo Bill' character in Ned Buntline's novels. But the real ideological connection lies in the same place as Adam Smith and Adam Ferguson: that a peaceful and commercial civilisation is in danger of losing the necessary virile fighting qualities. Roosevelt, notes Beale (*Theodore Roosevelt*, p. 48), thought 'there was something dull and effeminate about peace'.

62. The virtues in question are 'the very qualities which are fostered by manly, out-of-doors sports' – Theodore Roosevelt, 'Value of an Athletic Training', *Harper's Weekly*, Vol. 37, No. 3, 16 December 1893, p. 1236.

63. Theodore Roosevelt, 'Expansion and Peace', *The Independent*, 21 December 1899, in *The Works of Theodore Roosevelt, Vol. XV* (New York: Charles Scribner's Sons, 1925), pp. 282–92. Also 'The Law of Civilization and Decay', *Forum*, January 1897, pp. 575–89.

64. Frank Ninkovich, 'Theodore Roosevelt: Civilization as Ideology', *Diplomatic History*, Vol. 10, No. 3, 1986, pp. 221–45.

65. Theodore Roosevelt, *The Winning of the West, Vol 1: From the Alleghanies to the Mississippi 1769–1776* (New York: G. P. Putnam's Sons, 1889), pp. 1, 87, 89.

66. Theodore Roosevelt, 'National Life and Character' (1894), in Roosevelt, *American Ideals* (New York: G. P. Putnam's Sons, 1897), pp. 311–12.

67. Fritz Grob, *The Relativity of War and Peace: A Study in Law, History, and Politics* (New Haven: Yale University Press, 1949), p. 231.

68. William Edward Hall, *A Treatise on International Law*, 4th edn (Oxford: Clarendon Press, 1895), p. 297.

69. Vic Hurley, *Jungle Patrol: The Story of the Philippine Constabulary 1901–1936* (1938) (Salem, OR: Ceberus Books, 2010), pp. 30, 34, 47. For the figures, see Alfred W. McCoy, *Policing America's Empire: The United States, The Philippines, and the Rise of the Surveillance State* (Madison, WI: University of Wisconsin Press, 2009), p. 62.

70. McCoy, *Policing America's Empire*, p. 61.

71. Andrew J. Birtle, *US Army Counterinsurgency and Contingency Operations Doctrine 1860–1941* (Washington, DC: United States Army Center of

Military History, 2009), pp. 5, 102–6, 154, 156, 160–1; Jeremy Kuzmarov, *Modernizing Repression: Police Training and Nation-Building in the American Century* (Amherst: University of Massachusetts Press, 2012), p. 24.

72. The historical literature on this is now massive, but the central point still stands. For a sample, see McCoy, *Policing America's Empire*; Kuzmarov, *Modernizing Repression*; Sam C. Sarkesian, *America's Forgotten Wars: The Counterrevolutionary Past and Lessons for the Future* (Westport, CT: Greenwood Press, 1984); David M. Anderson and David Killingray, 'Consent, Coercion and Colonial Control: Policing the Empire, 1830–1940', in David M. Anderson and David Killingray (eds), *Policing the Empire: Government, Authority and Control, 1830–1940* (Manchester: Manchester University Press, 1991); Joan M. Jensen, *Army Surveillance in America, 1775–1980* (New Haven: Yale University Press, 1991); Martha K. Huggins, *Political Policing: The United States and Latin America* (Durham: Duke University Press, 1998).

73. T. J. Lawrence, *The Principles of International Law*, 3rd edn (Boston: D. C. Heath and Co., 1905), p. 299. Note the shift in the passage in the fourth edition eight years later: 'In cases where a strong state or group of states finds itself obliged to undertake what are potentially measures of police against weak and recalcitrant powers, one or other of the means just described may be a useful alternative to war'. The natives had moved from *barbarism* to mere *recalcitrance*. T. J. Lawrence, *The Principles of International Law*, 4th edn (London: Macmillan, 1913), pp. 343–4.

74. T. J. Lawrence, *International Problems and Hague Conferences* (London: J. M. Dent and Co., 1908), p. 51.

75. T. J. Lawrence, 'Is There a True International Law?', in *Essays on Some Disputed Questions in Modern International Law* (Cambridge: Deighton Bell and Co., 1884), p. 24.

76. Lawrence, *Principles*, p. 93.

77. Annelise Riles, 'Aspiration and Control: International Legal Rhetoric and the Essentialization of Culture', *Harvard Law Review*, Vol. 106, 1993, pp. 723–40, p. 727.

78. This was a phrase which came into wide use in the 1920s – see Quincy Wright, 'The Outlawry of War and the Law of War', *American Journal of International Law*, Vol. 47, 1953, pp. 365–76.

79. Lord Davies, *The Problem of the Twentieth Century: A Study in International Relationships* (London: Ernest Benn, 1930; revised edn, 1934), pp. 25–7, 379, 425.

80. Davies, *Problem*, p. 404.

81. Davies, *Problem*, p. 425.

82. Davies, *Problem*, pp. 703–4.

83. Davies, *Problem*, pp. 160–1, 484, 555.

84. John A. Hobson, *Towards International Government* (London: George Allen and Unwin, 1915); P. J. Noel Baker, *Disarmament* (London: Hogarth Press, 1926).
85. David Edgerton has shown this at length over several works: see 'Liberal Militarism and the British State', *New Left Review*, 185, 1991, pp. 138–69; *England and the Aeroplane: An Essay on a Militant and Technological Nation* (Basingstoke: Macmillan, 1991), pp. xv, 42; *Warfare State: Britain, 1920–1970* (Cambridge: Cambridge University Press, 2006), pp. 52–8, 313–18; *Britain's War Machine: Weapons, Resources and Experts in the Second World War* (London: Penguin, 2012), pp. 7, 147–52. Also see Waqar H. Zaidi, '"Aviation Will Either Destroy or Save Our Civilization": Proposals for the International Control of Aviation, 1920–1945', *Journal of Contemporary History*, Vol. 46, No. 1, 2011, pp. 15–78, and Brett Holman, 'World Police for World Peace: British Internationalism and the Threat of a Knock-out Blow from the Air, 1919–1945', *War in History*, Vol. 17, No. 3, 2010, pp. 313–32.
86. Davies, *Problem*, pp. 367–8, 396, 475–6, 487.
87. Baker, *Disarmament*, pp. 213–44; J. M. Spaight, *An International Air Force* (London: Gale and Polden, 1932); James H. Ashton, *International Police Force* (Leeds Central Committee of the League of Nations Union, 1932); C. R. Attlee, *An International Police Force* (London: New Commonwealth Society, 1934).
88. J. J. van der Leeuw, *Why a World Police is Inevitable* (London: The New Commonwealth Pamphlets, 1934); K Capper-Johnson, *The Relations Between Disarmament and the Establishment of an International Police Force* (London: New Commonwealth Institute, 1935); Rear Admiral Robert Neale Lawson, *A Plan for the Organisation of a European Air Service* (London: New Commonwealth Institute, 1935); Major General Sir Frederick (Barton) Maurice, *The First Stage in International Policing* (London: New Commonwealth Institute, 1935); H. R. G. Greaves, *An International Police Board* (London: New Commonwealth Institute, 1935); Pierre Cot, *Military Force or Air Police* (London: New Commonwealth Institute, 1935); Hans Wehberg, *Theory and Practice of International Policing* (London: New Commonwealth Institute, 1935); The New Commonwealth, *The Functions of an International Air Police* (London: The New Commonwealth Pamphlets, 1936), p. 8; Field Marshal The Right Hon. Viscount Allenby, *World Police for World Peace* (London: New Commonwealth Institute, 1936), reprinted in *International Conciliation*, Vol. 17, 1936, pp. 479–86.
89. Philip Noel Baker et al., *Challenge to Death* (London: Constable, 1934), pp. 186–239; W. Bryn Thomas, *An International Police Force* (London: Allenson and Co., 1936); Lord Davies, *Nearing the Abyss: The Lesson of*

Ethiopia (London: Constable, 1936); Squadron-Leader E. J. Kingston-McCloughry, *Winged Warfare: Air Problems of Peace and War* (London: Jonathan Cape, 1937).

90. 'Labour Party General Election Manifesto 1935', in Iain Dale (ed.), *Labour Party General Election Manifestos 1900–1997* (Abingdon: Routledge, 2000), p. 46.

91. Beaumont, *Might Backed by Right*, pp. 72–3; Syed Waqar Hussain Zaidi, *Technology and the Reconstruction of International Relations: Liberal Internationalist Proposals for the Internationalisation of Aviation and the International Control of Atomic Energy in Britain, USA and France, 1920–1950*, unpublished PhD, University of London (Imperial College), 2008, pp. 64–7; Edgerton, *Warfare State*, p. 315; Michael S. Sherry, *The Rise of American Air Power: The Creation of Armageddon* (New Haven: Yale University Press, 1987), p. 95.

92. D. W. Bowett, *United Nations Forces: A Legal Study of United Nations Practice* (London: Stevens and Sons, 1964), p. 328.

93. See Mathieu Deflem, *Policing World Society: Historical Foundations of International Police Cooperation* (Oxford: Oxford University Press, 2002), pp. 44, 124–52; Peter Andreas and Ethan Nadelman, *Policing the Globe: Criminalization and Crime Control in International Relations* (Oxford: Oxford University Press, 2006), pp. 79–96; Ben Bowling and James Sheptycki, *Global Policing* (Los Angeles: Sage, 2012).

94. Quincy Wright, 'National Security and International Police', *American Journal of International Law*, Vol. 37, 1943, pp. 499–505, p. 501.

95. Air Marshal William A. Bishop, *Winged Peace* (New York: The Viking Press, 1944), p. 148.

96. Allan A. Michie, *Keep the Peace Through Air Power* (London: George Allen and Unwin, 1944), pp. 9, 16, 119, 122, 123, 127–8, 139.

97. Michie, *Keep the Peace*, pp. 136, 139.

98. Ely Culbertson, *Total Peace: What Makes Wars and How to Organize Peace* (London: Faber and Faber, 1943), pp. 21–31, 190–1, 193, 196, 218–26, 235–8.

99. J. M. Spaight, *Bombing Vindicated* (Glasgow: The University Press, 1944).

100. F. de Barros Pimentel, *The International Police: The Use of Force in the Structure of Peace*, trans. Charles Lyon Chandler (Review of the Institute of Brazilian Studies, March 1944); James T. Shotwell, *The Great Decision* (New York: Macmillan, 1944), pp. 99, 128–31, 212; Julia E. Johnsen, *International Police Force* (New York: H. W. Wilson Co., 1944); Eugene E. Wilson, *Air Power for Peace* (New York: McGraw-Hill, 1945).

101. Lord Davies, *The Seven Pillars of Peace* (London: Longmans, Green & Co., 1945), pp. 57–92; Harold J. Laski, *Reflections on the Revolution of Our Time* (London: George Allen and Unwin, 1943), p. 244. On Chatham House, see Zaidi, *Technology and the Reconstruction*, pp. 93–5, 119.

102. See Culbertson's two articles on 'A System to Win This War', *Reader's Digest*, February 1943 and April 1943; Volta Torrey, 'Will Airborne Police Enforce World Peace?', *Popular Science*, September 1944, pp. 72–7, 222, 230.
103. Gill Robb Wilson, 'The Air World', *New York Herald Tribune*, 30 April 1945, cited on p. 291. A year later, Group Captain R. Fulljames would claim in a pamphlet that just as law needs police, so international law needs international police, and this in turn needs air power – *An International Police Force* (Southampton Branch of the UN Association: Shirley Press, 1946), pp. 5–7.
104. Zaidi, *Technology and the Reconstruction*, 2008, pp. 107, 125; Beaumont, *Might Backed by Right*, pp. 82–3, 95, 99.
105. This was picked up by Shotwell, *Great Decision*, p. 131: 'In short, if it [air power] can serve as an effective police force rather than as one of the arms in total war, it may well furnish the third step in the process of pacification'.
106. See in particular Edgerton, 'Liberal Militarism and the British State', but also his books and those by Zaidi cited above.
107. See Mark Neocleous, *The Fabrication of Social Order: A Critical Theory of Police Power* (London: Pluto, 2000), pp. 95–118.
108. See David H. Bayley, 'Policing: The World Stage', in R. I. Mawby (ed.), *Policing Across the World: Issues for the Twenty-first Century* (London: UCL Press, 1999), pp. 3–12, p. 4; Beth K. Greener, *The New International Policing* (Basingstoke: Palgrave Macmillan, 2009), p. 3; Beaumont, *Might Backed by Right*, pp. 126, 155.
109. Respectively: Vernon Nash, *The World Must be Governed* (New York: Harper and Brothers, 1949), p. 144; Richard A. Falk, *A Study of Future Worlds* (Amsterdam: North-Holland Publishing Co., 1975), p. 243.
110. Grenville Clark and Louis B. Sohn, *World Peace Through World Law*, 2nd edn (Cambridge, MA: Harvard University Press, 1960), pp. xxix; Hidemi Suganami, *The Domestic Analogy and World Order Proposals* (Cambridge: Cambridge University Press, 1989), pp. 23, 28–9; Chiaro Bottici, *Men and States: Rethinking the Domestic Analogy in a Global Age* (2004), trans. Karen Whittle (Basingstoke: Palgrave Macmillan, 2009), pp. 4, 7, 77.
111. Raymond Aron, *Peace and War: A Theory of International Relations* (1962) (New Brunswick, NJ: Transaction, 2003), p. 16.
112. The reader will recognise the refracted words of Walter Benjamin, 'Critique of Violence' (1920–1), trans. Edmund Jephcott, in *Selected Writings, Vol. 1: 1913–1926*, ed. Marcus Bullock and Michael W. Jennings (Cambridge, MA: Belknap/Harvard, 1996), p. 243. Also, Neocleous, *Fabrication*, p. 107.
113. Danilo Zolo, *Cosmopolis: Prospects for World Government* (Cambridge: Polity Press, 1997), p. 113.
114. Lee Kennett, *A History of Strategic Bombing* (New York: Charles Scribner's Sons, 1982), p. 2.

115. Respectively: William Mitchell, *Winged Defense: The Development and Possibilities of Modern Air Power – Economic and Military* (New York: G. P. Putnam and Sons, 1925), pp. 25–6; William Mitchell, *Skyways: A Book on Modern Aeronautics* (Philadelphia: J. B. Lippincott, 1930), p. 256.

116. Major Alexander P. de Seversky, 'What is Air Power?' (1955), in Eugene M. Emme (ed.), *The Impact of Air Power* (Princeton, NJ: D. Van Nostrand Co., 1959), p. 201.

117. Sir Alan Cobham, English aviator, commenting in 1927, cited in Thomas Lowell, *European Skyways: The Story of a Tour of Europe by Airplane* (New York: Houghton Mifflin Co., 1927), p. 90.

118. General John M. Shalikashvili, Chairman of the Joint Chiefs of Staff, Remarks at the Naval War College graduation, Newport, RI, 16 June 1995 – http://www.defense.gov/speeches/speech.aspx?speechid=1085 (accessed 25 December 2012).

CHAPTER 7

1. In autumn 2002 several American clothing outfitters, including Gap and Old Navy, featured 'primary colours' in their 'back-to-school' children catalogues, and presented khaki as one of the primary colours. For male 'military chic': National Outdoors declared militarised menswear 'a hip trend'; Armani has been selling camouflage clothing; a few hours after the first strike on Iraq in March 2003 the Guess online store announced that it had sold out of its cargo cadet pants; Old Navy's website sales pitch was 'military surplus-style for your action-packed days!' for its men's messenger bags, which came 'with army-style numbers and letters and metallic dog tab on adjustable strap'. See Susan Faludi, *The Terror Dream: What 9/11 Revealed About America* (London: Atlantic Books, 2007), pp. 137–8, and François Debrix, *Tabloid Terror: War, Culture, and Geopolitics* (London: Routledge, 2008), p. 91. Although these examples are relatively recent, for the longer trend, see Jane Pavitt, *Fear and Fashion in the Cold War* (London: V & A Publishing, 2008).

2. See the collection of essays in Elaine Cardenas and Ellen Gorman (eds), *The Hummer: Myths and Consumer Culture* (Lanham: Lexington Books, 2007), especially Cardenas and Gorman, 'Introduction'; Jeremy Packer, 'Auto Militarization: Citizen Soldiers, the Hummer, and the War on Terror'; James K. Walker, 'The Hummer: The Return of the Hard Body'; Randel D. Hanson, 'A Gated Community on Wheels: Sports Utility Vehicles, Privatization, and Global Capital'.

3. The literature on this is now vast, and we touched on it a little in previous chapters. Paul Virilio has made the more general theoretical claim concerning war and the city over several works – for example, Paul

Virilio/Sylvere Lotringer, *Pure War* (1983), trans. Mark Polizzotti (Los Angeles: Semiotext(e), 2008). The longer historical view can be found in Max Weber's account of the origins of the *polis* as a guild of warriors, in *Economy and Society*, ed. Guenther Roth and Claus Wittich (Berkeley: University of California Press, 1978), p. 1359. Recent developments in military urbanism have been comprehensively dealt with in Stephen Graham, *Cities Under Siege: The New Military Urbanism* (London: Verso, 2010). Graham's book, however, should be read in conjunction with Jennifer S. Light's important analysis of the urban crisis as a national security crisis, in which urban warfare and guerrilla warfare historically folded into one another – *From Warfare to Welfare: Defense Intellectuals and Urban Problems in Cold War America* (Baltimore: Johns Hopkins University Press, 2003). For a study of Cold War architecture, see Annabel Jane Wharton, *Building the Cold War: Hilton International Hotels and Modern Architecture* (Chicago: University of Chicago Press, 2001).

4. Steve Thorne, *The Language of War* (Abingdon: Routledge, 2006), pp. 10–11. On 'strategy', see Jeffrey Bracker, 'The Historical Development of the Strategic Management Concept', *Academy of Management Review*, Vol. 5, No. 2, 1980, pp. 219–24; David Knights and Glenn Morgan, 'The Concept of Strategy in Sociology: A Note of Dissent', *Sociology*, Vol. 24, No. 3, 1990, pp. 475–83; Martin Shaw, 'Strategy and Social Process: Military Context and Sociological Analysis', *Sociology*, Vol. 24, No. 3, 1990, pp. 465–73; Mikkel Vedby Rasmussen, *The Risk Society at War: Terror, Technology and Strategy in the Twenty-First Century* (Cambridge: Cambridge University Press, 2006), p. 14.

5. Patrick J. Bracken and Celia Petty, 'Introduction', in Patrick J. Bracken and Celia Petty (eds), *Rethinking the Trauma of War* (London: Free Association Books, 1998), p. 1.

6. Didier Fassin and Richard Rechtman, *The Empire of Trauma: An Inquiry into the Condition of Victimhood* (2007), trans. Rachel Gomme (Princeton, NJ: Princeton University Press, 2009), p. 10.

7. Mark Neocleous, *Critique of Security* (Edinburgh: Edinburgh University Press, 2008), pp. 106–41.

8. Cindi Katz notes the remarkable overlaps between anxious parenting and the anxious homeland security state. Both tend toward inappropriate targets, offer a false sense of security through either overkill in some areas and a blithe disregard of others, and thus divert attention from other, more pressing, issues. In this, the parallels between 'domestic' and 'national' security are revealing, both undergirded by a politics of anxiety – Cindi Katz, 'Me and My Monkey: What's Hiding in the Security State', in Michael Sorkin (ed.), *Indefensible Space: The Architecture of the National Insecurity State* (New York: Routledge, 2008), p. 307.

9. Sianne Ngai, *Ugly Feelings* (Cambridge, MA: Harvard University Press, 2005), p. 214.

10. *The WHO World Mental Health Survey: Global Perspectives on the Epidemiology of Mental Disorders* (Cambridge: Cambridge University Press, 2008); *Working Our Way to Better Mental Health: A Framework for Action* (London: HMSO, 2009), p. 14.

11. Franz Neumann, 'Anxiety and Politics' (1954), in Neumann, *The Democratic and the Authoritarian State* (New York: Free Press, 1957).

12. Uday Singh Mehta, *The Anxiety of Freedom: Imagination and Individuality in Locke's Political Thought* (Ithaca: Cornell University Press, 1992).

13. For this and other examples, see Mark Neocleous, '"Don't Be Scared, Be Prepared": Trauma-Anxiety-Resilience', *Alternatives: Global, Local, Political*, Vol. 37, No. 3, 2012, pp. 188–98. Some of the arguments in this chapter were first developed in that article and one which followed – 'Resisting Resilience', *Radical Philosophy*, 178, 2013, pp. 2–7.

14. Claudia Aradau and Rens van Munster, *Politics of Catastrophe: Genealogies of the Unknown* (London: Routledge, 2011), pp. 46–7. Also see Jeremy Walker and Melinda Cooper, 'Genealogies of Resilience: From Systems Ecology to the Political Economy of Crisis Adaptation', *Security Dialogue*, Vol. 42, No. 2, 2011, pp. 143–60.

15. OECD, *Concepts and Dilemmas of State Building in Fragile Situations: From Fragility to Resilience* (OECD, 2008), p. 17.

16. US National Security Council, *National Strategy for Homeland Security*, October 2007, pp. i, 25, 27, 28, 29, 31, 42, 47.

17. Barack Obama, 'Remarks at "A Concert for Hope" Commemorating the 10th Anniversary of the September 11 Terrorist Attacks', 11 September 2011.

18. Cabinet Office, *The National Security Strategy of the United Kingdom: Security in an Interdependent World* (London: HMSO, 2008), pp. 8, 9, 26, 41, 42, 43, 45, 55.

19. See 'Military Ethos in Schools', 15 November 2012 – http://www.education. gov.uk/childrenandyoungpeople/youngpeople/militaryethos/a00217000/ military-ethos-in-schools (accessed 1 December 2012).

20. Department of Defense, Defense Science Board, *Task Force Report: Predicting Violent Behaviour*, August 2012, para. 5.2. I am grateful to Tyler Wall for bringing this text to my attention.

21. On the sniffer dog, see Mark Neocleous, 'The Smell of Power: A Contribution to the Critique of the Sniffer Dog', *Radical Philosophy*, 167, 2011, pp. 9–14.

22. Aradau and Munster, *Politics of Catastrophe*; Stuart Price, *Worst-Case Scenario? Governance, Mediation and the Security Regime* (London: Zed Books, 2011).

23. Department for International Development, *Defining Disaster Resilience: A DFID Approach Paper* (London: DFID, 2011); United Nations, *Living With Risk: A Global Review of Disaster Reduction Initiatives, Vol. 1* (New York and Geneva, United Nations, 2004), p. 37, emphasis added.

24. *The 9/11 Commission Report: The Full Final Report of the National Commission on Terrorist Attacks Upon the United States* (New York: W. W. Norton and Co., 2004), p. 344.

25. Paul Virilio, 'Endo-colonization and the State-as-Destiny', in Virilio/ Lotringer, *Pure War*, p. 104.

26. These searches were conducted in February 2013. I predict that the number will rise and rise.

27. World Economic Forum, *Systemic Financial Resilience* – Network of Global Agenda Councils Report, 2011–12; United Nations Development Programme, *World Resources 2008: Roots of Resilience – Growing the Wealth of the Poor* (Washington, DC: World Resources Institute, 2008).

28. In April 2012, in the midst of a potential strike by fuel tanker drivers, British Health Secretary Andrew Lansley commented that the nation had to be prepared in order to better come through this and any other strike: 'we have got to build resilience in the system and that's what we're doing' – Dan Milmo and Juliette Jowit, 'Build Up Resilience Against Tanker Strike, Lansley Urges', *The Guardian*, 2 April 2012, p. 5. On the neoliberal underpinnings, see Walker and Cooper, 'Genealogies of Resilience'; Mark Duffield, 'Challenging Environments: Danger, Resilience and the Aid Industry', *Security Dialogue*, Vol. 43, No. 5, 2012, pp. 475–92; Julian Reid, 'The Disastrous and Politically Debased Subject of Resilience', *Development Dialogue*, No. 58, 2012, pp. 67–79.

29. See Carl Cederstrom and Peter Fleming, *Dead Man Working* (Winchester: Zero Books, 2012).

30. Pat O'Malley, 'Resilient Subjects: Uncertainty, Warfare and Liberalism', *Economy and Society*, Vol. 39, No. 4, 2010, pp. 488–509, p. 492. Also see David Chandler, 'Resilience and Human Security: The Post-interventionist Paradigm', *Security Dialogue*, Vol. 43, No. 2, 2012, pp. 213–29, p. 217.

31. Richard Layard, *Happiness: Lessons from a New Science*, 2nd edn (London: Penguin, 2011), p. 251; Derek Bok, *The Politics of Happiness: What Government Can Learn from the New Research on Well-Being*, (Princeton, NJ: Princeton University Press, 2010), pp. 114, 149; Matthieu Ricard, *Happiness: A Guide to Developing Life's Most Important Skill* (2003), trans. Jesse Browner (New York: Little, Brown and Co., 2007), pp. 69, 73, 115; Jessica Pryce-Jones, *Happiness at Work: Maximizing your Psychological Capital for Success* (Chichester: John Wiley, 2010), pp. 8, 74–8, 111. For a critique of the happiness agenda, see William Davies, 'The Political Economy of Unhappiness', *New Left Review*, 71, 2011, pp. 65–80.

32. Cited in Daniel Boffey, 'Labour Scorns Cameron "Happiness" Agenda', *The Observer*, 29 January 2012, p. 23.
33. On the increasing prevalence of the psy disciplines in IR more generally, see Alison Howell, *Madness in International Relations: Psychology, Security, and the Global Governance of Mental Health* (London: Routledge, 2011).
34. J. Daw, 'Documentary on Resilience Set to Air Sept. 11', *Monitor on Psychology*, Vol. 33, No. 7, 2002, p. 12; Sara Martin, 'Building Resilience from the Grassroots Up: APA Members take the "Road to Resilience" Campaign to the Public', *Monitor on Psychology*, Vol. 33, No. 11, 2002, p. 52.
35. Russ Newman, 'The Road to Resilience', *Monitor on Psychology*, Vol. 33, No. 9, 2002, p. 62.
36. For example: http://www.allbusiness.com/health-care-social-assistance/880919-1.html
37. I am playing here on Theodor Adorno, *The Jargon of Authenticity* (1964), trans. Knut Tarnowski and Frederic Will (London: Routledge and Kegan Paul, 1973).
38. Theodor Adorno, *Negative Dialectics* (1966), trans. E. B. Ashton (London: Routledge, 1990), pp. 17–18.
39. Franco Fornari, *The Psychoanalysis of War* (1966), trans. Alenka Pfeifer (Bloomington: Indiana University Press, 1975), p. xvii.
40. Sigmund Freud, 'Inhibitions, Symptoms and Anxiety' (1926), in *The Standard Edition of the Complete Psychological Works of Sigmund Freud, Vol. XX* (London: Vintage, 2001), pp. 165–7.
41. Allan Young, *The Harmony of Illusions: Inventing Post-Traumatic Stress Disorder* (Princeton, NJ: Princeton University Press, 1995); Wilbur J. Scott, *The Politics of Readjustment: Vietnam Veterans Since the War* (New York: Aldine de Gruyter, 1993), pp. 34, 238; Wilbur J. Scott, 'PTSD in DSM-III: A Case in the Politics of Diagnosis and Disease', *Social Problems*, Vol. 37, No. 3, 1990, pp. 294–310; Edgar Jones and Simon Wessely, *Shell Shock to PTSD: Military Psychiatry from 1900 to the Gulf War* (Hove: Psychology Press, 2005), p. 131. More generally, see Ben Shephard, *A War of Nerves: Soldiers and Psychiatrists 1914–1994* (London: Pimlico, 2002); Paul Lerner, *Hysterical Men: War, Psychiatry, and the Politics of Trauma in Germany, 1890–1930* (Ithaca: Cornell University Press, 2003). Note also Philip Cushman's argument concerning psychotherapy's socio-political function, not least due to its reliance on trauma theory – *Constructing the Self, Constructing America: A Cultural History of Psychotherapy* (Cambridge, MA: Da Capo Press, 1995), p. 343.
42. Fassin and Rechtman, *Empire*, p. 39. Also Michael R. Trimble, 'Post-traumatic Stress Disorder: History of a Concept', in Charles R. Figley (ed.), *Trauma and its Wake, Vol. 1: The Study and Treatment of Post-Traumatic Stress Disorder* (New York: Brunner/Mazel, 1985), pp. 5–14.

43. For a more recent and comparable case, see Paula Gody-Paiz, '"Canada's Troubled Troops": The Construction of Post-Traumatic Stress Disorder and Its Uses by the Canadian Armed Forces', *Alternate Routes*, Vol. 20, 2004, pp. 6–23.

44. See Jenny Edkins, *Trauma and the Memory of Politics* (Cambridge: Cambridge University Press, 2003), p. xv. For a similar claim concerning the reassertion of the authority of the British state following WWI, see Susan Kingsley Kent, *Aftershocks: Politics and Trauma in Britain, 1918–1931* (Basingstoke: Palgrave, 2009), p. 7. On the advantage that the powerful have over the powerless in the conduct of griefwork, see Jonathan Shay, *Achilles in Vietnam: Combat Trauma and the Undoing of Character* (New York: Scribner, 2003), p. 56.

45. Chester B. Scrignar, *Post-traumatic Stress Disorder: Diagnosis, Treatment, and Legal Issues* (New Orleans: Bruno Press, 1988), p. 2.

46. Both cited in James Palmer, 'Civilian Toll', *San Francisco Chronicle*, 19 March 2007.

47. Christopher J. Colvin, '"Brothers and Sisters, Do Not Be Afraid of Me": Trauma, History and the Therapeutic Imagination in the New South Africa', in Katherine Hodgkin and Susannah Radstone (eds), *Contested Pasts: The Politics of Memory* (London: Routledge, 2003), pp. 153–68.

48. Yael Danieli, Danny Brom and Joe Sills (eds), *The Trauma of Terrorism: Sharing Knowledge and Shared Care, an International Handbook* (London: Haworth Press, 2005); Yael Danieli (ed.), *International Handbook of Multigenerational Legacies of Trauma* (New York: Plenum Press, 2010); Raymond Monsour Scurfield and Katherine Theresa Platoni (eds), *Healing War Trauma: A Handbook of Creative Approaches* (London: Routledge, 2013).

49. Johan Galtung, 'Peace by Peaceful Conflict Transformation – The TRANSCEND Approach', in Charles Webel and Johan Galtung (eds), *Handbook of Peace and Conflict Studies* (London: Routledge, 2007), pp. 16, 30.

50. Derek Gregory, 'The Everywhere War', *The Geographical Journal*, Vol. 177, No. 3, 2011, pp. 238–50.

51. Young, *Harmony*; Derek Summerfield, 'The Social Experience of War and some Issues for the Humanitarian Field', in Bracken and Petty (eds), *Rethinking*; Austin Sarat, Nadav Davidovitch and Michael Alberstein, 'Trauma and Memory: Between Individual and Collective Experiences', in Austin Sarat, Nadav Davidovitch and Michael Alberstein (eds), *Trauma and Memory: Reading, Healing, and Making Law* (Stanford, CA: Stanford University Press, 2007).

52. Bruno Bettelheim, 'Trauma and Reintegration', in Bettelheim, *Surviving and Other Essays* (London: Thames and Hudson, 1979), pp. 33–5.

53. Tana Dineen, *Manufacturing Victims* (Montreal: Robert Davies, 1996), p. 56;

Ian Hacking, *Rewriting the Soul: Multiple Personality and the Sciences of Memory* (Princeton, NJ: Princeton University Press, 1995), p. 183; Kirby Farrell, *Post-traumatic Culture: Injury and Interpretation in the Nineties* (Baltimore: Johns Hopkins University Press, 1998), p. x; Joanna Bourke, 'Sexual Violence, Bodily Pain, and Trauma: A History', *Theory, Culture and Society*, Vol. 29, No. 3, 2012, pp. 25–51, p. 29.

54. Kali Tal, *Worlds of Hurt: Reading the Literatures of Trauma* (Cambridge: Cambridge University Press, 1996); Leigh Gilmore, *The Limits of Autobiography: Trauma and Testimony* (Ithaca: Cornell University Press, 2001); Farrell, *Post-traumatic Culture*, p. 153; Roger Luckhurst, *The Trauma Question* (London: Routledge, 2008), pp. 81–208; Lauren Berlant, *Cruel Optimism* (Durham: Duke University Press, 2011), pp. 9, 79; Jeffrey C. Alexander, *Trauma: A Social Theory* (Cambridge: Polity Press, 2012), pp. 3–4, 114. Writing about the imagination of disaster in science fiction films, especially the disaster of nuclear war (she was writing in 1965), Susan Sontag comments that 'most of the science fiction films bear witness to this trauma, and, in a way, attempt to exorcise it'. Susan Sontag, 'The Imagination of Disaster' (1965), in Sontag, *Against Interpretation* (London: Vintage, 2001), p. 218. Although in the light of the politics of planning and preemption, one might say that the current trauma culture is more an attempt to *exercise* it. Such exercise can be found in the breed of 'traumatized superhero' that has emerged in film since 2001 – see Dan Hassler-Forest, *Capitalist Superheroes: Caped Crusaders in the Neoliberal Age* (Winchester: Zero Books, 2012), pp. 69–112.

55. Laurie Beth Clark and Leigh A. Payne, 'Trauma Tourism in Latin America', in Ksenija Bilbija and Leigh A. Payne (eds), *Accounting for Violence: Marketing Memory in Latin America* (Durham: Duke University Press, 2011).

56. Frank Furedi, *Therapy Culture: Cultivating Vulnerability in an Uncertain Age* (London: Routledge, 2004), p. 4.

57. For example, Vanessa Pupavac, 'War on the Couch: The Emotionology of the New International Security Paradigm', *European Journal of Social Theory*, Vol. 7, No. 2, 2004, pp. 149–70. Also Michael Humphrey, 'New Wars and the Therapeutic Security Paradigm', in Damian Grenfell and Paul James (eds), *Rethinking Insecurity, War and Violence: Beyond Savage Globalization?* (London: Routledge, 2009), pp. 61–70. The term 'emotionology' is taken from Carol Zisowitz Stearns and Peter N. Stearns, *Anger: The Struggle for Emotional Control in America's History* (Chicago: University of Chicago Press, 1986). Emotionology, they claim (p. 14), 'normally governs what people think they should be experiencing', and Pupavac is right to say that this has now been projected onto international issues in a new therapeutic security paradigm. However, she also holds the view that this new

paradigm'may be said to represent a shift from ideology to emotionology' (p. 152). But it is surely the case that emotionology is now part of ideology. It is also the case that the analysis in the Stearns book is heavily driven by questions of class ('changes in the dominant emotionology do help explain class relationships' – p. 16), which is absent from many of the analyses of the therapeutic security paradigm.

58. Jacques Derrida,'Autoimmunity: Real and Symbolic Suicides – A Dialogue with Jacques Derrida', in Giovanna Borradori, *Philosophy in a Time of Terror: Dialogues with Jurgen Habermas and Jacques Derrida* (Chicago: University of Chicago Press, 2003), p. 97.

59. Susan J. Brison, *Aftermath: Violence and the Remaking of a Self* (Princeton, NJ: Princeton University Press, 2002); Cathy Caruth, *Unclaimed Experience: Trauma, Narrative, and History* (Baltimore: Johns Hopkins University Press, 1996); Ruth Leys, *Trauma: A Genealogy* (Chicago: University of Chicago Press, 2000); Shosana Felman, *The Juridical Unconscious: Trials and Traumas of the Twentieth Century* (Cambridge, MA: Harvard University Press, 2002); Allen Meek, *Trauma and Media* (New York: Routledge, 2010); Peter A. Levine, *Walking the Tiger: Healing Trauma* (Berkeley: North Atlantic Books, 1997); Mieke Bal, Jonathan Crewe and Leo Spitzer (eds), *Acts of Memory: Cultural recall in the Present* (Hanover: University Press of New England, 1999); Katherine Hodgkin and Susannah Radstone, 'Remembering Suffering: Trauma and History', in Hodgkin and Radstone (eds), *Contested Pasts*, pp. 97–102.

60. Don DeLillo, *Falling Man* (London: Picador, 2007), p. 138.

61. Stuart McLean, *The Event and Its Terrors: Ireland, Famine, Modernity* (Stanford, CA: Stanford University Press, 2004), p. 155.

62. See Mark Neocleous, *The Monstrous and the Dead: Burke, Marx, Fascism* (Cardiff: University of Wales Press, 2005).

63. Allan Young, 'Posttraumatic Stress Disorder of the Virtual Kind: Trauma and Resilience in Post-9/11 America', in Sarat, Davidovitch and Alberstin (eds), *Trauma and Memory*, pp. 21–48; Luckhurst, *Trauma Question*, p. 210.

64. There is a powerful argument that PTSD will, eventually, become superseded by resilience-based models for managing the anxious subject. See Alison Howell,'The Demise of PTSD: Governing Through Trauma to Governing Resilience', *Alternatives*, Vol. 37, No. 3, 2912, pp. 214–26.

65. See www.traumaweb.org. For discussion, see Keren Friedman-Peleg and Yehuda C. Goodman, 'From Posttrauma Intervention to Immunization of the Social Body: Pragmatics and Politics of a Resilience Program in Israel's Periphery', *Culture, Medicine and Psychiatry*, Vol. 34, No. 3, 2010, pp, 421–42.

66. Henri Barbusse, *Under Fire* (1916) (Teddington: Echo Library, 2007), p. 11.

67. Martin Jay, *Essays from the Edge: Parerga and Paralipomena* (Charlottesville: University of Virginia Press, 2011), p. 10.
68. Geoffrey Hartman, *Scars of the Spirit: The Struggle Against Inauthenticity* (New York: Palgrave Macmillan, 2002), p. 31.
69. I finished my book *Critique of Security* (2008) with a quote from a song by the Gang of Four, which looped back to a citation from the group with which the first chapter of that book had begun. The citation was designed to pick up on the theme of the song cited ('Return the Gift') and thus one of the themes of the book, namely: to return the 'gift'. The gift in the song is the 'prize' of commodities, which turns out to be not much of a gift at all; the commodity destroys human being. The gift in the book is the 'prize' of security, which turns out to be equally destructive. Too many readers seemed perplexed and quizzed me about this or missed it completely; I was clearly either trying too hard or not trying hard enough. As well as clarifying that point, this footnote is also meant to clarify a similar loop in this book: the final paragraph in this book is taken in part – that is, in phrases – from David Peace, *Occupied City* (2009), p. 160. The related quote from Peace's book with which the Introduction to this book began is on p. 156.

INDEX